PENGUIN BOOKS

THE NEW VEGETARIAN EPICURE

Anna Thomas was born in Germany of Polish parents in 1948 and the family emigrated to Michigan when she was still a baby. After graduating from the University of California at Los Angeles, she continued to study for several years there in the film department. *The Vegetarian Epicure*, her first book, was written during that period, both out of the need to support herself as a young film-maker and to provide herself and her friends with a more exciting repertoire of vegetarian recipes than had ever been collected before. The phenomenal success of this book has enabled Anna Thomas to further her career as a writer, producer and film director, and to expand her culinary horizons through much travel, and the tasting and testing of new recipes. In 1975 she married film director Gregory Nava and they have collaborated on numerous films and screenplays. They live with their two young sons in the orange-growing valley of Ojai, California.

Anna Thomas

The New Vegetarian Epicure

PENGUIN BOOKS

PENGUIN BOOKS

Published by the Penguin Group
Penguin Books Ltd, 27 Wrights Lane, London W8 5TZ, England
Penguin Books USA Inc., 375 Hudson Street, New York, New York 10014, USA
Penguin Books Australia Ltd, Ringwood, Victoria, Australia
Penguin Books Canada Ltd, 10 Alcorn Avenue, Toronto, Ontario, Canada M4V 3B2
Penguin Books (NZ) Ltd, 182–190 Wairau Road, Auckland 10, New Zealand

Penguin Books Ltd, Registered Offices: Harmondsworth, Middlesex, England

First published in the USA, under the title
The Vegetarian Epicure, Book Two, by Alfred A. Knopf, Inc. 1978
and simultaneously in Canada by Random House of Canada Ltd
Published in Penguin Books 1991
3 5 7 9 10 8 6 4 2

Printed in England by Clays Ltd, St Ives plc
Filmset in Monophoto Photina

For my husband, Greg

CONTENTS

ACKNOWLEDGEMENTS

I would like to acknowledge gratefully my friend Gail Hand, for her cheerful and efficient help in preparing countless recipes; Judith Jones, for all her clear-headed and tactful editing and advice; and Gregory Nava, for running to the store so many times.

INTRODUCTION

WHY A SECOND BOOK? Because we always itch to expand horizons. This book is not just a continuation of the first volume but an exploration of rich new lodes. The first book came out of my own past, and from the tremendous need for a collection of really good vegetarian recipes. This second volume is the result of new adventures: it broadens the scope of the gourmet vegetarian kitchen with forays into entirely different cuisines and cultures. It is a record of culinary discoveries that I'm eager to share, and a notebook of travels.

The writing of this book came about in a most enjoyable way. I spent the last four years travelling, eating, reading, taking notes, cooking, and writing. Work and whim took me through large parts of Europe – Portugal, Spain, Italy, France, Greece, Austria, Hungary, Poland – as well as on a brief sally into the Middle East and on a jaunt through Mexico. Everywhere I went I was delighted by the food, by the rewards of being eager to sample the new and unfamiliar.

I thought of each meal as a little adventure (and some turned out to be big ones). When I was lucky enough to be staying with relatives or friends, I followed them into the kitchen and pestered them for their best recipes. If, while touring, I discovered a particularly wonderful restaurant, I didn't mind staying a day or two longer in that city to do it justice.

Many people, I found, were curious how a vegetarian could survive, and even eat splendidly, while travelling abroad. The answer is, easily. Nearly everywhere I went I discovered that most restaurant menus commonly included some enticing dishes made of fresh vegetables or fruits, eggs, cheeses or grains. In all the *tavernas*, trattorias, *kellars*, cafés and *ristorantes* I visited, the choices offered me ranged from adequate to exciting.

In Italy, of course, the antipasto and pasta were a constant temptation; in France we discovered omelettes anew and ate dozens of cheeses that we had never tried before. In Madrid and Segovia every restaurant offered an array of vegetable dishes, along with the eggy Spanish tortillas, which appeared in endless variation.

In Poland and Hungary we found marvellous fruit soups, pancakes in wonderful new roles, subtle and cooling salads made of cooked vegetables, and a whole repertoire of tasty ways with simple, fresh cheeses. I also recall evenings in Greece, sitting by the Aegean at sunset, munching vine leaves stuffed with rice and dill and washing them down with ouzo. And during the long, hot summer days in Cairo, when we weren't devouring the sweet, juicy watermelons, we were sampling *tahini* and *baba ghanouj* and hotly spiced bean cakes.

The list goes on; really, the only problem was not to overdo the pleasures of the table so much that a new wardrobe would become necessary *en route*!

In hotel rooms and on long train rides my husband and I would reminisce and fill notebooks with descriptions of wonderful dishes we had eaten, along with the new ideas that cropped up constantly alongside these discoveries. Dining cars were best for this. Rumbling past slowly changing landscapes and thousands of telephone poles, we detailed the high points of a culinary odyssey.

Whenever we returned home, the serious cooking would soon begin. I would experiment with re-creating memorable dishes from our travels and adapting foreign ideas to my own style. Great eating became even better as family and friends joined us at the table in our little dining-room, under the mirrored globe, to sample the new fare. I would gauge their responses, make more notes and cook or bake things again if necessary – until it was all absolutely right.

Of course, not every recipe in this book is the fruit of travel. Often my friends share their particular specialities with me. Sometimes I feel the need of a little celebration or I have a house guest to pamper, and then I like to devise something new and, usually, write it down. It is just a matter of doing something I enjoy, and that's how I hope this book will be used by others.

In the course of all this testing and trying, my feelings about the main 'secret' of good cooking were constantly reaffirmed. The one piece of advice I invariably repeat when people ask me how one should go about cooking well is this: use good ingredients. Always, always start with the best possible ingredients – the freshest butter and milk and cream, the nicest vegetables, the finest pasta, the loveliest rice, vine- or tree-ripened fruit, aged cheeses, good wines.

You won't be sorry. With high quality at the outset, you have a fair chance of achieving superior results. Yes, it's possible to destroy even the best ingredients if you don't know what you're doing, but at least you can be confident that they won't destroy you! So procure the best you can, don't be shy in the kitchen and good things will follow.

As in the first *Vegetarian Epicure*, the good things in this book are meatless, but it is not a book for vegetarians only. It is for anyone who can enjoy foods like fettucine alfredo, pea soup with dumplings, fondue, pimiento and olive quiche, tomatoes filled with hearts of palm, Liptauer cheese, wild mushroom soufflé, Caesar salad and frozen strawberry mousse. It is true, however, that a great many people today are eating less meat, for reasons of health, economy or simply personal preference, and I am convinced that these new styles in dining, far from being dreary, can be infinitely varied and inspired. For those who want to expand their repertoire because they are eating less meat than they used to, and for those who, like myself, prefer not to eat meat at all but don't intend to compromise on the satisfaction of really delicious food, I hope this book provides a bonanza of pleasurable eating.

Arranging all this new material in a manner that made sense was an interesting task, so I'd like to say something about the way we finally did it. Several chapters are devoted to the foods of specific countries; most of the recipes, however, are grouped by type rather than by place of origin. With such an arrangement, there are bound to be a few things that fit into more than one category, so there is some cross-referencing. Gazpacho, for example, is included with the soups, but there is a note about it at the end of the section on Spanish foods.

Several readers of my earlier book have expressed concern about the use of Worcestershire sauce, pointing out that it contains a trace of anchovies. Life Worcestershire sauce, manufactured by St Giles' Foods and available in health-food shops, contains no anchovies. Similarly, some readers will prefer to use agar-agar in place of animal-based gelatin, and others will wish to avoid cheeses that may have been made with animal rennet.

I hope that this book will be as enjoyable for you as it has been for me. The most important thing about food, after all, is enjoyment, and what a grand thing it is that eating is such a renewable pleasure: we always do get hungry again! Preparing those delectable meals should be a pleasure as well. It's an act of creation that is all the more charming because it is so ephemeral. There's something pleasing about the fact that a great meal is not a lasting thing; that, rather, all the thought and work are enjoyed by one small group of people for one brief and delightful while, then vanish, to linger in memory only.

We all eat, and it would be a sad waste of opportunity to eat badly. It's true that the meals we consume in a lifetime number in the tens of thousands, but the number is finite; each one should be as nice as it can be, for it can never be regained.

So, have a good time, and *buon gusto!*

MEASUREMENTS

In this book many dry ingredients are measured by *volume*.

1. Spoons are standard cook's *level* measuring spoons, not just any household teaspoon or tablespoon.

2. A cup holds 8 fl oz/225 ml; this is not equivalent to a weight of 8 oz/225 g for all ingredients. Use cook's measuring cups for the best results.

Other quantities are given first in imperial and then in metric measurements. In any one recipe follow one set of measurements or the other; do not mix them.

Menus

A GOOD MENU IS LIKE A GOOD STORY. It must have the proper balance of dramatic elements, sorted out and arranged in such an order that each new course fulfils the promise of the one that came before while setting the scene for the one to follow, and everything must be resolved in the end, for, unlike some stories, all meals should have happy endings.

Before plunging on to the ways in which this is accomplished, I should say a word or two about vegetarian menus versus traditional ones. It makes sense that a pattern that works for meals designed primarily around meat won't work as well for a varied assortment of non-meat dishes. I won't say that vegetarian cooking has no 'main courses' because there clearly are meals that do have such a central dish. However, that is just one part of a flexible range of possibilities and, more often than not, a fine meatless menu will consist of two or three complementary courses of equal importance.

This is no new idea, nor is it particular to vegetarian cooking. The *primero* and *secundo* of an Italian meal are an example of this style of eating. Spain has a similar tradition: the typical restaurant menu there shows no special categories for soup, salad or entrée; rather, foods are listed in three groups, the last being the most substantial, both in weight and in price, and dinners are composed from these groups according to the diner's preference.

This sort of attractive flexibility should be kept in mind when planning a meatless menu. It allows for a real variety of satisfying meals, any of which can make delicious culinary sense on its own terms. As long as one doesn't try to force vegetarian cooking into a narrow form that does not suit it, then ideas can be found everywhere, and tasty meals devised according to a few basic rules.

Contrast, as a good storyteller knows, is an invaluable tool in creating effect. The simpler the dish preceding your *pièce de résistance*, the more wonderful the latter will seem. Surprise, too, is a dramatist's stock in trade. But the most effective surprise is the one that, once sprung, is quickly followed by the sense that it was inevitable. Of course, you should always consider the tastes of the diners, the time of year, the time of day and the setting. A candle-lit dinner in a formal dining-room on a nice crisp evening in November is quite a different story from a picnic in August or a family meal in the kitchen.

Practically speaking, the question is, with every meal, where exactly to begin? The best way is with a blaze of inspiration, but lacking that (and we all have our off days), start with one good, solid idea. It might be a particular dish, a type of dish or even a certain ethnic flavour for which you've developed a sudden craving. Then consider what is in season. There's nothing like seven or eight months' deprivation to whet the appetite for crisp stalks of asparagus in the spring or ripe, golden pumpkins and roasted chestnuts in autumn. Whatever your idea, seasonal planning is a sure-fire way to proceed. Having considered the possibilities, give a thought to the limitations as well. If it's going to be a buffet for twenty, then you'll want to concentrate on dishes that can be prepared in advance, will keep well and are served with a minimum of fuss. And for any kind of meal, try not to plan more than one or two dishes that will require your last-minute attention, unless you thrive on the edge of hysteria.

When preliminaries are decided, think in terms of balancing sweet dishes with tart ones, hearty with light, and creamy food with something that will afford a crisp, satisfying crunch. If it's pasta that you're hankering for, then you'll want to start with tangy marinated vegetables or salad with a vinaigrette dressing, and the dessert should be light. If you're celebrating a birthday and cake will be required after dinner, avoid starchy or overly heavy dishes. One rich and saucy course is generally all the sauce a meal will want, and the same is true, as a rule, of foods sautéed in decadent amounts of butter or olive oil.

All these suggestions, though, are merely suggestions, not laws. If an unusual combination of foods strikes you as being perfectly appetizing, go ahead and try it! If you know that the group for whom you are cooking develops a prodigious capacity for sweets at Christmas-time, indulge it and serve three desserts at your gala dinner. Or, if you're longing to do something that is deliberately out of season and are able to procure ingredients of high quality, by all means have fresh strawberries or melons in the middle of December.

Taste and circumstance will guide you, after all, but imagination will set you free.

There is only one rule that must never, under any circumstances, be broken: don't try to prepare something if you can't, for any reason, procure the highest quality ingredients for it. However good your idea, no dish is better than what goes into it, and the best planned menu won't save it.

When it comes time to cook, make everything as lovely to look at as you can, arranging colours and shapes with as much care as you do seasonings; keep your sense of humour; and enjoy yourself.

One final note. Even the best story needs the proper telling to bring it off, and so we come to the idea of timing. A meal should be served as thoughtfully as it is planned and prepared. Now, I'm not suggesting that you should starve anyone to ensure the proper reception for your food, but a little bit of a wait among pleasant company can be quite enjoyable and serves to heighten not only the appetite but the drama as well.

In the case of the omelette or the soufflé, hot crêpes, or pasta *al dente*, the timing is nothing short of critical, and it is far better for the diner to wait awhile for the soufflé than the other way round. Any time that food is being served in courses, hurrying from one to the next is not recommended. Remember the value of suspense! Allow enough time to savour each dish with the proper, leisurely absorption and to anticipate the following one deliciously.

In Florence, in restaurants like Che' Ce' Ce' and Fagioli, the antipasto was generally the heart and soul of a meal or even the whole of it. There the antipasto is not some insignificant tray of celery sticks and olives brought to your table by a waiter. No, indeed. The magnificent sight of it grips your attention from the moment you enter and dominates it thereafter. A table of awe-inspiring size is laden with an abundant assortment of raw and cooked salads, marinated dishes, pickles and olives and peppers of all sorts, mild and sharp concoctions, heavy and light ones. Once, at Che' Ce' Ce', we tried counting – and lost track somewhere around forty.

You probably don't have the facilities or the inclination to set out an antipasto of quite such wealth at home, but it's not too much trouble, really, to toss together a selection of four or five dishes, augmented by some good, vinegary things from jars or from a delicatessen. Then serve a great pasta, not overdone and not too saucy, and a light or fruity dessert.

The two meals that follow are reminiscent, in a scaled-down way, of the way we ate in Florence.

Menu 1	Menu 2
ANTIPASTO:	ANTIPASTO:
Pickled Peppers	*Marinated Mushrooms*
Flageolet Salad	*Chick-pea Salad*
Peperonata	*Fresh Mozzarella Salad*
Tomatoes with	*Frittata of Courgette*
Vinaigrette Dressing	*Pickled Peppers*
Cured Olives	*Cured Olives*
Sliced Provolone Cheese	*Sliced Tomatoes and Cucumbers*
	Spring Onions
Penne alla Cardinale	
(Pasta with	*Penne alla Boccalone*
Creamy Tomato Sauce)	*(Pasta with Spicy Herb Sauce)*
Melons in Vermouth	*Cherry and Amaretto Soufflé*
Almond Biscuits or Torrone	
	Espresso
Espresso	

A lovely and festive dinner, with a high amusement quotient, this is designed for a small group – four to six, ideally – sitting at a round table. The salads can be prepared well in advance and likewise the fabulous dessert. Only the fondue wants some last-minute stirring in the kitchen.

I like to put each antipasto in individual oblong bowls or dishes and ring them round the chafing dish or fondue pot in the middle of the table. If you have a lazy Susan large enough to carry this entire operation, then you're really in business. Pass a large basket of cubed bread first so that all can take as much as they like on to their plates, and pour the wine. Bring the fondue out, adjust the flame under it and the job is done. The idea is to nibble on bites of salads in between scoops of fondue.

ANTIPASTO:
Gnocchi Salad
White Bean Salad
Aubergine Caviar
Peperonata
Pickled Peppers
Cured Olives

Italian Fondue

Cubes of French or Italian Bread

Spumoni Cake

Espresso

Here is another kind of Italian dinner.

The dish that needs your real attention at the last moment is the Spaghetti e Cipolla, of course. Don't let the pasta cook a moment too long. Drain it as soon as it is *al dente*, have the onion sauce ready and steaming hot, toss them together and serve instantly on warmed plates. Don't make the portions too large, though, or the delicious stuffed aubergine (which can wait in the oven an extra 5 minutes with no harm done) could be too much.

After a filling meal, fruit is the best. In this case oranges and tangerines would be welcome or melons of any kind.

Insalatone
(*A Marinade of Cooked Vegetables*)

Spaghetti e Cipolla
(*Spaghetti and Onions*)

Melanzana al Forno
(*Baked Aubergine*)

Assorted Fresh Fruit

Espresso

For cold days and hearty appetites, Spanish Cocido is really a whole meal: the cooking broth combined with vermicelli makes a light soup, to be followed by the assorted stewed vegetables, chick-peas and dumplings, then a light salad to clear the palate before dessert.

Cocido
with Crusty Rolls or Garlic Bread

Tossed Green Salad

Caramel Custard

Coffee

In Spain *tapas* belong to *tapa* bars. They are, by definition, those snacks that are eaten, in small individual portions, to accompany a glass of wine while one is standing at the bar. I ate many fine dinners in Madrid by roaming through several good bars of this type and having a little of this here and a little of that there, with many glasses of red wine. Once back home, I sorely missed the *tapa* bars, so I'd prepare a little selection of my own *tapas* and serve them buffet-style to my friends – with Spanish wine, of course, or *sangría* in the summer.

Tortilla Española

Ensaladilla Russa

Champiñónes alla Plancha
(Steamed Mushrooms)

Barcelona White Bean Salad

Roasted Aubergine and Peppers in Oil

Cured Olives

Cheeses

Crusty Bread or Rolls

Hearty Red Spanish Wine

Croquettes, or *croquetas*, are a big favourite in the *tapa* bars of Madrid, and the Menestra de Verduras, a hearty and interesting assortment of stewed vegetables, is equally popular in the restaurants. Although this is a very Spanish meal, I find that a bit of tomato-apple chutney or even some cranberry relish goes very well with the rich, mild croquettes.

Tossed Salad with Herb Dressing

Egg Croquettes

Menestra de Verduras
(Spanish Steamed Vegetables)

Apple Tart

In Mexico tortillas often appear in every course. In this simple but interesting meal the popular starter Guacamole is served with tortilla crisps, followed by an unusual Tortilla Soup, and then Enchiladas, which are simply stuffed and sauced tortillas.

Guacamole

Tortilla Soup Tlaxcalteca

Enchiladas Salsa Verde
Mexican Rice

Fresh Fruit

With this Mexican dinner you can be very flexible. If you don't care for beer or tequila, the Cantaloup Water, a very cooling drink, can be served at the start of the meal and sipped throughout. It makes a pleasant foil for the hot sauce that accompanies everything. Or it can be served at the end as a very light sort of fruit dessert.

Avocado Tacos
Bean and Potato Tacos
Hot Sauce

Rajas con Queso
(Peppers with Cheese)
Fresh, Hot Tortillas

Cantaloup Water

The little *tortitas* that make the first course of this meal should be freshly made and warm, but you can shape the shells of corn dough, or *masa*, in advance and just do the actual baking and filling, which doesn't take long, at the last minute. *Tortitas* are one of the best accompaniments to a good margarita I've ever tasted, so have your glasses salted and a cold jug of margaritas ready when the shells come out of the oven. The rest of the meal is simple enough to prepare and serve if you only keep in mind that refried beans should be cooked for a long time and enchiladas only long enough so that they are piping hot all through.

Margaritas
Tortitas con Queso

Spinach Enchiladas Suizas
Spicy Refried Beans

Strawberry Water

The salad is satisfying but not heavy, and the Cheese Soup elevates it to a perfectly pleasant warm-weather meal. What's more, the order can be reversed. If it's a *very* hot day, start with salad and, once refreshed, move on to Cheese Soup and bread, with a cold, crisp-flavoured white wine.

*Cheese Soup
with Garlic Toast*

Watercress and French Bean Salad

Any Fruit Tart

Coffee

This is one of the best of simple meals – quiche and soup. And so easy to serve the two either together or one after the other (remember quiche is just as good at room temperature as hot). A delightful lunch or dinner to have in warm weather outdoors with a good, dry wine. Be sure to indulge in great, generous portions of whatever wonderful berries are at peak season.

Red Pepper and Olive Quiche

Aubergine Soup

Green Salad with Vinaigrette Dressing

*Fresh Berries with Cream
Coffee*

There are no courses in an Indian meal. So, although these two Indian menus are relatively simple, they will have the appearance of a banquet when everything is served all at once.

To make your Indian dinner into an exotic event, find a bright-coloured tablecloth and arrange the table in such a way that there is ample room in the centre for six or seven attractive serving dishes. If you have some nice-looking shallow copper pots or gratin dishes, polish them and put them to use. Set each place with a large plate and, for the soupy *dal* or the cold *raita*, an additional little bowl. Then bring on the feast.

The *pakoras* are a snack or hors-d'oeuvre and must be served hot, so plan on frying them at the last minute. They can be served first, by themselves, to nibble while sipping a gin and tonic or Pimm's and soda; both of these drinks, I've found, are excellent, cooling accompaniments to the spicy flavours of Indian cooking. Another fine choice is a good pale ale. If you'd rather forgo alcoholic beverages, a spicy hot tea with milk will do very nicely.

After the *pakoras*, everything but the sweet should be placed on the table at once, together with little dishes of nuts, raisins, spicy pickles and whatever other garnishes you desire.

Menu 1	Menu 2
Pakoras	Smothered Potatoes
(Hot Vegetable Fritters)	Purée of Scorched Tomatoes
Green Curry	Dal
Curried Chick-peas	Plain Pilau
Saffron Rice	Aubergine Raita
Banana and Coconut Raita	Fresh Fruit
Cachumber	Chutneys
Chutneys	Puris or Chapatis
Puris or Chapatis	Tea
Tea	
Any Fresh Fruit Dessert	

When you're feeling dramatic, have this dinner. It starts quietly but deliciously with the Artichoke Puff, which can be served cool but is really more wonderful hot out of the oven. The rich soup version of Pasta i Fagioli, an Italian combination of pasta and beans, is also modestly served, but the Caesar Salad is a performance, prepared and tossed at the table. Then, instead of bowing out with something simple, serve crêpes for dessert! They can be made in advance and reheated when you're ready for them; the lemon juice and icing sugar are passed separately and added to taste, so it's really much easier than it sounds.

Artichoke and Cheese Puff

Pasta i Fagioli
French or Italian Bread

Caesar Salad

Fresh Lemon Dessert Crêpes

————

This is a good autumn or winter menu, with hearty dishes made of leeks, potatoes and cabbage, though you could also enjoy it in the spring. But if you have a garden and freeze vegetables in the summer when they are abundant, it's fun to bring out some tender green peas in the middle of winter and treat yourself to this most delicate, fresh-tasting soup.

Drink a dry, somewhat spicy white wine with this meal, or an excellent Pilsner beer.

Marinated Leeks

Creamed Fresh Pea Soup with Dumplings

Mushrooms and Potatoes in Wine Sauce
Red Cabbage with Apples

Fresh Fruit
Cheese

The Cheese Pastries can be made early in the day, or even the day before, and chilled, then baked at the last minute and served hot. While everyone is nibbling, start the rice; then serve the Broccoli Mousse with no delay, and the rice should be just right when you are ready to serve the second course.

Cheese Pastries

Cold Broccoli Mousse

Mushroom Stew
with Steamed Rice

Pumpkin Pie with Whipped Cream

Coffee

In Warsaw, where some of the best restaurants are Hungarian, I ate stuffed pancakes of this type many times, and they were always a delight – but so filling! Consequently, I've found that a light touch is needed in the rest of the menu.

Have a Gewürztraminer with this. The dry, slightly spicy flavour of the wine will bring out the best in the food. And one word of warning: it takes too long to make the large potato pancakes at the last minute if you are serving more than two people (unless you have more than two hands), so make them a few hours before dinner. Just before filling and serving them, reheat them quickly on both sides in a very lightly oiled pan.

Chilled Ukrainian Stewed Aubergine
with Dark Rye Bread

Stuffed Potato Pancakes, Hungarian Style
with Hot Paprika Sauce

Coffee Mousse

Espresso

Here's a meal that keeps topping itself with one exotic delicacy after another. It takes an investment of advance preparation, but is well worth it.

The *Bibbelkäse* is fairly simple and might well be made a day or two in advance. The hearts of palm are an expensive but wonderful treat: they can marinate in their dressing all day, if it's convenient, before being spooned into the tomatoes. Some last-minute work must be done for the soufflé and its rich sauce, though. Mousseline sauce is hollandaise-based, so it must be made very carefully and can't be kept warm too long, but what a special sauce it is.

Many desserts would be anticlimactic after such an array, but Wenia's Mazurek, an elaborate torte, is splendid enough for any occasion. Make it the day before if you can – it will keep perfectly.

Bibbelkäse
(Spiced White Cheese)

Tomatoes Stuffed with Hearts of Palm

Wild Mushroom and Dill Soufflé
with Spicy Mousseline Sauce

Wenia's Mazurek

Coffee or Tea

———

A soup to celebrate the cherry season, a frankly baroque Crêpe Cake, which can be constructed in advance and baked at the last, and a salad to be tossed at the table. Only the elegant dessert must be assembled just before serving.

Cold Cherry Soup

Wild Mushroom Crêpe Cake

Salad Torcoloti

Crème à la Irena
Espresso

To enjoy the last of the courgettes and the first cold days, here's a hearty and interesting combination. The Stuffed Courgettes make a salad that is at once assertive and delicate, with its subtle taste of coriander. It will wake up the palate before you go on to more solid fare.

The Sauerkraut Soup, obviously, is at the heart of this plan – rich and satisfying, redolent of tomatoes, onions and hot paprika, it is a perfect foil for the *pierogi* with their cases of soft yeast dough wrapped round fillings of cheese, black mushrooms or buttery cabbage and egg. The meal ends with a light touch: Apricots in Brandy.

Avocado-stuffed Courgettes

Assorted Pierogi
(Cheese-filled, Mushroom-filled, Cabbage-filled)
Sauerkraut Soup

Whole Apricots in Brandy

Coffee or Tea

The croquettes are hot and a little bit spicy, a nice accompaniment to the cool, refreshing soup. The giant stuffed mushrooms are necessarily a rare dish, as it isn't every day that you can find mushrooms impressive enough in size to fit this bill. For the dessert, prepare the batter and the apples in advance. Then, when you take the mushrooms out of the oven, put the pudding in, and it will be ready at the perfect moment. No wine with the soup, but a light red wine or a full-bodied white will go well with the mushrooms.

Chick-pea Croquettes
Cold Buttermilk Soup

Giant Mushrooms Stuffed with Aubergine
on a Bed of Spinach and Dill Rice

Apple Pudding

Coffee or Tea

For autumn or winter, a meal that is easier to prepare than it seems and worthy of any occasion. The salad should be prepared a few days in advance, so that it can develop flavour. The Spinach Soup is uncomplicated, as is the dessert. Only the soufflé needs careful timing. Put it in the oven just before you sit down to eat, then take your time with the salad and soup. Just remember to heat the sauce five minutes before the soufflé is finished. Afterwards, enjoy cool, soft apples, juicy and slightly sweet, with a lick of cream.

Beetroot and Pineapple Salad
with Dark Bread and Butter

Spinach Soup

Spicy Cheese and Potato Soufflé
with Dill Sauce

Baked Apples with Cold Fresh Cream

Coffee or Tea

———————————

This is a meal to celebrate spring and indulge spring fever, a meal of subtle textures and fresh, delicate flavours. Drink Asti Spumante with it or another fruity Italian white wine and really celebrate.

Lettuce with Vinaigrette Dressing
Baked Stuffed Tomatoes
with Aubergine and Courgette Filling

Asparagus Crêpes
Cucumber-Avocado Sauce

Fresh Strawberries
Butter Biscuits

Coffee

As many Cheese Pastries as you care to serve is exactly the number that will be devoured, so be forewarned and don't make so many that appetites for the later courses will suffer! The Sweet Potato Soup is not very heavy at all – instead, quite delicate – but the Roulade with its sauce is delightfully rich.

Cheese Pastries
Celeriac Salad

Sweet Potato Soup

Courgette and Aubergine Roulade with Mornay Sauce

Rum Baba

Coffee

This dinner, largely Viennese in flavour, with some influence from parts of Eastern Europe, is elegant but still hearty. Allow two or three hours for this meal. First there are salads to sample and Liptauer Cheese to taste, and this should be an unhurried activity. After the velvety Carrot Soup, allow a little break, so the chattering that accompanied the hors-d'oeuvres can resume while a new bottle of wine is opened and glasses filled. Then the Cabbage Rolls; by now spirits are high, and plenty of time must be allowed, not only to eat, but to finish the wine and the arguments. By the time the fresh berries and melons are served, everyone has pushed his or her chair back a little and sighed with contentment to see a light and refreshing dessert. Afterwards, linger over fresh, hot coffee.

ASSORTED COLD HORS-D'OEUVRES:
Paprikasalat   Potato Salad
Liptauer Cheese   Black Bread   Pickles

Cream of Carrot Soup

Mushroom and Barley Stuffed Cabbage Rolls

Fresh Strawberries and Melons in Brandy with Whipped Cream

Coffee or Espresso

For a special dinner on a warm summer night, I suggest a menu that includes only one hot dish – the stuffed Crêpes.

Lay the table with linen and shining crystal; open the windows to the garden and chill an excellent white wine. The pâtés are a beautiful way to begin. It feels so luxurious to have an assortment and enjoy the variety of flavours, but cut them in thin, thin slices because this course must tease the appetite, not sate it. Next, one of the world's great salads, which is really a soup: the sharp, icy cold Gazpacho of southern Spain. Then the palate is ready for something warm, mild and a bit rich. The stuffed Crêpes, sautéd in butter to a golden brown just before serving, are perfect. For dessert, Frozen Strawberry Mousse, cool, light and ambrosial.

HORS-D'OEUVRES:
Mushroom Pâté
White Bean Pâté
Egg and Olive Mould
Thin-sliced French Bread

Gazpacho

Crêpes with Feta Cheese
Garnished with Thin Wedges of Cantaloup

Frozen Strawberry Mousse

Coffee or Espresso

There are times when a light, simple and quickly prepared meal is in order; something more than a snack but less than a serious dinner. Late suppers, planned for after the cinema or theatre, hot-weather lunches or other meals of that sort have their own requirements. Either the food must be something that can be largely prepared in advance or it must be very easy and quick to make – but just because a meal is not elaborate is no reason for it to be dull. Six menus follow that bear this out. They range from the unusual and sophisticated to the simple and unadorned.

The dessert must be prepared in advance and the sauce for the Fettucine Alfredo can be as well, so that leaves tossing and dressing a salad and boiling the noodles – no great task. Have a nice, chilled white wine, a Soave, for example, with the fettucine and this simple meal will be very agreeable indeed.

Tossed Green Salad with Herb Dressing

Fettucine Alfredo

Oranges in Wine

Espresso
Amaretto

A Cold Omelette Salad is no snap to prepare, but it can be finished up to six or seven hours in advance without suffering and then just brought out on your fanciest silver tray. The Cheese-filled Bread, of course, is made in advance, and so are the Baked Apples. The result is a light, pleasant meal that needs, by way of last-minute work, only to be carried out and served, yet is quite elegant.

Cold Omelette Salad
Cheese-filled Bread

Baked Apples

Tea or Coffee

Have some cold soup ready – it could be the Cold Avocado Soup or a gazpacho – and you can be eating this very tasty meal in about 20 minutes' time. The Potato and Courgette Omelettes are also an ideal choice for brunch; serve with any assortment of fresh fruit, some hot muffins or toast and fresh-brewed coffee.

Cold Avocado Soup

Potato and Courgette Omelettes

Fresh Fruit and Cheese
Biscuits

Coffee or Tea

Start with Ensaladilla Russa, the simple and tasty Spanish version of a Russian vegetable salad – it is the right preliminary to Garlic Soup, which must be eaten only among good, garlic-loving friends. Garlic Soup is made moments before it is served, but takes only 5 or 10 minutes to prepare (and packs a real punch for such a quickie). After this soup, fresh fruit is the obvious choice, but something a bit sweeter and richer might be wanted a little later, so serve another Spanish winter favourite, the thick hot chocolate, instead of coffee.

Ensaladilla Russa

Garlic Soup

Fresh Fruit and Cheese

Castilian Hot Chocolate

Although the mushrooms must be cooked just before serving, they take so little time that this does not present a problem. I've suggested the Paprika-Cucumber Salad here because it must be made in advance and keeps nicely, but almost any salad would do.

Paprika-Cucumber Salad

Mushrooms on Toast

Custard or Pudding

Coffee or Tea

Sometimes the absolutely simplest fare is the best, more suited to the mood and appetite than anything sophisticated or rich.

This menu was inspired by memories of my stay in England during the cold, dark month of November. There, late one night, in front of a bright, hot fire, I first feasted on William Bryan's pungent, spicy pickled onions and a good old English cheese, along with a crusty bread and an excellent bitter beer.

The preparation for this meal, except for the tart, is all in procuring a fine cheese and the very tastiest pickled onions. The best thing to do is to open a jar of the onions you pickled yourself (with the recipe on page 392) six or eight weeks before.

Pickled Onions

Sharp Cheddar Cheese

Crusty Rolls and Butter

Dark Beer or Ale

Apple Tart

Coffee

Breads

ALL THE FICKLENESS OF MY NATURE emerges on the subject of bread. There are at least a dozen different kinds that I could call my favourite without batting an eye. I can't help loving the light, long French baguettes, however many times I'm reminded that white flour is not as nutritious as whole wheat. On the other hand, my fondness for the dark, dense, shiny-surfaced ryes and pumpernickels of northern and eastern Europe remains undiminished. I could and often do make a meal of a thick, moist slice of Rye Bread with Fruit or Beer Bread.

On another day my favourite is Corn Bread, yellow and buttery and hot; a classic corn bread recipe is given in the first *Vegetarian Epicure*, but now I have new variations on that tasty theme: Pumpkin Corn Bread and Corn and Rye Muffins. Then, when nothing will do but a chewy oatmeal bread, I dicker between the filling Oatmeal Rye Bread and the slightly sweet Oatmeal Raisin Bread.

Rich-textured whole-wheat bread is certainly one of my continuing favourites, and I've added two excellent versions to my repertoire here: Whole-wheat Anadama Bread is an early American variety, a little heavier than others for the addition of some corn meal; and Whole-wheat Egg Bread, rich and mild, can be made into a fine cinnamon loaf with practically no extra effort.

Flat breads and fried breads, like the easy-to-make Indian puris and chapatis; beautiful, egg-varnished brioches or plaited Vienna Bread; quick soda breads, served warm, like the addictive Cranberry Bread; and elegantly coiled Sweet Coffee Bread, on its way to becoming cake, opulent with egg yolks, butter, raisins and lemon rind – they're all my favourites, and that without taking anything away from rolls, muffins and rusks. What's more, I'm always ready to be tempted by some new discovery.

As everyone seems to be noticing these days, making bread at home can be relaxing, enjoyable and gratifying in many ways. Most of us do little enough with our hands now and find that the chore of kneading, once we get the knack, is a pleasantly sensual experience (at least until the phone rings when both hands are immersed to the wrists in dough). Furthermore, baking bread is not nearly as complicated or time-consuming as many believe. The actual working time is usually no longer than half an hour; for the rest of it, the hours of rising and baking, the bread takes care of itself. Those hours can be arranged very conveniently, too, since you can always retard the rising of your dough by putting it in the refrigerator if you get the yen to go to the cinema, for instance.

The whole bread process, from kneading to shaping to baking, is progressively more delightful as you go along. But finally, whatever may be said about the joy of kneading and the mouth-watering aroma of baking bread, the real pay-off in making your own bread is in the last step, the ever-renewable joy of eating.

Making Bread

With a little practice, you will find making a yeast dough and forming loaves the easiest things in the world – they become practically second nature. The basic techniques are uncomplicated and only a few rules have to be kept in mind.

Remember, first of all, that yeast is a living organism and is affected by temperature. Active dried yeast should be dissolved in lukewarm water. Hot water will kill it and cold water will not activate it, so test the water on your hand or wrist: it should feel just comfortably warm.

When the yeast is dissolved, the liquids and flours can be combined with it immediately to make the dough, or else a soft 'sponge' can be made first and allowed to rise for a while before the rest of the flour is added. For this second method, the dissolved yeast is combined with enough warm liquid and flour to make a rather thick batter, which is left in a warm place for an hour or longer. During that time, it bubbles and expands very impressively, until it looks exactly like a big, soft sponge. The remaining flour and other ingredients are then stirred into the sponge, and a normal, stiff dough is formed, which is kneaded and left to rise as usual. Breads made with the sponge method take a little longer but have a wonderful flavour and texture.

The questions of exactly how much flour to mix into your bread dough and how long to knead cannot be answered except by the practised touch of your hands once you've made a few loaves. However, the techniques can be described, and applying them should lead you to a recognizably good dough.

First, flour is added to the liquid mixture in the bowl until it is too stiff to be stirred. The dough is then turned out on to a large, well-floured board and sprinkled with more flour. It is important at this stage to keep the entire surface of the dough, top and bottom, well coated with flour, as it can be very annoying to get your hands stuck in it when it is still in a soft, glue-like state. (That's when the phone rings.)

Keeping it well dredged in flour, press the dough down with the heels of your hands, then fold it over. Press down again, pushing it out a bit, and fold over from the other side. That's all there is to kneading. The dough, which starts out soft and a little lumpy, gradually becomes more elastic, smoother and less sticky as it is kneaded and the necessary flour is worked in. After about 10 or 15 minutes, it should be quite springy, very smooth and no longer sticky.

Now you pat the dough into a ball and place it in an oiled or buttered bowl to rise. Turn the dough over once or twice so that all of its surface is coated with the butter or oil – this will prevent its drying out. Cover the bowl with a tea-towel or cling film and leave it in a warm, draught-free place. The temperature of the dough during the rising is important. Left in a cosy place at about 75–85°F, the dough will rise quite speedily, perhaps in an hour or so, though the kind of flour used will affect rising time, too. If it's a bit chilly in the spot where the dough is left, it may take several hours, though the dough is not at all harmed by this. If it's cold, you can wait till the world looks level, and nothing will happen.

When the dough has doubled in size, it must be punched down. Just make a fist and plunge it into the dough. It will sigh and collapse softly round your hand. At this point the dough should be ready to be formed into loaves.

Making a simple loaf is just a matter of rolling out and rolling up. Roll the dough out into an oblong shape about ¾ in/18 mm thick with a rolling pin, making it just a little wider at one end of the oblong. Starting at the narrower end, roll it up tightly into a cylinder. Pinch the seam, pull the ends over, and pinch the end seams. Or, if you prefer, just pat the dough into a loaf shape with your hands, pull it together along one side, and pinch the seam securely. Put the formed loaf into a loaf tin, seam side down, and there you are. Round loaves can be made by gathering the dough into a ball and pulling the ends together in one spot, where they can be firmly pinched together. The ball is then placed on a prepared baking sheet, pinched side down.

Once shaped, the loaves are left to rise again, but this time it doesn't take as long. While they are rising, preheat the oven. If you brush a loaf with water just before you put it in to bake, the crust will be harder and crisper. If you brush it with butter or oil, the crust will be softer. If you brush it with a glaze of egg yolk and cream, it will be beautifully shiny and brown.

Baking time can vary slightly, but when a loaf looks big and golden brown and has been in the oven for about the right amount of time, you can assure yourself that it is done by using a simple test: take it out and, using oven gloves or a towel, turn it upside down. Tap it lightly on the bottom. If it sounds hollow, it should be done. Loaves baked in tins should be removed from the tins as soon as they are done and cooled on racks. Loaves baked on baking sheets can be cooled on them.

Of course, you will want to slice it up and eat it hot with no further delay, and since that's what I do myself, I can't tell anyone else not to. But be prepared for some ragged-looking slices if you cut the bread while it's still hot. If you want it to cut smoothly and prettily, you must wait – but who can wait?

PLAITED WHOLE-WHEAT EGG BREAD

MAKES 2 LARGE LOAVES

2 tbsp dried yeast	*1 tbsp salt*
2½ fl oz/70 ml warm water	*1 whole egg*
16 fl oz/450 ml milk	*4 egg yolks*
1½ oz/40 g butter	*1 tsp single cream*
2 tbsp sugar	*sesame seeds*
7–7½ cups whole-wheat flour	

Dissolve the yeast in the warm water. Scald the milk and stir the butter and sugar into it. Pour the hot milk mixture into a large mixing bowl and when lukewarm, stir in the yeast.

Mix together the flour and the salt. Add about 2 cups of flour to the milk and beat with an electric beater until the mixture is smooth. Beat the egg and the yolks together lightly. Reserve about 2 tablespoons of the beaten egg mixture and add the rest to the batter. Beat again until smooth.

Gradually stir in enough flour to make a stiff dough. When the dough is too stiff to be stirred with a spoon, turn it out on to a well-floured board and knead about 10–15 minutes, adding more flour as necessary, until the dough is smooth and elastic.

Form the dough into a ball and put it in a large, buttered bowl, turning it over once so that it is coated on all sides. Cover the bowl with a towel and leave it in a warm, draught-free place for about 1½ hours, or until the dough has doubled in size.

Punch the dough down and cut it into 2 pieces. Pat each piece into a smooth oblong, about 6 × 14 in/150 × 350 mm. Slice the oblongs into 3 even strips, leaving them connected at one end. Starting at the connected end, form a thick plait, tucking under the last bit and pinching it to the others.

Place the plaits in 2 buttered medium-sized loaf tins, cover them with a towel and let them rise for about 30 minutes, or until half as large again.

Stir about 1 teaspoon of cream into the reserved egg and brush the tops of the loaves with it. Sprinkle the loaves with sesame seeds and bake them in a preheated oven at 375°F/190°C/Mark 5 for 45–50 minutes.

Vienna Bread

MAKES 2 MEDIUM-SIZED LOAVES

2 tbsp dried yeast	1 tbsp salt
8 fl oz/225 ml warm water	1½ oz/40 g butter, melted
2 tbsp sugar	GLAZE
5½–6½ cups white flour	1 egg yolk
8 fl oz/225 ml milk	1 tbsp milk

Dissolve the yeast in the warm water and stir in 1 tablespoon of the sugar and 1¾–2 cups flour, enough to make a soft, spongy dough. Cover the bowl with a towel and put the sponge aside in a warm place to rise for about 45 minutes, or until it is puffed and soft.

Add the milk, the remaining sugar, salt, and melted butter, and stir the sponge down well. Work in as much of the remaining flour as is needed to make a fairly stiff dough. Turn the dough out on to a heavily floured board, sprinkle a little more flour over it and knead it for 10–15 minutes, or until it is smooth and elastic; add flour as needed to keep the dough from sticking.

Form the dough into a ball and put it in a large, buttered bowl, turning it over once so that it is coated with butter on all sides. Cover the bowl with a light towel and put it in a warm, draught-free place for about 45 minutes–1 hour or until the dough has doubled in size.

Punch down the dough and form it into 2 oblong loaves or large plaits (see previous recipe). Put the loaves on buttered baking sheets, cover them with a light towel, and leave them in a warm place to rise for about 30 minutes or until they have nearly doubled in size.

Beat together the egg yolk and the tablespoon of milk and brush the loaves delicately with the glaze. Put them in a preheated oven at 425°F/220°C/Mark 7 and after 5 minutes lower the heat to 375°F/190°C/Mark 5. Bake the loaves for 35–40 minutes more, until they are golden brown.

Cool the loaves on racks before slicing.

WHOLE-WHEAT ANADAMA BREAD

MAKES 1 LARGE LOAF

1 tbsp dried yeast
13 fl oz/370 ml warm water
1 tbsp sugar
3 tbsp molasses
3 cups whole-wheat flour

1 cup white flour
1 cup yellow corn-meal
1 tbsp salt
1 oz/25 g butter, melted

Dissolve the yeast in the warm water with the sugar and molasses. Mix together the flours, corn-meal and salt and add about 1½ cups of the dry mixture to the liquid. Stir vigorously until smooth and put this sponge in a warm place to rise for about 1 hour.

Stir down the sponge, add the melted butter and gradually stir in as much of the flour mixture as you can. When the dough is too stiff to be stirred, sprinkle the remaining flour mixture on a large board, turn the dough out on to it, turn it over and begin gently kneading. Knead the dough until it is even-textured and elastic, working in as much of the flour as necessary to keep it from sticking, but no more.

Form the dough into a ball, put it in a buttered bowl, turn it over once or twice and then cover the bowl with a towel and leave the dough to rise, in a warm, draught-free place until it is double in size. Punch it down, knead it a couple more times and form it into a high, round loaf, pinching the seams together on the bottom. Place the loaf on a baking sheet that has been buttered and coated with corn-meal, and leave it to rise until it has almost doubled in size.

Cut a shallow cross in the top of the loaf with a sharp knife and brush the loaf with cold water. Bake in a preheated oven at 400°F/200°C/Mark 6 for about 45 minutes.

BRIOCHES

MAKES 2 MEDIUM-SIZED BRIOCHES

4½ fl oz/125 ml warm milk	1 tsp salt
1 tbsp dried yeast	3 eggs
2 tsp sugar	GLAZE
2½ cups flour	1 tbsp milk
4 oz/115 g soft butter	1 egg yolk

There are two methods of making brioches: the hard way, which involves plenty of energetic beating by hand, and the delightfully easy way, with a food processor. Here's the hard way first.

Blend the warm milk, yeast and sugar, stirring until the yeast is dissolved. Beat in 1 cup of the flour. Add the soft butter and salt and continue beating, either with a heavy-duty electric mixer or by hand, until the mixture is perfectly smooth.

Add the eggs, one at a time, beating again after each. Then gradually add the remaining flour and beat vigorously until the dough is glossy and elastic. If you are using a wooden spoon or your hand, the best method is to slap the dough hard against the side of a large bowl, pulling it up high each time and flinging it back down. The dough is ready when it starts to blister and pull away from your hand or the side of the bowl.

Place the dough in a large, buttered bowl, cover it with a towel, and let it rise in a warm place until it has doubled in bulk, about 2½–3½ hours.

Stir the dough down, cover the bowl with cling film, and chill the dough in the refrigerator at least 6 hours or overnight.

Butter two 7½-in/190-mm brioche tins.

Divide the dough into 2 equal parts, and leave 1 in the refrigerator. Take the other part and, on a lightly floured board, form it into 2 smooth balls, 1 large one and the other about ⅕ its size. To shape the balls, flour your hands and pull the dough down gently to a point at the bottom of the ball, pinching the ends together there securely.

Place the large ball of dough in one of the brioche moulds, pinched side down, and cut a small cross in the top of it with a sharp, pointed knife. With floured fingers, pull the dough apart slightly where it has been cut, forming a hole almost large enough to hold the small ball of dough. Place the small ball of dough into that hole, nesting it gently inside. It should be about half-hidden.

Shape the remaining half of the dough the same way, and put the brioches in a warm place, covered with a light towel, to rise for 2½–3 hours or until nearly doubled in bulk.

Beat the egg yolk and milk together for the glaze and gently brush the brioches with it. Bake them for 45–50 minutes in a preheated oven at 350°F/180°C/Mark 4. Unmould and serve warm or allow to cool first on a wire rack.

Brioches must be eaten fresh!

FOOD PROCESSOR METHOD

Dissolve the yeast in the milk and stir in the sugar and 1 cup flour. Put the steel blade in the food processor and pour the yeast-flour mixture into the container. Process for 15–20 seconds or until smooth.

Add the soft butter and salt and process for another 20 seconds. Add the eggs and process again for about 20 seconds.

Add the remaining flour and process for about 3 minutes, stopping occasionally to scrape down the sides of the container. The dough should be velvety smooth, glossy and elastic. Proceed exactly as above in allowing the dough to rise, chilling it, shaping it, letting the brioches rise once more and baking them.

OATMEAL-RYE BREAD

MAKES 2 LOAVES

2 tbsp dried yeast	1 tbsp salt
24 fl oz/680 ml warm water	2 cups dark rye flour
2 fl oz/55 ml molasses	2 cups rolled oats
2 cups white flour	more white flour as needed
2 cups whole-wheat flour	(1–1½ cups)

Stir the yeast into the warm water in a large bowl. Add the molasses and stir until it is dissolved. Add the white flour and the whole-wheat flour, about 1 cup at a time, stirring well after each addition. When all 4 cups of flour have been stirred in, beat the mixture vigorously with a wooden spoon for about 10 minutes. It should be smooth and very soft.

Cover the bowl with a dry tea-towel and put it in a warm, draught-free place for 45 minutes–1 hour. The yeast sponge should rise considerably and be rather bubbly at the end of this time.

Now sprinkle the salt over the sponge and fold it in. Add the rye flour and the oats, a little at a time, and fold them in. The dough should be quite thick. If it is not thick enough to handle, add a little more white flour. As soon as the dough is manageable enough to be removed from the bowl in more or less one piece, turn it out on to a floured board and begin kneading. Knead in only as much additional flour as is necessary to form a reasonably non-sticky dough. When the dough is smooth and elastic (about 20 minutes of kneading), form it into a ball and put it in a large, buttered bowl, turning it over once so that it is coated with butter on top as well.

Cover the bowl with a tea-towel and put it aside for about 1 hour to rise. The dough should be doubled in size.

Punch the dough down and divide it into 2 parts, forming each into a loaf. Put the loaves in buttered, medium-sized loaf tins, cover them with tea-towels and put them aside to rise for about 50 minutes. Bake the bread in a preheated oven at 350°F/180°C/Mark 4 for 1 hour. When it is done, remove the loaves from the tins and allow them to cool on a rack.

Rye Bread with Fruit

This is a dense, rich bread, meant to be cut in thin slices. It is very good buttered, excellent with a mild cheese and keeps well for a couple of weeks.

MAKES 2 LARGE LOAVES

2 tbsp dried yeast
8 fl oz/225 ml warm potato water*
2 cups warm mashed potatoes
4 fl oz/115 ml molasses
approximately 4 cups whole-
    wheat flour
2½ cups dark rye flour
2 tsp salt

½ cup wheat germ
⅔ cup chopped prunes
⅔ cup sultanas
⅔ cup currants
⅔ cup chopped walnuts
GLAZE
1 egg yolk
2 tbsp water

Dissolve the yeast in the warm potato water and stir it into the mashed potatoes in a large bowl. Add the molasses and 2 cups of the whole-wheat flour and blend well. Cover the bowl with a light towel and put it away in a warm, draught-free place for 1½ hours to let the sponge rise.

Stir down the sponge. Mix together the rye flour and the salt, and stir them in along with the wheat germ, fruit and nuts.

Turn the dough out on to a heavily floured surface and knead in as much more of the whole-wheat flour as is necessary to make a manageable dough. Continue kneading the dough until it feels elastic and springs back when pushed down.

Form the dough into a ball and put it in a large, lightly buttered bowl, turn it over once, cover the bowl with a towel and put it aside in a warm place for 1½ hours or until the dough has risen to about twice its former size. Punch the dough down, form a ball again and let the dough rise again for about 45 minutes.

Divide the dough into 2 parts and shape each into a ball. Place the balls, smooth side up, on buttered baking sheets. Cover them with a light towel and let them rise for 45 minutes. Brush the loaves with the glaze and bake them in a preheated oven at 375°F/190°C/Mark 5 for 1 hour.

Allow the loaves to cool before slicing.

* Just the water in which
you've cooked the potatoes.

RAISIN-RYE BREAD

MAKES 2 MEDIUM-SIZED LOAVES

2 tbsp dried yeast
12 fl oz/340 ml lukewarm water
1 tsp sugar
1⅓ cups raisins
8 fl oz/225 ml milk
¼ cup brown sugar
grated rind of 2 oranges

½ tsp fennel seeds, crushed
4½ cups rye flour
1½ oz/40 g butter, melted
1 tbsp salt
2½ cups white flour
corn-meal

In a small bowl dissolve the yeast in 4 fl oz/115 ml of the luke-warm water and stir in the sugar. Leave the yeast to prove for about 10 minutes.

Pour boiling water over the raisins and let them plump up in it for 10 minutes, then drain.

Combine the milk with the remaining 8 fl oz/225 ml water and heat the liquid until it is lukewarm. In a large bowl, stir together the milk and water, the yeast mixture, brown sugar, raisins, orange rind, fennel seed and 2 cups of rye flour. Beat this mixture with a wooden spoon until there are no lumps of flour left, then stir in the melted butter and salt.

Beat in the remaining rye flour, ½ cup at a time, plus 1 cup of the white flour. The dough should now be getting a bit too stiff to be beaten with a spoon. If not, add a little more of the white flour until it is.

Sprinkle 1 cup of white flour over a large, flat wooden or marble surface and dump the dough out on top of it. Sprinkle the remaining white flour on top of the dough. Carefully start kneading, keeping the dough well coated with flour at first, as it will be sticky. Knead in as much flour as is necessary to make a smooth, elastic dough. The kneading should take about 15 to 20 minutes.

Form the dough into a ball and put it in a large, buttered bowl. Turn the dough over once or twice so that it is completely coated with butter. Cover the bowl with a tea-towel and leave the dough to rise in a warm, draught-free place for 1 hour or until it has doubled in size.

Punch the dough down, knead it a few times and cut it in half. Form each half into a smooth ball, pinching it together firmly at the seams. Put the loaves, seam side down, on buttered baking sheets that have been sprinkled with corn-meal. With a sharp, serrated knife, cut a large X in the top of each loaf. Cover the loaves with a tea-towel and leave them to rise again for another hour or until almost doubled in bulk.

Brush the loaves with water and bake them in a preheated oven at 375°F/190°C/Mark 5 for 1 hour or a little longer, until they sound hollow when tapped on the bottom.

Cool the loaves on racks.

EASY HERB BREAD

This is a yeast bread, but it doesn't take as long to make as most of them and is wonderful to serve warm with dinner.

MAKES 3 SMALL LOAVES

8 fl oz/225 ml water
8 fl oz/225 ml milk
¼ cup sugar
2 tbsp dried yeast
2 fl oz/55 ml vegetable oil
1 clove garlic, finely minced
3 tbsp minced onion

approximately 5 cups whole-
    wheat flour
1¼ tsp salt
½ tsp dried basil, crushed
½ tsp dried oregano, crushed
¼ tsp dried thyme, crushed
1 egg

Heat together the water and milk until lukewarm, then stir in the sugar and the yeast.

Heat the oil in a small frying pan and sauté the garlic and onions in it until they just begin to colour.

In a large bowl, combine the yeast mixture with about 1½ cups of the flour and beat with an electric mixer until smooth. Add the salt, the herbs, the oil mixture and the egg and beat again. Gradually add approximately another 1½ cups of flour and beat for 5 minutes. The dough should be soft and smooth.

Stir in another cup of flour, then turn the dough out on to a floured board and knead it for 5 minutes, working in as much of the remaining flour as is necessary to keep it from sticking. The dough should be smooth and elastic and still quite soft. Form it into a ball and put it in an oiled bowl, turning it over once so that it is evenly coated with the oil. Cover the bowl with a towel and leave it in a warm place for 45 minutes or until the dough has nearly doubled in size.

Punch down the dough and form it into 3 small loaves. Place them in small, oiled loaf tins, cover them with a towel and leave them to rise again for about 30 minutes. Bake the loaves in a preheated oven at 375°F/190°C/Mark 5 for 35 minutes or until they sound hollow when tapped on the bottom.

BEER BREAD

If you like hard-crusted, coarse-textured breads, go no further. This is the bread for you. It has a beautiful dark colour, a rich flavour, and a combination of chewiness and crunch that few loaves can claim. However, you must give it ample time to rise before baking or it will come out of the oven like a regular little brick.

MAKES 1 LARGE LOAF

½ cup whole-wheat berries	1½ cups white flour
24 fl oz/680 ml water	1 tbsp salt
8 fl oz/225 ml dark beer, warmed	½ tsp fennel seeds, finely crushed in a mortar
2 tbsp dried yeast	2¾–3 cups stone-ground dark rye flour
2 fl oz/55 ml molasses	

Put the wheat berries and the water in a medium-sized, heavy-bottomed saucepan, bring to a boil, then lower the heat and leave the wheat berries to simmer very gently for about 2–3 hours, or until they are very tender and bursting open.

In a large bowl combine the warm beer, yeast and 1 tablespoon of the molasses, and leave it for about 10 minutes, or until it foams up.

When the yeast mixture foams, stir in the remaining molasses and the white flour and beat vigorously with a wooden spoon until the mixture is smooth. Cover the bowl with a tea-towel and leave it in a warm place for about 40 minutes to let the sponge rise. It should be bubbly and doubled in size.

Stir down the sponge and mix in the salt and fennel seeds. Gradually add the rye flour, stirring it in until the dough is too stiff to mix with a spoon. Sprinkle some of the rye flour on to a large, flat wooden surface and turn the dough out on to it. Sprinkle more rye flour over the dough and begin kneading. Knead the dough for at least 10 minutes, working in as much of the flour as necessary to keep it from sticking. When the dough is elastic, form it into a ball and put it in a buttered bowl, turning it over once so that it is coated with butter all over. Cover the bowl with a towel and leave it in a warm, draught-free place for 1 hour or until the dough has doubled in size.

Punch down the dough, turn it out on to the floured board and flatten it slightly. Drain the cooked wheat berries thoroughly, spread some of them on the flattened dough, fold the dough over and start kneading them in, Continue flattening the dough, adding more wheat berries and kneading until they are all incorporated into the dough.

Form the dough into a smooth, round ball, pinching the seams together securely, and place it, seam side down, on a buttered baking sheet. Brush the loaf lightly with butter, cut a shallow cross in the top with a sharp knife, cover it with a tea-towel, and leave it in a warm, draught-free place to rise until it has nearly doubled in size.

Bake the loaf in a preheated oven at 425°F/220°C/Mark 7 for 10 minutes, then reduce the heat to 375°F/190°C/Mark 5 and bake it for another 55 minutes–1 hour or until it sounds hollow when tapped on the bottom.

Brush the hot loaf again with butter and let it cool. Slice the bread with a very sharp, serrated knife.

OATMEAL-RAISIN BREAD

MAKES 4 LOAVES

2 cups rolled oats
2 pt/1.1 l water
2½ fl oz/70 ml honey
2 tbsp salt
⅔ cup wheat germ

2 tbsp dried yeast
6 cups whole-wheat flour
1 cup raisins
2 cups white flour

Cook the oats in 1⅔ pt/950 ml boiling water until they are just soft (5–10 minutes). Stir in the honey, salt and wheat germ and let the mixture cool to lukewarm.

Dissolve the yeast in the remaining water, which should be warm, and stir it into the oats along with 3 cups of the whole-wheat flour. Beat the sponge with a wooden spoon for a few minutes, then cover the bowl with a tea-towel and let the sponge rise in a warm, draught-free place for about 1 hour or until it has doubled its volume.

Stir down the sponge and stir in the raisins and the remaining whole-wheat flour. Sprinkle 1 cup of the white flour over a flat wooden or marble surface and turn the dough out on to it. Sprinkle the remaining white flour on top of the dough.

Knead the dough for about 10 minutes or until it is smooth and elastic. Form it into a ball and put it in a large, buttered bowl, turning it over so that it is evenly buttered. Cover the bowl with a tea-towel and put the dough away to rise for 1 hour or until it has doubled in size.

Punch down the dough, cut it into 4 even parts and form each part into a loaf. Place the loaves in 4 buttered medium-sized tins, cover them with a tea-towel and let them rise for about 30 minutes. Bake the loaves in a preheated oven at 400°F/200°C/Mark 6 for 15 minutes, then turn the heat down to 350°F/180°C/Mark 4 and bake them for another 30–40 minutes.

Variation: Cinnamon Bread

Prepare the bread dough as described above. When you are ready to form the loaves, take each portion of the dough and roll it out in an oval shape until it is about ½ in/12 mm thick. Brush it with melted butter, evenly sprinkle about 1 teaspoon cinnamon over it, then sprinkle about 2 tablespoons sugar over the cinnamon. Starting at one of the narrow ends of the oval, roll it up into a loaf and pinch together the bottom. Place in buttered pans and bake as described above.

CHEESE-FILLED BREAD

MAKES 1 LARGE LOAF

DOUGH
1 tbsp dried yeast
2 fl oz/55 ml lukewarm water
2 tbsp plus 2 tsp sugar
8 fl oz/225 ml milk,
  scalded
1½ tsp salt
4½–5½ cups flour
2 eggs
4 oz/115 g butter, melted

FILLING
1½ lb/675 g Munster cheese,
  grated
2–3 oz/55–85 g Roquefort or
  blue cheese
1 oz/25 g butter, melted
2 eggs
GLAZE
1 egg
1 tbsp single cream

Dissolve the yeast in the water and stir in 2 teaspoons of the sugar. Combine the scalded milk in a large bowl with the remaining sugar and the salt, and allow it to cool to lukewarm. Stir in the yeast and 2 cups of the flour, and beat the mixture vigorously with a wooden spoon for about 10 minutes.

Beat the eggs lightly and add them to the dough. Beat with a wooden spoon again until the eggs are completely incorporated and then stir in the butter. Continue beating, slapping the dough up against the sides of the bowl, until it blisters. Gradually beat in 2 more cups of flour.

Sprinkle a large board with the remaining flour, turn the dough out on to it and knead it gently until it is perfectly smooth, elastic and no longer sticky. Form the dough into a ball, put it in a large, buttered bowl, turning it once so that it is coated with butter. Cover the bowl with a tea-towel and put the dough in a warm, draught-free place to rise for about 1½ hours or until it has doubled in bulk.

While the dough is rising, prepare the filling. Put the grated Munster cheese in a medium-sized bowl. Mash the Roquefort cheese with a fork until it is a soft paste and stir in the melted butter. Beat the eggs lightly, beat in the Roquefort-butter mixture, then pour it over the grated Munster and stir the whole thing up thoroughly.

When the dough has risen, punch it down and turn it out on to a lightly floured board. Roll it out into a circle about 24 in/610 mm across, dust it lightly with flour and transfer it carefully on to a buttered 9–10-in/230–255-mm cake tin. Press the dough evenly into the pan, leaving the edge hanging over the sides.

Spread the filling over the dough in the tin and fold the sides of the dough up over it, pleating it as you bring it in to the centre. Gather the edges up to the centre and twist them together, forming a little knob on top of the loaf.

Let the loaf rise for about 30 minutes. Make the glaze by beating the egg with the cream and brush the loaf with it. Bake the loaf in a preheated oven at 350°F/180°C/Mark 4 for about 1½ hours. Serve the bread warm, cut into wedges.

ANOTHER WAY: MAKES 2 MEDIUM-SIZED LOAVES

To make smaller, less spectacular but more manageable loaves, cut the dough in half. Roll out one portion into a rectangle about ½ in/12 mm thick. Spread half the filling over the dough, leaving a 1-in/25-mm border round the sides and the near end, and a 2-in/50-mm border at the far end. Roll the dough up over the filling, finishing at the end with the wider border. Tuck under the ends, moisten the edge lightly with water and pinch the seams together securely. Fill and shape the second portion of the dough the same way.

Place the loaves, seam side down, on buttered baking sheets and let them rise in a warm, draught-free place for about 30 minutes. Brush them with egg glaze and, just before putting them into the oven, make a very shallow slash with a sharp knife lengthways down the centre of each loaf. Bake in a preheated oven at 350°F/180°C/Mark 4 for about 1¼ hours.

Sweet Coffee Bread

Not quite a coffee cake, but a delicious, sweet bread to have with tea or coffee.

MAKES 1 LARGE LOAF

DOUGH
1 tbsp dried yeast
4 fl oz/115 ml lukewarm water
6 tbsp sugar
3 cups white flour
1 cup whole-wheat pastry flour
1 tsp salt
1 cup raisins
3 whole eggs
2 egg yolks
2½ fl oz/70 ml milk

4 oz/115 g soft butter
FILLING
1½ cups cottage cheese
6 tbsp sugar
2 egg yolks
2 tsp finely grated, fresh lemon
  rind
3 tbsp flour
melted butter
icing sugar

Dissolve the yeast in the lukewarm water, add 2 tablespoons of the sugar and ¾ cup of the white flour, and stir well. Put this sponge aside in a warm place for 30 minutes or until it begins to puff and bubble.

In a large mixing bowl, sift together 2 cups of the white flour, the whole-wheat flour, remaining sugar and the salt. Add the raisins. In another bowl beat together the eggs, egg yolks and milk. Stir this mixture into the dry ingredients along with the yeast sponge and then begin working in the soft butter.

When all the butter has been incorporated, beat the dough vigorously with a wooden spoon, slapping it up against the sides of the bowl, until it becomes glossy and starts to blister. It should come away from the sides of the bowl pretty easily at this point.

Cover the bowl with a towel and put it in a warm, draught-free place for about 1½ hours or until the dough has doubled in size. Punch the dough down and turn it out on to a well-floured board. Sprinkle the dough with the remainder of the white flour and knead it gently a few times, just until it is smooth enough to handle.

Force the cheese through a sieve or spin it in a food processor to make it smooth.

Make the filling by combining the sieved cheese, sugar, egg yolks, lemon rind and flour. Stir well until the mixture is completely blended and free from lumps. It should be thick enough to hold a shape.

On a floured board, roll the dough out into a rectangle about 12 × 20 in/305 × 510 mm. Spread the cheese filling over it, leaving a 2-in/50-mm border at the ends and along one side, and a 3–4-in/75–100-mm border along the other side.

Roll up the dough lengthways over the filling, towards the side with the wide border. When it is almost completely rolled up, pull up the wide-bordered edge and stretch it slightly over the top of the roll. Moisten the edge with a bit of water and pinch the seam together securely. Turn up the ends and pinch them as well.

Turn the roll over carefully so that the seam is on the bottom. Transfer it carefully to a buttered baking sheet and shape it into a circle or a nearly closed horseshoe. Cover it with a tea-towel and set it aside in a warm place to rise for about 45 minutes or until it has nearly doubled in size. Brush the top with melted butter and bake it in a preheated oven at 350°F/180°C/Mark 4 for 70 minutes. Check it once, about 20 minutes before it is done, and if the top is getting very dark, cover it with a loose sheet of aluminium foil.

Allow the bread to cool and dust the top with icing sugar.

SOFT DINNER ROLLS

MAKES ABOUT 36

1 tbsp dried yeast
2 fl oz/55 ml warm water
½ pt/285 ml warm milk
1 egg, lightly beaten
4 cups unbleached white flour

¼ cup sugar
2 oz/55 g butter, melted
1 tsp salt
melted butter for brushing rolls

Dissolve the yeast in the warm water and combine it in a large, warm bowl with the milk, egg and a scant 2 cups of the flour. Beat by hand or with an electric mixer until all the lumps of flour are gone and the mixture is perfectly smooth. Add the sugar, melted butter and salt and beat again until smooth and glossy.

Stir in another cup of flour. The dough should now be getting stiff enough to hold together. Sprinkle half the remaining flour on to a large board, turn the dough out on to it and sprinkle the rest of the flour over the dough. Gently begin kneading the dough, keeping it coated with flour at all times to prevent sticking. Knead in as much of the flour as is needed to make a dough that is manageable but still soft.

When it is smooth and elastic, form the dough into a ball and put it in a warm, buttered bowl, turning it over once so that it is coated with butter on all sides. Cover the bowl with a towel and leave the dough to rise in a warm, draught-free place for about 1 hour or until it has doubled in volume.

Punch the dough down, place it on a lightly floured board, and roll it out into a rectangle about 9 × 18 in/230 × 460 mm. Cut the rectangle in half lengthways, and then cut each half into 1-in/ 25-mm strips crossways. To form a roll, pick up one of the strips, stretch it out slightly, twist it around a few turns, then tie it in one loose knot, and a second one next to it. Put the roll down on a buttered baking sheet, tucking the ends underneath.

These rolls will have an uneven oval shape. Of course, the rolls can be shaped any way that you prefer and they'll be just as tasty – this is just my way of forming rolls, preferred because it is so fast and simple.

When all the dough is shaped into rolls and arranged several inches apart on buttered baking sheets, cover the rolls with light towels and leave them in a warm place to rise for about 25 minutes or until nearly doubled in size. Brush the rolls lightly with melted butter and bake them in a preheated oven at 425°F/220°C/Mark 7 for 10 minutes, just until they begin to turn golden brown. Don't let them get too dark!

Serve hot or cool.

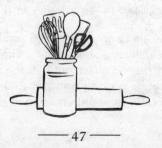

Buttermilk Dinner Rolls

MAKES ABOUT 15

1 tbsp dried yeast	1½ cups whole-wheat flour
8 fl oz/225 ml warm buttermilk	1 cup white flour
	1 tsp baking powder
1 tbsp brown sugar	1 tsp salt
¼ tsp bicarbonate of soda	1½ oz/40 g butter, melted

Dissolve the yeast in the warm buttermilk and stir in the brown sugar and bicarbonate of soda. Put this mixture aside for a few minutes until it starts to foam and bubble.

Sift together the whole-wheat flour, white flour, baking powder and salt. Stir about 1 cup of this into the yeast mixture, then stir in the melted butter and beat with a wooden spoon for a few minutes. Gradually add as much of the remaining flour as you can stir in, then sprinkle the rest on to a large board. Turn the dough out on to it and begin kneading. Knead the dough until it is smooth and elastic, working in only as much flour as is necessary to keep it from sticking. Form the dough into a ball and put it in a buttered bowl, turning it over once.

Cover the bowl with a tea-towel and leave it in a warm place to rise until the dough has doubled in size. Punch it down and turn it out on to a lightly floured board.

Roll the dough out to a thick rectangle about 8 × 14 in/205 × 355 mm. Cut it crossways in 1-in/25-mm strips. Take a strip, twist the ends around in opposite directions a couple of times, then tie it in a simple knot and loosely tuck under the ends. Form all the rolls this way (or any way you like if you have a preference!) and arrange them widely spaced on a buttered baking sheet.

Cover them lightly with a tea-towel and leave them to rise in a warm place for about 45 minutes or until they have nearly doubled in size. Bake the rolls for 15–20 minutes in a preheated oven at 425°F/220°C/Mark 7.

PUMPKIN CORN BREAD

Despite the amount of sugar, this bread is not too sweet or cakey to eat with dinner.

MAKES 2 LOAVES

1½ cups whole-wheat flour
5 tsp baking powder
¾ tsp ground cinnamon
¼ tsp ground allspice
½ tsp salt
1 cup yellow corn-meal
4 oz/115 g soft butter

⅔ cup brown sugar
3 eggs
3 tbsp lemon juice
12 fl oz/340 mm puréed cooked
   pumpkin
8 fl oz/225 ml milk

Sift together the flour, baking powder, cinnamon, allspice and salt. Stir in the corn-meal.

Cream the soft butter until it is smooth. Beat in the sugar and continue beating until the mixture is fluffy. Add the eggs and lemon juice and beat again until smooth. Finally, thoroughly mix in the pumpkin purée.

Continue to beat as you alternately add the flour mixture and the milk, until everything is combined.

Spoon the batter into 2 buttered medium-sized loaf tins and bake in a preheated oven at 350°F/180°C/Mark 4 for about 80 minutes or until a knife inserted in the centre comes out clean and dry.

Let the loaves cool in their tins for 5 minutes, then carefully remove them and let them finish cooling on racks.

CRANBERRY BREAD

MAKES 1 LOAF

1 cup white flour
1 cup whole-wheat flour
¾ cup sugar
1½ tsp baking powder
¾ tsp salt
½ tsp bicarbonate of soda
¼ tsp ground cinnamon

¼ tsp ground cloves
grated rind of 1 orange
6 fl oz/170 ml orange juice
1 large egg
2 oz/55 g butter, melted
1 cup firm, fresh cranberries
½ cup chopped walnuts

Sift together the flours, sugar, baking powder, salt, bicarbonate of soda and spices. Lightly beat together the orange rind, orange juice, egg and melted butter. Stir the wet ingredients into the dry ingredients.

Coarsely chop the cranberries and add them to the batter along with the chopped nuts. Mix everything together thoroughly and pour the batter into a buttered medium-sized loaf tin.

Bake the bread in a preheated oven at 350°F/180°C/Mark 4 for 1 hour or until a toothpick inserted near the centre comes out clean and dry. Cool on a rack and wrap tightly to store.

ORANGE-DATE BREAD

MAKES 1 LARGE LOAF OR 2 SMALL ONES

1½ cups whole-wheat flour
1 cup white flour
½ tsp salt
2 tsp baking powder
2 oz/55 g soft butter
¾ cup sugar

1 egg
8 fl oz/225 ml fresh orange
    juice
2 tbsp fresh-grated orange rind
½ cup chopped dates
½ cup rolled oats

Sift together the whole-wheat flour, white flour, salt and baking powder. Cream together the butter and sugar, then beat in the egg. Alternately add the flour mixture and the orange juice, beating after each addition, until you've used all but 2 tablespoons of the flour (use all of the juice). Add the grated orange rind.

Sprinkle the chopped dates with the reserved flour and roll them around in it, separating the bits from each other until they are no longer sticking together in clumps. Add the coated dates and the oats to the batter and stir well.

Spoon the batter into 1 large buttered loaf pan or 2 small ones, and bake in a preheated oven at 350°F/180°C/Mark 4 for 1 hour or until a toothpick inserted near the centre of a loaf comes out clean. Serve warm or cool with cream cheese.

CHEESE PASTRIES

These pastries, served warm, are a wonderful accompaniment for a soup, a cold vegetable mousse or any salad.

MAKES SEVERAL DOZEN

1 cup flour
½ tsp salt
½ tsp paprika
a bit of fresh-ground black
  pepper
4 oz/115 g butter
⅓ cup grated Parmesan cheese

4 oz/115 g Cheddar cheese,
  grated
2 tbsp double cream, well
  chilled
1 egg beaten with 1 tbsp cold
  water

Stir the flour together with the salt, paprika and some fresh-ground black pepper. Cut the butter in with a pastry cutter or spin briefly in a food processor until the mixture resembles coarse breadcrumbs. Toss it together with the grated cheeses, then sprinkle the cream over it and work the mixture with your hands until you have a smooth dough. Chill it for about 1 hour.

Roll the dough out on a lightly floured board to a thickness of a little less than ¼ in/6 mm. Cut it into strips ½ × 1½ in/12 × 37 mm. Brush the strips with the beaten egg, arrange them on un-greased baking sheets and bake them in a preheated oven at 325°F/170°C/Mark 3 for 12–14 minutes or until they are slightly puffed and beginning to brown on top.

CHAPATIS

These are the simple breads which accompany almost every Indian meal. Their delicious flavour and chewy, soft texture depend on their freshness, and ideally the chapatis should be served hot off the griddle, like tortillas. They can, however, be made an hour or two before dinner and reheated.

MAKES 12, ENOUGH TO SERVE 6 PEOPLE

2 cups whole-wheat flour
½ tsp salt
2 tbsp vegetable oil

4 fl oz/115 ml water
ghee (clarified butter; see page
    317) for brushing chapatis

Mix together the flour and salt, then add the vegetable oil and rub it into the flour with your fingers until the mixture is fairly homogeneous. Quickly stir in the water and start working the dough with your hand in the bowl until it holds together easily. If the dough continues to crumble, add a bit more water, 1 tablespoon at a time, adding just enough to allow the dough to hold together.

Take the dough out of the bowl and knead it energetically on a lightly floured surface until it is smooth and elastic, about 5–10 minutes.

Divide the dough into 12 equal-sized pieces and form each piece into a ball. Roll the balls out as evenly as possible into thin circles about 7 in/180 mm across. Stack them and keep them covered to prevent them from drying out.

Heat a cast-iron frying pan and have a little bowl of ghee and a pastry brush handy. Do not butter or oil the pan. Cook the chapatis one at a time, for a minute or so on each side. If they puff up, just press them down gently with a spatula. The chapatis are done when brown spots show evenly over both sides.

As the chapatis are finished, stack them on a plate, brushing each one lightly with ghee. If it is necessary to reheat the chapatis, place them in a very hot pan for a few seconds on each side or wrap them tightly in foil and put them in a hot oven just until they are warmed through.

PURIS

Puris are made of the same type of dough that is used for chapatis, but these little Indian breads are deep-fried in hot oil and puff up like balloons. They should be eaten almost immediately.

MAKES 10–12 LARGE PURIS, ENOUGH TO SERVE 4–6 PEOPLE

1 cup whole-wheat flour   *2 fl oz/55 ml water*
¼ tsp salt   *vegetable oil for deep frying*
1 generous tbsp vegetable oil

Sift together the flour and the salt, then add the vegetable oil and rub it into the flour with your fingers until the mixture is fairly homogeneous. Quickly stir in the water and start working the dough with your hand in the bowl until it holds together easily.

Take the dough out of the bowl and knead it vigorously on a lightly floured board for 5–10 minutes, or until it is smooth and elastic. Add a bit more flour or a few drops more water as necessary if the dough seems either too sticky or too dry to hold together well.

Divide the dough into 10–12 equal-sized pieces and roll each piece into a smooth ball. Roll the balls out into circles about 4 in/ 100 mm across, stacking them on a plate and keeping them covered to prevent drying out.

Heat about 16 fl oz/450 ml of vegetable oil in a wok or heavy, deep frying pan, and when it is very hot, slide in one of the dough circles. It should bubble up to the surface almost immediately and start to inflate like a balloon. Very gentle pressure with a flat spatula on top of the puri will help it inflate evenly.

Turn the puri over gently, using a slotted spoon or spatula, and cook it until both sides are golden brown – this will take only a few minutes. Lift it out, let the oil drip back into the wok for a few seconds, and put it on a plate lined with paper towels. Continue frying the puris in this manner until all of them are done, then serve immediately. The puris can be kept warm in a low oven for a short time.

To make small puris such as are used in Potato Chat Puris (p. 334), divide the dough into about 18 small pieces, roughly the size of little walnuts. Roll them out into circles approximately 2–2½ in/ 50–62 mm across and continue as above. Several small puris can easily be fried at one time.

SCONES

MAKES ABOUT 20

2 cups white flour	*4 oz/115 g butter*
4 tsp baking powder	*4–5 fl oz/115–140 ml cold*
¾ tsp salt	*milk*

Sift together the flour, baking powder and salt. Slice the butter while it is very cold, add it to the dry ingredients and cut it in with a pastry blender or two knives until it is in bits the size of split peas. The texture of this mixture should be a little more coarse than that of a short-crust mixture before the liquid is added. This could be done in a food processor but blend for only a few seconds.

Sprinkle 4 fl oz/115 ml of cold milk over the flour and butter, and stir it in quickly with a fork. Add only as much more of the milk as is necessary to make the dough hold together.

Gather the dough up into a ball, working it together with your hands very briefly, and then roll it out ½ in/12 mm thick on a floured board. Cut out small rounds and place them on ungreased baking sheets. If you aren't going to put them in the oven immediately, chill them in the refrigerator until ready to bake.

Bake the scones in a preheated oven at 450°F/230°C/Mark 8 for 10–12 minutes or until puffed and lightly browned on top. Serve them hot with butter.

SWEET FINNISH RUSKS

MAKES ABOUT 24–30

4 oz/115 g soft butter	*2 eggs*
⅔ cup sugar	*2½ cups white flour*
grated rind of 1 orange	*1½ tsp baking powder*

Cream the butter with the sugar and orange rind until it is fluffy, then beat in the eggs. Sift 2 cups of the flour with the baking powder, and add this mixture gradually to the butter mixture, beating it in till smooth.

Sprinkle the remaining flour over a large board or other smooth surface and turn the dough out on to it. Knead the dough for several minutes, incorporating the remaining flour; the dough should be smooth and easily manageable.

Break off pieces of dough the size of very large walnuts and roll them into smooth balls. Flatten the balls with a spatula until they are about ¾ in/18 mm thick. They will have the shape of miniature English muffins.

Arrange them 1 in/25 mm apart on lightly greased baking sheets and bake in a preheated oven at 400°F/200°C/Mark 6 for 10 minutes, just until they are beginning to turn golden brown and are puffing up a bit.

Take the rusks out of the oven, let them cool for a couple of minutes – just until you can handle them. While they are still warm, slice them in half with a sharp, serrated knife. Arrange them on baking sheets, cut side up, and put them back into the oven, reducing the heat to 350°F/180°C/Mark 4. Bake them for another 8–10 minutes, or until they are dried and golden but not brown.

Serve the rusks with coffee or tea.

CORN AND RYE MUFFINS

MAKES 12

1 cup whole-wheat flour	*12 fl oz/340 ml buttermilk*
¾ cup yellow corn-meal	*1 egg*
¼ cup dark rye flour	*2 fl oz/55 ml vegetable oil*
1 tsp baking powder	*2 fl oz/55 ml honey*
¾ tsp bicarbonate of soda	
½ tsp salt	

Sift together the dry ingredients. Beat together the wet ingredients.

Stir the two mixtures together just until they are well combined, then spoon the batter into buttered muffin tins.

Bake the muffins in a preheated oven at 400°F/200°C/Mark 6 for about 20 minutes or until a toothpick inserted in the centre of one comes out clean and dry. Serve warm.

FOUR-GRAIN MUFFINS

MAKES 12

¾ cup whole-wheat flour   ½ cup rolled oats
¾ cup yellow corn-meal   12 fl oz/340 ml milk
½ cup dark rye flour   1 egg
2 tsp baking powder   2 fl oz/55 ml vegetable oil
½ tsp salt   2 fl oz/55 ml honey

Sift together the wheat flour, corn-meal, rye flour, baking powder and salt. Stir in the rolled oats.

In another bowl beat together the milk, egg, oil and honey. Stir the two mixtures together vigorously just until they are well combined. Then spoon the batter into buttered muffin tins.

Bake the muffins in a preheated oven at 400°F/200°C/Mark 6 for 20 minutes. Serve warm.

OATMEAL MUFFINS

MAKES 12

1½ cups whole-wheat flour   8 fl oz/225 ml milk
2 tsp baking powder   1 egg
½ tsp salt   1½ oz/40 g butter, melted
¾ cup rolled oats   2 tbsp molasses
¼ cup ground hazelnuts   ½ cup currants
  (optional)

Sift together the flour, baking powder and salt. Mix in the rolled oats and ground nuts.

In another bowl beat together the milk, egg, melted butter and molasses. Add the currants and stir the two mixtures together just until they are well combined; then spoon the batter into buttered muffin tins.

Bake the muffins in a preheated oven at 400°F/200°C/Mark 6 for about 20 minutes. Serve warm.

SOUPS

ANYTHING SO SENSIBLE AND VERSATILE AS SOUP should not be too difficult to prepare, and for once things are as they should be. The great majority of soups are so little trouble to make and so economical that there is hardly any excuse at all for canned soups. But the flavour, the tantalizing aroma, the downright goodness of good home-made soup would be a bargain at twice the exertion or twice the price.

The idea that a home-made soup must take hours of time should be laid to rest right now. Garlic Soup (Sopa de Ajo), for instance, is a marvel of convenience (for garlic lovers only, though). It is ready in about twice the time it takes to poach an egg, costs pennies, can easily be prepared just one serving at a time and makes a nourishing, warming meal. In Madrid and Segovia, where winters are bitter, Sopa de Ajo takes its place on all the menus when gazpacho is taken off till the next summer, and we used to eat it nearly every day. One might think that something so practical would have no right to be delicious as well, but it's just one of those things.

Soups based on stocks, or broths, will never be as quick as that, but the actual work time required for most of them is not great. All the ingredients for a good broth can be put together in a quarter of an hour and after that it doesn't bother anyone for a long while as it simmers. Once it's finished, just a little extra attention can transform it into one of any number of delicacies, simple or fancy. In Mexico I found out about Tortilla Soup, made of a lightly creamed, tomato-flavoured broth with crisp-fried strips of corn tortillas, chunks of hot, half-melted cheese and morsels of onion and chilli. It was such a simple soup to make when I set about doing it in my own kitchen and has a wonderfully intriguing, slightly exotic flavour.

Some of my other long-time favourites are the soups that make a meal and satisfy a big hunger, like the Pistou, with its combination of beans and big chunks of fresh vegetables, all flavoured with that incomparable paste of olive oil, basil, pine nuts, garlic and Parmesan cheese. Another one to satisfy body and soul is Sauerkraut Soup. It was devised one chilly evening for a friend who had a stubborn craving for sauerkraut; we went down to the kitchen and got right to work with whatever supplies were on hand. The result was wonderful. Others of that type are Garlic Soup, Pasta i Fagioli (both recipes), Cheese Soup, Dutch Cheese and Potato Soup, Beer and Onion Soup, Split Pea Soup, and Green Chilli and Cheese Soup. No matter what the season of the year, and no matter what you may have on hand, chances are that a very palatable soup can be concocted from it. Inventive cooks are in their element with soup, and for the novice who wants to experiment, this is the place to begin. If you know a few basics of proportion and technique, which are quickly learned with the first few pots, it's hard to go wrong.

But right along with all this practicality, soups can still rise to the most elegant occasion. Nothing suits me as well for the start of an elaborate meal as a delicate Clear Beetroot Borscht, with slivers of wild mushroom, or the Creamed Avocado Soup, which is still unusual enough to be a nice surprise. And in the summer I like to serve the most ambrosial cold soup of them all, one that is well worth a little extra effort – Cold Cherry-Lemon Soup. It's a show stopper and wonderful with champagne.

Since almost every imaginable food can find its way into a soup, there should be something for everyone, and I can't imagine the person who doesn't like soup at all. In my own enthusiasm for all these delicious hot and cold liquids I've compiled here no less than thirty-six new soup recipes, and I think of it as just a nice sampler of what's possible.

VEGETABLE BROTH: I

This and the other broths that follow are pleasant just as they are. However, they are tremendously useful as stocks in the making of other soups, sauces, etc. They will keep well in the refrigerator for 2 to 3 days and can be frozen.

SERVES 4

8 pt/4.5 l water
4 medium-sized stalks celery,
   thickly sliced

2 medium-sized onions, peeled
   and halved, stuck with 2
   cloves

2 medium-sized potatoes,
  scrubbed and thickly sliced
2 turnips, scrubbed and cut in
  1-in/25-mm dice
5–6 large carrots, scraped and
  thickly sliced

several large sprigs parsley
2 bay leaves
8–10 peppercorns
4–5 cloves garlic, peeled
salt

Combine all the ingredients in a large saucepan or stock-pot, bring the water to a boil, lower the heat and simmer uncovered 3–4 hours. Strain the broth in a colander or large sieve and taste it. If it is weak, return it to the pot and continue simmering until it is reduced to the proper strength of flavour. Season to taste with salt.

VEGETABLE BROTH: II

Serve the broth with dumplings or use it as a base for other soups.

SERVES 6

½ oz/15 g dried wild
  mushrooms
3 medium-sized leeks
about ½ medium-sized head
  cabbage
2 large stalks celery
3 large carrots
1 turnip
1 large potato
10 medium-sized cloves garlic

4⅗ pt/2.7 l water
several sprigs parsley
2 bay leaves
10–12 peppercorns
large pinch of thyme
dash of Tabasco sauce
2 tbsp olive oil
juice of ½ lemon
1 tbsp salt

Pour a small amount of hot water over the dried mushrooms and let them soak in it while you prepare the other vegetables.

Trim the green parts off the leeks, cut them in half lengthways just to the base and wash them carefully. Cut the cabbage into wedges. Thickly slice the celery. Scrape and thickly slice the carrots. Peel and slice the turnip. Scrub and cube the potato. Separate the garlic cloves, but do not peel them.

As soon as the dried mushrooms are somewhat softened, wash

them very carefully, one by one, to get rid of all the sand and grit.

Put all the vegetables and garlic in a large stock-pot with the water. Add the parsley, bay leaves, peppercorns, thyme, Tabasco sauce, olive oil, lemon juice and salt and bring the water to a boil.

Reduce the heat until the liquid is just simmering and allow it to simmer, uncovered, for 1½ hours or slightly longer; the broth is ready when the flavour is full and strong.

Strain the broth through a colander and again through a fine sieve, and correct the seasoning if necessary.

POTATO PEEL BROTH
GARLIC BROTH

Potato Peel Broth and Garlic Broth, those fragrant liquids with the amusing names, are such good, basic stocks for soups and sauces that I couldn't leave them out. Both recipes are repeated here essentially as they appeared in the *Vegetarian Epicure*, with a few slight alterations that I developed in my repeated use of these broths and that strike me as improvements.

The Potato Peel Broth is a bit richer in flavour by the addition of some herbs and oil, which I had formerly added only to the sweeter Garlic Broth. And monosodium glutamate, about which we know too little but enough to scare us, has been deleted. To make Garlic Broth, it is necessary to add only a full head of garlic, split into cloves, to the Potato Peel Broth recipe.

So, back by popular demand, here they are.

Potato Peel Broth

SERVES 4

*peels from 6 to 7 large, healthy
  brown-skinned potatoes*
1 large onion
2 carrots
1 medium-sized stalk celery
3⅓ pt/1.8 l water

1 large sprig parsley
*1½ tbsp olive or mild vegetable
  oil*
½ to 1 bay leaf
¼ tsp dried whole thyme
pinch of sage

salt and pepper to taste *dash of Tabasco (optional)*
1 clove garlic (optional) *dash of lemon juice (optional)*

First scrub the potatoes very thoroughly and cut away any blemishes, then peel them, cutting off strips at least ¼ in/6 mm thick. Reserve the peeled potatoes for another use. Peel the onion and quarter it. Wash the carrots and celery and slice them.

Combine all the ingredients but the Tabasco and the lemon juice in a large stock-pot and simmer for about 1½ hours or until all the vegetables are very soft. If too much water evaporates during the cooking, add enough to keep all the vegetables covered with liquid. When the broth is done, there should be about 2½ pt/1.4 l of it, but this may vary slightly. The most important thing is to taste it, smell it, look at it. If it is light brown, fragrant and delicious, it's ready; if it seems weak, simmer it a bit longer and reduce it; if it seems too strong, add a bit of water.

For a clear broth, strain out all the vegetables through a sieve and correct the seasoning if necessary. For a soup with the consistency of a thin purée, first fish out the celery, garlic and bay leaf, then press everything through a fine sieve until only a rather dry pulp is left.

Garlic Broth

Proceed exactly as for Potato Peel Broth, but add a full, large head of garlic rather than just one puny clove, and be sure to use olive oil. Break the head of garlic up into separate cloves and peel them if you wish, though they can also be used unpeeled – a method that many people feel yields a richer flavour. Simmer the broth gently for a long time – 1½–2 hours – and then strain everything out through a sieve for a fine, clear and delicate broth.

Finally, for giving both Potato Peel Broth and Garlic Broth that final touch of seasoning, I've found that a delightful flavour is brought out by the addition of a few drops of Tabasco or a few drops of lemon juice, or both.

DUMPLINGS FOR SOUP

These dumplings are good with any broth, and they are a must
with creamed fresh pea soup (p.85).

SERVES 6–8

3 oz/85 g soft butter
2 eggs
1½ cups flour
2½ fl oz/70 ml milk

½ tsp salt
⅛ tsp nutmeg
⅛ tsp cayenne pepper

Cream the butter in a deep bowl and beat in the eggs. Add the flour
and milk alternately, beating after each addition, until all the flour
and milk are incorporated. Beat in the salt, nutmeg and cayenne.
The mixture should be smooth and creamy but fairly stiff.

Bring a large saucepan of heavily salted water to a boil and drop
the dough in by ½ teaspoonfuls. Boil the dumplings, covered, for
about 15 minutes and transfer them to the soup with a slotted
spoon.

The dumplings can also be boiled in a broth.

A VERY SIMPLE NOODLE SOUP

SERVES 6–8

2½ pt/1.4 l Vegetable Broth
  I or II (p. 60).
24 fl oz/680 ml broth from
  cooking flageolets,
  kidney beans or chick-peas
1 oz/25 g butter

1 tsp paprika
dash of cayenne
salt and pepper
2–3 oz/55–85 g fettucine or
  other noodles

Heat the broths together in a pot. When they are simmering, stir in
the butter, paprika, cayenne and salt and pepper to taste. Raise the
heat and add the noodles, breaking them up to whatever length
you prefer. Simmer for about 20 minutes or until the noodles are
perfectly tender.

Vegetable Soup: I

This was put together by clearing out all the odds and ends left in the vegetable bins after a busy couple of days of cooking. It is the simplest kind of soup to make and a delicious, hearty supper dish for a cold evening. You can invent your own versions easily by rummaging through the kitchen and putting together whatever you think will make a pleasing combination. The proportions I've given here are flexible.

SERVES 6–8

kernels from 1 ear of sweet-corn
½ medium-sized aubergine (8 oz/225 g), cubed in 1-in/25-mm pieces
1 large pale-skinned potato, washed and cubed
1 large red pepper, seeded and cut in 1-in/25-mm pieces
2 medium-sized courgettes, thickly sliced
1 onion, peeled and cut in 1-in/25-mm squares
5–6 mushrooms, sliced
4 cloves garlic, peeled and thinly sliced

3 spring onions, coarsely chopped
1 cup shredded cabbage
1 dill pickle, very thinly sliced
1½ cups chopped fresh spinach
2 tomatoes, cut in thin wedges
approximately 5 pt/2.8 l water
salt
black pepper
2 tbsp olive oil
2 tbsp red wine vinegar
ground cumin
cayenne pepper
oregano

To prepare the soup, just wash and trim the vegetables as required, chop or slice them and put them all together in a very large saucepan with the water. Salt and pepper to taste and season with olive oil, vinegar and spices to taste. Simmer the soup for at least 30 minutes and serve piping hot with bread and cheese.

VEGETABLE SOUP: II

SERVES 6–8

1 ear of sweet-corn
½ medium-sized aubergine
  (about 8oz/225g)
2 medium-sized carrots
1 stalk celery
1 large pale-skinned potato
1 fresh red pepper
2 medium-sized courgettes
1 onion
5–6 medium-sized mushrooms
¼ head cabbage
1 small dill pickle
4 cloves garlic

2 tbsp olive oil
3 spring onions
1½ cups shredded fresh spinach
2 tomatoes
salt
fresh-ground black pepper
cumin seeds, crushed
cayenne pepper
oregano
red wine vinegar
OPTIONAL GARNISH
croûtons

Wash the sweet-corn and scrape the kernels off the ear. Cube the aubergine, scrape and slice the carrots, slice the celery, and scrub and cube the potato. Remove the ribs and seeds from the pepper and cut it into medium-sized squares or strips. Wash and slice the courgettes and peel and very coarsely chop the onion. Wash the mushrooms thoroughly and slice them. Shred the cabbage, and thinly slice the pickle.

Put all these prepared vegetables in a large saucepan and add enough water to cover them amply. Simmer the soup over a medium heat.

Peel and mince the garlic and sauté it in the olive oil. Slice the spring onions, including the tops, and add them to the garlic and oil. When the onions are quite soft and the garlic golden, add this mixture to the soup.

When the other vegetables are about half-cooked, add the shredded spinach and the tomatoes, cut in thin wedges. Let it all cook together for a few minutes, stirring often; then season to taste with salt, pepper, crushed cumin seeds, cayenne, oregano and 1–2 teaspoons red wine vinegar. Continue cooking until all the vegetables are tender, adding more water if necessary.

Serve steaming hot, with *croûtons* if desired.

SPINACH SOUP

This is such a light and refreshing soup that it makes a perfect foil for a hearty or especially rich dish, like stuffed crêpes or filled potato pancakes.

SERVES 6

3⅓ pt/1.8 l water
1 lb/450 g fresh spinach
2 medium-large potatoes
¾ cup sliced spring onions
salt and pepper to taste

4 fl oz/115 ml soured cream
2 tbsp fresh lemon juice
GARNISH
soured cream (optional)

Heat the water in a large saucepan. Wash the spinach leaves carefully and remove the stems. Peel the potatoes and cut them in ½-in/12-mm dice. Add the spinach leaves, potatoes and half the onions to the water with a little salt and pepper, and simmer the soup very gently for about 1 hour, stirring occasionally.

Add the remaining onions and ladle out about a cup of the hot broth into the soured cream. Whisk the soured cream and broth together and stir it back into the soup. Add 1½ tablespoons of the lemon juice and let the soup simmer for another hour. Taste, add more salt and pepper as needed, and the remainder of the lemon juice if the soup is not tart enough for your taste.

Serve this soup hot or cold, with additional soured cream if desired.

GARLIC-TOMATO SOUP

SERVES 6

2½ tbsp olive oil
3 cloves garlic, pressed or
  minced
2 tbsp paprika
1⅘ pt/1 l Garlic Broth or
  Potato Peel Broth (p. 62)
1⅗ pt/900 ml puréed fresh
  tomatoes, strained

salt to taste
Tabasco sauce to taste
butter to taste
6 slices French bread
Parmesan cheese, grated

Heat the olive oil in a large, heavy frying pan and sauté the garlic in it for a minute or two. Remove the pan from direct heat and stir the paprika into the oil. Return to low heat and continue stirring the paprika and oil for another moment. The instant it begins to sizzle, add the broth and the puréed tomatoes. (If it's winter and you can't get good, fresh tomatoes, canned tomatoes can be substituted: purée them in a blender or food processor with all their juice, and strain through a sieve to get rid of the seeds.)

Simmer the soup for 10–15 minutes, taste it and season with salt and a little Tabasco.

Butter 6 slices of French bread and sprinkle them generously with grated Parmesan cheese. Rub the cheese lightly into the butter with a knife. Bake these *croûtons* in a hot oven for about 10 minutes, or put them under the grill for 2–3 minutes. They should be lightly browned round the edges. Put 1 in each of 6 bowls, pour the hot soup over them and serve immediately.

CLEAR BEETROOT BORSCHT
WITH MUSHROOMS

SERVES 12

1 oz/25 g of the best dried wild
   mushrooms*

5⅔ pt/3.1 l water

2 medium-sized potatoes,
   scrubbed and sliced

2 medium stalks celery, sliced

2–3 cloves garlic, peeled

1 large turnip, peeled and sliced

4 medium-sized carrots, scraped
   and sliced

1–2 bay leaves

1 tbsp salt

8–9 peppercorns

1½ lb/680 g beetroots

3 tbsp lemon juice

1 tbsp sugar

GARNISH

soured cream

Soak the dried mushrooms in 12 fl oz/340 ml water for about 2 hours or overnight.

In a large stock-pot combine 5 pt/2.8 l water, the potatoes, celery, garlic, turnip, carrots, bay leaves, salt and peppercorns. Simmer gently for about 1–2 hours. The broth should be subtle but flavourful.

Strain the broth and discard the cooked vegetables.

Drain the mushrooms and reserve the liquid in which they have been soaked. Wash the mushrooms carefully, one by one, and slice them in julienne strips.

Strain the mushroom liquid through several layers of muslin or through a paper coffee filter. Add the strained liquid and the mushrooms to the broth.

Peel the beetroots and cut them in julienne strips. Add them to the broth, as well as the lemon juice and sugar.

Simmer the soup for another 20–25 minutes or until the beetroots are quite tender; then taste, correct the seasoning and serve, garnishing each bowl with a spoonful of soured cream.

* *Boletus edulis*, which are called *porcini* in Italy and *cèpes* in France, are the best. These are also imported from Eastern Europe. As an alternative, dried Japanese forest mushrooms are also fine.

TORTILLA SOUP TLAXCALTECA

SERVES 6

2½ pt/1.4 l Garlic Broth
  (p. 63)
5 Tortillas (p. 296)
vegetable oil for frying
10 oz/285 g fresh mozzarella
  cheese

½ red onion
12 fl oz/340 ml puréed fresh
  tomatoes
4 fl oz/115 ml single cream
paprika
fresh chilli sauce

While the Garlic Broth is cooking, cut up the tortillas in strips about ½ × 1½ in/12 × 37 mm, and fry them in hot oil until they are crisp. Drain them well on kitchen towels and put them to one side.

Cut the cheese into ¼–½-in/6–12-mm cubes. Peel and slice the red onion and cut the slices into 1-in/25-mm lengths.

Add the puréed fresh tomatoes and the cream to the hot Garlic Broth, as well as the onion slices. Cook over a low heat for about 15 minutes, stirring occasionally. Season the soup to taste with paprika and fresh chilli sauce. The soup should not be too terribly hot with chilli, but its flavour should be subtly present.

Just before the soup is to be served, divide the fried tortilla strips and the cubes of cheese among the warmed soup bowls. Then ladle the steaming hot soup over them and serve immediately.

SWEET POTATO SOUP

SERVES 5–6

1¼ lb/570 g sweet potatoes
3 small carrots
1 large stalk celery
1 bay leaf
2½ pt/1.4 l water

1½ tsp salt
2 tbsp lemon juice
1 tsp paprika
¾ oz/20 g butter
4 fl oz/115 ml double cream

Peel the sweet potatoes and cut them in small dice. Scrape and thinly slice the carrots. Slice the celery. Put all the vegetables and the bay leaf in a saucepan with the water. Bring the water to a boil, then lower the heat and let the soup simmer for about 1 hour, stirring occasionally.

Add the remaining ingredients and simmer the soup for another 10 minutes or so.

CHEESE SOUP

Be sure to use good, properly aged cheeses for this soup. A cheese that is too 'green', or young, will curdle and turn rubbery when heated, but a mature cheese will melt beautifully as long as it is not boiled.

SERVES 6

3 oz/85 g butter
5 tbsp flour
1⅘ pt/1 l hot milk
8 fl oz/225 ml single cream
9 oz/255 g Gouda cheese, grated
4½ oz/125 g smoked Edam cheese, grated

2 tbsp Worcestershire sauce
1 tsp paprika
dash of Tabasco or cayenne pepper
salt and pepper to taste
garlic toast (optional)

Melt the butter in a large saucepan and stir in the flour. Cook this roux over very low heat for a few minutes, stirring. Add the hot milk and stir with a whisk over medium heat until the mixture is thickened and perfectly smooth.

Add the cream. Adjust the heat so that the soup stays hot but does not boil. Gradually add the grated cheeses, stirring constantly with a wooden spoon.

When all the cheese is melted and the soup has a smooth, velvety consistency, add the Worcestershire sauce, paprika, Tabasco, and salt and pepper.

Serve hot with garlic toast.

PASTA I FAGIOLI: I

(Pasta with Beans)

SERVES 6–8

1½ cups dried red kidney beans,
  washed
3⅕ pt/1.8 l water
2 large carrots, scraped and
  chopped
1 large onion, chopped
1 large stalk celery, thinly
  sliced
1 bay leaf
large pinch of basil

pinch of rosemary, crushed
4 cloves garlic, thinly sliced
1 tbsp olive oil
4 tbsp tomato paste
salt and pepper
6 oz/170 g fettucine noodles
GARNISH
grated Parmesan cheese
fresh-ground black pepper
olive oil

Boil the washed beans in lightly salted water for 30 minutes. Add the carrots, onions, celery, herbs, and olive oil. Simmer for at least another 30 minutes or until the beans are tender.

Ladle half the beans and vegetables into a blender or food processor with some of the broth and blend to a purée. Return the purée to the soup and stir in the tomato paste. Season to taste with salt and pepper.

Twenty minutes before serving, add the fettucine noodles, as well as a little boiling water if the soup seems too thick. Cook until the noodles are *al dente* – tender but still firm – and serve very hot.

Pass grated Parmesan cheese, a pepper mill and a jug of very good olive oil to garnish the soup.

PASTA I FAGIOLI: II

SERVES 6–8

1½ cups dried red kidney beans,
  washed
5 pt/2.8 l water
1½ tsp salt, and more to taste
2 small carrots, scraped and

  finely diced
4½ tbsp olive oil
1 small onion, peeled and
  chopped
2 small cloves garlic, minced

½ tsp rosemary, crushed
4 oz/115 g thin fettucine
  noodles

⅓–½ cup grated Parmesan
  cheese
fresh-ground black pepper

Put the beans in a saucepan with 3½ pt/2 l of the water and 1½ teaspoons salt. Bring the water to a boil, then lower the heat and simmer the beans for 1 hour. Add the diced carrots and simmer another 10 minutes.

Heat the olive oil in a pan and sauté the onions and garlic in it until they begin to colour. Add them to the soup along with the crushed rosemary and let it continue cooking for 10 minutes more. By this time the kidney beans should be tender and the liquid should be becoming quite thick.

Add the remaining water, bring the soup back to an easy boil and add the noodles. Cook them for 12–15 minutes or until they are tender, then stir in the Parmesan cheese, season to taste with more salt and fresh-ground black pepper, and serve.

GARLIC SOUP
(Sopa de Ajo)

PER SERVING

4 small cloves garlic
1 tbsp olive oil
1 tsp paprika
½ tsp salt
12–16 fl oz/340–450 ml hot
  water

dash of Tabasco sauce (optional)
dash of Worcestershire sauce
  (optional)
approximately 1½-in/37-mm
  thick slice dry French bread
1 egg

Peel the cloves of garlic and slice them thinly. Heat the olive oil in a saucepan or an earthenware casserole and sauté the garlic in it until it is just beginning to turn golden. Add the paprika and salt and stir quickly for about 30 seconds, then add the hot water. Simmer the broth for a few minutes, taste and add a dash of Tabasco and a dash of Worcestershire if you like.

Break the bread up into chunks or, if it is still soft enough, cut in paper-thin slices. Add the bread to the broth. When the bread is quite soft and the broth is simmering again, break in the egg and ladle some broth over it. Turn down the flame and continue to simmer the soup until the egg is poached to your taste.

SPLIT PEA SOUP

SERVES 6–8

1 lb/450 g green split peas
5 pt/2.8 l water
1½ tsp salt
1¼ oz/35 g butter
1½ cups finely chopped carrots
1 cup finely chopped sweet potato
1 cup finely chopped onions
½ cup finely chopped celery
½–¾ tsp ground marjoram

1 tsp dried basil
1–2 cloves garlic, crushed or minced
½–¾ tsp ground cumin
4 fl oz/115 ml dry white wine
fresh-ground black pepper to taste

OPTIONAL GARNISH
croûtons

Put the split peas in a large saucepan with the water and salt, bring the water to a boil, then lower the heat and simmer for about 1 hour. Skim off the foam from the top and discard it.

Sauté the finely chopped or minced carrots, sweet potato, onions and celery in the butter for about 10 minutes, stirring almost constantly. Add the herbs and cook the vegetables for another 5 minutes, then add them to the soup. Simmer the soup, stirring occasionally, for another 45 minutes–1 hour.

Ladle out approximately ½ the soup and purée it in a blender or force it through a sieve. Return the purée to the saucepan, add the wine and pepper, stir and bring the soup back to a simmer. Serve hot, alone or with *croûtons*.

Dutch Cheese and Potato Soup

SERVES 6

5–6 potatoes
2½ oz/70 g butter
2 large onions
2 bay leaves
1 tsp dill seeds, crushed in a
    mortar
2 tbsp flour

16 fl oz/450 ml milk
6 oz/170 g Gouda cheese,
    grated
1 tbsp paprika
1 tbsp Worcestershire sauce
salt
fresh-ground black pepper

Peel the potatoes and cut them into small cubes. Boil them in just enough lightly salted water to cover until they are tender. Do not discard the cooking water.

Meanwhile, melt 1½ oz/40 g of the butter in a large, deep frying pan or saucepan. Cut the onions in half crossways and slice them thinly. Sauté the sliced onions in the melted butter along with the bay leaves, stirring often, until the onions just start to turn golden. Add the crushed dill seeds and stir 1 minute more, then add the cooked potatoes along with their water.

Melt the remaining butter in a heavy-bottomed frying pan, stir in the flour, and cook 1–2 minutes over low heat. In a separate saucepan heat the milk, and then stir it into the roux. Stir constantly with a whisk until the sauce has thickened and is completely smooth. Add it to the soup.

Bit by bit, add the grated cheese, stirring slowly all the while. Then add the paprika, Worcestershire sauce, and salt and pepper to taste. Keep the soup barely simmering on a low heat, stirring often, for about 15 minutes more. Serve hot.

BEER AND ONION SOUP

SERVES 6–8

3 lb/1.25 kg onions
2–3 cloves garlic, minced
6 oz/170 g butter
16 fl oz/450 ml Vegetable
    Broth I or II (pp. 60–62)
1 pt/570 ml dark beer or stout
½ pt/285 ml single cream
2 tsp salt
2 tsp paprika
dash of Tabasco sauce

fresh-ground black pepper to
    taste
2–4 tsp sugar (depending on the
    bitterness of the beer used)
2 tsp cider vinegar
4 egg yolks
OPTIONAL GARNISH
hot paprika
toasted croûtons and grated
    Parmesan cheese

Peel the onions, halve them crossways, and slice them. Cook them slowly with the garlic in the butter until all the onions are transparent and soft – about 1 hour. Add the vegetable broth and purée the mixture, about 1 pt/570 ml at a time, in a blender or food processor.

Pour the purée into a large saucepan with the beer and cream. Add the salt, paprika, Tabasco, pepper, sugar and vinegar, and simmer the mixture, stirring often, for about 20 minutes.

Beat the egg yolks with a whisk. Continue to beat them as you add a small amount of the hot soup, then pour the egg yolk mixture into the pot with the rest of the soup and whisk it all together quickly. Cook the soup a few minutes more over very low heat, stirring constantly. It should be slightly thickened.

Serve the soup very hot and sprinkle a little hot paprika on top if you like, or garnish it with *croûtons* and Parmesan cheese.

SAUERKRAUT SOUP

SERVES 6–8

4 tbsp olive oil
2 oz/55 g butter
3 large onions, coarsely chopped

3 cloves garlic, peeled and
    minced
2 tbsp sweet paprika

¼ tsp hot paprika
2 lb/900 g sauerkraut
2½ pt/1.4 l water (more if
  needed)
1 stalk celery, sliced
1 carrot, peeled and sliced
3 cups sliced peeled tomatoes,
  with their juice

1 tsp caraway seeds
2–3 oz dried wild mushrooms
3 tsp sugar
4 fl oz/115 ml red wine
1 tsp dill weed
1½ tsp salt, or more to taste
pepper to taste

Heat the olive oil and butter in a large, heavy-bottomed frying pan. Add the chopped onions and garlic, and sauté them until they begin to turn golden. Add the 2 paprikas, stir for a moment, then add the sauerkraut, water, celery, carrot and tomatoes.

Pound the caraway seeds lightly in a mortar and add them to the soup. Soak the black mushrooms in water for a few minutes. Drain them, discarding the water, and wash each one very carefully. Then cut them into thin strips and add them to the soup.

Season the soup with sugar, red wine, dill weed and salt and pepper. Let the soup simmer gently for at least 1 hour, longer if possible. Add a little more water if the soup becomes too thick.

PISTOU

SERVES 8–10

4 pt/2.25 l water
1½ cups scrubbed, diced
  potatoes
1½ cups peeled, sliced carrots
1¾ cups cleaned, sliced leeks
  (white parts)
2 tsp salt
1 cup sliced courgettes
1 small red pepper, diced or cut
  in strips
2 cups cut French beans
1½ cups cooked kidney beans

¼ cup dry breadcrumbs
⅛ tsp saffron
PISTOU SAUCE
about ½ cup grated Parmesan
  cheese
3 oz/85 g tomato paste
⅓ cup pine nuts
1½ tbsp dried basil or ¼ cup
  chopped fresh
4–5 cloves garlic
2½ fl oz/70 ml olive oil
fresh-ground black pepper

In a large saucepan, combine the water, potatoes, carrots, leeks and salt and simmer for 40 minutes.

Add the courgettes, red pepper, French beans, kidney beans, breadcrumbs and saffron. Simmer the soup for another 20 minutes.

Meanwhile, prepare the pistou sauce. Grate the Parmesan cheese and stir it into the tomato paste. Grind the pine nuts finely and add them to the tomato-cheese paste, along with the basil. Crush the garlic and stir it in. Finally, add the olive oil and process the sauce in a blender at high speed until it is perfectly smooth and homogeneous. Lacking a blender, pound all but the olive oil with a pestle or a wooden spoon until you have a smooth paste, then gradually beat in the oil. Season with pepper to taste.

Ladle out about a cup of hot broth from the soup and stir it into the pistou sauce. Now add the mixture to the soup, stir and serve.

GREEN CHILLI AND CHEESE SOUP

SERVES 4

¾ oz/20 g butter
1½ tbsp olive oil
1½ medium-sized onions
4–5 cloves garlic
2 tsp paprika
1⅖ pt/800 ml water or
  Vegetable Broth I (p. 60)
1½ lb/675 g fresh, ripe
  tomatoes

4 oz/115 g medium chillis, seeded
  and skinned
2 small white-skinned potatoes
¼ tsp ground cumin
1 tbsp chopped fresh coriander
  leaves
1 tsp salt, plus more to taste
4 oz/115 g mild Cheddar
  cheese

Melt the butter in a large saucepan and add the oil. Peel the onions and cut them into 1-in/25-mm chunks. Peel and chop or thinly slice the garlic. Add the onions and garlic to the butter and oil and sauté for several minutes. Then add the paprika and sauté 1–2 minutes more, stirring constantly.

Add the water or broth. Cut the tomatoes into wedges and spin them briefly in a blender or food processor. They should be partly puréed and partly chopped. Cut the chillis into small strips or coarsely chop them. Scrub the potatoes and cut them into ½-in/ 12-mm cubes. Add the tomatoes, chillis, potatoes, ground cumin and chopped coriander leaves to the soup and simmer until the potatoes are tender, about 30 minutes.

Season to taste with salt.

Cut the cheese into small chunks and divide it among 4 large soup bowls. Ladle the soup, bubbling hot, over the cheese in the bowls. Serve immediately.

SPICED LENTIL SOUP

SERVES 6–8

2½ cups lentils
5⅗ pt/3.2 l water
1½ tsp salt, and more to taste
2 fl oz/55 ml olive oil
2 onions, peeled and chopped
4–5 large cloves garlic, peeled and sliced
2 large bay leaves
½ tsp ground cinnamon
½ tsp ground cloves
½ tsp ground ginger

1½ tsp ground cumin
2½ tbsp minced green chillis
2–3 tbsp chopped fresh coriander leaves
¼ cup chopped fresh parsley
1–1½ oz/25–40 g butter
lots of fresh-ground black pepper

OPTIONAL GARNISH
paprika
sprigs of coriander leaves

Put the lentils in a large saucepan with the water and the salt. Bring the water to a boil, then lower the heat and simmer the soup for 1 hour.

Heat the olive oil in a frying pan, add the onions, garlic and bay leaves and sauté them, stirring often, until the onions begin to colour. Add the cinnamon, cloves, ginger and cumin to the onions and stir over low heat for about 2 minutes. Stir the onions and spices into the soup, along with the chillis, coriander leaves and parsley. Let the soup simmer for another hour, stirring it occasionally.

When all the lentils are completely soft, purée at least half the soup in a blender, about 1 pt/570 ml at a time, or force it through a sieve. Return the puréed soup to the saucepan and stir in the butter. Grate in a generous amount of black pepper, stir, taste and add more salt or pepper as needed.

Serve the soup hot and, if you like, sprinkle a little paprika on it just before serving, or garnish each bowl with sprigs of coriander leaves.

CREAM OF CARROT SOUP

SERVES 8

3 cups scraped, sliced carrots
1 large onion, peeled and
  chopped
4 oz/115 g butter
1 tsp sugar
1 tsp salt, and more to taste
1 medium-sized potato, peeled
  and diced
4 fl oz/115 ml water
12 fl oz/340 ml single cream

4 tbsp flour
1⅘ pt/1 l milk
fresh-ground black pepper
paprika
cayenne pepper
1 clove garlic, minced (optional)
brandy
GARNISH
croûtons or chopped parsley

Sauté the carrots and onions in a large frying pan or stock-pot in 2 oz/55 g of the butter for a few minutes. Add the sugar, 1 teaspoon salt, the diced potato and the water. Cover tightly and simmer until the vegetables are just tender.

Purée the vegetables in a blender with the cream.

Melt the remaining butter in a frying pan and stir in the flour. Cook the roux until it is golden. Heat the milk and stir it into the roux with a whisk. Cook the white sauce over a very low heat, stirring often, until it is thickened.

Combine the carrot purée and the white sauce in a large saucepan. Grate in some pepper and add paprika and cayenne to taste, as well as a little minced garlic if you like. Add a little brandy and salt to taste.

Simmer the soup gently for another 10–15 minutes, stirring occasionally. Serve hot, garnished with croûtons or chopped parsley.

AUBERGINE SOUP

SERVES 6–8

3 lb/1.25 kg aubergines
2½ tsp salt
2 tbsp olive oil
4 cloves garlic, minced
1 tbsp paprika
¾ tsp ground cumin
1 pt/570 ml hot water
¾ cup finely chopped celery

1 cup finely chopped onions
1½ oz/40 g butter
4 fl oz/115 ml single cream
16 fl oz/450 ml milk
pinch of hot paprika
GARNISH
fresh-grated Parmesan cheese
   and croûtons

Prick the aubergines in several places with a fork and bake them in the oven at 375°F/190°C/Mark 5 for 40–50 minutes, depending on their size. The skins should be wrinkled and the aubergines soft. As soon as they are cool enough to handle, cut them open and scrape all the flesh out of the skins. Purée the flesh with 2 teaspoons of the salt in a blender and put it aside.

Heat the olive oil in a large saucepan and add the minced garlic. Cook the garlic, stirring often, until it is golden and then stir in the paprika, cumin and the remaining salt. Heat the spices in the oil for about 30 seconds, then add the hot water and simmer the broth gently for several minutes.

In a frying pan sauté the celery and onion in the butter until the onion is golden and beginning to brown. Combine these vegetables with the aubergine purée and stir all of it into the hot garlic-paprika broth.

Add the cream, milk and a little pinch of hot paprika. Simmer the soup for another 10–15 minutes, stirring occasionally, then taste it and correct the seasoning if necessary.

Serve the soup hot with *croûtons* and grated Parmesan cheese.

CARROT-YOGHURT SOUP

SERVES 4–5

2 oz/55 g butter
1 onion, peeled and chopped
1–2 cloves garlic, minced
½ tsp mustard seeds
½ tsp turmeric
½ tsp ground ginger
¼ tsp cayenne pepper, and more
    to taste
½ tsp salt, and more to taste
½ tsp ground cumin

¼ tsp ground cinnamon
1 lb/450 g carrots, scraped and
    sliced
1 tbsp lemon juice
1⅗ pt/800 ml water
16 fl oz/450 ml yoghurt
1 tbsp honey
black pepper to taste
GARNISH
chopped fresh coriander leaves

Melt the butter in a frying pan and sauté the onions and garlic until they are golden. Add the spices and cook for several minutes, stirring constantly. Add the carrots and lemon juice. Continue cooking for several more minutes, stirring often, then add 16 fl oz/ 450 ml of the water, cover tightly, and simmer for at least 30 minutes or until the carrots are tender.

Purée the spiced carrots in a blender with the remaining water. Return the purée to the frying pan and whisk in the yoghurt and honey. Heat the soup, but do not allow it to boil.

Taste, correct the seasoning with black pepper and more cayenne and salt as desired, and serve hot, with chopped coriander leaves sprinkled on top.

CREAMED AVOCADO SOUP

SERVES 6

2 oz/55 g butter
2 tbsp flour
24 fl oz/680 ml hot Potato Peel
    Broth (p. 62)
1 lb/450 g ripe avocados (about
    2 medium sized)
12 fl oz/340 ml single cream

4 fl oz/115 ml yoghurt
6 tbsp fresh lemon juice
½ tsp salt, and more to taste
½ tsp sugar
fresh-ground black pepper to
    taste

GARNISH
fried tortilla strips (p. 296)

any good hot chilli sauce
(optional)

Melt the butter in a medium-sized, heavy-bottomed saucepan and stir in the flour. Cook the roux over low heat for several minutes, stirring constantly, until it begins to turn golden brown. Pour in the hot broth and continue stirring until the mixture is slightly thickened and smooth.

Peel and remove pits of the avocados and purée the flesh in a blender or food processor with the cream, yoghurt and lemon juice. Combine the broth and the avocado mixture in an enamelled saucepan and stir in the salt, sugar and pepper. Heat the soup just to the simmering point, but don't let it come to a boil. Taste and correct the seasoning if necessary.

Serve the soup hot, putting a few crisp-fried tortilla strips in each bowl. Hot sauce can be passed separately and added as desired.

Note: I don't recommend making this soup too far in advance, keeping it hot for a long time, or reheating it more than once. Avocados can be a little bit fussy once they are removed from their skin and pit.

WATERCRESS SOUP

A lovely soup for a big party, but the proportions can easily be cut in half.

SERVES 8–10

4 oz/115 g butter
1⅓ cups chopped onions
6 tbsp flour
4 pt/2.25 l hot Potato Peel
*   Broth (p. 62)*
6 cups packed watercress leaves,
*   washed*

8 fl oz/225 ml double cream
4 eggs
2 tbsp lemon juice
1 tbsp sugar
salt to taste
pepper to taste

Melt the butter in a large saucepan and sauté the onions in it until they just begin to turn golden. Stir in the flour and lower the heat. Cook the roux, stirring constantly, for a few minutes. Continue stirring as you gradually add the hot broth. If you detect any lumps forming, stir briskly with a whisk.

Add the cleaned watercress leaves and simmer the soup for about 10 minutes. Taking the soup in 1-pt/570-ml batches, purée it in a blender until it is perfectly smooth. Return the soup to the saucepan.

Beat together the cream and the eggs, and continue beating as you pour in about ¾ pt/425 ml of the hot soup. Stir this mixture back into the soup, off the heat. Season the soup with the lemon juice, sugar, salt and pepper.

Over a moderate heat, stir the soup for about 3–4 minutes, or until it is quite hot through but not simmering. Serve immediately.

CREMA DE VERDURAS
(Puréed Vegetable Soup)

SERVES 6–8

1½ cups chopped leeks (white parts)
1½ cups sliced carrots
4 cups diced potatoes (with or without peel, according to preference)
1⅓ cups cut French beans
several large sprigs parsley
1–2 cloves garlic, minced

4 tsp salt
4 pt/2.25 l water
1 cup cooked artichoke hearts
½ cup peeled, seeded, diced red pepper
fresh-ground black pepper to taste
4 fl oz/115 ml double cream
1½ oz/40 g butter

In a large saucepan, combine the leeks, carrots, potatoes, French beans, parsley, garlic, salt and water. Simmer the vegetables for about 40 minutes, then add the artichoke hearts (reserving 2–3 for the garnish) and the diced red pepper (reserving about 2 tablespoons for the garnish). Simmer the soup for another 5–10 minutes.

Purée the soup in a blender in small batches, or press it through a sieve, and return it to the saucepan. Grind in a generous amount of black pepper, add the cream and butter and reheat the soup, stirring occasionally, until the butter is melted. Taste and correct seasoning if necessary.

Chop the reserved artichoke hearts and red pepper rather finely and sprinkle a little of both on each serving.

CREAMED FRESH PEA SOUP

SERVES 6–8

3½ lb/1.6 kg fresh peas (about
   4 cups shelled)
2⅖ pt/1.4 l water
½ medium-sized onion, chopped
3–4 good-sized sprigs parsley
1 tsp salt
½ tsp sugar
1 small head round lettuce
   (5–6 oz/140–170 g)

2 oz/55 g butter
4 fl oz/115 ml dry white wine
2 fl oz/55 ml double cream
dash of white pepper
GARNISH
small dumplings for soup
   (p. 64)

Shell the peas and put them in a large saucepan with the water, onion, parsley, salt and sugar. Bring to a boil, lower the heat and simmer the soup for about 40 minutes.

Wash and coarsely chop the lettuce. Melt 1½ oz/40 g of the butter in a frying pan and sauté the lettuce in it until the lettuce is completely soft and most of the excess liquid has evaporated. Add the lettuce and butter to the soup and continue simmering it for another 10 minutes.

Purée the soup in a blender, about ¾ pt/425 ml at a time, and return it to the saucepan. Add the wine and the cream, adjust the seasoning with more salt and a dash of white pepper, and stir in the remaining butter. Heat to the simmering point and serve with small dumplings.

CHILLED TOMATO SOUP
WITH CANTALOUP

SERVES 6

6–8 medium-sized tomatoes
1 large cucumber, peeled, seeded
    and chopped
½ cup finely chopped onion
8 fl oz/225 ml soured cream
2½ tsp salt
½ tsp ground ginger

pepper to taste
4 tsp lemon juice
1 tbsp fresh-grated lemon rind
1 large cantaloup
1 tbsp dried basil, crushed, or 2
    tbsp chopped fresh

Put the tomatoes in boiling water for a few minutes, until the skins start to crack and peel. Remove the tomatoes and peel them. Purée them in a blender or food processor at high speed. You should have 2 pt/1.1 l of fresh tomato purée.

Purée the cucumber and onions in a blender or food processor and add this to the tomatoes. If you are using a blender, you could 'prime' it with a bit of the puréed tomatoes. Stir in the soured cream and season the soup with salt, ginger, pepper, lemon juice and lemon rind.

Halve the cantaloup, remove all the seeds and either cut it into small balls with a melon scoop or peel and cut it into chunks. Toss the melon with the chopped basil and chill both soup and melon for several hours.

To serve, pour the soup into chilled bowls and put a few spoonfuls of the melon into each one.

COLD CUCUMBER AND SPINACH SOUP

SERVES 6

1¼ oz/35 g butter
1 large onion
1 lb/450 g fresh spinach
1⅘ pt/1 l Potato Peel Broth
  (p. 62)
3 long, slender cucumbers (about
  1½ lb/675 g)
8 oz/225 g cream cheese
pinch of nutmeg

pinch of hot paprika
2 tbsp lemon juice
salt and pepper
4 fl oz/115 ml single cream
GARNISH
sweet paprika
soured cream (optional)
fresh snipped dill (optional)

Melt the butter in a large frying pan. Chop the onion and sauté in the butter until golden. Meanwhile, carefully wash and remove coarse stems from the spinach.

Add the spinach to the onions and butter and stir until wilted. Combine the cooked vegetables with the broth in a large saucepan. Peel, seed and dice the cucumbers and add them to the broth. Simmer the soup for about 20 minutes, then purée it in a blender, in batches, and return it to the saucepan.

Slice the cream cheese and stir it into the hot soup. Continue stirring, over low heat, until all the cheese is completely melted and thoroughly incorporated into the soup.

Season the soup with a tiny bit of nutmeg, a tiny bit of hot paprika, the lemon juice and the salt and pepper to taste. Remove the soup from the heat, stir in the cream and chill the soup for several hours.

When the soup is completely cold, taste it again and correct the seasoning if necessary.

Sprinkle a little sweet paprika on the soup after it is ladled into bowls to add a bit of colour. This soup may also be garnished with a spoonful of soured cream in the centre of each bowl, and a sprinkle of fresh snipped dill.

GAZPACHO TOLEDANO

SERVES 6–8

7–8 medium-sized ripe tomatoes
2 medium-sized cucumbers
1 green pepper
1 small onion
2–3 cloves garlic
1½ slices French bread
12 fl oz/340 ml cold water
6 tbsp olive oil
4–5 tbsp wine vinegar, or to taste
3 tsp salt, or to taste

2 tsp paprika
pinch of ground cumin
fresh-ground black pepper to taste
GARNISH
croûtons
chopped onions
chopped red and green peppers
chopped cucumbers
chopped tomatoes

Cut the tomatoes into quarters. Peel and seed the cucumbers and cut into approximately 1-in/25-mm pieces. Seed the green pepper and cut into approximately 1-in/25-mm pieces. Peel and coarsely dice the onion. Put the garlic cloves through a press. Cube the bread.

Now put the prepared ingredients, 2–3 cups at a time, into a blender, adding a little of the water each time. Blend at medium or high speed until the vegetables and bread are puréed. Pour the purée into a large bowl.

Add the oil and vinegar, the remaining water and the seasonings and whisk vigorously until all is very well blended. Taste and correct seasoning. If the soup is too thick, thin it with a little more cold water.

Chill the soup in the refrigerator for several hours before serving. Arrange the garnishes attractively on a large platter and pass them round the table as you serve the soup.

MY GAZPACHO

SERVES 6

5–6 large ripe tomatoes (vine ripened if possible)

1 large cucumber
½ onion

	GARNISH
1 clove garlic	
½ cup coarsely chopped watercress	chopped cucumbers
	chopped red and green peppers
3 tbsp olive oil	chopped onions
3 tbsp red wine vinegar	sliced hard-boiled eggs
2 tsp salt	croûtons
1 pt/570 ml ice water	chopped tomatoes

Cut the tomatoes into wedges. Peel and seed the cucumber and cut it into chunks. Chop the onion and garlic.

Purée the tomatoes, cucumber, onions and garlic in a blender, about 2–3 cups at a time. Add the watercress to the last batch and blend until smooth.

Pour the puréed vegetables into a large bowl and add the oil, vinegar and salt. Blend these seasonings in with a whisk until the soup is smooth. Taste and correct seasoning. Now whisk in the ice water, and perhaps add an ice cube or two. Chill in the refrigerator until it is time to serve and then give it another quick stir with the whisk just before ladling into bowls.

Pass round the tray of garnishes as the soup is being served.

COLD AVOCADO SOUP

SERVES 4–6

2 medium-sized ripe avocados (about 1 lb/450 g)	1 tsp sugar
	⅛ tsp ground cumin
4 medium-sized tomatoes	8 fl oz/225 ml yoghurt
½ medium-sized onion	4 fl oz/115 ml single cream
1 clove garlic	12 fl oz/340 ml Vegetable
1 cucumber	Broth I (p. 61)
4 tbsp chopped green chillis	GARNISH
¾ tsp salt	chopped spring onions
3½ tbsp lemon juice	chopped fresh coriander leaves
1 tbsp red wine vinegar	fried tortilla strips (p. 296)
1 tbsp vegetable oil	

Peel, remove pits from and coarsely chop the avocados. Cut the tomatoes in thin wedges. Chop the onion and mince the garlic.

Peel, seed and cut up the cucumber. Combine all the vegetables and the chillis and purée them in a blender until no large chunks are left.

Add the salt, lemon juice, vinegar, oil, sugar and cumin. Run the blender again until the mixture is smooth.

Pour the avocado mixture into a bowl, add the yoghurt, cream and vegetable broth, and beat it lightly with a whisk until it is smooth once more. Taste the soup and correct the seasoning if necessary. Chill the soup thoroughly.

Chop up a few spring onions and about ¼ cup of fresh coriander leaves and put them aside in small bowls. Cut several corn tortillas into short strips and fry them in oil until they are crisp. Drain them on a paper towel, salt them lightly and put them in a napkin-lined bowl or basket.

Serve the soup ice-cold, in chilled bowls if possible, and pass the onions, coriander leaves and tortilla strips separately.

CHŁODNIK

(Cold Beetroot Soup)

SERVES 6–8

approximately 2 bunches fresh,	*3 tbsp chopped fresh dill*
young beetroots with leaves	*12 fl oz/340 ml soured cream*
2⅕ pt/1.25 l water	*1 medium-sized cucumber*
1 tbsp salt	*5 hard-boiled eggs*
1½–2 tbsp cider vinegar	*12 fl oz/340 ml beer*
1 tbsp sugar	

Peel and cut in julienne strips enough beetroots to fill 3 cups. Wash the stems and tender leaves carefully and chop up enough to fill 2 cups solidly. Put the beetroots, stems and leaves in a large enamelled saucepan with the water, the salt, the vinegar and the sugar. Bring the water to a boil, lower the heat and simmer until all the beetroots are completely tender, about 1 hour.

Taste the soup and add a little more vinegar or sugar as needed. Chill.

In a medium-sized bowl, combine the chopped dill with a little salt and pound it with a wooden pestle until it is moist and very fragrant. Add the soured cream and mix thoroughly. Pour in about 8 fl oz/225 ml of the beetroot broth and stir it in with a whisk until the mixture is smooth. Pour the soured cream mixture into the soup and mix everything together completely.

Peel and seed the cucumber and chop it coarsely. Peel the eggs and chop them rather coarsely as well. Add the cucumber and 3–4 of the chopped eggs to the soup. Reserve the remaining eggs for a garnish.

Finally, stir in the beer. Taste the soup and correct the seasoning to your own taste, adding more vinegar or sugar to get the right sweet-sour balance – but go easy! A little bit of vinegar or sugar will go a long way.

Serve the soup very cold, in chilled bowls if possible, and put a little ice cube in each bowl. Pass the reserved chopped eggs separately, to be sprinkled on top.

COLD CHERRY-LEMON SOUP

SERVES 6

grated rind of 3 lemons
juice of 4 large lemons (about
    8 fl oz/225 ml)
⅔ cup sugar, or more to taste
8 fl oz/225 ml water
8 fl oz/225 ml dry white wine

1 lb/450 g fresh, sweet dark
    cherries
5 egg yolks
10–12 ice cubes
8 fl oz/225 ml soured cream
    sweetened with 2–3 tbsp
    sugar

Combine the lemon rind, lemon juice, sugar, water and white wine in a large enamelled saucepan. Heat the mixture until the sugar is dissolved completely, stirring constantly.

Wash the cherries, remove their stems and pit them. Set aside 18 of the cherries, and add the rest to the soup. Simmer them gently until they are soft, then put them through a fine sieve or purée them in a blender. Return the purée to the soup. Add the egg yolks and beat them in with a whisk. Continue whisking gently for several minutes, over very low heat, as the soup thickens.

Allow the soup to cool somewhat, giving it an occasional stir. Taste and add more sugar if you like. When the soup is no longer steaming hot, put in 10–12 ice cubes and stir. Then put the soup in the refrigerator and chill it until it is time to serve – at least 1 hour.

To prepare the sweetened soured cream, just add the sugar and beat it in thoroughly.

To serve, put 3 of the reserved cherries into each bowl, ladle in the well-chilled soup and put a nice round dollop of the sweetened soured cream on top.

CHILLED BUTTERMILK SOUP

SERVES 6

1½ lb/680 g potatoes (about 2 large)
2⅕ pt/1.25 l buttermilk
⅔ cup chopped spring onions
2–3 tbsp chopped fresh dill weed, or 1 tsp dried
3 cloves garlic, minced

1 large cucumber, peeled, seeded and chopped
1 tbsp finely chopped fresh coriander leaves
¾–1 tsp salt, to taste
pinch of ground cumin

Peel the potatoes and cut them in ½-in/12-mm dice. Boil them in salted water until they are just tender, then drain them.

Combine in a blender 16 fl oz/450 ml of the buttermilk, ½ the cooked potatoes, ½ the chopped spring onions, the dill weed and the minced garlic. Blend at high speed until vegetables are puréed.

In a large bowl or tureen, stir together the purée, the remaining buttermilk, potatoes and onions, and the cucumber, coriander leaves, salt and cumin. Chill well before serving.

COLD CHERRY SOUP

A perfect first course for a summer supper.

SERVES 6

2½ lb/1.1 kg fresh, sweet dark
* cherries*
2 pt/1.1 l water
4 tbsp sugar, or more to taste

2½ fl oz/70 ml white wine, or
* to taste*
juice of 1–2 lemons, or to taste
8 fl oz/225 ml double cream

Wash the cherries, remove their stems, pit them and put them in a large enamelled saucepan along with the water and the sugar. Bring to a boil and simmer for about 15–20 minutes. Drain the cherries, and reserve the liquid. Remove 24 cherries and put them aside.

Rub the remaining cherries through a fine sieve and return the purée to the cherry liquid. Add a little white wine and fresh-squeezed lemon juice. If the soup is too sour, add a little more sugar.

Chill the soup. When it is quite cold, whip the cream. Put 4 of the reserved cherries into each of 6 bowls and divide the soup equally among them. Finish each serving with a generous spoonful of the whipped cream.

Sauces and
Salad Dressings

To BE A GOOD COOK, you will absolutely need some basic sauces, for they are often the very base of a dish. Soufflés, for instance, and croquettes and many desserts begin with a sauce, which is then added to and altered in various ways. Many other dishes take on their entire character with the addition of a sauce: where would we be without all those delicious pasta dishes and good things like asparagus hollandaise, pizza and apple-sauce crêpes?

You will have to make these sauces carefully to make them well. As a rule, sauces take a little more skill and concentration than other preparations. You can't stroll away to answer the phone while you are stirring the hollandaise, or turn round to do something else while the roux for the Béchamel scorches. Nevertheless, they are not so mysterious as some cooks like to suggest. If you're a beginner and all this makes you nervous, here's the good news: there really are only a few sauces. All the hundreds of others that can be imagined and concocted are actually variations of those few. When you know how to make a Béchamel sauce, you know essentially everything you need to know about flour-thickened sauces; when you can make one custard sauce, you can make any of them – and so on.

Once you understand the basics, you can unleash all your creativity. Herbs and spices can be used to great advantage; fresh herbs, as always, are best, and if you keep a herb garden, you have a real gold mine of flavour with which to enliven your sauces. I also like to use strong-flavoured broths or vegetable purées, reduced to a concentrated richness, and grated cheeses of all kinds. And don't forget the drinks cabinet: judicious amounts of the right wines or liqueurs can make all the difference for some foods, giving them an irresistible taste and perfume.

To make your sauces, you will want good heavy saucepans, some wooden spoons, a whisk, presence of mind and some practice. For hollandaise, you will need a double boiler. The quickest and tastiest mayonnaise can be made in a blender or food processor.

Once you know how to make sauces, it's important to learn how to use them properly. The Spanish have a saying: the sauce is worth more than what's under it. It's a clever saying, but the idea can too often be carried to extremes. Diamond Jim Brady once said to his cook, 'George ... if you poured some of that sauce over a Turkish towel, I believe I could eat all of it,' and in that case the saying would undoubtedly hold true. But as a rule, while I eat sauces enthusiastically, I apply them discreetly. Even when the sauce is the most important element of a dish, there's no excuse for drowning a food in it. The flavour of the eggs, the spaghetti or the vegetable is important, and a sauce should be used to enhance it, never to mask it. A good lesson can be taken from the Italians and the Mexicans too, who use delicious and sometimes potent sauces sparingly and to great advantage. You'll find that a good sauce, properly used, does not merely add to the savour of a dish, it multiplies it.

Ultimately, the real value of sauces lies in the way that even just a fundamental knowledge of them can increase your culinary repertoire. Quite ordinary foods can be turned into pleasing new dishes. A simple cheese and chilli omelette, for instance, took on an entirely new aspect one night when I spooned a little Cucumber-Avocado Sauce over it. A dish of ice cream becomes a distinctive dessert with the addition of some Raspberry Sauce. A Hot Paprika Sauce like the one I use for Stuffed Potato Pancakes, Hungarian Style, could also be added, in small amounts, to hot, buttered noodles or steamed cauliflower or drizzled over poached eggs on dark bread or served with any of several soufflés. In this way, with a little imagination, the mastery of sauces can vastly improve and expand your cuisine.

Making Sauces

One of the most important things to remember in making sauces is timing: a sauce cooked too long or too fast can curdle or separate, scorch or become pasty. On the other hand, an undercooked sauce can have a raw taste or be too thin. Good timing is not difficult to achieve once you realize that keeping your eye on the clock is not as important as keeping your eye on the sauce. You will soon learn to recognize how a sauce should taste and feel.

The other thing to remember is the basic rule for all good cooking, and that is to use good ingredients. If you start with fresh butter, eggs and milk, rich cream, good fruity olive oil, tasty wine vinegar, fragrant herbs, good aged cheeses and the highest-quality produce of all types, you are already well on the way to being a good cook. For fine sauces, just keep these things in mind, follow directions carefully and don't spare the whisk.

FLOUR-THICKENED SAUCES

The basic white sauce and its most popular refinement, Béchamel, are simplicity itself if the easy rules are followed. The thickening agent for this type of sauce is the roux, which is nothing more than a mixture of melted butter and flour. The butter is melted in a heavy-bottomed saucepan over a very low heat. This is important. A flimsy saucepan will not distribute heat evenly or keep it low and steady, and an even, gentle heating is what the roux needs. When the butter is melted, the flour (usually an amount equal to the butter) is stirred in. I use a wooden spoon for this and throughout the making of hot sauces. Wooden spoons do not scratch saucepans, nor do they conduct heat, during prolonged stirring, to the hand that holds them. I keep a large crock of them in every size near my cooker and find this a very satisfactory arrangement for both convenience and aesthetics.

When the flour is stirred into the butter, you have a pale roux. Continue stirring it over very low heat and keep a sharp eye on it. In a moment it will start to foam slightly. Two or three minutes' stirring over the low heat is all it needs: less, and the flour will taste raw; more, and it will scorch. It should not turn brown, but stay a pleasant golden yellow.

At this point, you must remove the saucepan from the heat and stir in the previously heated milk or cream, then beat energetically with a wire whisk. Here some beginners are plagued by lumps, but if you make sure the milk or cream is hot before adding it, and if you beat it in well enough, your sauce will be smooth. Run a spoon round the side of the saucepan and across the bottom to get out any bits of roux that are sticking there, and whisk again. I have not yet seen the lump that could not be beaten into submission with a good wire whisk.

Return the sauce to the heat, a little hotter this time, and stir gently with the whisk as the sauce comes to a boil. Continue stirring for about 2 minutes, then just season with salt and pepper and you have a white sauce, nicely thickened and perfectly smooth.

This sauce is the basis for many others, as well as for soufflés, croquettes and many fillings. It can be enriched with the addition of egg yolks, cream or butter – or all three.

Béchamel sauce is made by the same basic method, with the additional flavouring of a bit of onion and some herbs. Mornay sauce is essentially just a white sauce or Béchamel to which some cheese has been added, though it may also be enriched.

If egg yolks are added to a hot sauce, it is a good idea to beat them with a bit of cream or some other cold liquid first. Then a little bit of the hot sauce should be beaten into them before they are added, away from direct heat, to the rest of the sauce and beaten in with a whisk. This method will prevent curdling by allowing the egg yolks to heat up gradually. Once egg yolks have been incorporated into a flour-based sauce, the sauce may be brought to a boil once more without fear of curdling; however, the same is not true of a custard sauce, made without flour, so don't get them confused.

EMULSION SAUCES

Emulsion sauces depend on the ability of egg yolks to absorb butter or oil. When they are correctly handled, the yolks will thicken the fats and obligingly turn them into the creamiest, richest sauces possible. There are two main categories of emulsion sauces. They are the mayonnaise type, which is made without heat, and the hollandaise type, made with warmed egg yolks and hot melted butter. Mayonnaise made in a blender or a food processor is one of the fastest, easiest sauces to make – a stunned monkey could do it. Hollandaise is trickier, but again, if the timing and the proportions are right, you needn't have any problems.

The only things you need to know about making mayonnaise are that it is better to have the ingredients at room temperature, and that the egg yolks, or whole egg, must be beaten to a creamy consistency before the oil is added. In a blender this takes a few seconds. The oil is then added gradually while the blender is on and in moments you have a perfect, thick mayonnaise.

For hollandaise, or any variation of it, the process is more involved. Firstly, the egg yolks must be heated very gradually and *only* until they start to thicken. While it is possible to do this in a heavy saucepan over direct, low heat, it is far safer to use a double boiler.

If the egg yolks are heated too quickly or too long, they will curdle. Secondly, the yolks must be beaten constantly with a wire whisk as they are heated to ensure that they heat up evenly and stay smooth. Thirdly, the butter should be added very gradually, also with continuous whisking, or the sauce will not emulsify. If you are patient and add the butter in very small quantities, beating conscientiously with your whisk until it starts to look thick and creamy, and watch the temperature carefully, your sauce will be a success. Finally, it is important not to add any more butter than the recipe indicates and not to overcook the sauce, as either of these errors will curdle the sauce.

In general, the common pitfalls in making a hollandaise are easily avoided if you just familiarize yourself with the whole process before beginning, follow directions, and do not allow yourself to be interrupted – in other words, if the phone rings, ignore it. But if it happens that the sauce does curdle for some reason, chances are that it can still be saved. The best method to re-emulsify a curdled hollandaise is to beat a spoonful of it in a warm bowl with 1 teaspoon of lemon juice until it thickens. Then add small amounts of the sauce, beating in each addition until it is thick. The whole sauce can be reconstituted this way.

If you want to reheat a hollandaise that has been refrigerated, put a small amount of the cold sauce into a double boiler and whisk it over hot water until it is creamy, then very gradually whisk in the remaining sauce. Under no circumstances can the sauce be allowed to simmer or boil.

Mayonnaise and hollandaise both lend themselves to a number of variations, and once you have mastered the basic techniques, you will be able to make any of them with ease.

REDUCTION SAUCES, SALAD DRESSINGS

Certain sauces, for instance tomato sauces, are thickened by simmering slowly until enough moisture has evaporated from them. These are the most foolproof of all, as it is necessary to stir them only occasionally and keep an eye on them to see that they don't reduce too much and scorch. They take time, sometimes as much as an hour or two of gentle simmering, but it is time during which your attention can mainly be given to other things, so don't let that put you off.

Vinaigrette sauces and any kind of salad dressing also do not require the mastering of any special technique. About salad dressings I want to say only that they stand or fall on the quality of the ingredients used and on their freshness. Since they are so easy to make, there is no reason why they should be prepared any earlier than a few hours before they are to be served and, in general, can be mixed just before being added to the salad.

BÉCHAMEL SAUCE

This milk-based, roux-thickened sauce is so basic and has so many tasty and useful variations that it cannot be left out of this book. Here is essentially the same recipe that was given in the first *Vegetarian Epicure*, with additional comments and some variations.

MAKES ABOUT I–I ⅕ PT/570–680 ML

1½ oz/40 g butter
½ medium-sized onion, minced
3 tbsp flour
1 pt/570 ml hot milk
several peppercorns

large pinch of whole thyme
1 small bay leaf
salt to taste
dash of nutmeg

Melt the butter either in the top of a large double boiler or in a medium-sized, *heavy-bottomed* enamelled saucepan. (If you are not using a double boiler, keep a very sharp eye on the heat and on the sauce to avoid scorching.) Add the minced onions and cook them over low heat, stirring frequently, until they are soft but not brown.

Stir in the flour and continue cooking what is now a roux for a few minutes more, stirring often. Add the hot milk, beating it in with a whisk until the sauce is perfectly smooth and is beginning to thicken.

Add a few peppercorns, a good pinch of whole thyme, a tiny bay leaf, a little salt and a little nutmeg. Cook the sauce over very gentle heat, stirring often, for at least 10–15 minutes or for as long as 1 hour. The longer the cooking time, of course, the thicker and stronger flavoured the sauce.

Strain the sauce through a sieve and dot it with small shavings of butter, which will melt and keep a skin from forming on top. *Voilà* – you have basic Béchamel, and now you can spoon it over eggs, omelettes, vegetables, croquettes or pasta; or you can put it aside for a while, then gently reheat it, stirring it up with a whisk; or you can even refrigerate it for a day or two in a tightly covered container, and no harm done. Furthermore, you can make other good sauces with it, such as the following ones.

Rich Béchamel

4 fl oz/115 ml double cream	*salt to taste*
2 egg yolks	*½ tsp lemon juice*
hot Béchamel Sauce	*1 oz/25 g butter (optional)*

Beat together the cream and the egg yolks in a bowl and gradually beat in about 8 fl oz/225 ml of the hot Béchamel Sauce. Add this mixture to the remaining Béchamel Sauce in the saucepan, beating it in with a whisk. Heat the sauce very gently, stirring constantly with a whisk, until it comes to a simmer, then continue simmering and stirring for a couple of minutes. Be sure to run a spoon round the bottom and edges of the pan occasionally to prevent lumping there.

Remove the pan from the heat, taste the sauce, and add salt as needed. Stir in the lemon juice and beat lightly with the whisk again.

Béchamel can also be enriched with butter. To do this, simply beat in about 1 oz/25 g butter, a little at a time, just before the sauce is to be served. Butter-enriched Béchamel is delicious, but this method should not be used if the sauce is going into a dish that will be gratinéed in the oven, as excessive heat will make butter separate and float to the top.

Mornay Sauce

4 tbsp grated Gruyère cheese
3 tbsp grated Parmesan cheese
hot Béchamel Sauce

dash of cayenne pepper
(optional)

Add the grated cheeses to the hot Béchamel and beat them in with a whisk until they have melted and the sauce is perfectly smooth. A dash of cayenne can be added to this sauce with very nice results.

Rich Mornay Sauce

Proceed exactly as for ordinary Mornay Sauce, only use Béchamel that has been enriched with the cream and egg yolk mixture described above.

Mild Paprika Sauce

Add about 2 teaspoons of paprika to either basic Béchamel or Rich Béchamel (see above). Whisk the sauce lightly until the paprika is thoroughly blended.

HOLLANDAISE SAUCE

Hollandaise is tricky. If you haven't had a lot of experience with it, do go back and reread the general information and specific hints on pp. 100–101.

MAKES ABOUT 6 FL OZ/170 ML

3 large egg yolks
1–1½ tbsp lemon juice
pinch of white pepper

½ oz/15 g butter
3½/100 g butter, melted
salt

Put the yolks into the top of a double boiler* and beat them, cold, until they are creamy. Beat in 1 tablespoon of the lemon juice and a pinch of white pepper.

* If you don't have a double boiler, you can rig one up by fitting a stainless steel bowl snugly into the top of a saucepan, so that the bottom of the bowl clears the bottom of the pan by about 3 in/75 mm, leaving room for the water.

Put the top of the boiler over hot, but not boiling water. Add the unmelted butter and beat the egg yolk and lemon juice mixture steadily with a whisk until the butter has melted and the egg yolks have thickened. Be sure to scrape the egg yolks down from the sides and out of the corners of the saucepan frequently. The yolks should stay perfectly smooth and creamy as they thicken. At any indication of curdling or lumping up, immediately remove the saucepan from above the hot water and stand it in a shallow bowl of cool water for a moment as you continue to beat.

When the egg yolks have thickened, add a tiny bit of the melted butter and continue beating with the whisk, over hot water, until the butter is absorbed. Add another tiny bit and beat again.

When the sauce thickens and becomes glossy-smooth in texture, the emulsion has formed. Overheating at any point will undo it, however, and so will adding the butter too quickly. Keep beating in the butter gradually, until it is all incorporated. Season to taste with salt and additional lemon juice if desired.

If the sauce does not want to thicken, or if it separates, put 1 tablespoon of it into a smaller bowl with 1 teaspoon of lemon juice, beat till thick and glossy, then gradually beat in the rest of the sauce, a spoonful at a time.

Serve the sauce warm with eggs or vegetables.

SOURED CREAM HORSERADISH SAUCE

A good sauce for Broccoli-Walnut Soufflé (p. 122).

MAKES ABOUT 1 PT/570 ML

1 oz/25 g butter	8 fl oz/225 ml soured cream
2 tbsp flour	1 tbsp prepared horseradish
8 fl oz/225 ml hot milk	½ tsp Dijon mustard
2 egg yolks	salt
½ cup grated Wensleydale or	pepper
other mild cheese	

Melt the butter in a heavy frying pan and stir in the flour. Lower the heat and cook the roux for a few minutes, stirring constantly.

Gradually add the hot milk, stirring with a whisk as the sauce thickens. Then whisk in the egg yolks, one at a time, and stir in the grated cheese.

Continue stirring with the whisk until all the cheese is melted. Do not let the sauce boil.

Add the soured cream, horseradish, mustard and salt and pepper to taste. Cook over a very low heat for about 5 minutes more, still gently stirring. Serve hot.

SPICY MOUSSELINE SAUCE

Serve the sauce warm with vegetables or eggs. It is great with Wild Mushroom and Dill Soufflé (p. 124).

MAKES ABOUT ½ PT/275 ML

1 recipe hot Hollandaise Sauce ·   *¼–½ tsp hot paprika, or ½ tsp*
(p. 104)   *sweet paprika plus ¼ tsp*
4 fl oz/115 ml double cream   *cayenne pepper, to taste*

Make the Hollandaise Sauce according to instructions. When it is finished, but before it has time to cool, beat the cream in a bowl until it holds firm peaks. Stir it into the warm hollandaise until they are completely blended.

Add the hot paprika, or the sweet paprika and the cayenne, stir and taste. Add more paprika or cayenne to taste.

SIMPLE TOMATO SAUCE

Serve this sauce hot with soufflés, pasta, omelettes or plain cooked vegetables.

MAKES ABOUT 1 PT/570 ML

3 lb/1.25 kg fresh, ripe   *1½ oz/40 g butter*
tomatoes (about 5 cups   *1 large clove garlic, minced*
chopped, with juice)   *1 large pinch thyme*

½ tsp salt, or more to taste
3 tbsp dry red wine
fresh-ground black pepper to
  taste

1 tsp flour
2 fl oz/55 ml double cream
  (optional)

Scald the tomatoes in boiling water and peel them. Chop them finely or purée them.

Melt the butter in a medium-large saucepan and sauté the minced garlic in it for 2 minutes. Add the thyme, the puréed tomatoes with their juice and the salt. Simmer the mixture for 1 hour over medium heat or until it is reduced by half.

Stir in the wine, a little pepper and more salt if necessary. Sprinkle the flour over the sauce, whisk it in until the sauce is perfectly smooth and simmer another 5 minutes or so.

For milder and richer sauce, add double cream and cook a few minutes longer.

HOT PAPRIKA SAUCE

Ladle this over mushroom-filled crêpes or Stuffed Potato Pancakes, Hungarian Style (p. 197).

MAKES ABOUT 1 PT/570 ML

2 oz/55 g butter
4 tbsp flour
1 pt/570 ml heated Vegetable
  Broth II (see p. 61)
¼–½ tsp hot paprika or
  cayenne pepper, to taste

2 tsp sweet paprika
salt to taste
2 fl oz/55 ml double cream

Melt the butter in a medium-sized, heavy-bottomed saucepan and stir in the flour. Cook the roux for several minutes over very low heat, then stir in the vegetable broth and continue to stir with a whisk until the sauce has thickened. Add the hot and sweet paprikas, some salt and the cream and simmer the sauce gently, stirring often, for about 20 minutes; it should be slightly reduced and thickened.

CUCUMBER-AVOCADO SAUCE

Good on filled crêpes, omelettes or vegetables.

MAKES ABOUT 1 ⅕ PT/675 ML

2 large cucumbers (about
  1 ¼ lb/570 g)
2 ½ oz/70 g butter
2 tbsp flour
8 fl oz/225 ml milk, heated
½ tsp salt, or more to taste

white pepper to taste
1 small ripe avocado (about
  6 oz/170 g)
1 tsp finely grated lemon rind
3 ½ tbsp lemon juice
1 ½ tbsp minced onion

Peel and seed the cucumbers and cut them up in fine dice. Sauté them in 1 ½ oz/40 g of the butter, stirring often, for about 20 minutes – all the excess moisture should be evaporated.

Melt the remaining butter in a medium-sized, heavy-bottomed saucepan and stir in the flour. Cook the roux for 2–3 minutes over low heat, stirring constantly, and then whisk in the milk. Continue stirring over medium heat until the sauce is thick. Season with the salt and some white pepper.

Remove the sauce from the heat. Scoop the avocado out of its shell and mash or chop it. Add the avocado, cucumber, lemon rind and lemon juice to the sauce and purée.

Return the sauce to the pot, add the minced onion and heat it up just short of simmering – do not let it boil or the flavour of the avocado will be affected. Serve immediately.

DILL SAUCE

MAKES ABOUT 18 FL OZ/510 ML

1 oz/25 g butter
2 tbsp flour
2 tsp dried dill weed or 2 tbsp
  minced fresh
8 fl oz/225 ml warm milk
6 fl oz/170 ml soured cream

2 fl oz/55 ml dry white wine
2 tbsp lemon juice
½ tsp sugar
pinch of nutmeg
pinch of cayenne pepper
salt and pepper

Melt the butter in a heavy-bottomed saucepan and stir in the flour and the dill weed. Stir the roux over very low heat for a few minutes, then whisk in the milk and soured cream. Continue stirring with a whisk over low heat until the sauce is thick and smooth.

Add the wine, lemon juice, sugar, nutmeg, cayenne and salt and pepper to taste, and simmer the sauce for about 10 minutes more, stirring often.

Serve with soufflés, omelettes, or vegetables.

FRESH TOMATO HOT SAUCE

MAKES 12 FL OZ/340 ML

2 large, ripe tomatoes (about
  1¼ cups chopped)
4 tbsp chopped fresh coriander
  leaves
1 jalapeño chilli pepper (see
  p. 301)

5 tbsp minced onion
1 tbsp vinegar
salt to taste (about ½ tsp)
minced garlic (optional)

Chop the tomatoes rather finely and add the chopped coriander leaves. Peel and seed the chilli pepper and mince it. Stir it well into the tomatoes, add the onions, vinegar and a generous amount of salt. Add minced garlic and more salt to taste. Serve cold.

TARATOUR SAUCE
(Tangy Sesame Seed Sauce)

Serve this with hot, quartered pitta bread or use in preparing Hommos bi Tahini (p. 160) and Baba Ghanouj (p. 160).

MAKES ABOUT 16 FL OZ/450 ML

1 cup tahini (*sesame seed paste*)
3 large cloves garlic, crushed or finely minced
4 fl oz/115 ml fresh lemon juice
1 tsp salt
4 fl oz/115 ml cold water

Stir the *tahini* and the garlic together in a deep bowl. Beat in the lemon juice, salt and water. If the sauce is much thicker in consistency than mayonnaise, beat in a little more water, 1 tablespoon at a time, until it resembles a rather solid mayonnaise. Add more salt or garlic if desired.

VINAIGRETTE DRESSING

MAKES ABOUT 8 FL OZ/225 ML

3 tbsp white wine vinegar
¼ tsp dry mustard
½ tsp salt
⅛ tsp pepper
pinch of cayenne pepper
5 fl oz/140 ml olive oil

Whisk together the vinegar, mustard, salt, pepper and cayenne. Gradually add the olive oil, beating it in as you add it. If you prefer the taste of lemon juice, it can be used instead of the vinegar, and if you want a milder dressing, omit the mustard or use just a pinch.

HERB DRESSING

Herb dressing is best on a salad of mixed greens or a spinach salad, but can be used, in general, much as you would use a regular vinaigrette.

MAKES ABOUT 8 FL OZ/225 ML

3 tbsp white wine vinegar
¼ tsp dry mustard
½ tsp salt
⅛ tsp pepper
pinch of cayenne pepper
5 fl oz/140 ml olive oil

1 tbsp minced fresh chives
1 tbsp minced fresh parsley
1 small clove garlic, minced
½ tsp basil, crushed
¼ tsp oregano, crushed
¼ tsp tarragon, crushed

Whisk together the vinegar, mustard, salt, pepper and cayenne. Pour the olive oil in gradually, beating it in as you do, and then stir in the herbs. If you can get fresh basil, oregano and tarragon, or if you grow them in your garden, then by all means use them, just doubling the quantities.

CHIFFONADE DRESSING

Try this dressing on a salad of cos, round lettuce and watercress.

MAKES ABOUT ½ PT/275 ML

2 fl oz/55 ml white wine
    vinegar
¼ tsp dry mustard
½ tsp salt
fresh-ground black pepper to
    taste
6 fl oz/170 ml olive oil

2 hard-boiled eggs, finely
    chopped
2 tbsp finely chopped fresh
    parsley
2 tbsp minced pickled beetroot
1 tbsp minced onion
1 tbsp minced green olives

Whisk together the vinegar, mustard, salt and pepper. Very gradually beat in the olive oil. When the dressing has a creamy consistency, stir in the eggs, parsley, beetroot, onions and olives.

MAYONNAISE

Along with the basic mayonnaise recipe, here's the way to do it in a blender or food processor, as well as a nearly basic variation – green mayonnaise – which is delicious on sandwiches, hard-cooked eggs or cold cooked vegetables.

MAKES ABOUT 10–12 FL OZ/285–340 ML

1 egg
½ tsp salt
½ tsp dry mustard
2 tsp cider vinegar
1½ tbsp lemon juice

⅛ tsp Tabasco or dash of
*   cayenne pepper*
4 fl oz/115 ml olive oil
4 fl oz/115 ml vegetable oil
if needed: 1 tbsp hot water

BLENDER METHOD

Put the egg, salt, mustard, vinegar, lemon juice and Tabasco or cayenne into a blender and blend until smooth. With the blender still on, gradually pour in all the oil in a smooth, steady stream. If the mayonnaise starts becoming very thick immediately, push it down the sides of the container with a spatula. Continue blending at high speed until all the oil is emulsified.

A tablespoon of hot water may be blended in to stabilize the sauce if it shows any sign of separating. Store in the refrigerator, covered.

FOOD PROCESSOR METHOD

Flawless mayonnaise can also be made in a food processor. Using the steel blade, put the egg, salt, mustard, vinegar, lemon juice and Tabasco or cayenne in the container and process for a few seconds. Combine the oils and, with the processor on, pour them gradually into the feed tube. The oil should be completely emulsified within several seconds.

Green Mayonnaise

1 recipe basic Mayonnaise
*   (above)*
2 tbsp minced watercress

2 tbsp minced parsley
1–2 tbsp minced chives

Proceed exactly as for regular mayonnaise, adding the watercress and minced herbs to the egg mixture in the blender. Give it a good spin before starting to pour in the oil, to make sure that the herbs are really minced and not just finely chopped.

Other herbs can be used and quantities increased for subtly different flavours – basil, tarragon, chervil, small amounts of spinach leaves. Use *only* fresh herbs.

SOURED CREAM DRESSING: I

MAKES ABOUT 12 FL OZ/340 ML

8 fl oz/225 ml soured cream
2 fl oz/55 ml fresh-squeezed
  lemon juice
3 tbsp sugar
1 tsp cider vinegar

¼ tsp salt
1 tsp dried dill weed or 2–3 tsp
  snipped fresh
fresh-ground pepper to taste

Stir all the ingredients together in a bowl until they are completely blended. Do not beat with a whisk, as this will cause the soured cream to become quite foamy.

Be sure that your salad greens are patted dry and have no moisture clinging to them before putting on this dressing. Use the Soured Cream Dressing by itself or, for another delicious salad, toss the salad with a few tablespoons of olive oil first, then add some Soured Cream Dressing and toss again.

SOURED CREAM DRESSING: II

Serve this dressing with Cold Omelette Salad (p. 169) and with cold cooked vegetables, or combine it with more mayonnaise and serve it on tossed salads.

MAKES ABOUT 1 PT/570 ML

1 cup minced radish
¾ cup minced or grated
  cucumber
6 fl oz/170 ml soured cream

2 fl oz/55 ml home-made
  Mayonnaise (p. 112)
½ tsp salt, or more to taste
2 tbsp yoghurt

fresh-ground pepper to taste   *1 clove garlic, minced*
¼ tsp hot paprika   *1 tbsp lemon juice*

Trim, wash and mince enough radishes to fill 1 cup. Peel and seed 1 large cucumber and mince or grate it. You should have about ¾ cup of cucumber. Drain the vegetables well in sieves for about 15–20 minutes before using.

When the radishes and cucumber are drained, combine all the ingredients in a large bowl and whisk together. Taste, and correct seasoning if necessary. Chill.

AVOCADO SALAD DRESSING

Don't make this dressing more than a couple of hours in advance, and use it on a fairly simple tossed green salad: for instance, cos and round lettuce with some thin-sliced green pepper and red onion.

MAKES ABOUT 12 FL OZ/340 ML

1 medium-sized ripe avocado   *1 clove garlic, minced or*
  (about ½ lb/225 g)   *crushed*
2 fl oz/55 ml fresh lemon juice   *2 tbsp minced onion*
2 fl oz/55 ml olive oil   *2 tbsp white wine vinegar*
2 fl oz/55 ml vegetable oil   *½ tsp sugar*
½ tsp salt   *dash of Tabasco*
½ tsp fresh-ground black pepper

Cut the avocado in half, remove the pit and scoop the flesh out of its shell into a bowl. Immediately add the lemon juice and mash with a wooden spoon until you have a soft, smooth mixture. Whisk in the olive and vegetable oils, then add all the remaining ingredients and stir well. Taste, and correct the seasoning if necessary.

Eggs, Soufflés, Omelettes

THE MARVELLOUS THING ABOUT EGGS is that they are never out of place, no matter what the time of day, no matter how elegant or simple the meal. But there are two meals for which it seems that nothing else will do but a plate of eggs in one of their simplest forms, and both of them are breakfast. One is the breakfast that good, hard-working and sober citizens enjoy at an early hour in the morning before launching into another day. The other is that body-and-soul satisfying breakfast that a less temperate group enjoy at an even earlier hour, following a night of revelry. I don't know why eggs and toast should be so indispensable after a bright night on the town, full of eating, drinking, singing, dancing and laughing, or any combination of those happy employments, but it's so.

At times like those, the less an egg is tampered with, the better. Scrambled, poached, soft-cooked and fried are the simplest ways of preparing eggs; uncomplicated by sauce and flavourings, they are ideal for the hours between two and eight in the morning, when reasonable people are asleep.

At more wide-awake and elaborate meals, eggs can reach the heights of sophistication. What is higher and more sophisticated, after all, than a towering soufflé? Nor are they without their humorous moments, as Baked Alaska (known in Spain as soufflé Alaska) has shown us. Between these extremes, we relish eggs in a near-infinity of styles and combinations.

The omelette, which has been called 'the egg in its sublime state', is in itself sufficient claim to an egg's fame. I've served them for breakfast, brunch, lunch and at dinner and supper, and I've dressed them with so many cheeses, vegetables, herbs, spices, creams, sauces, jams, fruits and liqueurs that I'm hard put to think of anything edible that will not harmonize with the flavour of an egg.

Making Soufflés

Not long after Christopher Columbus made his historic discovery of the New World, believing it to be the East Indies, he was being fêted by Ferdinand and Isabella of Spain. A nobleman seated next to the hero was not inclined to allow him his share of glory and commented that he didn't think it was such a great thing to have reached the East Indies by sailing west. It struck him as a rather simple task, once one knew that the world was round, to reach a place from another direction.

Columbus, so the story goes, picked up a hard-boiled egg, handed it to his aristocratic companion and asked him if he could make it stand on end. The nobleman tried very hard but couldn't do it. At last he declared it impossible. Columbus took the egg from him, wrapped his hand firmly around it and brought it down hard on the table, thereby crushing its blunt end – and leaving it standing solidly in place. 'You see,' he said, 'it's easy. It's quite simple, when you know how.'

Almost as easily as Columbus made an egg stand on its end (and more easily, I hope, than the way he discovered America), you can turn a few of your eggs into a soufflé – when you know how. For in spite of its awe-inspiring mystique, a soufflé is something that can be easily produced by an ordinary mortal like you or me. No conjuring or witchery is involved. As long as you follow the rules and use the right equipment, you can produce beautiful soufflés every time. And once you know the principles at work, the rules will be easy to understand and follow because soufflés only look like all magic, while they are really all logic.

Every hot soufflé consists of two parts, which are put together at the last moment before baking. One part is a sauce, which is made of butter, flour, a liquid and egg yolks and is usually flavoured with something. The second part consists of two indispensable ingredients: egg whites and air. The egg whites, when they are beaten, form thousands of tiny cells or bubbles, each one of which contains some trapped air.

When the beaten egg whites are folded into the sauce and the soufflé is put into a hot oven, the air bubbles in the egg whites expand with the heat, and the soufflé rises. It's just that simple. Of course, the soufflé must be removed from the oven at the right moment or the bubbles of hot air will expand so much that they burst – and then it falls. But there's no need for that ever to happen.

Now that you understand soufflés, you can fearlessly set about making them, and here's how:

First, get some things ready. Preheat your oven to the correct temperature and prepare the soufflé dish. If your oven is temperamental, get an oven thermometer so you can be sure that the temperature is right. And be sure that the racks in your oven are adjusted so that the soufflé has plenty of room to rise without hitting the roof!

The choice of soufflé dish is important. A dish that is too wide means that a larger area must be held up by the air bubbles, and thus it will not give you the attractive height you're after. The soufflé dish should be a little wider than it is deep and have straight, smooth sides. It should be just large enough so that the uncooked soufflé mixture fills between ¾ and ⅞ of its capacity.

To prepare the soufflé dish, butter it generously and make a 'collar' for it. Tear off a sheet of aluminium foil long enough to wrap round the soufflé dish and overlap by a few inches. Fold it in half lengthways. Butter a 3-in/75-mm strip on one side of the foil, from the edge approximately to the middle. Wrap the foil round the soufflé dish with the buttered strip extending 3 in/75 mm up over the top of the dish and facing in. Tie a piece of heavy string round the wrapped dish to hold the foil in place. Straighten the foil if necessary. This collar will keep the soufflé in place as it rises. When you remove the soufflé from the oven, you will take off the collar – by that time, the soufflé will be firm enough to keep its shape and will be beautifully high.

MAKING THE SOUFFLÉ BASE

The soufflé base is a rather thick sauce, sometimes with solid chunks of food in it. The important thing to keep in mind about this sauce is that its consistency must be right. The proper consistency for this base is somewhere between a thick sauce and a thin custard. It should not be stiff, but neither should it be runny. I have given exact proportions for each soufflé, so just follow them carefully.

To make the sauce, first melt the specified amount of butter in a heavy-bottomed saucepan, then stir in the flour. Cook this butter-flour mixture, or roux, for 2–3 minutes over very low heat, stirring constantly. Stir in the heated milk or cream, raise the heat to medium and continue stirring with a whisk until the sauce has simmered for 1–2 minutes. The sauce should be very thick and perfectly smooth.

Remove it from the heat and whisk in the egg yolks, one by one. At this point, you will add the cheese, the chopped or puréed vegetables, the seasonings or liqueurs – in short, whatever you are going to use to flavour the soufflé. If, after you have stirred everything in, the sauce is smooth (allowing for the bits of solid food if the recipe calls for them) and about as thick as a good mayonnaise, all is well.

If you like, you can prepare this much of the soufflé ahead of time and keep the sauce in the refrigerator for several hours or a day, in which case you should brush a film of melted butter over the top to keep a skin from forming. However, if you do store it for a while, don't try to proceed with a cold, stiff sauce. Heat it up very gently, stirring with a whisk, until it is just lukewarm and smooth, then go on.

THE EGG WHITES

And now the all-important beating of the egg whites. A pinch of cream of tartar is added to them because this helps to stabilize them and prevents them from 'tearing', or separating, when beaten. The number of egg whites in a soufflé is usually one or two more than the number of yolks. This ensures the lightness of the finished product and compensates for the few bubbles that are burst in combining the whites with the sauce.

Be sure that the egg whites have no specks of yolk in them, as any extraneous matter in the whites will inhibit their ability to beat up stiffly. If a bit of egg yolk sneaks into the whites, just scoop it out with a piece of egg shell. Furthermore, the egg whites should be at room temperature before being beaten. If they are cold, you may have trouble whipping them up into the big, shiny puff you need. Cold egg whites can be safely warmed up a bit by putting them in a bowl and setting it in hot water. Stir them for a minute or two and test. As soon as they are at room temperature, take the bowl out of the water and beat them.

Beat the egg whites with a wire whisk, bringing it down into the bowl with a firm, circular motion. Or you can use an electric beater – just move it around in the bowl. The whites will foam up, then they will form soft peaks and then stiff peaks. As soon as the egg whites form stiff peaks, stop beating. At this point, they have a shiny surface and velvety texture. If you overbeat them, they will become dry, start to break up into clumps, and, finally, revert to liquid, at which time you may as well throw them out and start over because no amount of persuasion will ever puff them up again.

Once the egg whites have been beaten until they are stiff but not dry, stir about a quarter of them into the sauce. This step will lighten the texture of the sauce sufficiently so that the remaining whites can be folded in easily. Put the lightened sauce into a large bowl and pile the remaining egg whites on top of it. Using a small spatula, gently fold the whites into the sauce until they are just blended. Don't overmix, as this breaks the bubbles and deflates the egg whites. Just keep your eyes open and stop folding the whites when the soufflé mixture appears reasonably homogeneous.

Pile the mixture into the prepared soufflé dish, smooth the top a little and put it into the centre of your preheated oven. Gently close the door, wait for the minimum amount of time given in the recipe, then take a peek. If you have faithfully followed instructions, made sure of your oven temperature and there was no earthquake in the course of the baking, the soufflé will be high, puffy and golden. It is done when the top is browned, stiff and wobbles just slightly when the dish is gently shaken. Some people like their soufflés runnier than others, so the exact moment at which you want to call it done may vary by about five minutes.

When it's done, serve it immediately. In its moment of glory a soufflé is a breathtaking sight, but it takes away your breath only as long as it holds its own, which is a mere few minutes. It is the very brevity of its life that is one of its charms. One moment it is there, proud, lofty and delicately trembling, the next moment it is served, tasted – vanished. And so it must be. Making a hot soufflé wait is certain disaster. One French chef who was forced to wait with a soufflé because of some unforeseen delay in the course of the meal and watched his creation sink into an irreparable mess was so undone by the incident that he plunged a knife into his belly and died as a result of it. No lost soufflé, however splendid, could be worth such a reaction, but why risk frustration and ill humour? Keep your guests waiting for a few minutes. No one will mind, for they will all be flattered that you went to the trouble to make them that airy, magical creation.

BROCCOLI-WALNUT SOUFFLÉ

SERVES 5–6

2 oz/55 g butter
4 tbsp flour
12 fl oz/340 ml hot milk
5 egg yolks
1½ cups chopped cooked
    broccoli
½ cup finely chopped or sliced
    walnuts
3 tbsp minced onion

2 tbsp grated Parmesan cheese
½ tsp salt
fresh-ground pepper to taste
7 egg whites
pinch of cream of tartar
GARNISH
Soured Cream Horseradish Sauce
    (p. 105)

Butter a 3-pt/2-l soufflé dish and tie a buttered collar round it (see p. 119).

Melt the butter in a heavy saucepan and stir in the flour. Cook the roux over medium heat for a minute or two, stirring constantly. Then add the hot milk and stir with a whisk as the sauce thickens.

When the sauce is perfectly smooth, remove it from the heat and whisk in the egg yolks, one by one. Then add the cooked broccoli, the walnuts, the onions and the cheese. Stir well and season with salt and pepper.

In another bowl add a pinch of cream of tartar to the egg whites and beat them with a clean whisk or beater until they are stiff enough to form peaks. Do not overbeat them or they will be too dry.

Stir about 8 fl oz/225 ml of the beaten egg whites into the warm sauce. Now add the remaining egg whites and gently fold them in. Do this carefully, as you want to lose as little air as possible.

Pile the soufflé into the prepared soufflé dish, place it in the middle of a preheated oven at 375°F/190°C/Mark 5, and bake it for 40–45 minutes.

Serve immediately with hot Soured Cream Horseradish Sauce.

ONION AND CHEESE SOUFFLÉ

SERVES 4–6

6 medium-sized onions (about
   1½ lb/675 g)
2 oz/55 g butter
4 tbsp flour
4 fl oz/115 ml cream
½ tsp salt
white pepper to taste
dash of nutmeg

dash of cayenne pepper
2 tbsp grated Parmesan cheese
4 egg yolks
5 egg whites
pinch of cream of tartar
GARNISH
any good light tomato sauce

Peel the onions, and cut 5 of them in quarters. Place the quartered onions in enough lightly salted water to cover them and boil them until they are completely tender. Drain them and reserve the water. Mince the cooked onions.

Finely chop the last raw onion and, in a medium-sized, heavy-bottomed saucepan, sauté it in the butter until it begins to colour. Lower the heat and stir in the flour. Cook the roux for a few minutes, stirring constantly, then add 2½ fl oz/70 ml of the reserved onion water and all of the cream. Stir the mixture over low heat until it is perfectly smooth and very thick.

Remove the sauce from the heat and stir in the minced cooked onions, salt, a little white pepper, nutmeg, cayenne and the grated Parmesan cheese, and beat in the egg yolks.

In a bowl, beat the egg whites with the cream of tartar until they form stiff, shiny peaks. Stir about 8 fl oz/225 ml of the beaten egg whites into the onion sauce, then gently fold in the remaining whites.

Pile the mixture carefully into the prepared soufflé dish (see p. 119) and bake in a preheated oven at 350°F/180°C/Mark 4 for 35–40 minutes. Serve immediately, with a simple, light tomato sauce.

WILD MUSHROOM AND DILL SOUFFLÉ

SERVES 6

*2 oz/155 g dried wild
   mushrooms*
2¾ oz/75 g butter
4 tbsp flour
8 fl oz/225 ml hot milk
4 fl oz/115 ml soured cream
salt to taste
pepper to taste
pinch of cayenne pepper
6 egg yolks
2 tbsp chopped fresh dill weed

1 small onion, finely chopped
¼ cup chopped shallots
8 egg whites
pinch of cream of tartar
*1–2 tbsp grated Parmesan
   cheese*
GARNISH
*Hollandaise Sauce (p. 104) or
   Spicy Mousseline Sauce (p.
   106)*

Pour about 12 fl oz/340 ml of boiling water over the dried mush-rooms and let them soak in it for several hours. When they are rehydrated, drain them and reserve the liquid in which they were soaked. Wash the mushrooms very carefully to remove every last bit of sand, and chop them coarsely.

Melt 1¾ oz/50 g of the butter in a saucepan and stir in the flour. Cook this roux over low heat for several minutes, stirring constantly. Mix together the hot milk and the soured cream, blend them quickly with a whisk and pour the mixture into the roux. Continue stirring with a whisk over low heat until the sauce is very thick and smooth.

Season the sauce with a little salt and pepper and a pinch of cayenne. Remove it from the heat and beat in the egg yolks, one at a time. Stir in the chopped fresh dill weed and put the sauce aside.

Melt the remaining butter in a medium-sized frying pan and add the chopped onions and shallots to it. Sauté them until the onions are golden, then add the chopped mushrooms and salt and pepper. Pour the reserved liquid from the mushrooms through a filter or through muslin to remove the grit and add 8 fl oz/225 ml of it to the mushroom mixture. Cook this mixture, stirring often, until all the liquid is absorbed or evaporated. Add the hot mushrooms to the white sauce, mixing it thoroughly.

Prepare a 3-pt/2-l soufflé dish by buttering it and sprinkling the

Parmesan cheese over the butter. Tie a tall, buttered, stiff-paper or aluminium-foil collar round the dish (see p. 119).

In a large, clean bowl, beat the egg whites with a little salt and a pinch of cream of tartar until they hold stiff peaks.

Preheat the oven to 400°F/200°C/Mark 6.

Add a few spoonfuls of the stiffly beaten whites to the sauce and blend them in gently. Now pour the sauce over the remaining egg whites and fold them in, using a spatula or a large spoon. Pour the mixture into the prepared soufflé dish, place it carefully in the middle of the oven, and lower the temperature to 375°F/190°C/Mark 5.

Bake the soufflé for about 35–40 minutes, and serve it immediately with Hollandaise Sauce or Spicy Mousseline Sauce.

ARTICHOKE AND CHEESE PUFF

Serve the puff hot or cool, cut in wedges or squares. It makes a very nice hors-d'oeuvre or can be combined with a rather hearty salad for a perfectly tasty little supper.

SERVES 8–10 AS AN HORS-D'OEUVRE, 4–6 AS A MAIN COURSE

*12 oz/340 g marinated
  artichoke hearts
1 medium-sized onion, coarsely
  chopped
5 eggs
¾ tsp salt
fresh-ground black pepper to
  taste*

*2 tbsp flour
6 oz/170 g Cheddar cheese,
  grated
1 oz/25 g Parmesan cheese,
  grated*

Drain off 2 fl oz/55 ml of oil from the artichoke hearts and heat it in a large frying pan or shallow, fireproof casserole. Sauté the onions in it until they are beginning to colour.

Thickly slice the artichoke hearts or quarter them. Beat the eggs with the salt, some fresh-ground black pepper and the flour until the mixture is perfectly smooth. Stir in the grated cheeses.

Add the artichoke hearts to the onions and stir them round a little, then transfer them (if you are using a frying pan) to a warm casserole. Distribute the artichokes and onions evenly over the base of the casserole. Spoon the egg and cheese mixture over the vegetables, spread it round gently and bake the puff in a preheated oven at 350°F/180°C/Mark 4 for 20–25 minutes, or until it is completely set, golden brown and slightly crusty on top.

COTTAGE CHEESE SOUFFLÉ

This is not really sweet enough for a dessert, but a good dish for brunch or lunch.

SERVES 4–5

1 cup small-curd cottage cheese	½ oz/15 g butter, melted
4 fl oz/115 ml soured cream	5 egg yolks
5 tbsp flour	5 egg whites
5 tsp sugar	pinch of cream of tartar
½ tsp salt	GARNISH
¼ tsp ground cinnamon	cranberry relish or
crushed seeds from 2 cardamom	apple sauce or
pods	fresh fruit

Butter a 3-pt/2-l soufflé dish and tie a buttered collar round it (see p. 119).

Combine the cottage cheese and the soured cream in a medium-sized, heavy-bottomed saucepan. Add the flour gradually, stirring it in thoroughly after each addition. Add the sugar, salt, cinnamon, cardamom, melted butter and egg yolks. Beat the mixture with a whisk to make sure that everything is well blended and there are no lumps of flour.

Heat the mixture over very low heat, stirring constantly, until it begins to thicken. Continue stirring, without letting it come to a boil, for about 3 minutes. The sauce should have a custard-like consistency. Remove it from the heat and let it cool to lukewarm, stirring occasionally.

In a clean bowl beat the egg whites with the cream of tartar until they hold stiff peaks. Stir about ⅓ of the beaten whites into the cottage cheese sauce, then gently fold in the rest.

Pile the mixture into the prepared soufflé dish and bake it in a preheated oven at 350°F/180°C/Mark 4 for 35–40 minutes. Serve immediately, garnished with cranberry relish, apple sauce or fresh fruit.

SPICY CHEESE AND POTATO SOUFFLÉ

SERVES 4–6

2½ oz/70 g butter
3 tbsp flour
10½ fl oz/300 ml hot milk
6 egg yolks
6 oz/170 g Munster cheese, grated
1 medium-sized potato (about ½ lb/225 g)
1 medium-sized onion, peeled, quartered and thinly sliced

4–5 tsp crushed dried red peppers (depending on how hot they are)
1 tsp salt
8 egg whites
pinch of cream of tartar
GARNISH
Dill Sauce (p. 109)

Butter a 3-pt/2-l soufflé dish and tie a buttered collar round it (see p. 119).

Melt 1½ oz/40 g of the butter, stir in the flour and cook the roux for a few minutes over low heat, stirring constantly. Whisk in the hot milk and continue beating with a whisk until the sauce is thick and smooth.

Remove the sauce from the heat and beat in the egg yolks, one by one, then stir in the grated cheese. Stir the sauce over low heat until the cheese is just melted, then put it aside.

Peel the potato, cut it in ¼-inch/6-mm dice and boil it in salted water for a few minutes, then drain immediately. Melt the remaining butter in a medium-sized frying pan and sauté the onions in it on fairly high heat until they start to colour. Add the potatoes and continue sautéing, stirring constantly, until the potatoes are golden brown and tender. Add the crushed red peppers and stir for 2–3 minutes more.

Stir the vegetable mixture into the cheese sauce, along with the salt.

In a clean bowl beat the egg whites with the cream of tartar until they hold stiff peaks. Stir about ⅓ of the egg whites into the cheese and vegetable mixture, then fold in the rest. Pile the mixture into the prepared soufflé dish and put it in the middle of a preheated oven at 375°F/190°C/Mark 5. Lower the heat to 350°F/180°C/Mark 4 and bake the soufflé for about 40 minutes.

Serve the soufflé with Dill Sauce.

COURGETTE SOUFFLÉ

SERVES 4–6

1 lb/450 g fresh courgettes	10½ fl oz/300 ml warm milk
1 small onion	6 egg yolks
2½ oz/70 g butter	2 tbsp grated Parmesan cheese
¾ tsp salt, and more to taste	7 egg whites
¼–½ tsp dried basil, crushed	pinch of cream of tartar
fresh-ground black pepper to	GARNISH
taste	Hollandaise Sauce (p. 104) or
3 tbsp flour	a cheese sauce

Butter a 3-pt/2-l soufflé dish and tie a buttered collar round it (see p. 119).

Trim, wash and grate the courgettes. Peel and chop the onion. Melt 1 oz/25 g of the butter in a medium-sized frying pan and sauté the onion in it until it is just soft. Add the grated courgettes and toss and stir over fairly high heat until they are tender and the excess moisture has evaporated. Add the salt, basil and some fresh-ground black pepper, stir for a few minutes more and remove from the heat.

Melt the remaining butter in a medium-sized, heavy-bottomed saucepan and stir in the flour. Cook the roux over very low heat for a few minutes and then stir in the warm milk. Beat the sauce lightly with a whisk over medium heat until it is thick and smooth.

Remove the sauce from the heat and beat in the egg yolks, one at a time, then stir in the Parmesan cheese and the cooked courgettes. Season to taste with more salt and pepper.

Beat the egg whites with a pinch of cream of tartar until they hold stiff peaks. Stir about ¼ of the beaten egg whites into the sauce, then gently fold in the rest. Pile the mixture into the prepared soufflé dish and bake in a preheated oven at 350°F/180°C/Mark 4 for 35–40 minutes. The top should be golden brown.

Serve the soufflé immediately, with Hollandaise Sauce or a cheese sauce.

SPINACH SOUFFLÉ

SERVES 4–6

2 lb/900 g fresh spinach
2 tsp salt
⅓ cup chopped spring onions
1 tbsp olive oil
½ tsp cider vinegar
¼ tsp dried dill weed
1½ oz/40 g butter
4 tbsp flour
8 fl oz/225 ml hot milk
pinch of nutmeg

pinch of cayenne pepper
6 egg yolks
3 tbsp grated Parmesan cheese
black pepper to taste
7 egg whites
pinch of cream of tartar
GARNISH
Hollandaise Sauce (p. 104) or
    Mornay Sauce (p. 104)

Wash and trim the spinach and toss the leaves with 1½ teaspoons of the salt. Cook the spinach leaves in just the water that clings to them, tossing constantly over medium heat, until they are wilted and tender. Drain the spinach thoroughly and chop it finely.

Sauté the spring onions in the olive oil until they are soft, then stir in the chopped spinach, cider vinegar and dill weed.

Melt the butter in a heavy-bottomed saucepan and stir in the flour. Cook the roux over very low heat for several minutes, stirring often, then whisk in the hot milk. Cook the sauce until it thickens, season it with a little nutmeg and cayenne, then remove it from the heat and beat in the egg yolks, one by one. Return the sauce to very low heat, add the Parmesan cheese, and stir for about 2–3 minutes. Remove it from the heat and stir in the spinach mixture, seasoning it with the remaining ½ teaspoon salt and a little black pepper.

Beat the egg whites with a pinch of cream of tartar until they hold stiff peaks. Stir $\frac{1}{4}$ of the beaten egg whites into the spinach sauce, then fold in the remaining egg whites.

Pile the mixture into a buttered 3-pt/2-l soufflé dish or a $2\frac{1}{2}$-pt/ 1.5-l soufflé dish prepared with a collar (see p. 119). Bake in a preheated oven at 350°F/180°C/Mark 4 for 35–40 minutes and serve with Hollandaise Sauce or Mornay Sauce.

Making Omelettes

A good omelette is a wonderful thing and can play a fine role at breakfast, lunch or even dinner. Among the simplest of all foods in their composition, omelettes require a certain amount of practice and a light touch in their preparation. If you are ready to invest a little time, though, and to eat scrambled eggs when those first efforts don't result in perfection, there is no reason why you shouldn't soon master the art and turn out tender, golden omelettes every time, as pretty to look at as they are good to eat.

The first requirement for making a good omelette is to use good ingredients, and that means fresh eggs and plenty of real butter. (There was a dieters' fad, which seems to be passing off, I'm grateful to notice, for cooking eggs with little or no butter in a 'non-stick' frying pan, a thoroughly barbaric idea.) In addition to the eggs and butter, you will want only some salt and pepper, and perhaps just a bit of milk or cream, but that is strictly a matter of preference. Those are the ingredients of a plain omelette, and you can make that plain omelette as elaborate as you like with any of a great variety of fillings and sauces.

The equipment is simple as well. Every kitchen has mixing bowls and a whisk or eggbeater, but pay attention to the pan. An omelette pan should have a heavy bottom and gently sloping or curved sides – a properly seasoned cast-iron or a non-stick pan. One more thing is needed to make the whole operation much easier, and that is a long, narrow and flexible spatula.

To make an individual omelette, two eggs are generally sufficient, but three can be used if the appetite warrants it. Beat the eggs briefly in a bowl with a pinch of salt and a smaller pinch of pepper, as well as a dash of milk or cream if you like. Heat an 8–9-in/ 200–225-mm omelette pan and melt about $1/2$ oz/15 g butter in it, swirling the butter all over the bottom of the pan. When the butter has melted and foamed and the foam has begun to subside, set a medium heat, pour in the beaten eggs and tilt the pan round gently so that the eggs spread evenly over the bottom. In a moment the eggs will begin to set. When they do, run the spatula once round the edge of the omelette to loosen it, and shake the pan a bit. Then start carefully lifting the edges with your spatula and tilting the pan to let the uncooked eggs on top run to the bottom.

In less than a minute, the omelette will be nearly done. Give the pan another quick shake to keep the eggs from sticking. The top of the omelette, at this point, should be moist but not runny. If you are filling your omelette, spoon in some of the prepared filling now. Then slip a spatula under one side and fold it over the other. Leave the omelette in the pan just a few seconds more before sliding it out on to a warm plate. The omelette should be golden in colour and tender and creamy inside. And it must be served immediately!

The commonest pitfall in making an omelette is overcooking the eggs, so do move quickly when they are starting to set. Overcooked eggs are tough and rubbery, even less acceptable than overcooked vegetables.

An omelette large enough for two can be made the same way, just by doubling the ingredients and using a slightly larger pan. Smaller omelettes, however, are a great deal easier to handle if you're just beginning, and so I advise starting with the individual size and moving on to larger ones when you're an experienced hand.

Because omelettes take so very little time to prepare, they are an ideal dish for impromptu meals, and because eggs are so democratic in the way they successfully associate with nearly every other kind of edible, you can make an omelette to fit practically any taste or mood. Omelettes with cheese, with vegetables, with hollandaise or tomato sauce are all justly popular, but don't ignore the possibilities of sweet omelettes either. A delicious dessert or elegant brunch omelette can be made by using marmalade or sautéd apple slices as a filling, for example.

MUSHROOM OMELETTES

SERVES 4

FILLING
1 oz/25 g dried wild
  mushrooms
1½ oz/40 g butter
2 tbsp minced onion
8 fl oz/225 ml soured cream
5–6 large, fresh mushrooms,
  sliced
pinch of thyme
½ tsp salt

pepper to taste
½ tsp dried dill or 1 tsp chopped
  fresh parsley
OMELETTE
8 eggs
salt and pepper to taste
2 fl oz/55 ml milk or cream
butter for frying
GARNISH
chopped fresh parsley

Soak the dried mushrooms in about 16 fl oz/450 ml of hot water for several hours, then wash them very carefully and reserve the water in which they have been soaked. Strain the liquid through several layers of cheesecloth or through a filter and reserve. Coarsely chop the mushrooms.

Melt 1 oz/25 g of the butter in a frying pan and sauté the minced onions in it until they begin to colour. Add the chopped mushrooms, the soured cream, and 8 fl oz/225 ml of the strained mushroom liquid. Lower the heat and simmer the mixture, stirring occasionally, until the mushrooms are very tender and the liquid is reduced to a thick sauce.

Melt the remaining butter in a small frying pan and sauté the fresh mushrooms in it for 5–6 minutes. Sprinkle them with a little thyme, toss briefly over high heat, then add them to the soured cream mixture.

Season the sauce with the salt, pepper and dill, and continue cooking it until the sauce is no longer runny.

Make 2 medium-sized omelettes, or 4 small, individual omelettes according to the directions on p. 131. Divide the mushroom mixture evenly between them, rolling the omelettes up over it. Sprinkle the omelettes with parsley and serve immediately.

POTATO AND COURGETTE OMELETTES

This is one of my favourite omelettes. It's quick to prepare and makes a hearty, satisfying meal for any time of day. Try it for one of those 4 a.m. breakfasts, after a night of serious partying, or else for the 1 p.m. brunch the next day.

SERVES 2–3

½ lb/225 g potato (about 1¼ cups diced)
½ lb/225 g courgettes (about 1½ cups diced)
½ oz/15 g butter
2 tbsp olive oil
⅔ cup chopped onion (1 small)
¼ tsp dried dill weed
¼ tsp dried basil, crushed

½ tsp crushed dried red pepper
salt to taste
fresh-ground black pepper to taste
5–6 eggs
butter for frying
GARNISH
soured cream

Peel or scrub the potato and cut it in ½-in/12-mm dice. Wash, trim and finely dice the courgettes. Drop the diced potato into boiling salted water and cook for 5 minutes, then drain it and set it aside. Cook the diced courgettes in boiling water for 3–4 minutes, drain and set aside.

Heat the butter and the olive oil in a medium-sized frying pan and sauté the onions in it until they start to colour. Add the partially cooked potato and courgettes, the dill weed, basil, crushed red pepper and salt. Cook this mixture over medium heat, stirring often, until the potatoes are just tender. Grind in some black pepper and add more salt if needed.

Make either 2 medium-sized or 3 small omelettes according to the directions on p. 131. When the eggs are almost set, spoon some of the hot vegetables on to one side and fold the other side of the omelette over the filling. Slide the omelettes on to warm plates and serve immediately with soured cream.

CHEESE AND CHUTNEY OMELETTE

SERVES 2

¼ lb/115 g white Cheshire
cheese
4 tbsp preserved chutney
4–5 eggs

salt to taste
fresh-ground black pepper to
taste
butter

Crumble the cheese coarsely. Spoon out the chutney (you can use a little more or less, depending on how spicy it is) and if it has particularly large pieces of fruit in it, cut them into smaller bits.

Make 1 large or 2 individual-sized plain omelettes according to the directions on p. 131. When the eggs are nearly set, but still moist on top, sprinkle the crumbled cheese over one side of the omelette and spoon the chutney on top of the cheese.

Fold the other side of the omelette over the filling and leave it in the pan over low heat for another minute as the cheese and chutney warm up. Serve immediately on warmed plates.

TOMATO OMELETTES PROVENÇALE

SERVES 4–5

2¼ lb/1 kg tomatoes
1 tsp salt, and more to taste
1 medium-sized onion
2 cloves garlic
3 tbsp olive oil
2 bay leaves
½ tsp dried basil, crushed
½ tsp dried tarragon, crushed

2 tbsp chopped fresh parsley
5 cured black olives, pitted and
sliced
coarse-ground black pepper to
taste
8–10 eggs
milk
butter for frying

Blanch the tomatoes in boiling water for about 2 minutes and then peel them. Chop the tomatoes very coarsely and put them aside in a bowl with the salt.

Chop the onion, mince the garlic and sauté them in the olive oil in a large frying pan until they begin to colour. Add the bay leaves and sauté a few minutes more. Add the tomatoes, basil, tarragon, parsley and sliced olives, and cook over medium heat, stirring occasionally, until the sauce is thick. It should take about 40–45 minutes.

Make individual omelettes according to the directions on p. 131. Spoon on some of the hot Provençale sauce just when the eggs are nearly set and fold the omelettes over the sauce. Serve immediately.

AVOCADO OMELETTES

SERVES 2

1 medium-sized ripe avocado
(about ½ lb/225 g)
1½ tbsp mayonnaise
1 tbsp fresh lemon juice
1 tbsp finely chopped red onion
salt

fresh-ground black pepper
4–5 eggs
1–1½ oz/25–40 g butter
OPTIONAL GARNISH
soured cream
hot chilli sauce

Halve the avocado, remove the pit, peel off the skin and trim away any hard or brown spots. Chop the avocado in small bits and combine it in a bowl with the mayonnaise, lemon juice and chopped onions. Mash slightly and stir everything together thoroughly. Season to taste with salt and pepper.

Make 2 individual omelettes according to the directions on p. 131. When the eggs are nearly set but still moist on top, spoon half the avocado filling on to each omelette.

Fold one side of each omelette over the other and leave them in their pans over low heat for another minute or so, then serve immediately on warmed plates. Soured cream and any hot chilli sauce can be passed separately.

BELL PEPPER AND
CREAM CHEESE OMELETTES

SERVES 4–5

1½ lb/680 g red or green bell
  peppers (about 4 medium-
  sized)
1 large onion
3 tbsp olive oil
1 large tomato, coarsely
  chopped

¾ tsp salt
fresh-ground black pepper to
  taste
4 oz/115 g cream cheese
8–10 eggs
salt and pepper to taste
butter for frying

To make the filling, first grill the peppers, turning them often, until they are evenly charred and blistered all over. Hold them under cool running water as you slip off their skins, then remove the cores, seeds and ribs. Cut the peppers into short strips, about ½ × 1 in/12 × 25 mm.

Peel the onion, quarter it and thickly slice it. Sauté in the olive oil in a fairly large frying pan until soft and translucent and barely starting to colour. Add the chopped tomato, the pepper strips, salt and fresh-ground pepper and stir over medium heat until the tomato is soft. Cut the cream cheese into small chunks, add it to the vegetable mixture and continue stirring over medium heat until the cheese has melted and formed a smooth sauce around the vegetables. Keep the filling hot while making the omelettes.

Make 4 or 5 individual omelettes, according to directions on p. 131. When the eggs are nearly set but still moist on top, spoon some of the hot filling over one side of each omelette and fold the other side over it. Leave the omelette in the pan for another 30 seconds or so, then serve immediately.

CHEESE AND CHILLI OMELETTE

FOR EACH INDIVIDUAL OMELETTE

2–3 eggs
salt and pepper to taste
½–1 oz/15–25 g butter
2 oz/55 g mild Cheddar cheese,
  grated

1 large spring onion, chopped
2 tbsp chopped medium-hot
  green chillis
OPTIONAL GARNISH
soured cream

Make an individual omelette according to instructions on p. 131.
When the eggs are nearly set and just moist on top, quickly spread
the grated cheese over one side of the omelette. Sprinkle the
chopped onion and green chillis evenly over the cheese and fold the
other side of the omelette over the filling. Leave the omelette in the
pan on medium-low heat for another minute or so, just long
enough for the cheese to melt.

Slide the omelette on to a warmed plate and serve immediately,
garnished with soured cream if desired.

ONION AND MOZZARELLA OMELETTES

SERVES 2

1 very large red onion (about
  1 lb/450 g)
3 tbsp olive oil
½ tsp salt
½ tsp crushed dried red chillis
¼ tsp oregano, crushed

black pepper to taste
4 eggs
salt and pepper to taste
butter for frying
3 oz/85 g mozzarella cheese,
  grated

Peel the onion, quarter it and slice it thickly. Cook in the olive oil
over medium-low heat, stirring often, until completely soft and
beginning to colour. Add ½ teaspoon salt, crushed red chillis,
oregano and black pepper and stir over medium heat for a few
minutes more.

Make 2 individual omelettes, or 1 large one, according to the
directions on p. 131. When the eggs are set but still moist on top,
spoon the hot onions over one side of the omelette (divide them

evenly between the 2 omelettes if making individual ones). Sprinkle the grated mozzarella over the onions and fold the other side of the omelette over the filling. Leave the omelette over medium-low heat another minute until the cheese is melted, then serve immediately.

See ITALIAN PASTAS, VEGETABLES AND FRITTATAS for Frittata of Courgette, and Onion and Herb Frittata. See SPANISH SPECIALITIES for Tortilla Española, Aubergine Tortilla, Tortilla alla Paesana, and Asparagus Tortilla.

Salads and Cold Vegetables

FRESHNESS IS THE ESSENTIAL INGREDIENT OF A SALAD. The simpler the salad, the more essential its freshness becomes, and this holds for the dressing as well, which should be custom-made for the salad, not poured out from a bottle. Beyond that, it is pointless to quibble about what a salad should or shouldn't be.

At many European tables the most familiar salad consists of lettuce and other greens tossed with a vinaigrette dressing. In the Middle East, on the other hand, salads are made of sesame seed paste, aubergine, tomatoes, cucumber, oil, spices – many things, but never a leaf of lettuce. I've had warm salads as well as cold; sweet salads; and hearty, filling entrée salads.

My taste in salads is broad but never indifferent. There are times when a leafy salad of crisp cos or soft round lettuce with an uncomplicated dressing of fruity olive oil and wine vinegar has a place in the menu that no other dish could fill as well. At other times, I prefer salads that are elaborate and filling enough to make a meal in themselves, and I am really inordinately fond of the various marinated, cooked and pickled dishes that enliven a good antipasto or buffet.

Under no circumstances will I allow that the essential freshness can be dispensed with just because a salad is cooked or marinated. I like flavours that still remember their origins. Even a salad that improves from marinating for a day or so, for instance, one of flageolets or chick-peas, cannot be successfully concocted from tired ingredients. But soaked and newly cooked dried beans can make an admirable salad when they are combined with fresh chopped parsley, slivers of sharp onion and an excellent oil and vinegar.

I firmly draw the line at bottled dressings and soggy coleslaws. And though I admit that through the years I have swallowed many things in the name of courtesy, I really just bail out completely when faced with a sticky, syrupy fruit salad obviously from a can.

If you are lucky enough to have room for a kitchen garden, and industrious enough to grow one, then a rare treat of a salad is at your fingertips. My parents live in the country and every spring my mother plants a bountiful assortment of vegetables. Like any reasonable being, she grouses at the constant watering and weeding that her garden demands, and she thinks uncharitable thoughts about the deer who will come and nibble away a tender harvest if measures aren't taken to deny them access. Nor does she subscribe to the popular notion that vegetables come much cheaper when you grow your own, because when she allows for the value of her time and labour, there is ultimately no great saving in it. But year after year, the garden flourishes under her care because, quite simply, she delights in the garden-fresh flavours and the otherwise unobtainable crisp and tender textures.

The salads we eat there are designed in the garden, not too long before mealtime. Late in the afternoon, when the sun is already dipping down behind the hills and the air begins to cool, is my favourite time to pick the salad. We pluck off crisp young lettuces and pull up carrots as thin as my little finger and radishes that are tiny, hard and stingingly sharp. The smallest spinach leaves are chosen and sometimes the tops of infant beetroots. The vegetables that make such impressive displays in supermarkets are often urged to a mature, large size before being picked, but in my mother's vegetable garden we can indulge ourselves by picking them while they are still young and delicate and exploding with the flavour that only vine or bush ripening can produce.

We find bell peppers the size of eggs, so thin and crisp that they are almost brittle and with a pungent taste that makes the bigger ones pale by comparison. We dig up new potatoes, no larger than walnuts, pull up some spring onions and snip off fragrant chives, flat-leaf parsley and feathery stems of dill weed. The French beans and yellow wax beans are slender, and we hunt through the jungle of courgette vines carefully, so that we can harvest the bright green vegetables while they are still so small that they hardly need slicing. Tomatoes that have ripened in the hot sun until they are ruby-red are added to the baskets, as well as sweet cucumbers, young enough not to require seeding. Invariably hauling in twice as much as we can consume, we take our cornucopia to the house and hose it off in colanders outside the kitchen door. Then we rinse, trim, dry and slice, and the big wooden salad bowl begins to fill up.

Sometimes, after a day of scorching heat, the salad becomes our main course. A particularly memorable one was composed of French beans, courgettes and new potatoes, all boiled till they were just tender and then cooled under running water, combined with hearts of round lettuce and thin-sliced cucumbers, mushrooms and red onions. The salad was tossed first with just a hint of olive oil, wine vinegar and fresh herbs, then finished with a bit of light soured cream dressing and garnished with quartered hard-boiled eggs. Everyone devoured heroic portions, accompanied by fresh, buttered rolls, and though it was over a year ago, I can recall with clarity the distinct, vivid flavours we relished that night.

The recipes here don't necessarily depend on the abundance of a garden such as my mother's. If you find a good market, you can enjoy lovely salads the year round. Here I've collected samples of the many salads I've enjoyed. Any of them will bolster appetites on a warm day (or even a cool one), but some are perfectly suited to be the heart of a meal. There is also an assortment of salads that are especially good for grouping in an antipasto, but each of them could also stand alone as a nice first course. Between the big, leafy tossed salads and the meticulously arranged, elegant ones there is ample choice; if only everything that is so good for you could also be so tasty and attractive, what a happy world this would be.

Tossed Salads

The making of a good, simple salad is a straightforward operation, but it requires strictest attention to quality and seasoning.

First, choose the greens – and there is usually a wealth to choose from: round, cos, iceberg, Batavian endive, chicory, curly endive, various red-leafed lettuces, rocket, lamb's lettuce, mustard greens, and watercress to name some of the best known. Personally, I like my simple salads really simple. One of the nicest I ever tasted consisted of nothing but the inner, tender leaves of round lettuce, a few thin slices of raw mushroom, and a delicate oil and vinegar dressing. It was ambrosial. Any number of combinations can be equally pleasing if you only remember that the more assertive ingredients, such as watercress or endive, are best used sparingly with a larger proportion of one or two mild-flavoured lettuces.

If you can pick your greens fresh from the garden, all the better. If you're picking them at a market, choose with a sharp eye for the youngest, crispest, freshest-looking of the lot, avoid the plastic-wrapped ones and don't keep them in your refrigerator longer than a few days. When it comes time to clean and tear the greens, take another good look: tough or wilted leaves? Throw them out instantly! Use only the best or suffer the consequences, for they will not be disguised.

Wash the greens in cool water, handling them gently, and either shake or spin them dry in a salad basket, or very lightly pat them dry on tea-towels. Wet lettuce in a salad will make a soggy mess. Once clean, very large pieces should be torn apart with your fingers, the smaller left whole.

If you want to accent your salad with some slices of raw mushroom or radish, a little cucumber, celery or tomato, prepare these ahead of time. Test the vegetables for firmness, clean and trim them, cut them in thin, tossable slices and use them in moderation.

As far as onion and garlic are concerned, there is generally no middle road. If you like them, you probably love them and will relish their flavour in salad more than anywhere. If you don't like them, no amount of talk can convert you, and that's fine too. For those who do, I recommend red onion, cut in paper-thin slices. Spring onions are also delightful in a salad, but go easy: they are more potent than they look. For a subtle hint of garlic, rub a wooden bowl with a cut clove before tossing the salad in it. For the true garlic lover, minced fresh garlic should be added to the olive oil.

Fresh herbs are, along with good olive oil, the best thing that can happen to a salad. If you have parsley, dill, basil, chervil or tarragon growing somewhere in your garden or in pots on the windowsill, this is their big moment. Mince small quantities with a sharp knife and toss them in with the prepared greens, but exercise some discretion because too many kinds mixed together can drown out the flavours of all.

Finally, the all-important dressing of the salad. You may prefer to make a dressing in advance (but not too much in advance), in which case you will now pour a little of it over your salad, toss, taste, add a bit more and so on until precisely the right balance of flavour is obtained. Each leaf and sliver should glisten, but no soupy excess must be found lurking in the bottom of the bowl.

I prefer to dress a salad by combing the oil and vinegar directly on the salad. Begin with pure, fruity olive oil; a first-pressing oil, called 'virgin olive oil' on the bottle or can, will have the most olivey taste. Pour it on carefully and toss the salad with the oil before adding anything else. When all the lettuce leaves are shiny, add just a bit of wine vinegar and a very niggardly amount of salt, then toss again and taste. Adjust your quantities of oil and vinegar (or lemon juice), give it a few grinds of black pepper, add your herbs and fresh-toasted *croûtons* if you like them, and serve at once.

PAPRIKASALAT

Served cold with pumpernickel bread and Liptauer cheese, it makes a great first course.

SERVES 4–6

3 *large red peppers*	2 *tbsp white wine vinegar*
½ *medium-sized onion*	1 *tsp sugar*
2 *tbsp olive oil*	*salt and pepper to taste*

Quarter, seed and derib the peppers. Using a very sharp knife or a vegetable slicer with a good blade, slice the peppers very, very thinly. Peel and quarter the onion and slice it thinly.

Toss together the pepper slices, the onion slices and the remaining ingredients. Taste and correct for seasoning. Put the salad aside for a few hours before serving.

SALAD TORCOLOTI

One of the best salads I ever ate was served to me in a restaurant called Torcoloti, in Verona. I took careful notes and enjoyed it again at home.

SERVES 6–8

1½ lb/680 g small, new
   potatoes
9½ fl oz/270 ml fruity olive
   oil
¼–⅓ cup fresh-minced parsley
salt
fresh-ground black pepper
1 lb/450 g slender young
   courgettes

1 lb/450 g thin French beans
2 large heads oak-leaf lettuce
6 fl oz/170 ml wine vinegar
½ tsp basil, crushed
2 cloves garlic, minced
1 cup paper-thin carrot slices

Boil the potatoes in their jackets in salted water until they are just tender. Drain the potatoes and chill them. When they are cold, peel and thickly slice them. Put them in a bowl with 3 tablespoons of the olive oil, the parsley and some salt and pepper. Toss and put aside until you are ready to serve the salad.

Slice the courgettes ¼ in/6 mm thick, cutting on a slant if they are particularly slender, and drop the slices into boiling salted water. Cook the courgettes for 5 minutes exactly, drain and run cold water over them. Chill them.

Trim and wash the French beans and cut them in 1-in/25-mm lengths. Boil them in salted water until tender but still crunchy. Drain the beans, run cold water over them and chill them.

Wash the lettuce, dry the leaves by patting them gently with a tea-towel and tear them into manageable pieces.

Combine the remaining olive oil, the vinegar, basil, garlic and some salt and pepper, and beat them all together with a whisk or blend in a blender.

Just before serving, combine all the vegetables, including the carrots, in a bowl, pour the dressing over them and toss lightly until everything is evenly coated. Add salt and fresh-ground pepper to taste.

WATERCRESS AND FRENCH BEAN SALAD

Serve with rye or pumpernickel bread.

SERVES 4–6

1 medium-small potato	1 medium-sized cucumber
1 lb/450 g French beans	8–9 large, firm mushrooms
1 large bunch watercress (about	(about 1 cup sliced)
¼ lb/115 g trimmed)	6 fl oz/170 ml Soured Cream
½ medium-sized red onion	Dressing I (p. 113)
4 eggs, hard-boiled	4 fl oz/115 ml mayonnaise

Peel and dice the potato, cook it in boiling salted water until it is tender, drain and run cold water over it until it is cool. Put it in the refrigerator.

Wash and trim the French beans, cut them in 1-in/25-mm pieces and boil them in salted water until they are just tender – not a minute longer. Run cold water over them until they are cool and put them in the refrigerator. Wash the watercress, trim off the heavy stems and cut any very large pieces in half.

Quarter and thinly slice the red onion. Peel and coarsely chop the hard-boiled eggs. Peel the cucumber, halve it lengthways and slice it.

Clean the mushrooms, trim off the stems and slice them thinly.

Toss all the vegetable ingredients together in a bowl. Blend Soured Cream Dressing I with the mayonnaise, pour the dressing over the salad and toss again until everything is evenly coated.

PRESSED CUCUMBER-SOURED CREAM SALAD

SERVES 6–8

3½ lb/1.6 kg cucumbers	2 tbsp lemon juice
1 tbsp salt, and more to taste	1 tsp sugar
4 fl oz/115 ml soured cream	

Peel the cucumbers, cut them in half lengthways, remove any large seeds and slice the cucumbers as thinly as possible. Toss the slices with the salt and leave them in a colander to drain for at least 30 minutes.

Taking the slices a handful at a time, squeeze out the excess moisture between the palms of your hands. Combine the slices in a bowl with the soured cream, lemon juice, sugar and a tiny bit more salt if it is needed. Toss together until all the slices are evenly coated, chill briefly and serve.

PAPRIKA-CUCUMBER SALAD

SERVES 6–8

4–5 cucumbers
salt to taste
2½ fl oz/70 ml white wine
  vinegar
½ large onion, sliced paper-thin
2 tsp sweet paprika

1 tbsp minced fresh dill weed or
  1 tsp dried
1½ tsp sugar
fresh-ground pepper to taste
pinch of hot paprika (optional)

Peel the cucumbers, cut them in half lengthways and seed them. Slice the cucumber halves thinly, toss them with a generous amount of salt and leave them to drain in a colander for 30 minutes.

Prepare the dressing by combining the vinegar, onion slices, paprika, dill weed, sugar and pepper. Stir it up well and put it aside for 30 minutes.

Give the cucumbers a quick rinse and pat them dry with a tea-towel. Combine the cucumbers and the dressing in a medium-sized bowl and toss until all the cucumber slices are evenly coated. Taste and correct the seasoning if necessary. Chill the salad for at least 20 minutes and stir up again before serving.

SPINACH SALAD

SERVES 6

1¼ lb/570 g fresh spinach
½ lb/225 g mushrooms
½ lb/225 g crumbly white
    cheese, such as Cheshire,
    Caerphilly or feta
1 red onion
5 fl oz/140 ml olive oil

2½ fl oz/70 ml wine vinegar
oregano to taste
salt to taste
fresh-ground black pepper to
    taste
GARNISH
Guacamole (p. 310)

Wash the spinach carefully, trim off the stems and pat the leaves dry in a tea-towel. Tear the larger leaves into pieces.

Clean, trim and thickly slice the mushrooms. Crumble the cheese and peel, quarter and thinly slice the red onion.

Combine the spinach, mushrooms, cheese and onions in a large mixing bowl. Whisk together the olive oil, vinegar, oregano and a little salt. Pour the dressing over the salad and toss gently until every leaf is evenly coated. Grind some black pepper over the salad and toss again lightly.

Divide the salad among 6 shallow bowls and top each one with 2–3 rounded tablespoons of Guacamole.

MARINATED LEEKS

SERVES 4–6 AS AN HORS-D'OEUVRE

8–10 slender leeks (about
    ¾ lb/340 g trimmed)
2½ fl oz/70 ml olive oil
4 fl oz/115 ml white wine
    vinegar
4 fl oz/115 ml white wine

2 small (inner) stalks celery
2 bay leaves
10–12 peppercorns
10–12 whole coriander seeds
½ tsp salt
3 sprigs parsley

Carefully trim off all the dark green parts and wash the leeks. If they are very long, cut them into 3-in/75-mm lengths.

Arrange the leeks in a shallow enamelled fireproof casserole. Pour the olive oil, wine vinegar and wine over them. Add enough water to cover the leeks.

Cut the celery stalks in 3-in/75-mm lengths, then slice them lengthways into strips the size of French beans. Add them to the leeks, along with all the remaining ingredients. Simmer, covered, on a medium heat for about 20 minutes, then chill them overnight.

FLORENTINE BREAD SALAD

This green salad, the Tuscan brainstorm for using up yesterday's bread, is unlike most others in that it can be made several hours in advance and will still be perfectly wonderful. Just toss it again shortly before serving. Serve it as a first course on its own or as part of an antipasto.

SERVES 6–8

1 lb/450 g cos lettuce (1 large head or 2 smaller ones)
1 large cucumber
2–3 stalks celery, thinly sliced
1 large tomato, cut in thin wedges
1 cup sliced radishes
½ lb/225 g slightly stale French or Italian bread, cut in 1-in/25-mm cubes (about 4 cups)

½ red onion, thinly sliced
8 fl oz/225 ml olive oil
4 fl oz/115 ml wine vinegar
1 tsp crushed basil
2–3 cloves garlic, minced or crushed
½ tsp salt
ground black pepper to taste
½ cup fresh-grated Parmesan cheese

Wash the lettuce, pat the leaves dry, and tear them into bite-sized pieces. Peel the cucumber, cut it in half lengthways, seed it by scooping out the centre with a small spoon and slice it thinly.

Put the lettuce and cucumber in a large bowl along with the celery, tomato, radishes, bread cubes and onions.

Put the oil, vinegar, basil, garlic, salt and some pepper in a blender and blend at high speed for about 1 minute. Pour the dressing over the salad, sprinkle on the Parmesan cheese and toss the salad gently for several minutes. The bread will soak up a lot of the dressing. Taste and correct the seasoning with more salt and pepper if desired.

Chill the salad for at least 30 minutes before serving it.

CAESAR SALAD

There are now many versions of this famous salad being prepared all over the world. Quite a few are very good, but this recipe, according to reliable sources, is very much like the original Caesar Salad – and, of course, that must be the best.

SERVES 4–6

6 oz/170 g French bread (about 15–18 slices from a thin baguette)
4 tbsp olive oil for frying
2 cloves garlic, crushed
2 eggs
3 large heads of fresh, crisp cos lettuce
6–8 fl oz/170–225 ml fruity olive oil, to taste

juice of 2 large lemons (about 2½ fl oz/70 ml)
salt to taste
fresh-ground black pepper to taste
dash of Worcestershire sauce, or more to taste
½ cup fresh-grated Parmesan cheese

Slice the bread and cut each slice in half or in thirds. Dry the bread out in a medium-hot oven for about 20 minutes. Heat the olive oil in a large saucepan and add the garlic to it. Toss the dried bread in the olive oil, over low heat, for 5–10 minutes. Set aside.

Boil 2 eggs for exactly 1 minute, run cool water over them for an instant and put them aside.

Remove the large outer leaves from the lettuces and save them for some other salad. Take apart the inner leaves, wash them and dry them on tea-towels. Chill them.

To prepare the salad at the table, assemble all the ingredients in attractive bowls on a tray. Put the lettuce leaves in the largest salad bowl you have. If you want to keep the leaves whole (as in the original), arrange them all in one direction so that you can roll them over and over each other without breaking them. Have two large wooden spoons ready for this operation.

Pour about ½ the fruity olive oil over the lettuce and toss or lift from one side, rolling the leaves over to the other side several times. Break the eggs over the lettuce and flip all the lettuce over several times more. Continue in this fashion, adding some more olive oil, then the lemon juice, then some salt and fresh-ground black pepper, a dash of Worcestershire sauce and the Parmesan cheese, tossing or rolling over the leaves between each addition. Finally, add the *croûtons* and toss again. Taste one of the smaller leaves. Correct the seasoning with a little more oil, salt, pepper or Worcestershire sauce if needed. Serve immediately.

CHICK-PEA SALAD

SERVES 8–10

8 fl oz/225 ml olive oil
4 fl oz/115 ml red wine vinegar
4 cloves garlic, minced
1 tsp sugar
salt to taste
fresh-ground black pepper to taste

3 tbsp liquid from cooking chick-peas
6 cups cooked and drained chick-peas*
1½ small red onions, peeled, quartered and thinly sliced

Make a dressing from the oil, vinegar, garlic, sugar, salt, pepper and chick-pea liquid. While the chick-peas are still quite warm, combine them with the onions and pour the dressing over them. Toss until all the chick-peas are evenly coated, then put aside for several hours before serving.

Serve cool or at room temperature.

---

*To cook dried chick-peas, soak them overnight in enough water to keep them covered, with a pinch of baking soda in it. The next day, add more water if needed, salt it well and bring it to a boil. Reduce the heat and simmer the chick-peas until they are tender, about 1–1½ hours. Chick-peas can also be cooked without pre-soaking, but the cooking time will be longer by ½–1 hour. When they are tender, drain and use as directed.

PEPERONATA

This makes a very good addition to an antipasto, or it can be served as a separate course.

SERVES 2–4 AS A FIRST COURSE

2 large green peppers
2 large red peppers
1 tbsp olive oil
1 tsp white wine vinegar

1 tsp fresh lemon juice
salt to taste
fresh-ground black pepper to
taste

Grill the peppers, turning them frequently, until the skins are blistered and brown. Remove the peppers and put them in a paper bag; let them cool there until you can handle them easily.

Peel the charred, papery skin from the peppers carefully, then cut them open and remove the seeds and ribs. Slice the peppers evenly into pieces about 2 in/50 mm long and ½ in/12 mm wide and put them in a bowl.

Add the oil, vinegar, lemon juice, salt and black pepper to the pepper slices, mix well and chill before serving.

FLAGEOLET SALAD

SERVES 8

2 cups large dried flageolet
  beans
2½ pt/1.4 l water
salt
2½ fl oz/70 ml olive oil

2 fl oz/55 ml white wine
  vinegar
plenty of fresh-ground black
  pepper

Put the beans in a large pot with the water and 1 teaspoon salt, bring to a boil, then reduce the heat. Simmer the beans gently for about 1 hour or until they are just tender. Drain them while they are still hot, reserving the liquid.

In a frying pan, boil the bean liquid vigorously for a few minutes until it is substantially thickened. Measure out 5 fl oz/140 ml of the thickened liquid into a bowl.

Add 1 tablespoon salt plus all of the other ingredients to the warm liquid and whisk until well blended and you have a smooth sauce.

Pour the sauce over the beans while they are still warm and mix them up gently with a wooden spoon, being careful not to mash them. Refrigerate for several hours.

Before serving, stir the salad again so that all the beans are well coated with the dressing.

Gnocchi Salad

SERVES 6–8

¾ cup fresh peas
1 lb/450 g chilled cooked gnocchi*
1½ cup red, yellow and green
   peppers, cut in thin, short
   strips
3 tbsp finely chopped red onion

2 tbsp olive oil
2 tbsp thick tomato purée or
   1½ tbsp tomato paste
1 tbsp red wine vinegar
salt and pepper to taste
basil, chopped, to taste

Drop the peas into boiling salted water and cook them until they are barely tender and not yet soft. Drain them and run cold water over them to cool them.

Combine the cold gnocchi, the peas, the peppers and the chopped onions in a bowl. Make a dressing of the olive oil, tomato purée, wine vinegar, salt and pepper and basil, and pour it over the gnocchi and vegetables. Toss everything together until the dressing is very evenly distributed, then put in refrigerator to chill for several hours. Serve cold as part of an antipasto.

*For this salad you can use cold Potato Gnocchi (p. 265), or buy some good fresh or frozen gnocchi, cook them and chill them a while.

RICE SALAD VINAIGRETTE

Serve with an antipasto or as a separate course.

SERVES 4–6

⅓ cup finely diced carrots
¾ cup French beans, cut in
 ¼-in/6-mm bits
¼ cup diced celery
¼ cup diced green pepper
½ cup chopped red onion
3 tbsp minced fresh parsley
2½ cups cooked rice, warm or
 cold

4 tbsp grated Parmesan cheese
4 tbsp olive oil
3 tbsp white wine vinegar
salt to taste
fresh-ground black pepper to
 taste
pinch of thyme
pinch of basil
pinch of oregano

Cook the carrots and French beans in a minimum of salted water until they are barely tender and drain immediately.

Combine the first 7 ingredients in a large bowl and toss together.

Combine the cheese, olive oil, vinegar and seasonings and whisk until smooth. Pour the dressing over the salad, toss until everything is thoroughly combined and put in the refrigerator to chill for several hours.

WHITE BEAN SALAD

SERVES 8–10

1 lb/450 g small dried white
 beans (about 2 cups)
2 medium-sized tomatoes,
 coarsely chopped
⅓ cup finely chopped red onion
⅓ – ½ cup cured black olives,
 sliced
6 tbsp olive oil

6 tbsp white wine vinegar
1–2 cloves garlic, minced
½ cup chopped fresh parsley
 (slightly packed)
¼ tsp dried basil – or fresh
¾ tsp salt, or more to taste
fresh-ground black pepper to
 taste

Rinse the beans and combine in a large pot with about 4–5pt/2–3 l salted water, bring to a boil, then lower the heat and simmer until the beans are quite tender, about 1 hour. Drain the beans and allow them to cool slightly.

Combine the beans in a bowl with all the other ingredients and toss gently until everything is thoroughly combined. Taste, and correct the seasoning with more salt and pepper if necessary. Chill the salad and serve it cold as a first course or as part of an antipasto.

MARINATED MUSHROOMS

SERVES 6

1 lb/450 g fresh white
mushrooms
12 fl oz /340 ml water
12 fl oz/340 ml cider or white
wine vinegar
1 tbsp pickling spice, or:
4 cloves, 4 peppercorns, ¼
tsp mustard seeds, ½-in/12-
mm stick cinnamon, pinch of
dried rosemary, 1 bay leaf

2½ tbsp olive oil
¼ tsp basil, crushed
¼ tsp oregano, crushed
1 clove garlic, minced
pinch of thyme
¼ cup chopped fresh parsley
salt and papper to taste

Wash the mushrooms and trim stems. If the mushrooms are very large, cut them in half. Put them in an enamelled saucepan and cover them with equal parts of water and cider or vinegar. Add the pickling spices in a muslin or cheesecloth bag.

Cover the saucepan and bring the mixture to a boil. Let it boil for about 5 minutes, then turn off the heat and leave the mushrooms covered in the hot liquid for 1–2 hours.

Drain the mushrooms thoroughly, rinse them and pat them dry with a paper towel. Put them in a bowl and toss them with the olive oil, herbs and salt and pepper until each mushroom is well coated. Put them aside for several hours before serving.

The mushrooms can be served chilled or at room temperature. They are excellent as part of an antipasto.

INSALATONE

Insalatone is one of the Italian salads I had in Bologna, a sort of marinade of cooked and raw vegetables. It's a good dish to include in a varied antipasto, but wonderful enough to serve all by itself as a first course.

SERVES 6–8

1½ lb/680 g potatoes
½ lb/225 g courgettes (about 3 medium-small)
1½ cups sliced celery hearts and inner stalks
2 red tomatoes
2 green tomatoes
7 tbsp olive oil
4 tbsp white wine vinegar
3 tbsp minced fresh parsley

½ tsp salt
½ tsp basil, crushed
½ tsp oregano, crushed
fresh-ground black pepper to taste
MARINADE
5 fl oz/140 ml red wine vinegar
2–3 tbsp olive oil
salt to taste
12 fl oz/340 ml water

Boil the potatoes in their jackets until they are just tender; do not overcook. Allow them to cool completely before peeling.

Trim and slice the courgettes ¼ in/6 mm thick. Put the slices in an enamelled saucepan with the marinade, using just enough water to completely cover them. Bring the marinade to a boil, then lower the heat slightly. Boil the courgettes for exactly 5 minutes, remove them with a slotted spoon (reserving the marinade) and run cold water over them. Chill in the refrigerator until needed.

Put the sliced celery hearts and stalks in the marinade, bring it to a boil again and cook the celery for 8–10 minutes. Drain the slices, run cold water over them, then put them in the refrigerator until needed. Discard the marinade.

Peel the potatoes, quarter them lengthways and thickly slice them. Quarter and slice the tomatoes. Combine all the vegetables in a large bowl, add all the remaining ingredients and toss gently until the dressing is evenly distributed. Taste, and correct the seasoning.

Chill the salad for at least 1–2 hours and toss it once more before serving.

AUBERGINE CAVIAR

Serve as a salad, on savoury biscuits or as part of an antipasto.

SERVES 6–8 AS A FIRST COURSE

2½ lb/1.1 kg firm aubergine
1 large, firm tomato
½ cup minced onion
2 cloves garlic, minced
½ cucumber, peeled, seeded and
  grated
12–15 pitted cured black olives,
  sliced off the pits

1½ tbsp olive oil
1 tbsp wine vinegar
1 tbsp lemon juice, or more to
  taste
salt to taste
fresh-ground black pepper to
  taste

Prick the aubergines a few times with a fork and bake them at 400°F/200°C/Mark 6 for 50–60 minutes. Allow them to cool until you can easily handle them.

Split the aubergines lengthways with a sharp knife and scrape out all the pulp. If the seeds are dark brown and starting to separate from the rest of the flesh, they will be bitter – discard them. Discard the skins. Chop the pulp coarsely and drain off the excess moisture.

Chop the tomato coarsely. Combine all the ingredients and mix thoroughly. Taste and correct seasoning. Chill before serving.

CELERIAC SALAD

SERVES 4–6

1 lb/450 g celeriac
2½ pt/1.4 l water
4 fl oz/115 ml milk
2 tbsp lemon juice
1½ tbsp white wine vinegar

2½ tbsp mayonnaise
2 tsp Dijon mustard
1 tbsp double cream
salt and pepper to taste

Peel the celeriac and cut it in julienne strips. Combine the water, milk and lemon juice in a large saucepan and bring to a boil. Add the celeriac strips to the boiling liquid and leave them submerged until the liquid boils again. Then drain them and run cold water over them. Squeeze out any excess moisture.

In a bowl, toss the celeriac strips with the vinegar. Mix together the mayonnaise, mustard, cream and some salt and pepper. Pour the mayonnaise sauce over the celeriac and toss again until the strips are evenly coated. Taste and correct the seasoning.

Chill the salad for 1–2 hours before serving.

GINGERED AUBERGINE SALAD

SERVES 4–6

2 lb/900 g firm young aubergine	2 small cloves garlic, minced
1 tbsp peanut oil	2 tbsp finely minced onion
2 tbsp cider vinegar	2 generous tsp grated fresh ginger
2½ tbsp brown sugar	2 tsp fresh lemon juice

Prick the aubergines in several places with a fork and bake them at 400°F/200°C/Mark 6 until they are quite soft.

When the aubergines are cool enough to handle, cut them in half and scrape the pulp carefully out of the skin. If the seeds are dark brown and starting to separate from the pulp, they will be bitter and must be removed (meaning the aubergine wasn't quite young or fresh enough). If the seeds are pale and small, leave them.

Drain the pulp thoroughly in a large sieve and mince it. Combine the minced aubergine in a bowl with all the remaining ingredients, mix well and chill for several hours.

Serve small portions of the chilled aubergine on lettuce leaves as a first course or with savoury biscuits as a dip.

HOMMOS BI TAHINI

This salad has the consistency of a dip or a spread and is served cool or at room temperature with savoury biscuits or pitta bread on the side.

SERVES 4–6 AS A FIRST COURSE

3 cups cooked chick-peas (reserve
   a little bit of the cooking
   liquid, as it may be needed)
2 large cloves garlic, finely
   minced
5 tbsp fresh lemon juice

1½ tsp salt, or more to taste
6 fl oz/170 ml Taratour Sauce
   (p. 110)
1 tbsp olive oil
approximately 2 tbsp chopped
   fresh coriander leaves

In a large bowl, mash the cooked chick-peas with a pestle until they are puréed or force them through a coarse sieve. Stir in the crushed garlic and beat in the lemon juice, salt and Taratour Sauce.

The *hommos* should have a consistency similar to that of mayonnaise; it should be easily spreadable. If it is too thick, add a few tablespoons of the cooking liquid from the chick-peas, beating it in a little at a time until the consistency is right.

Spread the *hommos* in a shallow dish, gently spread the olive oil over and sprinkle with chopped coriander leaves.

BABA GHANOUJ

Serve with savoury biscuits or with hot pitta bread as a first course.

SERVES 4–6

1 lb/450 g aubergine
2 fl oz/55 ml Taratour Sauce
   (p. 110)
2 fl oz/55 ml fresh lemon juice
1 tsp salt, or more to taste

¼ tsp pepper
1 tbsp plus 1 tsp olive oil
2 tbsp chopped fresh coriander
   leaves, or more to taste

Prick the aubergine with a fork in several places and bake it in a preheated oven at 400°F/200°C/Mark 6 for 45–55 minutes, or until it is soft throughout. When the aubergine is cool enough to handle, cut it in half and scrape out all the pulp.

Mince the pulp and add to it the Taratour Sauce, lemon juice, salt, pepper and 1 tablespoon of the olive oil. Stir the mixture thoroughly, taste it and correct the seasonings.

Spread the mixture evenly in a shallow serving dish, drizzle the remaining olive oil on top of it, sprinkle with chopped coriander leaves and chill for several hours before serving.

FRESH MOZZARELLA SALAD

This antipasto salad is made from fresh, new mozzarella cheese, which is very white, much lighter in texture than a mature mozzarella and is stored in water. It is available at well-stocked delicatessens.

SERVES 6

1 lb/450 g fresh mozzarella
  cheese
3 small tomatoes (about ¾ lb/
  340 g)
¾ lb/340 g courgettes
½ cup very thinly sliced red
  onion

6 tbsp olive oil
3 tbsp wine vinegar
1 tsp salt
approximately ¼ cup chopped
  fresh parsley
¼ tsp oregano
black pepper to taste

Cut the mozzarella into strips or small, ¼-in/6-mm-thick slices. Slice the tomatoes in thin wedges. Cut the courgettes in ¼-in/6-mm slices and drop them into boiling, salted water. Cook 2 minutes, then drain and cool briefly under running water.

Combine all the ingredients in a bowl and toss gently until well combined.

Serve immediately or marinate for several hours. Toss again before serving.

FLAGEOLETS IN
TOMATO AND GARLIC SAUCE

SERVES 8–10

1 lb/450 g large dried flageolets
3 tbsp olive oil
5–6 cloves garlic, crushed or
    minced
½–1 tsp rosemary, crushed
16 fl oz/450 ml thick tomato
    purée
3 peeled tomatoes, coarsely
    chopped

2½ fl oz/70 ml dry red wine
1 tsp salt
2 fl oz/55 ml lemon juice
1 tsp sugar
fresh-ground black pepper to
    taste
3 tbsp minced onion

Put the beans in a large saucepan with about 3 pt/1.8 l of water
and some salt. Bring the water to a boil, then reduce the heat and
simmer the beans until they are tender, but don't let them get
mushy. Drain them and save the broth to use in a soup – it's
delicious.

Heat the olive oil in a very large frying pan and sauté the garlic
and rosemary in it for a few minutes. Add the tomato purée,
chopped tomatoes, red wine, salt, lemon juice, sugar and a generous
amount of black pepper. Simmer the sauce, stirring often, for about
15 minutes.

Add the drained beans and continue simmering, stirring now
and then with a wooden spoon, for another 5–10 minutes. The
sauce should be quite thick.

If you want to serve the beans hot, stir in the minced onions
shortly before serving. If you want to serve them cold, as a salad,
allow them to cool before stirring in the minced onions and chill
them for a few hours or overnight – the flavour improves.

TOMATOES STUFFED WITH HEARTS OF PALM

SERVES 6–10 AS A SALAD

2½ cups hearts of palm, cut in
    ¼-in/6-mm slices
2 fl oz/55 ml fruity olive oil
3 tbsp white wine vinegar

fresh-ground black pepper to
    taste
⅓ cup chopped fresh parsley
salt to taste
10 medium-sized tomatoes

Drain and rinse the hearts of palm and slice them. Combine them in a bowl with the olive oil, vinegar, pepper, parsley and salt. Toss the mixture gently until all the hearts of palm are evenly coated, then cover the bowl and chill the mixture for several hours.

Slice the tomatoes in half crossways. With a small, sharp knife, scoop out a shallow bowl in each tomato half. Save the scooped-out tomato pulp for another use. Lightly salt and pepper the tomato shells. Dividing the marinated hearts of palm evenly among the 20 tomato shells, mound a couple of spoonfuls evenly in each one.

POTATO SALAD WITH CARAWAY SEEDS

SERVES 6

3 large white-skinned potatoes
½ onion
7 tbsp white wine vinegar
¼ tsp caraway seeds

7 tbsp olive oil
salt
pepper
3 tbsp chopped fresh chives

Boil the potatoes in their jackets until they are tender, then drain and cool them until you can handle them. Peel them while they are still warm and cut them in medium-sized dice. Mince the onion.

Combine the diced potatoes and minced onions in a large bowl. Heat the vinegar with the caraway seeds and pour it over the potatoes. Gently toss the mixture until well combined.

Pour the olive oil over the potatoes, add salt and pepper to taste and the chopped chives. Toss again, always carefully, and taste. Correct the seasoning.

Chill the salad for several hours and stir once more before serving.

GERMAN POTATO SALAD

SERVES 8–10

4 lb/1.8 kg potatoes
1 large onion, finely chopped
1 cup white wine vinegar
4 fl oz/115 ml mayonnaise

2 fl oz/55 ml olive oil
1½ tsp dried dill weed
salt
pepper

Boil the potatoes in their jackets until they are just tender. Drain them and let them cool slightly. When they are just cool enough to handle, peel them and cut them into ½-in/12-mm cubes. Spread them evenly in a large, shallow bowl and pour the vinegar over them while they are still warm. Sprinkle the onions over them. Set them aside for a while to absorb the vinegar, turning them gently with a spatula now and then.

After about 30 minutes, drain off any excess vinegar. Toss the potatoes carefully with the mayonnaise, olive oil and dill weed. Season to taste with salt and pepper. Serve warm or chilled.

POTATO SALAD TZAPANOS

I came across this salad at the Taverna Tzapanos, in Athens, hence the name.

SERVES 8–10

3 lb/1.25 kg white-skinned
  potatoes
1½ lb/680 g carrots
2 fl oz/55 ml olive oil
2½ fl oz/70 ml white wine
  vinegar

2 tsp salt
4 tsp dried dill weed, or 3 tbsp
  minced fresh
2 cloves garlic, minced or
  pressed

Boil the potatoes in their jackets until they are just tender. Drain them immediately and allow them to cool.

Scrape the carrots, cut them into large pieces, and boil them until they are tender; drain them and let them cool.

Cut the potatoes into ½-in/12-mm dice and coarsely chop the carrots. Combine them in a large bowl with all the remaining ingredients and toss the mixture until everything is thoroughly blended. Chill the salad for several hours and toss it once more before serving.

Avocado-Stuffed Courgettes

SERVES 6 AS A FIRST COURSE

6 plump, evenly shaped
  courgettes (about 1¾ lb/
  800 g)
2 medium-sized ripe avocados
  (about ¾ lb/340 g)
1 tbsp fresh lemon juice
1 tbsp olive oil
1 tbsp wine vinegar

2 tbsp chopped fresh coriander
  leaves
½ small onion, finely chopped
1 tsp salt
GARNISH
paprika and fresh coriander
  sprigs

Trim the stem ends of the courgettes and cut them in half lengthways. Put them in a saucepan of boiling salted water for 4 minutes, then drain them and run cold water over them for a minute. Working carefully with a small spoon, scoop out the pulp, leaving a shell about ¼ in/6 mm thick. Put the pulp in a sieve to drain and turn the shells upside down on a rack for about 10 minutes.

Chop the well-drained courgette pulp. Peel the avocados, remove the pits and chop or mash the flesh with a fork. Add the avocado to the courgette pulp. Stir in all the remaining ingredients and mix thoroughly.

Fill the courgette shells with the avocado mixture and sprinkle a line of paprika down the centre of each one. 'Plant' a small sprig of fresh coriander leaves in the stuffing of each courgette, arrange them on a platter and chill for 1–2 hours before serving.

ASPARAGUS MOUSSE

A rather rich salad that works best as a first course.

SERVES 8

2 tbsp gelatin
4 fl oz/115 ml cold water
12 fl oz/340 ml hot milk
4 fl oz/115 ml water from
  cooking asparagus
1 oz/25 g butter
3 eggs
16 fl oz/450 ml puréed cooked
  asparagus (about 1½ lb/
  680 g fresh asparagus,
  trimmed)
8 fl oz/225 ml mayonnaise

4 fl oz/115 ml soured cream
2 tbsp lemon juice
1 tsp sugar
½ tsp salt
large pinch of cayenne pepper
pinch of nutmeg
pepper to taste
OPTIONAL GARNISH
red pepper strips
thinly sliced cucumber
sliced black olives

Soften the gelatin in the cold water. Stir the gelatin into the hot milk along with the asparagus water and the butter. Stir the mixture over very low heat until both the gelatin and the butter are completely dissolved. Remove the liquid from the heat and beat in the eggs. Beat the mixture with a whisk for about 2 minutes. Chill the mixture until it just begins to thicken but can still be easily stirred.

Combine the puréed asparagus, the mayonnaise, soured cream, lemon juice, sugar, salt and other seasonings and stir until all is thoroughly smooth. Stir in the gelatin mixture.

Pour the entire mixture into an oiled, 3-pt/2-l mould and chill it for 3 hours or until it is firm.

Turn the mousse out on to a well-chilled serving dish and, if you like, decorate it with strips of red pepper, thin slices of cucumber and sliced black olives.

COLD BROCCOLI MOUSSE

Serve the mousse with hot Cheese Pastries (p. 51).

SERVES 6–8

2 lb/900 g broccoli
1½ tsp salt, and more to taste
½ lb/225 g mushrooms
1 oz/25 g butter
fresh-ground pepper to taste
2 tbsp gelatin
2 fl oz/55 ml cold water
8 fl oz/225 ml single cream
6 fl oz/170 ml Vegetable
  Broth II (p. 61)

2 eggs, beaten
1 tsp prepared horseradish
2 fl oz/55 ml lemon juice
8 fl oz/225 ml mayonnaise
GARNISH
cherry tomatoes
parsley sprigs

Trim the broccoli, cut the tops into florets, and peel and slice the stems. Boil the florets and stems in salted water until they are tender, then drain immediately. Chop half the cooked vegetable finely, and purée the other half in a blender or food processor.

Wash the mushrooms and mince them or put them through a food mill. Sauté the mushrooms in butter, stirring constantly, until they are completely tender and all the moisture has evaporated. Season them with salt and pepper.

Soften the gelatin in the water. Heat together the cream and the vegetable broth and add the gelatin, stirring over low heat until it is completely dissolved. Remove the liquid from the heat and beat in the eggs.

Combine the mushrooms, the chopped and puréed broccoli, 1½ teaspoons salt, the horseradish, pepper, lemon juice and mayonnaise, and mix everything together thoroughly.

Allow the gelatin mixture to cool, stirring it occasionally, until it just begins to thicken. Then stir in the broccoli mixture, taste and correct the seasoning if necessary. Spoon the mousse into 6–8 individual oiled moulds or ramekins and chill them for several hours or until the mousse is completely set.

Unmould each mousse on to a medium-sized plate and garnish with cherry tomatoes and parsley sprigs.

Beetroot and Pineapple Salad

SERVES 8

4 large beetroots (about 1½ lb/ 680 g or 3½ cups when cooked and diced)

1½ cups chopped, drained fresh pineapple

1 cup thinly sliced inner celery stalks

¼ cup minced onion

2 tbsp olive oil

6 tbsp red wine vinegar

salt to taste

Boil the beetroots, unpeeled, until they are tender (about 45–60 minutes). Cool them, peel them and cut them in ¼-in/6-mm dice. Combine the beetroots with the pineapple, celery and onions. Pour the oil and vinegar over them and toss until everything is evenly coated with dressing. Taste and add salt as needed. Toss again.

Chill the salad for several hours, then stir it up again and take it out of the refrigerator at least 30 minutes before serving, so that it is cool but not ice-cold. Serve in small bowls or on lettuce leaves.

Filled Cantaloup Salad

Serve as a first course with thin, buttered slices of bread or crisp Cheese Pastries (p. 51).

SERVES 4

1 large cucumber

1 medium-sized avocado

2 cups sliced fresh strawberries

4 fl oz/115 ml lemon juice

2 tbsp vegetable oil

4 tsp sugar

¼ tsp salt

2 medium-sized cantaloups

Peel the cucumber, quarter it lengthways, remove the seeds with a small spoon and discard, and slice the cucumber quarters thinly. Cut the avocado in half and remove the pit. Peel it and cut it in medium dice. Combine the cucumber, avocado and strawberries in a bowl and sprinkle them with the lemon juice, oil, sugar and salt. Toss gently until everything is evenly coated with the dressing and refrigerate for about 1 hour.

Cut the cantaloups in half crossways with a zigzag pattern: using a sharp, pointed knife, push the point of the knife into the centre of the cantaloup, making an angled cut slightly less than 1 in/25 mm long. Pull the knife out and make another cut next to it at about a 90° angle. Continue round the centre of the cantaloup this way, making the cuts as even as possible, until you come all the way round. Pull the two halves apart and scoop out the seeds.

Fill the cantaloup halves with the marinated fruit-and-vegetable mixture and chill them briefly before serving.

COLD OMELETTE SALAD

SERVES 4–6

6 eggs
1½ oz/45 g butter
salt and pepper to taste
4 tbsp minced fresh parsley
3 tbsp minced fresh chives
3 tbsp minced fresh dill weed
½ tbsp minced fresh coriander
    leaves
2 tbsp home-made mayonnaise

red leaf lettuce
3 fresh, ripe tomatoes
1¼ cups sliced pickled beetroots
1 recipe Soured Cream
    Dressing II (see p. 113)
GARNISH
parsley sprigs
radish rosettes

Make 3 thin, plain 9-in/225-mm omelettes, using 2 eggs and ½ oz/ 15 g butter for each, according to the directions on p. 131. Turn them out of the pan without folding, stack them on a plate and set them aside.

Combine the minced parsley, chives, dill and coriander leaves with the mayonnaise and a little salt and pepper. Spread ⅓ of this mixture evenly over 1 of the omelettes and roll it up tightly. Place it seam side down on a plate so that it will not unroll. Spread and roll the other 2 omelettes the same way. Put the omelettes in the refrigerator to chill for 1–2 hours.

The salad can be arranged on individual plates or on a serving dish. First arrange the lettuce leaves on the plate, then slice the tomatoes and put a layer of tomato slices over the lettuce in a pretty pattern. Put a slice of pickled beetroot on top of each tomato slice.

Cut the chilled omelette rolls in slices about ¾ in/18 mm thick. Arrange the omelette slices over the tomato and beetroot slices. Garnish the plate with parsley sprigs and radish rosettes and pass the chilled Soured Cream Dressing separately as you serve.

See SPANISH SPECIALITIES for Ensaladilla Russa.

STEWS, CASSEROLES,
HOT VEGETABLE DISHES

IN THE HEART OF THE TOWN OF VERONA is the beautiful Piazza delle Erbe. It is bounded at one end by the medieval civic buildings and at the other end by a palazzo from a later period. Stretching across the piazza, from one elegant side to the other, are the dozens of white, umbrella-topped stalls of the vegetable market, and everywhere the happy commotion that always accompanies the choosing of shiny, purple aubergines, earth-coloured mushrooms, plum-shaped tomatoes, ruffled lettuces, juicy, sweetly perfumed berries, and cut flowers for the table.

In a sunny, open spot near the middle of the square is a graceful thirteenth-century fountain. A slender medieval lady gazes serenely across the piazza from above the trickling water, and at her feet several little plastic hoses have been slipped into the pool from which to siphon water into buckets and sprinkling cans to keep all the bright-coloured flowers, fruits and vegetables fresh.

The Piazza delle Erbe is one of my favourite open-air markets, not only because it is filled with such an opulent array of beautiful foods and flowers in an exquisite setting, but also because it expresses something fundamental to the Italian spirit, their unerring aesthetic sense, which built the lovely town, piazza and the fountain, and their ease and practicality, which allows them to siphon water casually from the priceless fountain in order to keep their vegetables sprinkled.

I always find the atmosphere of open-air produce markets captivating and seek them out wherever I go. Each one is like a crazy salad, with its own special flavour, but all express the same ebullient spirit, as the seasonal abundance of vegetables and fruits is brought to town. In Warsaw the market is everywhere. In every square and on every street, alone or grouped in cosy pairs or trios, the little wooden stalls offer whatever the season dictates in the way of food and flowers. It isn't possible to walk more than a few streets without passing something very inviting – maybe just a small cart entirely filled with dark red cherries or maybe a large stall already aspiring to be a shop, with a dozen fresh vegetables arrayed in front and long ropes of dried black mushrooms hanging from the little roof.

In Cairo a sprawling street market stays open all night, and the turbaned and caftaned stall keepers sit calmly by their treasuries of vegetables, spices, herbs and fruits, and by great hills of the reddest, juiciest, absolutely best watermelons in the world. And in Barcelona the big San Juan Market spills out of its great halls and trails along part of the wide, flowery Ramblas, a beautiful avenue so ideally suited for strolling that it is gradually metamorphosing into a park.

Walking through markets like that was frustrating for me sometimes. I wanted to buy everything and take it right home to a kitchen. Instead, I imagined, translated, took notes in hotel rooms and carried the notebooks back home. But more than once I've devised dishes and whole meals while rambling through the market at home and watching the good cooks pinch their cucumbers and sniff their melons. That was the way I thought of the Giant Mushrooms Stuffed with Aubergine: on one of those forays, I spotted enormous fresh mushrooms – huge, firm and round. I couldn't keep from buying them, so I then proceeded to scout other stalls for something that could do them justice as a stuffing. At the same time, I was already mulling over how to work out a menu round them and deciding that we should ask someone over to help us eat them. A nice party developed that evening.

Like the mushrooms, most of the hot vegetables here are not side dishes but are rather suited to central importance in a meal. Many of them are hearty winter foods, the kind you long for when it starts to rain and blow and turns dark at four o'clock. Then you want a stew and dark home-made bread to go with it, and a fireplace to sit by while you eat them. Even among such plain, straightforward stock-pots from humble origins are a few combinations made with a light touch. Sweet and Sour Stuffed Cabbage Balls, from my friend Flora Mock's old, unwritten recipe, have an unexpectedly delicate flavour, piquant but subtle.

A dish like that, or like the Squash and Tomato Stew, with its soft, golden corn-meal dumplings, makes a fine dinner, needing only the addition of an interesting salad and, the easiest of desserts, fruit and cheese. And because stews and casseroles are generally so uncomplicated to prepare and serve, they lend themselves well to large dinner parties or buffets. A festive but easy-to-handle menu can be designed by making the first course one of the more elegant cold dishes, like Broccoli Mousse, and finishing with a party dessert – a torte or the sinfully rich Crème à la Irena.

In the summertime, when a lighter hot dish is required to set off a cold soup or big salad, try French Fried Mushrooms. Serve them hot from the oil, crisp on the outside and juicy inside, with a fresh tartar sauce, and wash them down with a chilled white wine. Then bring on the peaches or the fresh raspberries sprinkled with kirsch to complete a perfect alfresco luncheon or supper.

MUSHROOM STEW

SERVES 6

2½ oz/70 g butter
1 tbsp olive oil
2 bay leaves
2 cloves garlic, minced
1 large onion, chopped
2 tbsp flour
8 fl oz/225 ml Vegetable Broth
  (see pp. 60–61)
8 fl oz/225 ml tomato juice
2 cups peeled, quartered
  tomatoes

1 tsp thyme
1½ lb/680 g mushrooms,
  washed
1 lb/450 g boiling onions
red wine to taste
chopped fresh parsley to taste
salt and pepper
1 cup pitted ripe green olives

In a medium-sized saucepan, melt 1 oz/25 g of the butter with 1 tablespoon olive oil and add to it the bay leaves, garlic, and onions. Sauté until the onions are golden and then stir in the flour and lower the heat.

Cook this roux for several minutes, stirring constantly, and then add the vegetable broth and tomato juice. Stir with a whisk to remove all lumps and add the peeled tomatoes.

In another, larger saucepan, melt the remaining butter and add the thyme and the washed mushrooms. Sauté the mushrooms over a high heat for several minutes, turning them over often, and then add the boiling onions and the tomato sauce. Turn down the heat and simmer the stew for about 20 minutes. Add a little red wine, some chopped parsley and salt and pepper to taste. Last, but not least, toss in the green olives. Cook only a few more minutes and serve hot with a good bread and some red wine.

WINTER VEGETABLE STEW

SERVES 8–10

4½ oz/125 g butter
4 medium-sized leeks
1 lb/450 g boiling onions
3½ oz/100 g parsley root
3–4 cloves garlic, minced
¼ tsp thyme
2 bay leaves
rosemary to taste
1 lb/450 g mushrooms
2 medium-sized turnips
1 pt/570 ml dry white wine
3 tbsp Worcestershire sauce

1 lb/450 g potatoes
½ lb/225 g small Brussels
  sprouts
3 tbsp flour
16 fl oz/450 ml hot Vegetable
  Broth (see pp. 60–61)
2 tbsp wine vinegar
3 tbsp molasses
3 tsp paprika
dash of Tabasco
salt and pepper

Melt 3 oz/85 g of the butter in a large, heavy saucepan. Trim off the green parts and wash and slice the remaining part of the leeks. Peel the onions. Scrape and thinly slice the parsley root.

Sauté the leeks, onions and parsley root in the butter, together with the garlic, thyme, bay leaves and rosemary, until the leeks begin to turn golden.

Wash the mushrooms and if they are particularly large, cut them in half. Peel the turnips and cut them in ½-in/12-mm dice. Add the mushrooms and turnips to the saucepan, as well as the wine and the Worcestershire sauce. Stir and lower the heat.

Peel and dice the potatoes and wash and trim the Brussels sprouts. Add them to the stew, stir again and cover.

In a small, heavy saucepan, melt the remaining butter and stir in the flour. Cook this roux for a few minutes, then add the hot vegetable broth and stir quickly with a whisk. Add the vinegar, molasses, paprika and a little Tabasco. Stir with the whisk again until the sauce is smooth and pour it over the stew.

Simmer the stew gently, covered, for about 1 hour or until all the vegetables are tender. Season to taste with salt and pepper and serve very hot.

STEWED AUBERGINE

SERVES 5–6

2 large aubergines	1 cup cooked, chopped spinach
olive oil to taste	¼ cup chopped chives
salt to taste	½ cup chopped celery leaves
2 large onions	1½ tsp oregano
3 cloves garlic, minced	plenty of pepper to taste
2½ fl oz/70 ml olive oil	2 tbsp lemon juice
3 large tomatoes	¼ cup sesame seeds

Peel and slice the aubergines lengthways, ⅓ in/8 mm thick. Cut each slice again into 2 or 3 lengthways strips. Arrange the slices on baking sheets, brush them with olive oil and salt them lightly. Put them under a preheated medium grill for about 7–10 minutes or until the aubergine starts to turn golden brown. Turn the slices over, brush the other side with olive oil, salt the slices and put them back under the grill till the other side is coloured as well.

Meanwhile, peel and chop the onions, mince the garlic and sauté them in the olive oil until the onions are translucent. Cut the tomatoes in thin wedges and add them to the onions, along with the spinach, chives and celery leaves. Simmer the mixture for about another 10 minutes, then stir in the oregano, salt and pepper and the lemon juice.

Put a few tablespoons of this sauce in the bottom of a fairly large, fireproof casserole and arrange ⅓ of the grilled aubergine slices over it. Spoon some more sauce over the aubergine and continue layering until all the aubergine is used up. Cover the last aubergine layer with the remaining sauce.

Put a close-fitting lid on the casserole and simmer the vegetables together on a medium heat for 10 minutes.

Toast the sesame seeds by spreading them on a baking sheet and putting them in the oven at 350°F/180°C Mark 4. Give them an occasional stir and remove them when golden brown.

Sprinkle the toasted sesame seeds over the aubergine just before serving.

UKRAINIAN STEWED AUBERGINE

SERVES 8

1 cup chopped onions
4 tbsp olive oil
½ lb/225 g carrots (4 medium sized)
2 medium-sized green peppers
2 lb/900 g aubergines
1½ lb/680 g tomatoes, peeled and quartered
2 cloves garlic, minced

2½ tsp salt
pinch of cayenne pepper
5 fl oz/140 ml lemon juice
2 tsp sugar
fresh-ground black pepper to taste
GARNISH
½ cup thin-sliced spring onions

Sauté the onions in the olive oil for 5 minutes.

Scrape and thinly slice the carrots. Trim and seed the peppers and cut them in thin 1-in/25-mm strips. Peel the aubergine and slice it lengthways ½ in/12 mm thick. Cut the slices, again lengthways, into strips ½ × 1½ in/12 × 37 mm.

Add the carrots to the onions and sauté another 5 minutes. Then add the peppers, aubergine, tomatoes, garlic, salt, cayenne, lemon juice, sugar and pepper. Simmer the mixture, covered, for about 30 minutes, then uncovered for about 15 minutes, stirring occasionally. The liquid from the tomatoes should be greatly reduced.

Serve the aubergine hot or cool, sprinkled with the spring onions.

STEWED VEGETABLES
WITH ANISE AND LEMON SAUCE

SERVES 6–8

1 lb/450 g dried flageolet beans
  (about 2 cups)
3½ pt/2 l cold water
2½ tsp salt, and more to taste
3 medium-sized heads anise
  (about 2–2½ lb/900 g–1 kg
  untrimmed) or fennel
2 large onions

12 oz/340 g French beans
½ lb/225 g carrots
½ lb/225 g mushrooms
4 oz/115 g butter
3 eggs
juice of 2 large lemons (about
  2½ fl oz/70 ml)
pepper to taste

Put the dried beans in a saucepan with 2¾ pt/1.6 l of the cold water and 1 teaspoon of the salt, bring the water to a boil, then lower the heat and simmer the beans gently for 1 hour. Skim off the foam from the top.

Trim the long stalks and tops off the heads of anise and peel off the outer leaves if they are blemished. Wash the anise carefully, getting out any dirt that may be trapped between the leaves. Cut the anise into chunks no more than 1 × 2 in/25 × 50 mm.

Peel the onions and cut them into 1-in/25-mm chunks. Trim the French beans and cut them into 1-in/25-mm pieces. Scrape the carrots and slice them thickly or, if they are slender, cut them in ¾-in/18-mm lengths. Wash and trim the mushrooms.

Melt the butter in a large saucepan and sauté the anise and onions in it for about 10–12 minutes, stirring frequently. Add the beans, carrots and mushrooms and stir for a few minutes more. Add the partially cooked flageolets with their liquid, the rest of the cold water and salt. Stir everything together gently, cover the saucepan and simmer over low heat for about 45 minutes or a little longer if necessary. All the vegetables should be tender.

Beat the eggs with the lemon juice. Ladle out about 8 fl oz/225 ml of the hot broth from the vegetables and beat it into the egg mixture. Add the sauce to the vegetables and stir over the lowest possible heat for a few minutes, until the liquid has thickened. Season with more salt and pepper, and serve.

SQUASH AND TOMATO STEW

SERVES 6–8

1½ large onions
4½ tbsp olive oil
5–6 cloves garlic, minced
¾ tsp ground cumin
¾ tsp ground cinnamon
¾ cup diced hot green chillis
2½ pt/1.4 l cooked tomatoes,
  with liquid
1¼ lb/570 g yellow winter
  squash, peeled and cut in
  ½-in/12-mm cubes

1½ tsp salt
12 fl oz/340 ml water
1 recipe Corn-meal Dumplings
  (below)
1¼ lb/570 g courgettes, cut in
  ¼-in/6-mm slices
3–4 tbsp fresh chopped coriander
  leaves
1½ tsp sugar

Peel, quarter and slice the onions. In a very large saucepan, sauté them in the olive oil until they are clear, then add the garlic, cumin, cinnamon and diced chillis. Sauté for a few minutes more, stirring constantly, then add the tomatoes and their liquid, the cubed squash, the salt and the water.

Lower the heat, cover the saucepan and simmer the mixture gently for about 1 hour.

Meanwhile make dumpling batter.

Add the courgettes, coriander leaves and sugar to the stew. Stir and cook for another 5–6 minutes.

Now drop dumpling batter on the stew by teaspoonfuls, cover the saucepan tightly and leave the stew simmering over very low heat for 20 minutes.

CORN-MEAL DUMPLINGS

MAKES ABOUT 24 DUMPLINGS

1 cup yellow corn-meal
⅓ cup white flour
1 tsp baking powder
¾ tsp salt

1 tsp sugar
1 egg
4 fl oz/115 ml single cream
¾ oz/20 g butter, melted

Sift together the corn-meal, flour, baking powder, salt and sugar. Beat together the egg and the cream and stir into the dry mixture. Add the melted butter and continue stirring until the batter is smooth.

Drop the batter by teaspoonfuls into simmering soup, stew or heavily salted water. Cover and simmer for 14–15 minutes.

MUSHROOMS AND POTATOES
IN WINE SAUCE

SERVES 6

*1½ oz/40 g dried wild
   mushrooms*
2½ oz/70 g butter
⅔ cup chopped onion
1 clove garlic, minced
2½ lb/1.1 kg potatoes
*14 fl oz/400 ml dry white
   wine*

1 tsp salt, and more to taste
½ lb/225 g fresh mushrooms
¼ tsp dried dill weed
¼ tsp dried whole thyme
4 tbsp chopped fresh parsley
fresh-ground black pepper

Put the dried mushrooms in a bowl and pour over them enough hot water to cover them amply. Let them soak for about 1 hour, or longer if you have the time, then drain them, reserving the liquid. Wash the mushrooms very carefully, cut them in wide strips and put them aside. Strain the liquid through several layers of cheese-cloth or through a paper filter and simmer it in a small saucepan until it is reduced to 8 fl oz/225 ml.

Melt 1½ oz/40 g of the butter in a large saucepan and sauté the onions and garlic in it until they begin to colour. Peel the potatoes, cut them in 1-in/25-mm cubes and add them to the onions and garlic. Pour in the white wine, add the salt, stir and cover the sauce-pan.

Simmer on medium-low heat for 10 minutes, then add the soaked mushrooms and the reduced mushroom liquid, stir and cover again. Continue simmering, stirring occasionally, for another 20 minutes. The potatoes should be completely tender.

Meanwhile, wash and slice the fresh mushrooms. Melt the remaining butter in a frying pan, add the dill weed, thyme, chopped parsley and the sliced mushrooms, and sauté them, stirring constantly, until the mushrooms are tender.

When the potatoes are cooked, add the sautéd, herbed mushrooms to the saucepan and simmer uncovered for a few more minutes, stirring often. Add fresh-ground black pepper to taste, and more salt if needed. The liquid should be reduced to a thick, gravy-like sauce. Serve hot.

ITALIAN POTATO
AND CHEESE CASSEROLE

SERVES 5–6

2 lb/900 g potatoes	10½ oz/300 g mozzarella
3 oz/85 g butter	cheese
½ tsp salt, and more to taste	6 hard-boiled eggs
1½ lb/680 g ripe tomatoes	⅔ cup chopped fresh parsley
pepper to taste	½ cup fresh-grated Parmesan
1½ tsp basil, crushed	cheese

Boil the potatoes until they are just barely tender, drain them, peel them and cut them crossways in fairly thick slices.

Melt the butter and pour 2 tablespoons of it over the bottom of a large, shallow casserole. Arrange the potato slices in the casserole in one layer and salt them.

Slice the tomatoes and arrange the tomato slices on top of the potatoes. Sprinkle the tomatoes with salt, pepper and basil.

Slice the mozzarella, cut the slices into wide strips and arrange them on top of the tomatoes.

Peel and coarsely chop the eggs, combine them in a bowl with the remaining melted butter, the chopped parsley, ½ tsp salt, and some pepper. Toss the mixture together until it is thoroughly mixed. Spread the egg mixture evenly over the cheese.

Sprinkle the casserole with the Parmesan cheese and bake it in a preheated oven at 350°F/180°C/Mark 4 for 25–30 minutes.

RED CABBAGE WITH APPLES

SERVES 6–8

2 lb/900 g red cabbage, cored
   and shredded
1 medium-sized onion, chopped
1½ lb/680 g tart green apples
   (about 3 large), peeled, cored,
   quartered and sliced
4 oz/115 g butter
1 tsp salt

2 tbsp brown sugar
2 tbsp cider vinegar
¼ tsp ground cloves
pinch of cinnamon
pinch of nutmeg
fresh-ground black pepper
6 fl oz/170 ml beer

Sauté the cabbage, onions and apples in the butter for about 10 minutes, stirring often. Add the salt, brown sugar, cider vinegar, cloves, cinnamon, nutmeg, black pepper to taste and the beer. Stir the mixture well, cover it, lower the heat, and let it simmer for 1 hour, stirring only occasionally.

The cabbage can be served at this point but improves if it is allowed to cool and is reheated several hours later or the following day.

POTATO KUGEL

A kugel is a pudding-like dish, best eaten hot or warm. Potato Kugel is generally a side dish, but it could be used as the basis of a light meal, with the addition of a soup or salad and some fruit.

SERVES 6–8

4 medium-sized potatoes (about
   2 lb/900 g)
1 large onion
2 eggs
1 tsp salt

pepper to taste
3 tbsp vegetable oil
GARNISH
soured cream

Peel the potatoes and grate them as quickly as possible. Peel and grate the onion, beat the eggs lightly and stir together the potatoes, onions, eggs, salt and pepper. If you are using a blender or food processor, cut the peeled potatoes and onions into chunks and process them, ½ batch at a time, together with the eggs, until no large pieces are left.

Preheat the oven to 350°F/180°C/Mark 4, pour the oil into a shallow, medium-sized casserole and heat it for a few minutes. Pour the kugel mixture into the hot oil in the casserole and bake it for 1 hour. The kugel should be puffed up and browned. Serve hot with soured cream.

MUSHROOMS ON TOAST

Use only fresh, firm, rather small mushrooms for this recipe, and don't try to substitute dried herbs for fresh. The flavour of this dish is wonderful, but it depends on just the right balance in seasonings.

SERVES 4–6

1½ lb/680 g fresh mushrooms
4 tbsp olive oil
4 tbsp finely chopped fresh parsley
2 medium cloves garlic, minced
salt to taste
fresh-ground black pepper to taste

1¼ oz/35 g butter
2 tbsp fresh lemon juice
1½ tbsp cider vinegar or wine vinegar
2 tbsp chopped fresh coriander leaves
4–6 large slices of French or pumpernickel bread, toasted

Wash the mushrooms, trim off the stems and cut them in half unless they are very small. Toss the mushrooms in a bowl with the olive oil, parsley, garlic and some salt and pepper. The mushrooms can be prepared in advance to this point and kept in the refrigerator, covered, for up to 1 day.

Melt the butter in a large frying pan and when it is sizzling, add the mushrooms. Sauté the mushrooms over high heat for 5–6 minutes, stirring constantly. They should be just tender and beginning to release water.

Add the lemon juice, vinegar and coriander leaves. Cook the mushrooms for about 5 minutes more, still over high heat and still stirring constantly. Mound the mushrooms on top of the toast, dividing them equally among the 4–6 slices, and drizzle the liquid that is left in the pan over them. Serve immediately!

FRENCH-FRIED MUSHROOMS

The mushrooms can be fried in advance and reheated for about 10 minutes in a very hot oven, but the crusts will lose just a bit of their crispy pizzazz that way.

SERVES 6

1½ lb/680 g fresh, firm
  mushrooms
1 cup dry breadcrumbs
⅓ cup minced fresh parsley
2 eggs
1 clove garlic, minced or
  crushed
salt to taste

fresh-ground pepper to taste
½ cup flour
vegetable oil for deep frying
GARNISH
tartar sauce or
  Hot Paprika Sauce (p. 107) or
  Simple Tomato Sauce (p. 106)
grated Parmesan cheese

Choose the mushrooms carefully for uniformity of size, picking medium-small mushrooms rather than very large ones. Wash them quickly, trim off the stems even with the bottoms of the mushrooms and pat them dry in tea-towels.

Combine the breadcrumbs and minced parsley in a shallow bowl. Beat the eggs and add to them the minced garlic, a generous amount of salt and some pepper. Put the beaten eggs in another small, shallow bowl.

Add some salt and pepper to the flour as well and put the mixture in a third shallow bowl.

Roll all the mushrooms in the flour first, tapping them lightly after you do to be sure there aren't any pockets of flour around the stems. Then dip each mushroom into the beaten egg and immediately roll it in the crumbs and parsley.

Fry the mushrooms in deep, hot vegetable oil until they are golden brown, drain them on paper towels and serve them hot with tartar sauce, Hot Paprika Sauce or Simple Tomato Sauce, and grated Parmesan cheese.

MUSHROOM STROGANOFF

This dish is made with both dried and fresh mushrooms. The dried mushrooms can be *Boletus edulis*, the wild black or dark brown ones that are imported from Italy or eastern Europe, but I've also had success using the Japanese forest mushrooms – a wonderful, pungent flavour.

SERVES 6

2 oz/55 g dried dark
    mushrooms
1⅗ pt/900 ml hot water
1 lb/450 g fresh, firm
    mushrooms
½ medium-sized onion, minced
2 oz/55 g butter
pinch of thyme
salt

fresh-ground black pepper
8–9 fl oz/ 225–255 ml soured
    cream
2 tbsp brandy
2 tbsp dry sherry
1 lb/450 g wide egg noodles
1½–2 oz/40–55 g butter,
    melted
2–3 tsp poppy seeds

Soak the dried mushrooms in the hot water for several hours. Drain them, reserving the liquid. Wash the mushrooms thoroughly under running water, one by one, and trim off the hard stems. Cut the mushrooms in wide strips. Strain the liquid through several layers of cheesecloth or through a paper coffee filter; there should be about 16 fl oz/450 ml of it now. Transfer the liquid to a saucepan and simmer it until it is reduced by slightly more than half.

Meanwhile, wash, trim, and thickly slice the fresh mushrooms. Sauté the minced onions in the butter until they are transparent, then add the sliced fresh mushrooms and toss over high heat until they have released their excess water and it is starting to evaporate. Season with a pinch of thyme and salt and pepper to taste. Add the soaked mushroom strips and reduce the heat to medium-low.

Gradually whisk the reduced mushroom liquid into the soured cream, and add this mixture to the mushrooms. Simmer gently, stirring often, for 15–20 minutes or until the soured cream sauce is slightly thickened and the mushrooms are tender. Stir in the brandy and sherry, taste and correct the seasoning if necessary.

Boil the noodles in a large amount of vigorously boiling salted water until they are just tender but not yet soft. Drain them immediately and toss them with the melted butter and poppy seeds in a heated bowl.

Serve the mushrooms with the poppy seed noodles and follow it with a tart, crisp salad.

COURGETTE AND AUBERGINE ROULADE

Crazy as it may sound, a roulade is really like a big, flat soufflé that has been rolled up around a filling, Swiss-roll style. It's served hot, cut into spiral-patterned slices with a sauce poured over them.

SERVES 6–8

1¼ lb/570 g courgettes
approximately 1 tsp salt, and
  more to taste
1 medium-sized aubergine (about
  1 lb/450 g)
2 tbsp olive oil
2 cups peeled, cooked tomatoes
  (with liquid)
2 tsp sugar
2 tsp lemon juice
2½ fl oz/70 ml single cream
salt and pepper to taste

4 oz/115 g butter
⅓ cup chopped onions
⅔ cup flour
8 fl oz/225 ml warm milk
4 eggs, separated
½ cup grated Parmesan cheese
fine, dry breadcrumbs
⅓ cup pine nuts
GARNISH
Mornay Sauce (p. 104) or
  drawn butter and extra
  Parmesan cheese

Wash and grate the courgettes and toss with the 1 teaspoon salt. Put the courgettes in a colander to drain for 20 minutes. Then squeeze out the excess moisture, rinsing first only if too salty.

Make the aubergine filling. Peel the aubergine, grate it and sauté it for 10–15 minutes in the olive oil, stirring often. Add the tomatoes, sugar and lemon juice and cook over medium-high heat, stirring almost constantly until the sauce is thick. Add the cream and the salt and pepper and continue cooking until the consistency is not at all runny.

Melt the butter in a medium-sized saucepan and sauté the onions in it until they are completely transparent. Stir in the flour and continue stirring over low heat until the flour is golden, about 5–6 minutes. Add the warm milk and stir vigorously until the mixture is smooth and thick. Remove it from the heat and let it cool for 5 minutes. Beat in the 4 egg yolks, then stir in the courgettes and the Parmesan cheese.

Beat the 4 egg whites until they hold fairly stiff peaks. Stir ¹/₂ the egg whites thoroughly into the egg-courgette-cheese mixture then fold in the other ¹/₂.

Butter a 10 × 14-in/250 × 350-mm Swiss-roll pan and sprinkle it with fine, dry breadcrumbs. Spread the egg-courgette-cheese mixture evenly over the entire surface of the pan.

Bake in a preheated oven at 375°F/190°C/Mark 5 for about 15 minutes or until it is puffed and coming away from the sides.

Turn the roulade out on a tea-towel and spread it with the aubergine filling, leaving a 1¹/₂-in/37-mm border along one side. Sprinkle the pine nuts over the filling and, starting with the end where the border has been left, roll it up lengthways. Use the towel to help roll it evenly.

Put the roulade back in the oven for 5 minutes and serve it with Mornay Sauce or drawn butter and extra Parmesan cheese.

MUSHROOM AND BARLEY
STUFFED CABBAGE ROLLS

SERVES 6–8

1 large head green cabbage
Mushroom-Barley Stuffing
  (p. 189)
2¹/₂ lb/1.1 kg fresh, ripe
  tomatoes
4 tbsp olive oil

1 large onion, chopped
3–4 cloves garlic, minced
1¹/₂ tsp paprika
red wine
salt
pepper

Place the whole head of cabbage in a large saucepan and pour boiling water over it. In a few moments, the outer leaves will soften. Lift the cabbage out and very gently peel off the soft leaves. Repeat this procedure until all the leaves large enough to wrap round a spoonful of stuffing have been removed. If the cabbage leaves are not pliable enough to fold without tearing, douse them with boiling water again and leave them in it until they are soft.

Cut off the very stiff core ends and trim the largest leaves just a little. Place a rounded tablespoon of stuffing near the thick end of a leaf. Fold the end over the stuffing, then fold over the sides, as if making an envelope. When the sides are neatly tucked over, roll up the cabbage leaf as tightly as possible without squeezing out the stuffing. Continue in this manner until all the stuffing is used. You should have enough for 12–15 cabbage rolls.

Blanch the tomatoes in boiling water and peel them. Purée them in a blender at low speed for a very short time – the resulting sauce should be thick and have bits of tomato in it.

Heat the olive oil in a large frying pan and sauté the onions, garlic and paprika in it until the garlic is golden. Add the tomato purée, a little red wine and salt and pepper to taste. Simmer the sauce gently until it is thickened, at least 30 minutes.

Lightly butter or oil a large, shallow (about 2 in/50 mm deep) baking dish. Put a few spoonfuls of the tomato sauce in the bottom. Arrange the cabbage rolls in one neat layer in the dish. Pour the remaining tomato sauce over them.

Bake the cabbage rolls in a preheated oven at 350°F/180°C/Mark 4 for about 40 minutes and serve piping hot.

MUSHROOM-BARLEY STUFFING FOR CABBAGE ROLLS

2 oz/55 g dried wild mushrooms	1 large onion
⅓ cup barley	2 oz/55 g butter
½ lb/225 g fresh mushrooms	salt
	fresh-ground black pepper

Put the dried mushrooms in a bowl with 16 fl oz/450 ml hot water and allow them to rehydrate for about 1 hour. Put the barley in a small saucepan with 8 fl oz/225 ml water and let simmer gently for 1½–2 hours, until tender.

When the mushrooms have plumped up, take them out of the bowl, one or two at a time, and wash them carefully under running water to get rid of all the gritty dirt that they conceal in such abundance. Set them aside.

Take the liquid in which the mushrooms were soaked and strain through muslin or through a good paper coffee filter. Measure out 8 fl oz/225 ml of the filtered liquid and add it to the simmering barley.

Put the soaked dark mushrooms through the medium blade of a food mill.

Wash the fresh mushrooms and halve them, then slice the halves thinly.

Peel and coarsely chop the onion.

Melt the butter in a large frying pan and add the onions and fresh mushrooms. Sauté them until the onions are transparent, then add the dark mushrooms and season with salt and fresh-ground black pepper to taste. Sauté this mixture for another 10–15 minutes, stirring often.

When the barley is quite tender, add it along with the remaining liquid to the mushroom mixture. Stir it all up well and simmer gently, covered, for another 30 minutes or so, stirring occasionally.

RICE-STUFFED CABBAGE ROLLS

SERVES 8

1 large head cabbage (about
  2½ lb/1.1 kg)
FILLING
2 oz/55 g dried wild
  mushrooms
1½ cups brown rice
1⅕ pt/ 680 ml water
1 tsp salt, and more to taste
1 oz/25 g butter
2 cups chopped onions
2 cloves garlic, minced
1 tsp sweet paprika
⅛–¼ tsp hot paprika

1 tsp dill seeds
½ cup raisins
⅔ cup finely chopped walnuts
2 eggs, lightly beaten
½ cup dry breadcrumbs
pepper to taste
SAUCE
2 oz/55 g butter
1 cup chopped onions
1⅗ pt/900 ml cooked tomatoes
  (with liquid)
4 fl oz/115 ml medium-sweet
  vermouth

2½ tbsp lemon juice   salt to taste
3 oz/85 g tomato paste   pepper to taste

Make the filling first. Soak the mushrooms in hot water for about 1 hour.

Bring the rice to a boil in the water with the salt, then lower the heat and simmer it for 25 minutes. Drain the rice.

Melt the butter in a frying pan and sauté the chopped onions and the minced garlic in it until the onions are transparent.

Drain the mushrooms, reserving the liquid. Wash the mushrooms carefully, one by one, to remove every speck of sand, and mince them. Add them to the onions and garlic and sauté the mixture for another few minutes.

Strain the liquid from the mushrooms through 5–6 layers of cheesecloth or through a paper filter and add 1⅕ pt/680 ml of it to the mushroom mixture, along with the cooked rice, the two paprikas, the dill seeds and the raisins. Simmer this mixture gently for about 30 minutes or until most of the liquid is absorbed. Then add the walnuts, eggs, breadcrumbs and salt and pepper. Continue cooking this filling, stirring often, until it is quite thick.

Core the cabbage and blanch it in boiling salted water for 5 minutes. Carefully peel off 14–15 leaves. If the inner leaves are still too stiff, put them back in the boiling water for 1–2 minutes. Trim 1½ in/37 mm off the bottom of each leaf and a little off the sides of the largest ones.

Put 2–3 tablespoons of filling in the centre of each cabbage leaf and roll it up, folding the sides in as you do.

Now make the sauce. Chop the remaining cabbage coarsely and sauté it in the butter with the chopped onions. When the onions are translucent, add the tomatoes, coarsely chopped, together with their liquid, the vermouth, the lemon juice, tomato paste and salt and pepper. Stir this sauce up thoroughly and heat it through.

Put several large spoonfuls of this sauce in the bottom of a large, fireproof casserole. Arrange a layer of the stuffed cabbage leaves in it, seam side down and close together. Cover them with more of the sauce and arrange another layer of cabbage rolls the same way on top of the others. Continue until all the cabbage rolls are used up and finish by pouring the remaining sauce on top. Cover the casserole tightly and simmer over a very low heat for about 1½ hours.

BAKED STUFFED TOMATOES

SERVES 6–8

¾ lb/340 g green peppers
  (about 2 large)
¾ lb/340 g courgettes
½ lb/225 g small Japanese
  aubergines (about 3
  aubergines)
1 small onion
2 fl oz/55 ml olive oil
1½ tsp salt, or more to taste

2 tbsp chopped fresh coriander
  leaves
1 tsp crushed dried red peppers
dash of oregano
1½ tbsp lemon juice
black pepper to taste
6–8 large ripe tomatoes
½ lb/225 g Munster cheese,
  grated
2 tbsp dry breadcrumbs

Grill the peppers, turning them often, until they are blistered and charred. Hold them under cold running water and peel off the skins. Remove the stems, seeds and ribs, and cut them in short, thin strips.

Trim and finely dice the courgettes and aubergines. Peel and chop the onion.

Heat the olive oil in a large frying pan and sauté the chopped onions in it over very high heat, stirring constantly, just until they begin to colour. Add the diced courgettes and aubergines and toss, still over high heat, for about 5–6 minutes. Add the salt, coriander leaves, red pepper, oregano, lemon juice and black pepper. Stir well and turn off the heat.

Cut out a 2-in/50-mm circle from the top of each tomato and scoop out the pulp, leaving a ¼-in/6-mm shell. Chop the tomato pulp coarsely, add it to the vegetables in the frying pan and stir again over high heat just until the liquid is reduced to a thick paste.

Remove the vegetables from the heat and quickly stir in about ¾ of the grated cheese.

Spoon the mixture into the tomato shells. Toss the remaining cheese with the breadcrumbs and put a little mound of it on top of each tomato.

Bake the tomatoes in a preheated oven at 350°F/180°C/Mark 4 for 15–20 minutes and serve immediately.

GIANT MUSHROOMS
STUFFED WITH AUBERGINE

SERVES 4

8 very large, firm mushrooms
(about 3 in/75 mm across)
1–1½ oz/25–40 g butter
1 medium-sized aubergine
1 tsp salt, and more to taste
1 medium-sized red pepper
2 tbsp olive oil
½ tsp ground cumin
1 tsp paprika

3 large cloves garlic, minced
3 tbsp white wine vinegar
3 tbsp tomato paste
2½ tbsp minced red onion
½ cup chopped walnuts
pinch of oregano
fresh-ground black pepper
1 cup grated Gruyère cheese

Clean the mushrooms carefully and take out the stems. Then, using a grapefruit spoon, melon baller or very carefully with a knife, hollow out the centres a little, leaving a thick shell. Sauté the mushrooms in butter for a few minutes only, first on one side, then the other. Remove them from the heat and set aside.

Peel the aubergine and slice lengthways into ¼-in/6-mm-thick slices. Cut these lengthways into strips ½-in/12-mm wide, then cut the strips to 1-in/25-mm lengths. Toss the strips with the salt and leave in a colander for 30 minutes.

Seed the red pepper and cut out the white ribs. Cut into julienne strips.

Heat the olive oil in a large frying pan and add the cumin, paprika and minced garlic.

Rinse the aubergine and press out all excess moisture. Sauté it and red pepper strips in the olive oil until they are just tender.

Stir in the vinegar, tomato paste, minced onions and walnuts. Season to taste with oregano, salt and fresh-ground black pepper. Sauté for a couple more minutes, then stir in ½ the grated cheese.

Spoon the filling into the hollowed-out mushrooms, shaping it into nice, even mounds. Sprinkle the remaining cheese on top.

Bake the mushrooms in a lightly buttered, covered baking dish in a preheated oven at 350°F/180°C/Mark 4 for about 25–30 minutes.

Serve hot, if you like with Spinach and Dill Rice (p. 198).

SWEET AND SOUR
STUFFED CABBAGE BALLS

SERVES 6–8

1 large head cabbage
3/4 cup white rice
3/4 cup barley
1 2/5 pt/800 ml water
1 tsp salt, and more to taste
1 tbsp vegetable oil
*3/4 cup coarsely chopped pine
   nuts or pistachio nuts*
2 eggs

*1/2 tsp dried dill weed or 1 tsp fresh
black pepper to taste*
*1 medium-sized onion, finely
   chopped*
1/2 cup raisins
*2 lb/900 g peeled tomatoes,
   sliced or coarsely chopped*
1/3 cup sugar
2 1/2 fl oz/70 ml lemon juice

Bring a large saucepan of salted water to a boil. Core the cabbage, put it in the boiling water, cover and let it simmer for about 20 minutes, or just until the leaves are tender enough to peel away easily. Drain the cabbage and allow it to cool enough so that it can be easily handled.

Meanwhile, combine the rice and barley in a medium-sized saucepan and add the water. Stir in the salt and vegetable oil and bring the water to a boil. Lower the heat and simmer, covered, for about 40 minutes. Turn off the heat and let the rice and barley stand, covered, for 30 minutes; all the water should be absorbed. Stir in the nuts, eggs, dill weed, black pepper, chopped onions and raisins, as well as more salt if it is needed.

Scoop out about 2 heaped tablespoons of the mixture and form it into a ball between the palms of your hands, the way you would form a snowball. Peel off one of the soft cabbage leaves and wrap it round the ball of filling, smoothing the cabbage against the rice ball with your hands and overlapping all the edges as securely as you can. The soft cabbage will cling to the rice ball as it is smoothed round. The rice ball must be completely wrapped in the cabbage, but as you continue and the cabbage leaves get smaller, you can use two of them to wrap round one ball of filling. It's all easier than it sounds.

Combine the tomatoes and all their juice with the sugar, lemon juice and salt to taste; stir well.

Spoon $1/3$ of this mixture into a large, heavy-bottomed enamelled saucepan or fireproof casserole.

Arrange a layer of cabbage balls on top of the tomatoes, fitting them snugly next to each other but not squeezing them. Spoon another $1/3$ of the tomato mixture over them and make a second layer of cabbage balls. Pour the remaining tomatoes over the top, together with any leftover cabbage, coarsely chopped.

Cover the saucepan or casserole tightly and simmer over lowest heat for 25 minutes. Put the stuffed cabbage away in the refrigerator for 12–24 hours, then simmer it for another 25 minutes on low heat or heat it in a preheated oven at 350°F/180°C/Mark 4 for 45–50 minutes.

AUBERGINE WITH CHEESE AND WALNUTS

SERVES 8

$2\frac{1}{2}$ lb/1.1 kg firm aubergine
salt
3–4 cloves garlic, sliced
4 fl oz/115 ml olive oil
2 red onions, peeled, halved and
   sliced

3 cups peeled plum tomatoes
   (with all their juice)
$2\frac{1}{2}$ fl oz/70 ml dry white wine
fresh-ground black pepper
$1\frac{1}{3}$ cup walnut pieces
$\frac{1}{2}$ lb/225 g fontina cheese
$\frac{1}{4}$ lb/115 g mozzarella cheese

Trim off the stem ends and slice the aubergines lengthways, $1/2$ in/12 mm thick. Salt the slices liberally on both sides and put them aside for about 30 minutes to drain.

In a large frying pan, sauté the garlic in the olive oil for several minutes, then remove and discard the garlic. Rinse the aubergine slices and press out the excess moisture between the palms of your hands. Brush the aubergine slices on both sides with the olive oil, and grill them for several minutes on each side until they show dark spots.

When all the slices have been grilled, add to the remaining oil the sliced onions and stir over high heat until they are limp and beginning to brown. Cut the plum tomatoes in very thick slices and add them, with all their juice, to the onions. Stir in the wine. Cook for several minutes over high heat, stirring often, and add about ½ teaspoon of salt and pepper to taste.

Pour the tomato sauce into a large, shallow casserole. Arrange the sautéd aubergine slices over it in one even, overlapping layer. Sprinkle the slices with a little salt and pepper, then spread the walnut pieces evenly over the aubergine.

Cut the fontina cheese in slices or strips and arrange it evenly over the walnuts. Grate the mozzarella and sprinkle it over the fontina.

Bake the casserole in a preheated oven at 350°F/180°C/Mark 4 for 20–30 minutes: it should be bubbling hot, and the cheeses should be melted and beginning to brown. Serve immediately.

LECAS

(Basque-style French Beans)

SERVES 4–6

1 lb/450 g fresh French beans
2 fl oz/55 ml olive oil
2 cloves garlic, minced
1 large onion, chopped
1 lb/450 g peeled tomatoes,
  coarsely chopped

½–¾ tsp salt
fresh-ground black pepper to
  taste
large pinch of oregano

Wash and trim the beans and cut them in 1-in/25-mm lengths. Bring a medium-sized saucepan of heavily salted water to a boil.

Heat the olive oil in a fairly large saucepan or frying pan and sauté the garlic and onions in it until they begin to colour. Add the chopped tomatoes, with all their juice, and simmer.

Plunge the cut beans into the boiling water and boil them for 5 minutes. Drain the beans and add them to the tomato sauce. A very small amount of water can be added if the tomato sauce seems too thick; it should just barely cover the beans. Add salt and pepper, and simmer covered for about 30 minutes.

Stir in the oregano, taste and add more salt and pepper if needed. Cook the beans a few minutes more, uncovered, and serve.

STUFFED POTATO PANCAKES HUNGARIAN STYLE

SERVES 6–8

4 lb/1.8 kg potatoes
4 eggs, beaten
1 cup flour
5 fl oz/140 ml single cream
½ cup chopped fresh parsley
1 tsp salt
fresh-ground pepper to taste
butter
MUSHROOM FILLING
16 fl oz/450 ml hot water

1½–2 oz/40–55 g dried wild
   mushrooms
¾ lb/340 g boiling onions
1 oz/25 g butter
1⅔ cups sliced celery
½ cup chopped walnuts
salt and pepper
approximately 12 fl oz/340 ml
   Hot Paprika Sauce (p. 107)

Peel the potatoes and soak them in cold water for 10 minutes, then grate them. Beat together the eggs, flour and cream and stir in the grated potatoes, chopped parsley, salt and pepper.

Melt about 2 teaspoons butter in a 10–11-in/250–275-mm pan and pour in about 4 fl oz/115 ml of batter. Spread it evenly over the pan and cook for several minutes, flip and cook 1–2 minutes more. The pancake should be golden brown on both sides. Prepare all the pancakes in this way, adding a little butter to the pan each time, and stack on a plate, keeping them covered with a light cloth to prevent drying out.

Make the filling. Soak the mushrooms in the hot water for about 1 hour. Drain them, reserving the liquid, and wash them very carefully, one by one. Slice the mushrooms in thick strips. Strain the liquid through a filter or through 2 layers of muslin.

Peel the onions and cut in half if large. Sauté the onions and celery in the butter in a large frying pan for about 5 minutes. Add walnuts, the mushrooms, their liquid and the Hot Paprika Sauce. Simmer the mixture, stirring occasionally, until the vegetables are tender and the sauce is thick and glazed, and then season.

To serve the pancakes, have additional sauce and the filling ready and heated. Reheat each pancake quickly on both sides in a very hot pan. Put one pancake on each plate, spoon some filling down the middle of it and fold over. Top with several tablespoons of Hot Paprika Sauce and serve immediately.

SPINACH AND DILL RICE

SERVES 8

1 lb/450 g fresh spinach
3 tbsp olive oil
2 cloves garlic, minced
2 tsp salt
1 tsp dried dill weed
2 tsp white wine vinegar

fresh-ground black pepper to taste
1⅔ pt/900 ml water
1½ cups long-grain white rice
½ cup finely crumbled feta cheese
½ cup fresh-grated Parmesan
  cheese

Wash and trim the spinach and mince it. Heat the olive oil in a small frying pan and add the minced spinach and minced garlic to it. Season the spinach with ½ teaspoon of the salt, the dill weed, vinegar and some black pepper.

Cook the mixture over medium heat for about 10 minutes, stirring often. All the excess liquid should have evaporated, leaving a thick purée.

Bring the water to a boil in a medium-large saucepan and stir in the remaining salt. Add the rice and lower the heat to a simmer. Cover the pot and leave the rice to cook over very low heat for 25 minutes. The rice will absorb all the water.

Add the spinach mixture and toss lightly with two spoons until the rice and spinach are well blended. Cover once more and leave over low heat for another 3–4 minutes.

Toss together the 2 cheeses. Spoon the green rice on to a warmed platter, sprinkle it with the cheeses and serve immediately.

GLAZED CARROTS

SERVES 4–6

1½ lb/680 g slender carrots
1½ oz/40 g butter
6 fl oz/170 ml water
2 tbsp lemon juice

salt to taste
1 tbsp cider vinegar
⅓ cup brown sugar
dash of nutmeg

Scrape and trim the carrots and cut them in 1-in/25-mm lengths. Melt 1 oz/25 g of the butter in a medium-sized frying pan and add the carrots, water, lemon juice and a little salt. Simmer, covered, for 20 minutes. Remove the cover and raise the heat. Cook over high heat, stirring often, until nearly all the liquid has evaporated – about 6–8 minutes.

Add the remaining butter, the cider vinegar, the brown sugar and a tiny bit of nutmeg. Lower the heat to medium and stir constantly until all the sugar is melted and the glaze is thick enough to coat the carrots.

Taste, add more salt if needed and serve.

CORN AND CHEESE PUDDING

SERVES 4–6

2 eggs
3 tbsp flour
4 fl oz/115 ml single cream
8 fl oz/225 ml milk
½ tsp salt
¼ tsp white pepper
1 tbsp sugar

1½ cups fresh-scraped
    sweetcorn (about 3 ears)
1½ oz/40 g butter, melted
3 oz/85 g sharp Cheddar cheese,
    grated
¼ cup finely chopped medium-
    hot green chillis

Beat the eggs and flour together to make a smooth paste, then beat in the cream, milk, salt, pepper and sugar. Add the sweetcorn, melted butter, grated cheese and chopped chillis, and stir the mixture together thoroughly.

Pour the mixture into a buttered medium-sized casserole, and place the casserole in a pan or larger casserole which is about ½ full of water. Bake the pudding for 50–55 minutes in a preheated oven at 350°F/180°C/Mark 4. It should be slightly puffed and golden on top. Serve hot.

SEE SPANISH SPECIALITIES for Cocido, Stewed Chick-peas, Menestra de Verduras, Champiñónes alla Plancha. See ITALIAN PASTAS, VEGETABLES, AND FRITTATAS for Pomodoro al Gratine and Melanzana al Forno.

CROQUETTES, PÂTÉS, CHEESES

CROQUETTES, PÂTÉS and the interesting hot and cold concoctions made from cheeses are among the most memorable treats that these past years of travelling, tasting and experimenting have yielded. They're hard to classify, but only because they're so well suited to so many purposes.

There are hors-d'oeuvres and first courses aplenty here, but also some dishes around which a substantial meal can be arranged. The Italian Fondue is a garlicky, pungent variation of the classic Swiss dish and can be served with an antipasto and lots of bread and wine for some superb eating. Croquettes of all types are most often a winning first course, but it's really a question of how hungry you are and how elaborate a meal you want because they also work perfectly well as a light supper, gently sauced and accompanied by a salad.

The pâtés and all the different spiced and potted cheeses, on the other hand, are among the ideal foods to gather together on a groaning board for a festive and opulent cold buffet. When I was planning a gala Christmas party once and wanted to enjoy myself with my guests rather than lurk in the kitchen, I devised a menu for a rich and varied supper that could be prepared entirely in advance, most of it *days* ahead of time. The only hot dishes were a selection of soups; for the rest, there were a couple of pâtés, sliced and prettily garnished, some filled Edam cheeses and a wide assortment of cold vegetable dishes and salads. To this I added baskets of dark and light breads and plenty of butter, cases of champagne, music, and an abundance of mistletoe in every room, as well as one gloriously lighted Christmas tree, of course.

For a small and simple family meal or a hot, comforting lunch on a cold day, the little Russian *vareniki* or the Noodle Kugel are unsurpassed. Only a clear soup (borscht is nice) or simple salad and dark bread is required to turn either into a satisfying meal.

But for that even simpler supper or snack when you have no time or inclination to cook at all I have to recommend again the pâtés and spiced cheeses that serve so well on elaborate occasions. It is at those busiest times that we get hungriest (part of the natural cussedness of life), and even scrambled eggs or omelettes seem like too much trouble. That is when it's a real joy to open the refrigerator, pull out a few things that have been hiding there, and sup both deliciously and instantly. The pâtés keep well, if tightly wrapped and chilled, for at least a week or two (I've never been able to keep one around any longer than that). The spiced cheeses, especially those with any beer or wine in the mixture, only improve with age for a good, long time. Both are a most welcome sight in those desperate 'I want it now' moments; add some bread and butter, a pickle or chutney from the shelf, an appropriate beverage and sit down. Since all this type of thing is as easy to make in a large quantity as a small, a few extra hours in the kitchen once a month or so can take care of quite a few hungry moments later, and why shouldn't your midnight snacks be as delicious as any other repast?

For more on cheeses, see the ITALIAN section and SAVOURY PASTRIES: QUICHES, PIZZAS, PIEROGI.

A note about the white cheese used in some of the recipes in this section. These recipes require a fresh white cheese, firm enough to slice in blocks, but not hard or dry, and easy to crumble into moist (not soggy) bits. If you can get only a hard white cheese, simply moisten that with a few spoonfuls of cream. Suitable cheeses include Wensleydale, Caerphilly, Lancashire as well as various French and Italian cheeses. You may get a slightly different flavour depending on which cheese you use, so you can vary the recipe by using different cheeses.

MUSHROOM PÂTÉ: I

This makes a nice first course with pumpernickel bread and can also be used as a spread for canapés.

*1 lb/450 g fresh mushrooms,
  chopped*
⅓ cup celery, chopped
¼ cup minced parsley
⅓ cup minced shallots
2 oz/55 g butter, melted
2 eggs, lightly beaten
*½ cup sieved white cheese (see
  p. 204)*
¾ cup fine, dry breadcrumbs
¼ tsp basil, crushed

¼ tsp oregano, crushed
¼ tsp rosemary, crushed
1 tsp salt
pinch of cayenne pepper
*fresh-ground black pepper to
  taste*
GARNISH
parsley
thin radish slices or
thin carrot slices

Combine the mushrooms, celery and parsley and put them through the fine blade of a food mill.

Sauté the minced shallots in ½ oz/15 g of the butter until they are soft.

In a large mixing bowl combine the mushroom mixture and the shallots. Add the rest of the butter and all the remaining ingredients. Stir until everything is thoroughly blended.

Butter a medium-sized loaf tin. Line it with greaseproof paper, leaving a large enough edge to fold over the top. Butter the grease-proof paper.

Spoon the mushroom mixture evenly into the tin and fold the ends of the buttered paper over the top.

Bake the pâté for 1½ hours in a preheated oven at 400°F/200°C/Mark 6. Allow it to cool in the tin until it is easy to handle.

Carefully take it out of the tin and peel away the paper. Chill for a few hours before serving.

Serve on a board, garnished with parsley and decorated with thin radish or carrot slices.

MUSHROOM PÂTÉ: II

1 oz/25 g dried wild
  mushrooms
1 lb/450 g fresh mushrooms
¼–⅓ cup chopped fresh parsley
⅓ cup chopped celery
⅔ cup chopped walnuts
⅔ cup sieved white cheese (see
  p. 204)
1 cup dry breadcrumbs
⅓ cup minced shallots

2 oz/55 g butter
2 eggs, beaten
3 tbsp sweet vermouth
¼ tsp basil, crushed
¼ tsp oregano, crushed
¼ tsp rosemary, crushed
1¼ tsp salt
pinch of cayenne pepper
fresh-ground black pepper to
  taste

Soak the dried mushrooms in hot water for several hours. Drain them and wash them carefully. Wash the fresh mushrooms. Combine all the mushrooms, parsley, celery, walnuts, cheese and breadcrumbs and put the mixture through the finest blade of a food mill or blend in a food processor.

Sauté the shallots in the butter until they are golden and add them to the mushroom mixture, along with all the remaining ingredients. Stir everything together thoroughly.

Butter a medium-sized loaf tin, line it with greaseproof paper, leaving a large edge of paper round the top, and butter the paper. Spoon the mushroom mixture into the pan and fold the buttered paper loosely over the top. Bake the pâté for 1½ hours in a preheated oven at 400°F/200°C/Mark 6. Allow it to cool until it is easy to handle.

Carefully remove the pâté from the tin and peel away the paper. Chill the pâté for several hours before serving.

WHITE BEAN PÂTÉ

3 cups cooked white beans
2–3 spring onions, chopped
2 oz/55 g butter
1½ cups finely grated carrots
½ cup minced onion

3 cloves garlic, minced or
  pressed
¼ cup chopped parsley
2 eggs, lightly beaten
½ cup dry breadcrumbs

4 fl oz/115 ml single cream
1½ tsp salt
¼ tsp ground coriander
¼ tsp basil

¼ tsp thyme
3 tbsp beer
fresh-ground black pepper to
  taste

Put the beans and spring onions through the fine blade of a food mill. Melt the butter in a large frying pan and sauté the carrots, onions and garlic until soft.

Combine everything in a large bowl and stir thoroughly. The mixture should be quite thick.

Butter a round baking dish, about 8–10 in/200–250 mm across, and spoon the mixture in evenly. Butter a round of greaseproof paper and place it, buttered side down, on top of the pâté. Cover the dish with a lid and bake it in a preheated oven at 400°F/200°C/ Mark 6 for 50–55 minutes.

This pâté may be served warm or cold, from its dish or turned out on a plate.

EGG AND OLIVE MOULD

This is nice for a cold buffet and can also be used as a spread for canapés or sandwiches.

6 hard-boiled eggs
5 tbsp chopped green, pimiento-
  stuffed olives
3 tbsp chopped celery
3 tbsp chopped onion
2 tbsp chopped parsley
2 oz/55 g soft butter
¾ tsp salt, or more to taste

fresh-ground black pepper to
  taste
cayenne pepper to taste
GARNISH
parsley
sliced pickles or radishes
paprika
thin-sliced red pepper
sliced olives

Combine all the ingredients. Put the mixture through a food mill, using the fine blade. It may be necessary to put it through more than once to obtain a nice, homogeneous mixture. Taste, and correct the seasoning.

If you are serving it in a buffet, mound it on a plate or board and, using a butter knife, mould it into a smooth dome. Garnish with parsley, sliced pickles or radishes, and decorate with paprika, thin slices of red pepper, and sliced olives. If you are using it as a spread, just serve it in a little bowl.

EGG CROQUETTES

SERVES 6–8

2½ oz/70 g butter	fresh-ground black pepper to
¾ cup flour	taste
16 fl oz/450 ml warm milk	dash of nutmeg
1 raw egg	dash of cayenne pepper
6 hard-boiled eggs, sieved or	⅔ cup fine, dry breadcrumbs
finely chopped	flour (about ½ cup)
5 tbsp grated Parmesan cheese	2 eggs, beaten
5 tbsp chopped parsley	breadcrumbs (about 1½ cups)
1½ tsp salt	vegetable oil for deep frying

Melt the butter in a medium-sized, heavy-bottomed saucepan. Stir the flour in gradually until the mixture forms a soft ball and cook it for 3–4 minutes more, stirring constantly over very low heat. Add the warm milk, beating it in energetically with a whisk until the sauce is very thick and smooth.

Remove it from the heat and beat in the raw egg. Then add the sieved or chopped hard-boiled eggs, the Parmesan cheese, parsley, salt, pepper, nutmeg, cayenne and enough of the breadcrumbs to make a stiff mixture.

Form the croquettes by scooping out 1 rounded teaspoonful of the mixture and sliding it off with a second teaspoon into a small bowl of flour. Roll each croquette in flour, dip it in the beaten eggs, then roll it in breadcrumbs. Dip it into the beaten eggs again and roll it in the crumbs a second time.

Chill the croquettes for about 30 minutes, then fry them in deep, hot vegetable oil (without crowding them) until they are golden brown. Drain them on kitchen towels. The croquettes can be fried in advance and reheated in a hot oven for about 10 minutes.

Serve the croquettes hot with a thick chutney or on a bed of rice or creamed vegetables.

BRIE CROQUETTES

SERVES 6

12 fl oz/340 ml milk
½ cup flour
1½ oz/40 g butter
2 egg yolks
8 oz/225 g Brie, without rind
  (about 9–10 oz/255–285 g
  with the rind)
4 oz/115 g white cheese (see
  p. 204)
⅛–¼ tsp cayenne pepper

¼ tsp paprika
dash of nutmeg
¼ tsp salt
fresh-ground black pepper to
  taste
flour (about ½ cup)
3 eggs, beaten
1½–2 cups fine, dry
  breadcrumbs
vegetable oil for deep frying

Beat together the milk and flour until the mixture is smooth. Heat it in a medium-sized, heavy-bottomed saucepan, stirring all the while with a whisk until it thickens. As the mixture thickens, beat vigorously to work out lumps.

Remove from the heat and whisk in the butter and the egg yolks.

Mash the Brie with a wooden spoon until it is a smooth paste, put the white cheese through a sieve and stir the cheeses into the white sauce.

Heat the sauce gently, stirring constantly, until the cheeses are melted. Stir in the cayenne, paprika, nutmeg, salt and pepper.

Spread the mixture out evenly on a large plate and chill it until it is firm.

Scoop up about 1 tablespoonful of the mixture at a time and drop it into a bowl of flour. Shape it into a round or oval croquette, dip it in the beaten eggs, then roll it in the breadcrumbs until it is evenly coated. Continue until the cheese mixture is entirely used up, then start over and dip each croquette again into the beaten eggs and roll it again in the breadcrumbs. It is important to have a solid and even coating of breadcrumbs or the croquettes will leak when fried.

Fry the croquettes in hot oil for only a few minutes. Do as many at one time as will fit in the pan without crowding. They should be golden brown in colour. Drain them on kitchen towels and serve immediately with seasoned rice, on a bed of cooked vegetables or with a light sauce.

The croquettes can be reheated in the oven if desired.

CHICK-PEA CROQUETTES

Loosely based on the flavour combination found in *felafel*, these croquettes have the same attractive spiciness but less of a tendency to absorb oil, so the effect is not quite so heavy.

SERVES 6–8

⅓ cup dried bulgur wheat
5 fl oz/140 ml water
2 cups cooked chick-peas (see
  p. 152)
2 fl oz/55 ml fresh lemon juice
3 tbsp chopped fresh coriander
  leaves
1½ tsp crushed dried red chillis
½ tsp ground cumin
1 tsp salt

1½ oz/40 g butter
⅛ tsp cinnamon
1½ tsp fresh-minced garlic
3 tbsp flour
6 fl oz/170 ml hot Vegetable
  Broth (see pp. 60–61)
2 cups fine, dry breadcrumbs
2 eggs, lightly beaten
flour (about ⅔ cup)
vegetable oil for deep frying

Soak the bulgur wheat in the water for 20 minutes, then drain it in a fine sieve, pressing out all the excess moisture.

Mash the chick-peas with a potato masher and stir in the lemon juice, coriander leaves, chillis, cumin and salt.

Melt the butter in a small saucepan and add the cinnamon and garlic to it. Sauté for about 2 minutes, then stir in the 3 tablespoons flour.

Cook the roux over low heat for several minutes, stirring often, then stir in the vegetable broth. Continue cooking and stirring the sauce until it is thick and smooth. Add it to the chick-pea mixture, along with the soaked bulgur and ½ of the breadcrumbs. Stir the mixture thoroughly, taste and correct the seasoning if necessary. Chill the mixture for about 2 hours.

Put the beaten eggs in a small, shallow bowl, the flour in another one and the remaining breadcrumbs in a third. Scoop up the croquette mixture by rounded tablespoonfuls and roll each one into a ball – they should be about the size of large walnuts. Roll each ball in flour until it is well coated. When all the balls have been floured, take one at a time and dip it first in the beaten eggs, then roll it quickly in the breadcrumbs until it is completely encrusted.

Cook the croquettes in deep, hot vegetable oil, about 7–8 at a time, for 6–8 minutes or until they are crisp and golden brown all over. Drain them on kitchen towels and keep them warm in the oven while cooking the rest.

Serve the croquettes hot with a salad or with Chilled Buttermilk Soup (p. 92).

VARENIKI

Russian *vareniki* are like Italian ravioli: little pockets of pastry are filled with cheese.

SERVES 6

DOUGH
1½ cups flour
½ tsp salt
1 egg
4 tbsp water
½ oz/15 g butter, melted
FILLING
12 oz/340 g white cheese (see
  p. 204)

4 fl oz/115 ml soured cream
1 egg
pinch of salt
2½ tbsp sugar
1 oz/25 g butter, melted
additional melted butter

To make the dough, mix the flour and salt in a bowl and make a well in the centre. Beat together the egg and the water, put it in the centre of the flour and stir the flour into it gradually; the dough will be a hard, sticky mass. Add a little more water if necessary to incorporate all the flour, then add the melted butter and knead the dough in the bowl until it is fairly smooth. Turn it out on to a lightly floured board and continue kneading for 5–10 minutes, or until the dough is perfectly smooth and starting to feel elastic.

Prepare the filling by putting the cheese through a sieve, beating together the soured cream, egg, salt, sugar and 1 oz/25 g melted butter, and mixing everything thoroughly. Adjust seasoning.

Roll the dough out as thinly as possible on a lightly floured board and cut out 2-in/50-mm circles. Place a small spoonful of filling in the centre of each circle, brush the edge of the dough with a little water and fold the dough over the filling, pressing the moistened edges together firmly to seal it in a half-moon shape.

To cook the *vareniki*, drop them into 3½–5 pt/2–3 l of boiling, salted water and boil them for 12–15 minutes. Drain them thoroughly and serve them with melted butter.

ITALIAN FONDUE

Fine with just a good tossed salad, but for a really special meal, try this: prepare an antipasto assortment of, for example, Marinated Mushrooms (p. 154), Peperonata (p. 153), Chick-pea Salad (p. 152) and Insalatone (p. 157). Add some hot *peperoncini* and a few cured olives and serve everything at once, with a good Italian white wine. For dessert, fresh strawberries and cream, then espresso and a liqueur.

SERVES 5–6

2–3 cloves garlic
2 tbsp olive oil
½ lb/225 g fontina cheese, coarsely grated
½ lb/225 g provolone cheese, coarsely grated

3 tbsp flour
12 fl oz/340 ml dry Italian white wine
pepper to taste
large loaf French bread, cubed

About 2–3 hours before you want to make the fondue, mince the garlic until it is almost a paste and stir it into the olive oil. Toss the grated cheeses together with the flour.

Half an hour before you want to eat, heat the wine in a fondue pot or a medium-sized enamelled saucepan. Be careful to keep the heat *below* a simmer.

Add the cheese mixture, a handful at a time, and stir slowly with a wooden spoon until it is melted. When all the cheese is melted, stir in the olive oil and garlic and some pepper. Continue stirring slowly over low heat for about 15 minutes, or until the fondue is perfectly smooth; it should have a velvety texture. Place the fondue pot over a candle or other food warmer. Spear bread cubes with long forks and dip them, stirring the fondue each time.

NOODLE KUGEL

A kugel is a pudding-like dish, best eaten hot. Noodle Kugel is slightly sweet, but not a dessert. Try it for lunch, with a salad or some fruit.

SERVES 6

¾ lb/340 g flat egg noodles
3 eggs
¼ cup sugar
10½ oz/300 g white cheese,
  crumbled (see p. 204)
½ tsp salt

½ tsp cinnamon, and more for
  garnish
¼ tsp nutmeg
2 oz/55 g butter
soured cream (optional)

Dump the noodles into heavily salted boiling water and boil them for 8–10 minutes, or until they are tender but still firm. Drain them immediately.

Beat together lightly the eggs, sugar, crumbled cheese, salt, cinnamon and nutmeg. Cut ½ the butter into small bits. Stir together the noodles, the egg and cheese mixture, and the cut-up butter.

Preheat the oven to 350°F/180°C/Mark 4. Put ½ oz/15 g butter in a medium-sized casserole and heat it in the oven until the butter is melted. Tilt the casserole around so that the sides are coated with butter and spoon in the kugel mixture. Sprinkle a little more cinnamon on top and dot it with the remaining butter.

Bake the kugel for 25–30 minutes or until the top is golden brown.

BIBBELKÄSE
(Spiced White Cheese)

MAKES ABOUT 16 FL OZ/450 ML

16 fl oz/450 ml small-curd
  cottage cheese
6 tbsp soured cream
3 cloves garlic, minced or
  mashed to a pulp

2½ tbsp minced fresh parsley
minced chives (optional)
fresh-ground pepper to taste
salt to taste

Press the cottage cheese through a sieve and stir in the soured cream, garlic and parsley. If you have fresh chives, a spoonful of minced chives could be added to the mixture. Stir the mixture well. Grind in some pepper, add salt, stir again and put away in a covered container to chill for several hours in the refrigerator.

Serve the cheese with black bread and warn all people who are afraid of garlic.

LIPTAUER CHEESE: I

SERVES 8–10

8 oz/225 g large-curd cottage
  cheese, drained
3 oz/85 g cream cheese
1½ oz/40 g butter
1–1½ tsp French mustard, to
  taste
2 tbsp beer
1 tbsp minced capers

5 tbsp finely minced onion
1½ tsp paprika
cayenne pepper to taste
¼–½ tsp ground cumin or
  caraway seeds to taste
GARNISH
paprika and sprigs of parsley

Put the cottage cheese through a sieve. Work in the cream cheese and butter until you have a smooth, homogeneous mixture.

Add all the remaining ingredients and combine thoroughly. Put the cheese into the refrigerator in a tightly covered container and let ripen for at least 24 hours.

To serve, mound the cheese on a plate, shaping it with the side of a knife until it is smooth. Sprinkle with a little paprika, garnish with parsley and serve with pumpernickel bread.

LIPTAUER CHEESE: II

Here is yet another version of Liptauer Cheese, for which so many variations have been devised. The rich flavour of this one is owed largely to the Camembert – but don't use a Camembert that is too ripe, or the mixture will be runny.

SERVES 10–12

8 oz/225 g Camembert cheese
  (medium ripe)
10 oz/285 g white cheese (see
  p. 204)
2 oz/55 g soft butter
2–3 tbsp dark beer
1 tsp paprika
1 tsp dry mustard

1½ tbsp minced capers
2 tbsp minced onion
salt
black pepper
½ tsp caraway seeds, crushed
GARNISH
paprika

Scrape or slice the crust off the Camembert and put the cheese in a bowl. Crumble the white cheese and add it to the Camembert, along with the soft butter. Mash the cheeses and butter together with a fork until the mixture is fairly smooth, then add a little beer, more or less depending on the consistency of the cheeses. With the addition of the beer, the mixture should be soft enough to spread, but stiff enough to hold a shape. Add the paprika, mustard, capers, onions, a little salt and pepper to taste and the caraway seeds. Mix thoroughly and mound the cheese on a plate, smoothing it with a wide, blunt knife to a nice round or oval shape. Cover and chill for several hours, or until the next day.

Sprinkle the cheese with a little more paprika to decorate it and serve it with thin buttered slices of black bread.

SPICED CHEDDAR
AND EDAM CHEESE

MAKES ABOUT 1¾ LB/800 G

½ lb/225 g Cheddar cheese
½ lb/225 g Edam cheese
4 oz/115 g soft butter
4½ fl oz/130 ml beer
1½ tsp caraway seeds

½ tsp dry mustard
¼ tsp ground cumin
½ tsp celery seeds, crushed
1 clove garlic, finely minced
dash of Tabasco sauce

Finely grate or grind the cheeses. Cream together the cheeses, butter and beer until the mixture is a smooth paste.

Dry roast the caraway seeds by spreading them in a frying pan and gently stirring them over a medium heat for a few minutes. Add the caraway seeds and all the rest of the spices to the cheese mixture and stir (or spin in a food processor) until everything is well blended. Pack into small crocks and store in the refrigerator.

For a milder version, omit the garlic, Tabasco and caraway seeds.

ANOTHER WAY
To make cheese balls, either 1 large one or a number of small ones for hors-d'oeuvres, first chill the mixture well and shape into a ball (or balls). Then roll in a half-and-half mixture of finely chopped walnuts and parsley and chill again.

FILLED EDAM

1½ lb/680 g round Edam
   cheese
½ lb/225 g soft butter
4 fl oz/115 ml brandy
2 tsp sweet paprika
pinch of hot paprika
½ tsp dry mustard

½ tsp celery seeds, finely
   ground in a mortar
salt to taste
3 tbsp sweet sherry
1 tsp sugar
GARNISH
strips of red pepper

Cut off the top third of a large, round Edam and carefully scoop out the cheese, leaving a ¼-in/6-mm shell. Grind or grate the cheese.

In a large bowl, work the butter into the grated cheese. Add the remaining ingredients and stir the mixture vigorously or work it by hand until everything is thoroughly combined. The cheese mixture should be quite smooth and light.

Spoon the cheese back into the large shell, piling it high on top and forming a smooth dome. Cover it with cling film or foil and put it away in the refrigerator for about 1 week.

Remove the cheese from the refrigerator several hours before serving and decorate it with strips of red pepper. Serve at room temperature with pumpernickel or rye bread.

MAMALYGA

This is one of those refreshing cold dishes so welcome during the summer heat: pleasant and filling but not overpowering. A Russian peasant dish, it goes well with a light, cool borscht or a fruit soup.

SERVES 8–10

¾ cup yellow corn-meal
2–2½ pt/1.25–1.4 l water
1–1¼ tsp salt, and more to
    taste
½ tsp sugar

2 oz/55 ml butter
¾ lb/340 g white cheese,
    crumbled (see p. 204)
8 fl oz/225 ml soured cream
black pepper

Stir together in a saucepan the corn-meal and 2 pt/1.25 l of water. Heat the mixture slowly, stirring often, until it is simmering. Add about 1 teaspoon of the salt, the sugar and the butter, and continue simmering the mixture gently, still stirring frequently, for 35–40 minutes. The corn-meal mush should have the consistency of a thin custard. If it feels stiff or very grainy, stir in a little more water.

Pour the mush into a smooth-surfaced bowl or casserole and allow it to cool completely. It will jell into a solid mould. Chill it if desired.

When it is quite cool and firm, turn the corn-meal mould out on to a plate and slice it thickly. For each serving, cover 1 thick slice of corn-meal with a few spoonfuls of crumbled cheese, a large dollop of soured cream and black pepper to taste.

Spiced Farmer Cheese

¾ lb/340 g white cheese (see
  p. 204)
8 fl oz/225 ml soured cream
1 tbsp minced fresh dill weed
⅓ cup chopped chives

1 tsp lemon juice
¼ tsp hot paprika
salt to taste
fresh-ground black pepper to
  taste

Combine the cheese and the soured cream and mash them together thoroughly with a fork until all the large lumps of cheese are broken up. Add the remaining ingredients and stir vigorously until the mixture is smooth and thoroughly blended. Chill the cheese lightly before serving it.

This makes a delicious spread for any kind of rye or pumpernickel bread and keeps for a couple of weeks if covered and refrigerated.

Cocktail Profiteroles

If there is a good bakery nearby which can supply you with cocktail-sized puffs, by all means buy them and save yourself the trouble. Your time will be better spent making the delicious filling. However, if you insist, here is a reasonably easy way of making puff pastry with the help of a food processor.

MAKES ABOUT 42 PROFITEROLES

PROFITEROLE PUFF DOUGH
8 fl oz/225 ml water
4 oz/115 g butter
½ tsp salt
1½ tsp sugar
1 cup plus 2 tbsp flour
4 eggs
FILLING
6 hard-boiled eggs, peeled and
  chopped

½ cup finely chopped fresh parsley
⅓ cup finely chopped marinated
  mushrooms
⅔ cup chopped cooked asparagus
2 oz/55 g butter, melted
¾ tsp salt
1 tbsp white wine vinegar
fresh-ground black pepper to
  taste

Put the water, butter, salt and sugar into a medium-sized saucepan and bring to a boil. As soon as the butter is melted, reduce the heat to a simmer and dump in the flour, all at once. Stir quickly with a wooden spoon until the mixture forms a smooth, homogeneous ball. Continue stirring and pressing the dough against the sides of the saucepan for about 3–4 minutes. Turn off the heat and let the dough rest for about 5 minutes.

Put the steel blade into the food processor and transfer the dough to the container. Process it for about 20 seconds. Add the eggs and process for about 50 seconds. The dough is now ready to use.

To make puffs for profiteroles, butter several large baking sheets and preheat the oven to 375°F/190°C/Mark 5. Using a pastry bag or 2 teaspoons, form balls of dough about the size of very small walnuts. If you are not using a pastry bag and have trouble forming smooth balls, butter your hands and roll the balls lightly and quickly between the palms of your hands until their shape is right.

Arrange the balls about 1½ in/37 mm apart on the buttered sheets and bake them for 20–30 minutes; they should be puffed and a light golden brown in colour. With the point of a sharp knife, make a little slit in the side of each puff and leave them in a warm, turned-off oven for another 15–20 minutes to dry out inside.

Slice off the top halves of the puffs, leaving them barely connected at one side so that they can be opened up and stuffed.

For the filling, combine the chopped eggs, chopped parsley, chopped marinated mushrooms and chopped asparagus in a large bowl. Pour the melted butter over this mixture and toss it lightly.

Add the salt and white wine vinegar, grate plenty of black pepper over it and toss again or stir carefully until everything is well combined. Taste and add more salt or vinegar if desired.

Place a slightly rounded teaspoonful of this filling inside each puff and press the top of the puff down just a bit into the filling so that it stays where it belongs.

Serve the cold Cocktail Profiteroles with cocktails (what else?), or with chilled white wine as a first course.

SAVOURY PASTRIES:
QUICHES,
PIZZAS, PIEROGI

To make a quiche you need only some rudimentary baking skills. As long as you have a decent oven, know how to make a pastry crust and see to it that the shell is large enough to hold the filling, the basic quiche is easily within your powers. All in all, when you consider how good a quiche can taste, what a pretty picture it makes when served and how altogether versatile and convenient it is, you will see that it doesn't cost much in effort for all those rewards. Besides making lovely lunches, hors-d'oeuvres and dinner or supper dishes, quiches are also many people's favourite picnic food, as they are nearly always just as tempting cold as they are hot.

While you should stick to the rules in preparing the crust and the custard, you can be as innovative as you like in dressing up the filling. A simple and mouth-watering quiche can be made with a filling of nothing but eggs, cream, cheese and a touch of flour, seasoned with a bit of salt and pepper. On the other hand, practically anything you happen to have in the larder can probably be successfully incorporated into the egg and cream mixture, so long as you use common sense.

I've used many different cheeses and vegetables, and combinations of both, and have never yet made a quiche that wasn't happily eaten down to the last crumb. I'm not sure why it's so, but there is something nearly irresistible about that combination of a baked dough or crust with a savoury filling or topping. It's an idea that is universally popular, and a hot, tender-crusted quiche is but one example. In Greece very flaky pastry is layered with feta cheese or spinach fillings and baked in the form of large pies or small turnovers. Polish and Russian cooking is full of *pierogi*, or *piroshki*, which are made by wrapping a yeast dough or shortcrust pastry around any of a variety of stuffings. In Hong Kong, Singapore and China *dim-sum* – filled dumplings that are usually steamed – are eaten with mid-morning tea.

The Italian pizza is one of the glories of the genre. I've heard that pizza first came into existence when bread was baked in large batches in a communal village bread oven. On bread-making day the busy housewife wouldn't have much time left to cook dinner, so she would take a piece of the bread dough, flatten it out, moisten it with a sauce and heap on it whatever left-overs she might have. Then it would be baked in the hot oven, together with the loaves, and supper was ready. It's one of those stories that makes so much sense that one can only say that if it isn't true, it should be.

When we were in Verona, in the elegant north and far from Naples, the world capital of pizza making, we saw an amusing picture of the popularity that pizza enjoys in its native land. We went to see the Scaligeri family tombs, which have been marked for seven centuries by the famous and beautiful equestrian statue of Mastino della Scalla, founder of the Scaligeri dynasty.* Depicted in his medieval armour, with a tall, pointed helmet dropped back off his head, Mastino is a stern-looking man. His armoured and hooded horse, however, looks down on passers-by with a droll, sleepy-eyed expression. The statue, one of Verona's major tourist attractions, is well loved by the Veronese people.

Nearby there is a popular pizzeria, and one of the large walls in this restaurant is painted with a mural of people from all over Italy happily eating their pizza. In the centre of the mural is an affection-ate, larger-than-life portrayal of Mastino, who has dismounted and is smilingly feeding his droopy-eyed horse a large slice of pizza. The mural is an appealing expression of the Italians' fondness for pizza – and of their wit.

*The original statue is now protected in a museum, but an exact replica stands in its traditional place.

BASIC SHORTCRUST PASTRY

MAKES ENOUGH DOUGH FOR
1 (11–12-IN/275–300-MM) QUICHE SHELL

1½ cups flour
½–¾ tsp salt

4 oz/115 g butter, well chilled
2½ fl oz/70 ml ice water

Sift together the flour and the salt. Slice the cold butter rapidly and drop the slices into the flour. With a pastry blender or two sharp knives, cut in the butter until the mixture resembles coarse breadcrumbs.

Sprinkle the ice water over the flour-butter mixture and stir it in very quickly with a fork, until the dough gathers together. Form the dough into a ball, wrap it in wax paper or foil and chill it for about 2 hours.

PREPARING A QUICHE OR TART SHELL

On a lightly floured surface, roll the chilled dough out in a circle about 2½ in/62 mm larger than your quiche or flan tin. (I like to use an 11–12-in/275–300-mm tin.) Roll the circle of dough loosely round your rolling pin and unroll it over the quiche tin, centring it as well as possible. Press the sides in against the rim of the tin, pushing the extra dough down a bit to make an edge that is slightly thicker than the bottom. Trim the dough off with a sharp knife, about ¼ in/6 mm above the rim of the tin.

Using a pastry crimper or the blunt end of a kitchen knife, crimp the ridge of dough neatly just above the rim of the tin. Prick the bottom of the shell all over with a fork and chill the shell for 30 minutes.

PRE-BAKING A QUICHE OR TART SHELL

Line the inside of the pastry shell with a piece of aluminium foil and fill it with dried beans or rice (which can be kept in a jar and reused for this purpose for ever). Bake the shell in a preheated oven at 450°F/230°C/Mark 8 for about 8 minutes, then remove the beans and foil, prick again with a fork and return to the hot oven for another 4–5 minutes or until the bottom of the shell begins to colour. Allow the shell to cool slightly on a rack, then fill and finish baking according to recipe.

ROQUEFORT QUICHE

SERVES 6–8

1 recipe Basic Shortcrust Pastry
  (p. 225)
¼ lb/115 g Roquefort cheese,
  crumbled
½ lb/225 g dry curd cheese,
  crumbled

6 fl oz/170 ml milk
4 large eggs
salt to taste

Prepare the pastry, line an 11-in/275-mm quiche tin with it and pre-bake according to instructions on p. 225.

Combine the crumbled cheeses. Beat together the milk and eggs, with a little pinch of salt. Spread the crumbled cheeses evenly over the bottom of the quiche shell and pour the custard carefully over them.

Bake the quiche in a preheated oven at 375 °F/190°C/Mark 5 for 40 to 45 minutes. The filling should be puffed and rather firm, and the top golden brown. Serve either warm or cool as a first course, or with ripe fruit for an unusual dessert.

LEEK AND TOMATO QUICHE

SERVES 6

1 recipe Basic Shortcrust Pastry
  (p. 225)
2 cups sliced leeks (3 or 4
  large)
1 oz/25 g butter
salt and pepper to taste
½ lb/225 g Gruyère cheese

1 oz/25 g pecorino romano or
  Parmesan cheese
1 tbsp flour
4 eggs
14 fl oz/400 ml single cream
  or rich milk
2 tomatoes, thinly sliced

Prepare the pastry, line an 11-in/275-mm quiche tin with it and pre-bake according to instructions on p. 225.

Split the leeks lengthways, wash them carefully, trim away the tough green parts and thinly slice enough to measure 2 cups. Sauté them in the butter until they start to turn golden, season them with salt and pepper.

Grate the cheeses and toss them with the flour. Beat together the eggs, cream and a little salt.

Spread the sautéd leeks evenly across the bottom of the quiche shell and spread the cheeses evenly over that. Pour the custard over the cheese and leeks and cover the top with a layer of thinly sliced, lightly salted tomatoes. Grind on a little pepper.

Bake the quiche for 15 minutes in a preheated oven at 400°F/200°C/Mark 6, reduce the temperature to 325°F/170°C/Mark 3 and bake for another 30 minutes or until a knife inserted in the centre comes out clean. Serve warm or at room temperature.

RED PEPPER AND OLIVE QUICHE

SERVES 6–8

1 recipe Basic Shortcrust Pastry
 (p. 225)
1 large onion, peeled, halved and
 sliced
2 cloves garlic, peeled and thinly
 sliced
2 tbsp olive oil
½ lb/225 g Gruyère cheese,
 coarsely grated

2 eggs
8 fl oz/225 ml single cream
salt and pepper to taste
½ cup sliced red pepper, grilled
 and peeled
¼ cup sliced, cured Greek black
 olives

Prepare the pastry, line an 11-in/275-mm quiche tin with it and pre-bake according to instructions on p. 225.

Sauté the sliced onions and garlic in the olive oil until they are golden brown. Distribute them evenly over the bottom of the pastry shell. Spread the grated cheese over the onions and garlic.

Beat the eggs and cream together with a little salt and pepper and pour them over the cheese. Arrange the sliced red pepper and olives on top of the cheese in an attractive pattern and bake the quiche for 15 minutes in a preheated oven at 450°F/230°C/Mark 8, then reduce the heat to 350°F/180°C/Mark 4 and bake for 10–15 minutes or until the top of the quiche is lightly browned in spots.

The quiche may be served hot, but I think it's better if it is allowed to cool to room temperature or chilled before serving.

CHEESE AND TOMATO PIE

Call it either a quiche or a pizza, it is one of the most delicious pies around.

SERVES 6–8

1 recipe Basic Shortcrust Pastry (p. 225)

3 lb/1.25 kg ripe tomatoes, peeled and seeded

3 tbsp olive oil

1 clove garlic, crushed or minced

¾ tsp salt

2 tbsp chopped fresh parsley

2½ tsp dried basil

fresh-ground black pepper to taste

1 lb/450 g onions

1 oz/25 g butter

⅓ cup grated Parmesan cheese

½ lb/225 g mozzarella cheese

12 cured black olives

Prepare the pastry, line an 11-in/275-mm quiche tin with it and pre-bake according to instructions on p. 225.

Chop the tomatoes coarsely, reserving their juice. Heat the olive oil in a large saucepan and sauté the garlic in it for a few minutes. Add the tomatoes and their juice, ½ teaspoon of the salt, the parsley, basil and a little fresh-ground black pepper. Simmer this sauce, stirring occasionally, until it is reduced by about half. It should be quite thick.

Peel, halve and thickly slice the onions. Sauté them in the butter until they are golden and sprinkle them with the remaining salt.

Sprinkle the Parmesan cheese over the bottom of the quiche shell. Arrange the sautéd onion slices over it in an even layer. Cover the onions with the tomato sauce.

Cut the mozzarella in thin strips and arrange them evenly on top of the tomato sauce. Slice the olives off their pits and sprinkle the olive bits over the mozzarella cheese.

Bake the pie for 35 minutes in a preheated oven at 375°F/190°C/ Mark 5 and serve it hot.

SWEET POTATO
AND CRANBERRY QUICHE

Here is an unusual quiche, somewhat sweet, somewhat savoury.
Serve it warm or cool, alone or with cream, as an hors-d'oeuvre, an
accompaniment to soup, with tea or even as a dessert. This is truly
the all-purpose quiche.

SERVES 6–8

1 recipe Basic Shortcrust Pastry
  (p. 225)
½ lb/225 g sweet potatoes
  (about 2 small)
½ lb/225 g carrots (about 3
  medium sized)
½ lb/225 g cranberries

⅔ cup sugar
4 fl oz/115 ml milk
4 eggs
½ lb/225 g soft cream cheese
dash of nutmeg
dash of salt

Prepare the pastry, line an 11-in/275-mm quiche tin with it, and
pre-bake according to instructions on p. 225.

Peel the sweet potatoes and carrots and either grate them or
chop them finely. Put the vegetables in a saucepan, douse them with
boiling, salted water, bring to a boil and cook the vegetables 5
minutes, then drain them.

Wash the cranberries and pick out any that are soft or blemished.
Put them in an enamelled saucepan with the sugar and cook them,
covered, over low heat for 10 minutes, stirring occasionally. Remove
the lid and cook the berries for 5 minutes more, stirring almost
constantly.

Add the potatoes and carrots and cook for 3–4 minutes more,
stirring constantly.

Beat together the milk, eggs, cream cheese, a little nutmeg and a
tiny bit of salt. Stir in the vegetable mixture and pour the filling
carefully into the prepared shell.

Bake the quiche in a preheated oven at 375°F/190°C/Mark 5 for
40 minutes or until the top is golden and the filling firm.

PIZZA

MAKES 2 LARGE PIZZAS

CRUST
1 tbsp dried yeast
½ pt/285 ml warm water
2 tsp sugar
3 cups flour
1½ tsp salt
1 tbsp olive oil
sesame seeds

SAUCE
16 fl oz/450 ml thick puréed
    tomatoes
4 fl oz/115 ml tomato paste
1½ cups coarsely chopped,
    peeled tomatoes
1 tsp salt
1 tsp oregano, crushed
1 tsp basil, crushed
¼ tsp thyme
dash of marjoram
dash of ground cinnamon
2 tbsp wine vinegar
1 tsp sugar
2 cloves garlic, crushed or
    minced
fresh-ground black pepper to
    taste

TOPPING
1 large aubergine
plenty of salt
2 tbsp olive oil
1 medium-sized onion
1 large green pepper
¾ lb/340 g mozzarella cheese

To prepare the crust, dissolve the yeast in 4 fl oz/115 ml of the warm water, add the sugar and leave it for 10 minutes. Put the dissolved yeast in a large, warm bowl with the rest of the water. Mix the flour and the salt together and start stirring it into the liquid gradually. Keep adding flour until the mixture is too stiff to stir. Knead it in the bowl briefly, then add the olive oil and continue kneading until the dough is smooth and elastic, adding a little more flour if necessary. Form the dough into a ball, brush it with oil, cover it and leave it to rise in a warm place for 1 hour or until it doubles in size.

Punch the dough down (see p. 29) and divide it in half. Put the 2 balls of dough on a large, lightly floured board and roll them out into circles. When the dough starts to pull back, cover it with a tea-towel and let it rest for 5–10 minutes, then roll it again. As the circles of dough start to approach the right size, about 16 in/ 400 mm across, they can be lifted up and gently stretched over the back of your hands.

When the dough is about ¼ in/6 mm thick, stop stretching it, adjust the shape as well as you can and prepare the tins by oiling them with olive oil and sprinkling them with sesame seeds. Put the circles of dough on the tins.

The sauce and the topping can be prepared while the dough for the crust is rising. To prepare the sauce, simply combine all the ingredients and stir them together very thoroughly. The sauce should be thick, not watery.

To prepare the topping, first peel the aubergine and slice ¼ in/ 6 mm thick. Salt the slices liberally and let them drain in a colander for 30 minutes. Rinse the slices quickly, press out the excess moisture between the palms of your hands and cut them in ½-in/ 12-mm dice. Heat the olive oil in a large frying pan and sauté the aubergine in it, tossing and stirring constantly, for about 5 minutes.

Peel and chop the onion. Core, seed and dice the green pepper. Grate the mozzarella cheese.

Spread the dough evenly with tomato sauce, aubergine, onions, peppers and, finally, grated cheese.

Bake the pizzas in a preheated oven at 425°F/220°C/Mark 7 for 15–20 minutes, or until the crust is crisp on the edges and bottom and the cheese is bubbling and turning golden brown.

YEAST PIEROGI

Pierogi are a Polish type of savoury pastry, which can be made with almost any kind of filling. Some are boiled in salted water, others fried in butter, but these are made with a yeast dough and baked. They can be served hot, warm or at room temperature and make a good accompaniment to soup, or they can be served as a course on their own. A selection of *pierogi*, served warm with a salad or a vegetable stew, makes a hearty supper.

YEAST DOUGH
1 tbsp dried yeast
2 fl oz/55 ml warm water
2½ tbsp sugar
6 fl oz/170 ml milk

4 oz/115 g butter
1½ tsp salt
4–5 cups flour
2 whole eggs
1 egg yolk

Dissolve the yeast in the warm water with 1 teaspoon of the sugar and leave it for 10 minutes. Heat the milk with the butter, the remaining sugar and the salt until the butter is melted. Allow the mixture to cool to lukewarm.

Gradually beat about 2 cups of the flour into the milk mixture and when the dough is smooth, stir in the dissolved yeast. Then beat in the eggs and the egg yolk, and continue beating, either by hand or with a heavy-duty mixer, for several minutes.

Turn the dough out on to a heavily floured board, cover it with more flour and begin kneading. Knead for about 10–15 minutes, working in as much of the remaining flour as needed to make a smooth, satiny, elastic dough.

Form the dough into a ball, brush it lightly with melted butter, put it in a bowl, cover it and chill it for several hours.

When you are ready to make the *pierogi*, take out the dough, punch it down (see p. 29) and roll it out on a floured board to a thickness of no more than ¼ in/6 mm. Cut out rounds about 3½–4 in/ 85–100 mm across. If the dough pulls together too much when the rounds are cut, roll each one a bit more, just before filling it, to make it thin again.

MUSHROOM FILLING
1½ oz/40 g dried wild
  mushrooms
½ lb/225 g fresh mushrooms
2 slices dark bread

1¼ oz/35 g butter
1 medium-sized onion, chopped
1 clove garlic, minced
plenty of salt and pepper
dill weed

Soak the dried mushrooms in hot water for about 1 hour, then rinse them carefully. Wash and trim the fresh mushrooms. Put all the mushrooms through a food mill, using the fine blade, and then put through the dark bread, torn into chunks.

Melt the butter in a large frying pan and sauté the onions and garlic in it until the onions are golden. Add the mushroom and bread mixture and season to taste with salt, pepper and dill weed. Cook the mixture over low heat for 20–30 minutes, or until the mushrooms are tender and the mixture is thick. Taste, and correct seasoning.

CABBAGE FILLING
1 large onion
1½ oz/40 g butter
3 cups finely shredded cabbage, packed

plenty of salt and fresh-ground black pepper
2 hard-boiled eggs
2 tbsp chopped fresh dill or 2 tsp dried

Finely chop the onion and sauté it in the butter until it is golden. Add the cabbage and a liberal amount of salt and pepper. Cover the pan and cook the vegetables over a low heat, stirring occasionally, for about 30 minutes.

Let the mixture cool slightly. Sieve the hard-boiled eggs and stir them into the cabbage along with the dill. Taste, and correct seasoning.

Note: The feta cheese filling for crêpes (see p. 241) can also be used as a filling for *pierogi*.

MAKING THE PIEROGI
Place a heaped tablespoon of filling in the centre of each round. Fold the top of the dough over the filling, bring up the sides and then bring up the bottom, overlapping the edges just slightly. Pinch the dough together where it meets and be sure that the seams are well sealed. When they are, shape the *pierogi* with your hands to make them smooth and rounded.

Place the *pierogi*, seam side down, on a buttered and floured baking sheet. Cover them with a towel and let them rise for about 30 minutes.

Make a glaze by beating together 1 egg and 1 tablespoonful of milk or single cream. Brush the *pierogi* with the glaze and bake them in a preheated oven at 375°F/190°C/Mark 5 for 30 minutes or until the crusts are golden brown and shiny.

Crêpes

Today everywhere one looks, one sees crêpe restaurants, crêpe cookery books, crêpe pans for sale. The delectable thin pancake that was too often reserved for dessert in a fancy restaurant, in the form of Crêpes Suzette, is now turning up with frequency at breakfast, lunch and supper, as well as brunch. I even had a friend phone me recently and say, 'Quick, give me some recipes for crêpe fillings. I'm going to a party today where the hostess is going to make crêpes and all the guests have to bring something good to put in them.'

You might think we'd all be sick of them soon, but because crêpes have such a mild, delicate flavour and commendable tenderness, there is hardly a soul who does not like to find a plateful of them served up, the more often the better. And since they combine so agreeably with almost any other food, there are always imaginative new ways of serving them, no two tasting quite alike.

What's more, crêpes are marvellously convenient. They all take a certain amount of preparation time, but most of the work can be done in advance. The crêpes themselves can be made a day or two ahead and kept tightly wrapped in the refrigerator. Since filled crêpes are nearly always heated again with their filling, it is not essential that they be warm, but they should be allowed to reach room temperature for easy folding or rolling. The fillings and sauces, likewise, can generally be prepared hours in advance, and usually the crêpes can be stuffed well before mealtime, leaving only the final sautéing and saucing for the last minute. This flexibility of preparation is a great boon, allowing an elegant and appetizing meal without keeping the cook in the kitchen, sweating and grumbling for hours before the meal and during great parts of it, while the others drink all the wine and enjoy themselves.

As for what can be done with a crêpe, the recipes in this chapter are only a beginning. Any filling that is delicious in an omelette, for example, will be equally tasty in a crêpe; flip through the omelette section and see what appeals. The amount of filling you use for one individual omelette is about what you'll need for one medium-sized crêpe, though the proportions will vary according to your own taste. In general, the mixtures from which you make croquettes will also make excellent stuffed crêpes. Place a few spoonfuls of such a stuffing in the middle of a crêpe and fold the crêpe round it envelope-style, rolling it up and tucking in the sides. Sauté the filled crêpes slowly on both sides, until they are hot all the way through, and there you are, with a new dish.

Delightful fruit crêpes can be made by cooking fresh fruit with a little butter and sugar, just until it is hot and tender, then folding it in a hot crêpe and serving with a little soured cream on top. These are marvellous for breakfast, but add a little liqueur to the filling and garnish the crêpes with whipped cream instead of soured cream and you've made an extravagant dessert. Sliced apples, strawberries, cherries, bananas, peaches and pears are all suitable for this method, and discreet additions of cinnamon or nutmeg can make a pleasant variation in flavour. If that seems too much trouble, you can also spread crêpes with a good jam or marmalade, fold them in quarters, sauté them quickly in butter on both sides, plop a spoonful of soured cream on top and you have a dessert so easy that it practically makes itself. (For more on dessert crêpes, see the DESSERTS section, where you'll find Hungarian Walnut Crêpes, Fresh Lemon Dessert Crêpes and Apple-sauce Crêpes.)

BASIC CRÊPES

This batter is slightly different from the one in my first book, and I've had great success with it. The crêpes are tender and easy to handle and reheat very well. A touch of sugar enhances the delicate flavour but isn't enough to make them actually taste sweet, and so they can be used for entrées or desserts equally well.

MAKES 15–18 7-IN/175-MM CRÊPES

3 large eggs	*1 cup flour*
5½ fl oz/155 ml milk	*½ oz/15 g butter, melted*
2½ fl oz/70 ml single cream	*1 tbsp sugar*
4 fl oz/115 ml water	*2 tbsp cognac*
½ tsp salt	*extra butter for the pan*

Beat the eggs, then beat in the milk, cream, water and salt. When the mixture is well blended, add the flour gradually, whisking it in until the batter is perfectly smooth. Or combine all these ingredients in a blender. Stir in the melted butter, sugar and cognac and leave the batter to rest for at least 2 hours.

Heat your crêpe pan and melt a piece of butter in it. As soon as the foam subsides, pour a small amount of batter into the pan, then quickly but gently tilt it around so that the batter spreads evenly over the bottom of the pan. (I use about 2½–3 tablespoons of batter for a 7-in/175-mm pan.)

Cook the crêpe over medium heat for about a minute. Loosen the edge by running a knife or thin spatula under it, turn the crêpe over and cook on the other side for just under 1 minute. The crêpe should be golden, with golden brown spots here and there.

Brush the pan with a tiny bit of butter between crêpes. If the butter sizzles violently and starts to brown immediately, the pan is too hot and the batter will not spread evenly in it. If, however, the batter does not start to congeal and coat the pan right away as it is swirled round, the pan is too cool. You may have to make 2–3 crêpes before the heat is perfectly adjusted, but after that it all goes quickly and smoothly.

The crêpes can be used immediately, kept warm in the oven for a while or refrigerated and reheated later. To keep crêpes warm, stack them on a plate, cover them with a very slightly damp tea-towel and put them in a warm oven. To reheat crêpes, wrap them air-tight in foil and put them in a moderate oven for 15–20 minutes, or until all of them are hot to the touch, even the ones in the middle of the pile.

PARMESAN CRÊPES

Parmesan crêpes are a treat just as they come from the pan and even better when doused with tomato or mushroom sauce. But they are also delicious when wrapped round almost any of the savoury fillings that follow.

MAKES 20–24 CRÊPES

1 cup flour	*1½ oz/40 g butter, melted*
1 tsp salt	*½ cup finely grated Parmesan*
6 eggs, beaten	*cheese*
1⅓ pt/680 ml milk	*butter for the pan*

Sift the flour and salt into a bowl and stir in the beaten eggs. Add the milk slowly, beating with a whisk, then beat in the melted butter and the grated Parmesan. The batter should be smooth and have the consistency of thick cream. Let the batter stand for 1–2 hours before making the crêpes.

Heat your crêpe pan and melt about ¼ oz/8 g butter in it. When the butter is melted and the foam has subsided, pour in about 3 tablespoons of the batter and swirl it round to the edges of the pan immediately. The crêpe should cook about 1 minute or so on each side.

Add a bit of butter to the pan between crêpes to avoid sticking. Stack the crêpes on a plate as you make them. The crêpes can be kept warm in the oven until all of them are done if you intend to eat them right away, or they can be reheated like any other crêpes (see Basic Crêpes), wrapped tightly in foil and put in a moderate oven for about 10 minutes.

Furthermore, they can be wrapped around asparagus, spread with feta cheese filling and folded up, rolled round a stuffing of hearts of artichoke and palm or of creamed mushrooms, and they can be used in constructing a savoury crêpe cake, to be cut in wedges.

CRÊPES WITH FETA CHEESE

SERVES 4–6

12 oz/340 g (about 2 cups),
  mild white cheese, crumbled
  (see p. 204)
6 oz/170 g (about 1 cup)
  feta cheese, crumbled
3 tbsp olive oil
2 eggs, lightly beaten
½ tsp dried oregano, crushed
½ tsp dried dill weed, crushed

2 cloves garlic, minced or
  crushed
fresh-ground black pepper to
  taste
12 crêpes (see p. 239)
butter for the pan
GARNISH
wedges of honeydew melon or
  cantaloup

Mash the cheeses with a fork until there are no large lumps left. Stir in the olive oil, eggs and seasonings, combining everything thoroughly. Do not add salt, as the feta cheese is already very salty.

Spread a heaped teaspoonful of the filling evenly on ½ of a crêpe and fold the other ½ over it. Now take a slightly rounded teaspoonful of filling and again spread it on ½ the surface of the folded crêpe. Fold the crêpe over this second layer of filling, so that it is folded in quarters, layered with cheese.

Fill all 12 crêpes in this manner. Just before serving, sauté the folded crêpes in butter for several minutes on each side. They should be lightly browned and hot through. Garnish each serving of crêpes with a wedge of honeydew or cantaloup melon.

ASPARAGUS CRÊPES

SERVES 6

1 ½ lb/680 g fresh asparagus
  (24–30 medium-sized stalks)
½ lb/225 g Gruyère cheese
12 crêpes (see p. 239)
butter for the pan

hot Cucumber-Avocado Sauce
  (p. 108)
GARNISH
thin wedges of melon and ripe
  strawberries

Trim the asparagus stalks so that they are an even length – about 7–8 in/175–200 mm. Peel the lower parts of the stalks thinly. Cook the asparagus in salted boiling water for 8–10 minutes (longer if they are thick) until tender but firm. Drain the stalks immediately.

Grate the cheese or cut it in small, very thin slices. Cut the asparagus stalks in half.

Place a small amount of cheese in the centre of a crêpe and arrange 4–5 pieces of asparagus on top of it. Fold the crêpe around the cheese and asparagus like an envelope. You should have rectangles about 2 × 4 in/50 × 100 mm.

Just before serving, sauté the filled crêpes in butter, briefly on both sides. They should be golden brown and hot through. Arrange them on a serving dish or on individual plates and pour hot Cucumber-Avocado Sauce over them. Garnish each plate with thin wedges of melon and a few ripe strawberries.

CRÊPES WITH HEARTS OF ARTICHOKE AND PALM

SERVES 6

2 cups sliced cooked artichoke
  hearts (about 1 lb/450 g)
1½ cups sliced hearts of palm
  (about 14 oz/400 g)
2½ oz/70 g butter, and more
  for the pan

2 tbsp lemon juice
2½ tsp sugar
1 egg, beaten
salt to taste
12 crêpes (see p. 239)
Hollandaise Sauce (p. 104)

If you are using canned artichoke hearts, be sure to rinse them in several changes of cool water after draining off the brine, and do the same for the hearts of palm. Cut fresh artichokes in half, scoop out the chokes and slice the hearts thinly. Slice the hearts of palm about ¼ in/6 mm thick, cutting them in half lengthways first if they are very thick.

Melt the butter in a large frying pan and heat the vegetables in it, stirring constantly, for about 10 minutes. Add the lemon juice and sugar, and some salt if it is needed, and stir again.

Remove the vegetables from the heat and quickly stir in the beaten egg. The heat of the vegetables will cook it slightly. Continue stirring for 1–2 minutes.

Divide the mixture among the crêpes, putting about 2 rounded tablespoonfuls down the centre of each one. Roll the crêpes up over the filling and sauté them in butter briefly on both sides before serving, just long enough so that they are hot through and lightly browned. Serve them with warm Hollandaise Sauce and a fresh fruit salad.

CRÊPES WITH CREAMED MUSHROOMS

SERVES 4–6

12 crêpes (see p. 239)
1½ lb/680 g mushrooms
2¼ oz/60 g butter
¼ cup finely chopped onion
2 tbsp flour
8 fl oz/225 ml double cream, heated

salt and pepper
1½ tbsp dry sherry
1 tbsp brandy
OPTIONAL GARNISH
fresh melon slices

Prepare the crêpes in advance and keep them warm, wrapped or covered, in a low oven, or reheat them before filling.

Wash and trim the mushrooms and slice them thickly. Sauté the onions in 1¼ oz/35 g of the butter for 2 minutes, then add the sliced mushrooms and sauté over high heat, tossing or stirring frequently until the mushrooms have released their excess liquid and it has evaporated. Season to taste with salt and pepper.

In a small saucepan, melt the remaining butter and stir in the flour. Cook this roux over low heat for about 2 minutes, stirring constantly, then stir in the hot cream. Beat lightly with a whisk until the sauce is smooth and simmer, stirring constantly, for several minutes. Stir in the sherry and the brandy.

Pour the sauce over the mushrooms and heat them together, stirring often, for a few minutes.

Spoon a small amount of the creamed mushrooms down the centre of each warm crêpe and roll the crêpes up over the filling. Serve hot, garnished with fresh melon slices or with a salad.

WILD MUSHROOM CRÊPE CAKE

SERVES 6–8

4 oz/115 g dried wild
  mushrooms
1½ oz/40 g butter
1 large onion, chopped
2 fl oz/55 ml red wine
salt and pepper
2 large heads round lettuce
1 pt/570 ml Béchamel Sauce
  (p. 102)
1 recipe Parmesan Crêpes
  (p. 240)
¾ lb/340 g Gruyère cheese,
  grated

TOMATO-PEPPER SAUCE
1½ tbsp olive oil
4 cloves garlic, minced
1⅕ pt/680 ml fresh tomato
  purée
⅔ cup finely chopped grilled red
  pepper
2 bay leaves
2–3 tbsp red wine
salt and pepper
GARNISH
paprika

Put the dried mushrooms in a large bowl and cover them completely with hot water. Let them soak while you prepare the sauce.

Heat the olive oil in a large frying pan and sauté the garlic in it until it is golden. Add the tomato purée, chopped red pepper, bay leaves and wine, as well as salt and pepper to taste. Simmer the sauce gently for 1–2 hours, until it is reduced by half and quite thick. Allow the sauce to cool slightly.

When the mushrooms have soaked for about 30 minutes, take them, one by one, from the bowl and wash them each with great care to get rid of all the sand and grit. Strain the water in which they were soaked through muslin or a paper coffee filter.

Put the mushrooms through a food mill, using the fine blade, or mince them finely with a knife. Melt the butter in a large frying pan and sauté the onions for a few minutes. Then add the ground mushrooms, a little red wine, some salt and pepper to taste and at least 1 pt/570 ml of the strained mushroom water.

Let this mixture simmer gently, stirring it occasionally, until most of the liquid has been absorbed and it has the consistency of a thick mush.

Blanch the lettuces in a large saucepan of boiling water, leaving them in for several minutes. When they are quite wilted, remove the heads, drain them thoroughly, squeezing out all the water, and chop the lettuce. Mix the chopped lettuce with a few spoonfuls of the Béchamel Sauce (just enough to bind it) and salt to taste.

Put a crêpe in the centre of an ovenproof serving dish or a shallow baking dish. Spread it with a thin layer of the mushroom mixture, extending it evenly to the edges. Place another crêpe over this and spread it evenly with a thin layer of the tomato sauce. Put down another crêpe, a layer of the chopped lettuce, another crêpe and an even, thin layer of grated cheese. Repeat this order twice more, just as if making a layer cake. Pour a little Béchamel over the cheese on the very top and sprinkle it lightly with paprika.

Prepare a second crêpe 'cake' in the same manner, using the remaining mushroom filling, tomato sauce and chopped lettuce. You should have about 12 fl oz/340 ml of Béchamel Sauce and a little grated cheese left over. Stir the cheese into the sauce.

Bake the crêpe cake in a preheated oven at 400°F/200°C/Mark 6 for about 20 minutes. Heat the remaining sauce. Serve the crêpe cake by cutting it in wedges and passing the sauce separately.

BLINTZES

SERVES 4–5 AS A LIGHT MEAL, 10 AS A DESSERT

¼ cup raisins
1 lb/450 g mild white cheese (see p. 204)
2 eggs
2 tbsp soured cream
1 oz/25 g butter, melted
3 tbsp sugar

¼ tsp salt
10 medium-sized crêpes (see p. 239)
butter for the pan
GARNISH
soured cream and apple sauce
or jam

The filling of these blintzes is very simple and a little bit richer than some with the addition of melted butter and soured cream. Because it has no spices, it depends completely on the quality and freshness of the cheese for its delicate but wonderful flavour.

First, pour some boiling water over the raisins and leave them to plump up in it for a while. Break the cheese up with a fork until it is coarsely crumbled and stir in the eggs, soured cream, melted butter, sugar and salt. Stir briskly with a fork until the mixture is well blended – the cheese will remain a bit lumpy, and that's as it should be.

Drain the raisins and mix them into the cheese filling. Place a heaped tablespoonful of the filling in the centre of a crêpe, fold one side of the crêpe over it and begin rolling it up. Fold the ends over, envelope-style, and finish rolling up the crêpe. It should have the shape of a short, plump cylinder. Fill all the crêpes this way.

Sauté the blintzes in butter on both sides until they are golden brown and hot through. Serve the blintzes with soured cream and apple sauce, or with jam.

See DESSERTS for Apple-sauce Crêpes, Hungarian Walnut Crêpes, Fresh Lemon Dessert Crêpes.

Italian Pastas, Vegetables and Frittatas

AFTER CROSSING THE ATLANTIC on an Italian ocean liner, I decided that eating oneself to death on Italian food might not be a bad way to go. We spent nine days on the calm seas, effectively unreachable by phone or post, surrounded by smiling, attractive Italians and sitting down four or fives times a day to delicious, bountiful meals of Italian food, cooked by someone else, with no dismaying bill to pay at the end of each repast.

At the beginning of the crossing everyone had big plans and all talk was full of activity – tennis, swimming, films every day, books to be read and letters to be written. Before long even the most energetic of us understood the real joy of ocean voyaging. By the third day no one even thought of shuffleboard or clay-pigeon shooting. We did two things: we ate and we sat in our deck chairs, watching the deck railing slowly dip below the blue horizon line and pause, then inch back up towards the paler blue sky. But mainly, we ate.

It was a bonanza for me. The Italians are very good at using interesting fresh vegetables in their cooking and combining them with cheeses, pastas and other good things, and there was always much more food than a normal being could consume, so I always found it easy to choose fine, meatless repasts from the dishes that were offered. There were nine glorious days of pungent olives and peppers, pastas made in innumerable amusing shapes, sauces redolent of herbs and fruity olive oil, soups full of tender vegetables – so luxurious in the middle of the ocean! – fine, aged cheeses, full-bodied wines, eggy frittatas tinted green with spinach, crusty breads, strong, fragrant espresso and an endless array of delicately flavoured, sinfully rich sweets. Early each afternoon and evening a low chime would sound, followed by a lovely voice intoning, *'Attenzione, prego . . .'* and the announcement of lunch or dinner. To this day I can't hear those words without salivating.

We tucked into each meal with an appetite sharpened by sea air, and when we debarked in Genoa, no one's clothes fitted very well, but no one minded. The pastas alone were a revelation. Made of hard, golden durum wheat and always served *al dente*, real Italian pasta will never dissolve into a glutinous mess and it has a sweet, delicious flavour. The Italians like to set it off with a great sauce or cheese, but never disguise it. Sauces are used sparingly and the effect is brilliant. The sauce can be as sharp and assertive as a peppery Boccalone or as mild and simple as a drenching of melted butter with a sprinkle of aged Parmesan tossed in, but it never overpowers the actual noodle.

The ocean voyage proved to be but a preview of the culinary treats we'd find in the cities and small towns of Italy. All up and down that rich peninsula we wandered into treasure troves, in museums and restaurants alike. Before long we realized that it was simply hard to miss. In Italy, unlike some places, wonderful food is available in unprepossessing, moderately priced *trattorias* as well as in the most elegant *ristorantes*.

In Florence we discovered the art of antipasto as we had never dreamed it possible. My brother-in-law, who had been living in Florence for two years, said, 'I've reserved a table at one of our favourite restaurants – it's terribly popular, but you won't find any tourists there.' Well, of course we were ready to love it because, as everyone knows, the one thing every tourist craves is the chance to pretend not to be a tourist. Following him down a maze of narrow streets, we arrived at a place so well hidden and unmarked that an unassisted tourist would never have known it was there, but inside the door everything was bright and full of laughter, and gorgeous aromas surrounded us. A sign above the door said, *'Una Trattoria Tipica . . . e Che C'è, C'è* ('A typical restaurant, and what there is, there is').

We sat down and took menus from the waiter. 'Don't order a main course,' instructed my brother-in-law and pointed to the far end of the room where the antipasto tables were arranged. That was when we blew our cover and gaped like the tourists we really were. A series of ample tables, grouped together and draped in crisp white linen, were laden with such a phantasmagoria of marinated, cooked, raw, pickled, sauced and simple, hot and cold dishes that we literally didn't know where to begin or, alas, where to stop. The gregarious proprietor waved his hand towards the forty-odd platters on display and told us to help ourselves. *'Prezzo per ochio,'* he explained, pointing a finger cheerfully at his eye; it was 'price by eye', but no matter how much you took, it was always 600 lire.

We learned about gnocchi salad, an idea that surprised us but shouldn't have. After all, if potatoes can be dressed with olive oil and vinegar and served as a salad, why not potato gnocchi? Tiny bits of grilled red pepper and a light dab of tomato sauce gave it crunch and colour. Grilled green and red peppers were bathed in a light, fruity olive oil, and olives of every size and description were gleaming in large bowls. Pickled onions, cucumbers and *peperoncini* set off milder dishes of subtly flavoured beans and scrumptious tiny roasted aubergines. Fresh white mozzarella, delicate in texture and flavour, was another discovery, tossed with slices of sweet red onion, wedges of ripe tomato and the always satisfying vinaigrette. Raw salads, real provolone and lightly cooked courgettes all tempted us in turn, and we never resisted. Wisely, we decided that there would be plenty of time to worry about our figures when we were visiting places with lesser gastronomic gifts.

Naples was without question the home of the greatest pizza in the world, as well as the most exuberantly flavoured tomato sauces, and could one expect less from the people who sing at the slightest whim and throw burning furniture out of second-storey windows on New Year's Eve? The personalities of all the different Italian provinces are reflected in their food, and Neapolitans are nothing if not bold and imaginative. Shops on crowded boulevards displayed in their windows thick-crusted pizzas, already cut in squares to be sold piece by piece, with dozens of different toppings in every conceivable combination. We pressed our noses against the glass, trying to decide among them and wondering how many slices we could eat with any pretence at decency.

By the time we arrived in Bologna we had great expectations, for we had heard that it was called the kitchen of Italy, and every other place we had visited impressed us as a very tough act to follow. Nevertheless, that ancient, arcaded city lived up to its promise. The cooks of Bologna have an aesthetic that is at once generous and refined. Their dishes are rich but never too heavy, and beautifully seasoned. We feasted on incredible pastas, gnocchi baked with butter and lots of that very famous cheese from nearby Parma. The most interesting meal I had in Bologna, however, was centred round an excellent risotto, ordered on the enthusiastic recommendation of the waiter. The Lombardy region, not too far from Bologna, produces some of the finest rice in the world and this particular Bolognese chef simmered it with a bounty of succulent wild mushrooms and tiny slivers of carrot and onion, with memorable results.

All through Italy I filled notebooks with descriptions and ideas. When I was home again, there was a wealth of good things I wanted to make. Often I worked on simply reproducing a dish that I'd tried and enjoyed during my travels. But there are many Italian dishes that use broths or small amounts of meat as a flavouring, and these often lent themselves well to adaptation. Knowledgeable use of fresh herbs, vegetable stocks, wines and the properly blended and concentrated flavours of vegetables produced from these ideas wonderful new versions of some old favourites. The guiding principle in these experiments was, of course, my memory of the times I spent with the Italians and of their style of doing things.

Everywhere we stopped in Italy we were caught up in the spirit of people who have a talent for enjoying whatever life happens to throw their way, who take everything seriously enough to do it well but nothing so seriously that they get stuffy about it. The trains didn't always get us to the next stop on time, but nobody cared because the opera and the cappuccino were unsurpassed. We finished each evening sated after a leisurely dinner, mellowed with one of the robust red wines or a crisp, dry one and in an altogether fine humour. In looking back on those travels (and forward to more), I can't remember a bad meal in Italy. Perhaps there were some that I've forgotten, buried as they were in an avalanche of gustatory pleasure, but most likely not. The Italians, from my experience, are people who believe that life is too short to spend a day without music or to eat a bad meal.

Cooking Pasta

Every good pasta recipe eventually comes round to insisting that the pasta must be cooked just until it is *al dente*, a simple Italian phrase that sums up one of the important secrets of those delicious spaghettis, fettucines and pennes. Literally translated, it means 'to the tooth'. It is a term used to describe pasta that has been cooked until it is just tender but still slightly firm; the pasta shouldn't taste raw, but it should have a little bite left.

Overcooked, mushy pasta is a sin: it loses its texture and a lot of flavour, becoming more like a glue than a food. In restaurants, unfortunately, busy cooks and waiters aren't always on the spot at the exact moment the pasta needs to be drained and then immediately served. But, on the bright side, there is no reason for such a fall from grace at home.

For a marvellous eating experience, first of all buy a good-quality pasta or make your own if you're the lucky owner of a pasta machine. Have your sauce ready and hot. Warm the plates and also the serving dish if you're going to use one.

Bring a large saucepan of salted water to a boil and put a few drops of oil in it. About 10–13 pt/5–7 l of water should be sufficient for 1 lb/450 g of dried pasta. No more than 10 minutes before you want to serve it, put the pasta into the energetically boiling water and stir it round a bit to make sure the noodles are not sticking together. After 8–9 minutes (less if the pasta is very thin; or if it's fresh pasta instead of dried, it needs only a few minutes once the water returns to a boil), pull out a strand and taste it. This test must be repeated every minute or so until one strand tells you that it is time to serve: it will be barely tender and will offer a slight, pleasant resistance to the tooth, rather than dissolving quickly into mush. *Al dente!* Drain the pasta immediately in a colander, transfer it to your heated serving dish and toss it briefly with the hot sauce, grated cheese or whatever it is that waits in readiness. Then serve and eat with no further ado.

Aside from overcooking, the most frequent mistake made by overzealous cooks is the drowning of their spaghetti in a veritable pond of sauce. Start with a little less than you think you need. If it's a strong-flavoured or very rich sauce, about 12 fl oz/340 ml might be enough for 1 lb/450 g of dried noodles. For a lighter sauce, you could increase the quantity to 4/5–1 pt/450–570 ml of pasta. More can be added to individual servings if desired, but I strongly urge moderation. If the pasta is good to begin with, after all, you will want to taste it.

PENNE ALLA BOCCALONE

SERVES 4–6

Penne are smooth, hollow pasta tubes about 1/4 in/6 mm in diameter, cut obliquely in lengths of about 1 1/2 in/37 mm.

3 tbsp olive oil
5 medium-sized cloves garlic, minced
1 tbsp finely minced small hot green chillis (2–3 small)
8 fl oz/225 ml fresh tomato pulp
2 tbsp tomato paste

1/2 cup chopped fresh parsley
1 tbsp wine vinegar
1/2 tsp dried basil, crushed
1/2 tsp salt
fresh-ground black pepper to taste
1 lb/450 g penne

Heat the olive oil in a saucepan and add the minced garlic and chillis to it. Sauté the garlic and chillis for 2–3 minutes, then add the tomato pulp (made by briefly whirling fresh tomato wedges in a blender), tomato paste, parsley, vinegar, basil, salt and pepper. Simmer the sauce for 15–20 minutes. It should be slightly reduced.

Boil 1 lb/450 g of penne in a large saucepan of salted water until they are *al dente*. Drain the pasta and put it quickly into a heated serving bowl with the sauce. Toss the pasta and sauce together thoroughly, then serve immediately on warm plates.

PENNE ALLA CARDINALE

SERVES ABOUT 6

6 medium-sized ripe tomatoes
2¼ oz/60 g butter
2 large cloves garlic, minced or
 pressed
½ tsp salt
½ tsp dried basil, crushed

12 fl oz/340 ml single cream
1½ tbsp flour
1 tbsp brandy
2 tbsp tomato paste
1–1½ lbs/450–680 g penne

Blanch the tomatoes in boiling water until the skins split and start to curl, about a minute. Remove them from the water and peel them.

Purée the tomatoes in a blender, a couple at a time. You should have about 24 fl oz/680 ml of thin purée.

Melt 1 oz/25 g of the butter in a saucepan and sauté the garlic in it until it is just golden. Add the tomato purée, the salt and the basil. Simmer gently until the purée is reduced by at least ⅓. It should be thick enough to coat a wooden spoon lightly.

In another saucepan, melt another ¾ oz/20 g butter, stir in the flour and cook this roux over a very low heat, stirring constantly, until it is golden.

Heat the cream until it is hot to the touch but not boiling and add it to the roux, stirring with a whisk. Cook this sauce until it is thickened, whisking it frequently, then stir in the brandy, the tomato paste and the remaining butter.

Combine the cream sauce and the thickened tomato purée, and cook them together for a while longer, until the desired consistency is reached.

The amount of pasta you cook will depend on what kind of pasta–sauce ratio you prefer and on how many people you're feeding. About 1¼ lb/570 g will serve 6 people generously.

Boil the pasta until it is *al dente*, or just tender.

Pour the hot sauce into a large, warm serving bowl. Add the drained noodles, toss until well mixed and serve at once.

CONCHIGLIE TUTTO GIARDINO

These shell-shaped pasta are served with a sauce made of fresh
vegetables –'the whole garden'.

SERVES 8–10

3½ oz/100 g butter
1½ cups thinly sliced carrots
1 cup chopped spring onions
1 large red onion, coarsely
   chopped
¾ cup thinly sliced radishes
½ cup coarsely chopped parsley,
   packed
2 tbsp fresh chopped basil
3 cloves garlic, crushed or
   minced
7 medium-sized tomatoes (about
   3 cups chopped)
3 cups thinly sliced courgettes
1 large green pepper, seeded and
   diced

12 fl oz/340 ml dry white
   wine, or more to taste
2 tsp salt
1 tsp pepper
1 tsp sugar
1 tbsp flour
8 fl oz/225 ml single cream
6 oz/170 g tomato paste
½ cup grated Parmesan cheese
1½ lb/680 g shell noodles
   (conchiglie)

GARNISH
additional Parmesan cheese

Melt 3 oz/85 g butter in large saucepan and add the carrots, the
spring and the red onions, the radishes, parsley, basil and garlic.
Sauté the vegetables, stirring often, until they begin to colour –
about 20 minutes. Cover the saucepan and simmer the vegetables
for about 15 minutes.

Add the tomatoes, courgettes, green pepper, wine, salt, pepper
and sugar. Simmer the sauce, uncovered, for about 45–60 minutes.

In a small saucepan melt ½ oz/15 g butter and stir in the flour.
Cook this roux for a few minutes over very low heat, stirring
constantly. Heat the cream and stir it into the roux with a whisk.
Add the tomato paste and whisk the mixture again until it is
perfectly smooth. Stir it into the vegetables and wine, along with
the grated Parmesan cheese.

Continue simmering the sauce over low heat, stirring often, until
it is as thick as you want it to be.

Cook the pasta in a large saucepan of boiling salted water until it is *al dente*, drain it completely and pour it into a large, heated serving dish. Ladle as much of the sauce over the pasta as you like, toss and serve immediately with more grated Parmesan cheese.

PENNE WITH
SWEET AND SOUR ONION SAUCE

SERVES 8

2 lb/900 g red onions
4 oz/115 g butter
2–3 tbsp olive oil, to taste
¾ tsp salt
1–2 cloves garlic, minced (optional)
1⅗ pt/900 ml peeled tomatoes (with liquid)
16 fl oz/450 ml dry red wine
½ tsp dried basil, crushed
½ tsp dried rosemary, crushed

1 large bay leaf
dash of marjoram
fresh-ground black pepper to taste
1 tsp sugar
dash of ground cinnamon
2 tsp red wine vinegar
¼ cup dried currants
1½–2 lb/680–900 g penne (or other pasta)

Peel the onions, halve them and slice them. Sauté them in the butter and the olive oil, stirring almost constantly, for 30–45 minutes – until they are evenly light brown. Add the salt and the garlic and cook for another few minutes.

Add the tomatoes, wine, herbs, pepper, sugar, cinnamon, vinegar and currants. Lower the heat and simmer the sauce for 1½–2 hours, until it is quite thick.

Boil the pasta in a large saucepan of salted water until it is just *al dente*, then drain it immediately. Toss together the pasta and sauce in a heated serving dish and serve immediately.

SPAGHETTI E CIPOLLA
(Spaghetti and Onions)

SERVES 6–8

2½ lb/1.1 kg red onions
4 oz/115 g butter
2 large bay leaves
3 cloves garlic, minced
1 tsp paprika
½ tsp salt, and more to taste
8 fl oz/225 ml good dry red
   wine
¼ tsp thyme
¼ tsp cayenne pepper
¼ tsp dried basil, crushed
¼ tsp dried oregano, crushed

1 tsp chopped fresh sage or ½
   tsp dried
16 fl oz/450 ml peeled,
   chopped tomatoes (with
   liquid)
2 fl oz/55 ml brandy
1 tsp lemon juice
2 tsp white wine vinegar
fresh-ground black pepper to
   taste
1¼–1½ lb/570–680 g thin
   spaghetti

Peel the onions, halve them and slice them rather thickly. Melt the butter in a large saucepan and add the bay leaves and the garlic and cook them, stirring constantly, for about 1 minute. Add the sliced onions and sauté them over fairly high heat, stirring almost constantly, for at least 30 minutes. The onions should be evenly light brown in colour. Add the paprika and the salt and stir for another few minutes. Add the wine, herbs, tomatoes, brandy, lemon juice, vinegar and pepper. Lower the heat and simmer the sauce, stirring occasionally, for about 45–60 minutes until thick but not pasty.

Taste the sauce and correct the seasoning if necessary.

Boil the spaghetti in a large saucepan of salted water until it is just *al dente* and drain it immediately. Pour the hot sauce over the spaghetti, toss them together quickly and serve.

FETTUCINE ALFREDO

SERVES 6

12 fl oz/340 ml double cream
1½ cups fresh-grated Parmesan
   cheese (about 5½ oz/155 g)

4 oz/115 g butter
2 egg yolks
salt

white pepper
1 lb/450 g fettucine noodles

GARNISH
½ cup chopped fresh parsley

Heat the cream in a medium-sized, heavy-bottomed saucepan. When it is just beginning to simmer, stir the cheese into it, bit by bit. Continue stirring constantly over low heat for about 10 minutes, then start adding the butter, a little at a time. When all the butter is incorporated and the sauce is smooth, remove it from the heat and beat a small amount of it into the egg yolks. Return the egg yolk mixture to the sauce and stir it in thoroughly with a whisk. Season to taste with salt and white pepper.

Bring 5–6 pt/3–3.5 l of heavily salted water to a rolling boil, add a tiny bit of butter or oil and cook the noodles in it until they are just *al dente* – barely tender and not yet soft.

Drain the noodles quickly in a colander and transfer them to a large, warm serving dish. Pour the hot cream sauce over the noodles. If the sauce seems too thick, it can be thinned with a tiny bit of cream or milk. Toss the noodles with two wooden spoons until they are all evenly coated. Sprinkle the noodles with the chopped parsley and serve them immediately.

SPAGHETTI ALLA CARBONARA

SERVES 4–6

6 medium-sized eggs
½ lb/225 g Parmesan cheese,
finely grated (about 2 cups)
3 medium-sized onions
6 tbsp olive oil

salt to taste
fresh-ground black pepper to
taste
1 lb/450 g spaghetti

Beat the eggs until they are fairly smooth and stir the grated Parmesan cheese into them. The mixture should have the consistency of a soft paste.

Peel, quarter and slice the onions, or chop them very coarsely, then sauté them in the olive oil in a very large frying pan over medium-high heat until they begin to turn golden brown round the edges.

Meanwhile, cook the spaghetti in 10–13 pt/5–7 l of vigorously boiling salted water until it is just barely *al dente*. If the onions are golden before the spaghetti is cooked, remove them from the heat until about a minute before the spaghetti will be drained, then quickly reheat them.

As soon as the spaghetti is tender (but not at all soft), drain it thoroughly in a colander. Remove the onions from the heat and add the spaghetti to them in the hot frying pan. Pour the egg-cheese paste over the spaghetti and stir it all together quickly, by lifting with two wooden spoons, for about 1 minute. The heat of the frying pan and the spaghetti will cook the eggs slightly and melt the cheese, and the result will be a creamy sauce that should coat all the pasta. Direct heat, however, will scramble the eggs, so be sure your pan is quite hot but off the heat, and pour the paste over the pasta, not directly into the pan. After about 1 minute of rapid lifting and stirring, the eggs should be sufficiently thickened, but if they are still runny, just continue the process for another 30 seconds or so.

Season with a little salt if needed, and grate on some black pepper. Serve immediately on heated plates.

LASAGNE

SERVES 6–8

2 lb/900 g fresh, ripe tomatoes
5 tbsp olive oil
1½ medium-sized onions, chopped
2 cloves garlic, minced
1 cup peeled, sliced Italian plum tomatoes
1 tsp salt, and more to taste
½ tsp basil
2½ fl oz/70 ml red wine

1½ lb/680 g aubergine
¾ lb/340 g flat lasagne noodles
1 lb/450 g fresh ricotta cheese
2 oz/55 g (about ¾ cup) fresh-grated Parmesan cheese
1 lb/450 g mozzarella cheese, sliced

GARNISH
additional Parmesan cheese and tomato sauce

Plunge the fresh tomatoes into boiling water for 2–3 minutes, then hold them under cool running water as you slip off their skins. Chop the tomatoes coarsely.

Heat 3 tablespoons of the olive oil in a medium-sized saucepan and sauté the onions and garlic in it until they begin to colour. Add the chopped fresh tomatoes, the sliced Italian tomatoes (fresh ones are preferable, but canned will do), the salt, basil and wine and simmer, stirring occasionally, for about 25 minutes. The sauce should be somewhat thickened, but still rather juicy.

Peel the aubergine and slice it ½ in/12 mm thick, lengthways. Salt the slices liberally on both sides and let them drain in a colander for about 40 minutes. Rinse them off, squeeze out the excess moisture, and cut them in ½-in/12-mm dice. Sauté the aubergine in the remaining olive oil over high heat, stirring or tossing constantly, until it is tender.

Boil the lasagne noodles, 6–7 at a time, in about 13 pt/7 l of salted water, with a tiny bit of oil, until they are *al dente*. Remove them from the water carefully, with tongs or 2 long forks.

Lightly oil a large, shallow baking dish, about 10 × 14 in/250 × 350 mm. Spoon ⅓ of the tomato sauce across the bottom and arrange ⅓ of the cooked noodles over it. Spread on ½ the ricotta cheese and sprinkle it with a few tablespoons of the Parmesan. Evenly distribute ½ the cooked aubergine over the 2 cheeses, cover it with ⅓ of the sliced mozzarella and spoon on another ⅓ of the sauce.

Make another layer of noodles, cover it with the rest of the ricotta, sprinkle on another few tablespoons of Parmesan, distribute the remaining aubergine over that, and arrange another ⅓ of the mozzarella slices over the aubergine. Make a third layer of noodles, cover them with the remaining mozzarella, spoon on the remaining sauce and sprinkle on the rest of the Parmesan.

Cover the dish and bake the lasagne in a preheated oven at 350°F/180°C/Mark 4 for about 30 minutes.

Serve hot with garlic bread and red wine. Additional Parmesan cheese and tomato sauce can be served separately if desired.

MELANZANA AL FORNO
(Baked Aubergine)

This recipe started out as an attempt to re-create a dish I ate in a very good restaurant in Bologna. It took off in a direction of its own, however, emerging as a new version of an old and popular dish, and met with rave reviews.

SERVES 6–8

2½ lb/1.1 kg firm aubergines (small are preferable)
4 tbsp olive oil
3 cloves garlic, minced
1 tsp salt
⅓–½ cup pine nuts
2 cups peeled tomatoes (with liquid)
2 tbsp minced fresh parsley

½ tsp basil
fresh-ground black pepper to taste
⅓ cup grated Parmesan cheese
½ cup dry breadcrumbs, and more if needed
2 eggs, well beaten
½ lb/225 g mozzarella cheese, cut into strips

For best results, choose aubergines of about ½–¾ lb/225–340 g size. Cut them in half lengthways and cut out the inside, leaving only a ¼-in/6-mm layer inside the skin. Put the scooped-out shells aside and chop the aubergine.

Heat the olive oil in a large pan and add the garlic to it. Stir for about a minute, then add the chopped aubergine and the salt. Sauté the aubergine over high heat, stirring almost constantly, for about 10 minutes or until it is just starting to colour.

Add the pine nuts, tomatoes (cut in chunks), parsley, basil and a generous amount of fresh-ground black pepper. Stir the mixture well, turn down the heat and simmer it for another 10 minutes. Add the cheese and the breadcrumbs and stir thoroughly. The mixture should be moist and thick – not at all runny. Add a little more breadcrumbs if needed, then stir in the beaten eggs. Taste, and correct the seasoning.

Spoon the mixture into the scooped-out aubergine shells filling them to the brim. Arrange strips of mozzarella cheese on top and bake the aubergine in a preheated oven at 350°F/180°C/Mark 4 for about 35–40 minutes. The cheese on top should be golden brown. Serve hot.

RAVIOLI WITH SPINACH AND HERB FILLING

SERVES 6

PASTA DOUGH
1 lb/450 g flour (about 3 cups)
1½ tsp salt
3 eggs
3 tbsp olive oil
approximately 4 fl oz/115 ml
    lukewarm water

SPINACH AND HERB FILLING
1½ lbs/680 g fresh spinach
3 hard-boiled eggs

1 oz/25 g butter, melted
2 tbsp fresh-grated Parmesan
    cheese
½ cup fresh ricotta cheese
2½ tbsp minced fresh parsley
½ tsp dried oregano, crushed
1 tsp dried basil, crushed
¾ tsp salt
fresh-ground black pepper to
    taste

To make the pasta, mix the flour and the salt together in a large bowl and make a well in the centre. Break in the eggs and add the oil and the water. Stir the flour into the wet ingredients until you have a moist, firm dough, adding a little more water if necessary. Alternatively, combine all the ingredients in the container of a food processor equipped with the plastic blade and process for just over 1 minute or until a homogeneous dough has been formed.

Turn the dough out on to a large, floured board and knead, working in a bit more flour if necessary, until the dough is smooth and satiny, about 8–10 minutes. Keep the pasta covered with cling film until it is needed

To make the filling, wash the spinach, remove the thick stems and cook it on high heat in a covered saucepan in as much water as clings to the leaves until it is soft and tender, about 8–10 minutes. Drain it thoroughly and chop finely or process briefly in a food processor with the steel blade.

Chop the hard-boiled eggs very fine and stir them into the spinach along with the remaining ingredients. Or, in a food processor, add the eggs, quartered, to the spinach and process for about 30 seconds. Then add the remaining ingredients and process again until the mixture is well blended, about 30–40 seconds.

MAKING THE RAVIOLIS
Divide the pasta dough into 4 equal parts. On a large board or tabletop, lightly dusted with flour, roll 1 part out as thinly as

possible; try to keep the shape of it as much like a rectangle as possible, though it will invariably try to make itself into a map of Italy or Africa. Keep the rest of the dough covered until you need it. If the dough sticks, peel it up carefully from the board and dust a little more flour under it.

When it is about $1/16$ in/2 mm thick, put it aside on a flat surface and roll out a second quarter of the dough to the same size and shape (within reason!). It is important to roll the dough out as smoothly and evenly as possible. If it is too thin in some places and too thick in others, parts will overcook and break apart in boiling, while other parts will remain undercooked.

Take one of the sheets of pasta and stretch it out on your lightly floured board. Place teaspoonfuls of filling on it in neat rows across and from top to bottom, about 2 in/50 mm apart from centre to centre. Using a pastry brush or your finger, moisten with water the pasta in between the mounds of filling, drawing wide lines between the rows.

Carefully lower the second sheet of pasta over the first and press down firmly along the wetted lines to seal the two pasta layers around the filling. If large air bubbles are trapped in the raviolis, prick through the pasta with the tip of a sharp knife, near the edge, then pinch together again securely when all the air has escaped.

Cut the raviolis apart with a pastry wheel, a ravioli cutter or a sharp knife.

Roll out, fill and seal the remaining 2 sections of dough in the same way. Be sure that all the seams are securely pressed together: Bad seals will ruin the raviolis in cooking. I've found that letting the raviolis rest for a while before cooking helps prevent breaking seals later. Leave the raviolis on a lightly floured board, in a single layer, for about 20 minutes before putting them in the saucepan.

To cook the raviolis, drop them in a vast saucepan of fast-boiling salted water and nudge them about very quickly with a wooden spoon for a minute or so to prevent them from sticking to each other. Boil them for 6–8 minutes, depending on their thickness, until the pasta is tender but not mushy. Drain them thoroughly and serve immediately, with a light tomato sauce, cream sauce or simply with butter and cheese.

POTATO GNOCCHI

SERVES 6–8

2 lb/900 g potatoes
1½ cups flour, and more if
 needed
2 tsp salt

1 egg, lightly beaten
approximately 4 oz/115 g
 butter, melted, to taste
Gruyère or Parmesan cheese

Boil the potatoes in their jackets until they are tender. Drain them and allow them to cool slightly, then peel them and put them through the finest blade of a food mill.

Work the potatoes, flour, salt and egg into a dough, kneading it with your hand, until smooth. Add a little more flour if necessary. The dough should be manageable but soft.

Take ⅓ of the dough at a time and, on a lightly floured board, shape it into a long, thick cylinder. Roll the cylinder and stretch it gently until you have a rope about 1 in/25 mm thick. With a sharp knife, cut it in ½-in/12-mm bits. Repeat with the remaining dough.

To cook the gnocchi, drop them into 10–13 pt/5–7 l of boiling salted water and boil them for 8–10 minutes, or until they are cooked through. Remove them with a slotted spoon and drain them.

Arrange the gnocchi in one layer in a well-buttered casserole or gratin dish, drizzle melted butter over them and sprinkle them to your taste with Parmesan or Gruyère cheese. Bake them in a preheated oven at 350°F/180°C/Mark 4 for 15–20 minutes, or until they are hot through and the cheese is beginning to brown.

SPINACH AND CHEESE GNOCCHI

SERVES 6

½ lb/225 g spinach leaves
4½ oz/125 g butter, melted
1 cup well-drained ricotta cheese
⅔ cup grated Parmesan cheese
3 egg yolks, beaten
7 tbsp flour, and more as needed
   for rolling

¾ tsp salt
fresh-ground pepper to taste
pinch of nutmeg (optional)
½ cup grated Parmesan cheese

Wash the spinach leaves carefully and cook them in 1½ oz/40 g of the melted butter on medium-high heat, stirring often, until they are completely tender and the liquid from them has evaporated completely. They should be just beginning to stick to the pan. This may take 10–15 minutes. Purée the cooked spinach in a blender or mince it with a large knife.

In a fairly large bowl combine the spinach purée with the ricotta cheese, ⅔ cup of Parmesan cheese, beaten egg yolks, 7 tablespoons flour, salt, pepper and nutmeg. Stir the mixture vigorously until it is perfectly blended and lump-free. Chill the mixture for at least 30 minutes.

Using two teaspoons, form little gnocchi about the size and shape of a pecan: scoop up a rounded teaspoonful of the mixture in one spoon, then cup the second spoon over it and slide it off to the side. Do this once or twice more to get an even shape and drop the little dumpling into a bowl of flour. Roll it in the flour, dust it off and put it down on waxed paper. Continue forming the gnocchi until all of the spinach–cheese mixture is used up.

To cook the gnocchi, drop them carefully into about 10 pt/5 l of simmering salted water. Allow them to simmer (not boil) for 10–12 minutes, stirring them very gently once or twice with a wooden spoon to make sure they don't stick to each other. Remove them from the water with a slotted spoon and drain them on a clean cloth.

Pour another 1½ oz/40 g melted butter into a large, shallow casserole or gratin dish. Brush it evenly over the bottom of the dish and arrange the gnocchi in it in one layer. Pour the remaining butter over them and sprinkle them with the remaining grated Parmesan cheese. Bake the gnocchi in a preheated oven at 350°F/180°C/Mark 4 for 15–20 minutes, or until they are hot through and the cheese is beginning to colour.

ITALIAN SPINACH AND POTATO ROULADE

This is like a giant rolled dumpling with a spinach filling. A potato dough reminiscent of gnocchi is rolled up around the filling, then the whole thing is wrapped in cheesecloth, boiled in salted water and served hot, in spiral-patterned slices.

SERVES 6 GENEROUSLY

FILLING
2 lb/900 g fresh spinach
1½ oz/40 g butter
1 large onion, chopped
1 large clove garlic, minced
1½ tbsp white wine vinegar
½ tsp salt
¼ tsp oregano, crushed
pinch of nutmeg
DOUGH
2 lb/900 g potatoes

2 whole eggs
1 egg yolk
1½ tsp salt
⅛ tsp nutmeg
2–2½ cups flour
GARNISH
4 oz/115 g butter, melted
¾ cup fresh-grated Parmesan
   cheese

To make the filling, wash the spinach carefully and cook it, covered, in the water that clings to the leaves until it is all completely wilted. Squeeze out the excess moisture and chop the spinach fine.

Melt the butter in a medium-sized frying pan and sauté the

chopped onion and minced garlic in it until they are golden. Stir in the chopped spinach, the vinegar, the salt, the oregano and the nutmeg. Stir and continue cooking for a few minutes, until the mixture is thick but still moist. Taste, and correct the seasoning if necessary.

To make the dough, boil the potatoes until they are tender, peel them and press them through a coarse sieve into a large bowl. Beat the whole eggs with the egg yolk and stir the beaten eggs into the potatoes along with the salt and the nutmeg. Stir in about 2 cups flour and begin working the dough with your hand until it is smooth (one hand will do – you don't want to have them both in there at once or you'll have trouble getting out). Work in as much flour as is necessary to form a dough that is stiff enough to hold its shape in a ball.

Sprinkle a large sheet of waxed paper with a generous amount of flour and roll the dough out on it in an even rectangle, 11 × 13 in/ 275 × 325 mm. Keep the dough dusted with flour to prevent it from sticking.

Spread the spinach filling over the rectangle of dough, leaving a 1-in/25-mm border on both shorter ends and one of the longer sides, and a 2-in/50-mm border on the other long side. Starting with the long side that has the 1-in/25-mm border, roll the dough up over the filling, peeling back the waxed paper as you go. Securely pinch together the seam and ends so that none of the filling can squeeze out. Now wrap the entire roulade in cheesecloth, 2–3 layers thick and long enough to extend past both ends of the roulade by several inches. Tie the cheesecloth with string at the ends, and tie another strip of cheesecloth, about 3 in/75 mm wide, around the middle of the roulade.

Place it in a large, fairly deep pan, such as a roasting pan, and cover it with boiling salted water. Simmer the roulade for 50 minutes, turning it over once, halfway through.

Lift out the roulade and let it rest for a couple of minutes, then carefully remove the cheese cloth; use a sharp knife to help peel away the cheesecloth if it should stick.

Cut ¾-in/18-mm slices and serve them immediately on warm plates, drenched with melted butter and sprinkled liberally with Parmesan cheese.

FRIED MOZZARELLA

SERVES 6

1½ lb/680 g mozzarella
  cheese
1⅓ cups fine, dry breadcrumbs
3–4 tbsp finely minced fresh
  parsley
2 eggs
salt to taste

pepper to taste
approximately 3–4 tbsp flour
approximately 2½–4 fl oz/
  70–115 ml olive oil
GARNISH
slices of melon

Cut the mozzarella into evenly sized slices about ¼ in/6 mm thick.

Combine the breadcrumbs and the parsley in a shallow bowl, mixing them together thoroughly.

Beat the eggs lightly with a little water and some salt and pepper, and pour the beaten eggs into another shallow bowl.

Put a few tablespoons of flour into a third bowl. Dredge the cheese slices in flour on both sides and on the edges. Take one of the floured slices and dip it first in the egg mixture, then in the breadcrumb mixture, then once more in the egg mixture and once more in the crumbs.

Bread all the cheese slices this way. Be sure that the slices of cheese are thickly and evenly breaded, including the edges, or else they will come to grief in the frying pan!

Pour a liberal amount of olive oil into each of 2 large frying pans and heat it. Put in the cheese slices, regulate the heat to medium and sauté the cheese for a few minutes on each side. The breading should be crispy and golden brown.

Remove them from the oil and place them on kitchen towels for an instant, then serve immediately. The cheese should be completely melted inside the crust.

Serve with a salad or garnished with slices of melon.

POMODORO AL GRATINE

Because it's so light and refreshing, this is an ideal hot hors-d'oeuvre for a dinner that includes a heavy pasta dish. It's also delightful as an accompaniment to croquettes.

SERVES 6

6 medium-sized, firm tomatoes
  (about 2 lb/900 g)
2 tbsp olive oil
3 tbsp minced fresh parsley
1 tsp dried basil, crushed
½ tsp dried oregano, crushed

1–2 cloves garlic, minced
½–¾ tsp salt, to taste
fresh-ground black pepper to
  taste
⅓ cup grated Parmesan cheese
⅔ cup dry breadcrumbs

Slice the tomatoes in half crossways and scoop out the pulp with a spoon, leaving a firm ¼-in/6-mm shell. Coarsely chop the pulp and put it in a bowl together with all the liquid, the oil, the herbs, salt and pepper, cheese and breadcrumbs. Stir everything together until it is thoroughly combined.

Lightly salt the inside of the tomato shells and spoon the prepared filling into them, dividing it evenly among the 12 shells.

Bake the tomatoes in a preheated oven at 350°F/180°C/Mark 4 for about 20–25 minutes and serve hot.

FRITTATA OF COURGETTE

SERVES 6

1½ lb/680 g young, firm
  courgettes (about 4½ cups
  chopped)
1 medium onion

3 tbsp olive oil
6 eggs
salt and pepper to taste
basil, chopped, to taste

Cut the courgettes into small dice and chop the onion. Heat the olive oil in a 10-in/250-mm frying pan and add the onions and courgettes to it. Sauté the vegetables, stirring often, until the onions are golden and the courgettes tender.

Meanwhile, beat the eggs lightly with some salt, pepper and a little chopped basil. When the courgettes are just tender, spread the vegetables round the pan evenly and pour the eggs over them. Lower the heat and cover the pan. Cook the frittata this way until the eggs are completely set, about 15–20 minutes. Check it occasionally to see if it is puffing up in a bubble, in which case pierce it once or twice with a sharp knife.

When the eggs are firm on top, loosen the frittata carefully by sliding a spatula under it. Then place a plate upside down over the top of the pan like a lid and invert them, dropping the frittata on to the plate. Slide it carefully back into the pan with the top side down and brown it for a few minutes. Then turn it out on to a serving plate.

Serve the frittata cut in wedges, as a first course or as part of an antipasto. It can be served hot but is best when served at room temperature. Do not serve it cold.

ONION AND HERB FRITTATA

SERVES 6 AS A FIRST COURSE OR AS PART OF AN ANTIPASTO

1 yellow onion	⅓ cup snipped chives
1 red onion	¼ tsp/dried basil or 2 tsp fresh
3 tbsp olive oil	6 eggs
½ cup chopped fresh parsley	salt and pepper to taste

Peel and coarsely chop the onions. Heat the olive oil in a large frying pan and sauté the onions in it until they just begin to colour. Add the parsley, chives and basil, and sauté a few minutes more, stirring often.

Beat the eggs lightly with a little salt and pepper.

Give the onions and herbs one more stir, then distribute them more or less evenly in the frying pan and carefully pour the eggs over them. Lower the heat as much as possible, cover the pan and cook until the eggs are barely firm on top; this should take 10–15 minutes on very low heat.

Turn a large plate upside down over the frying pan like a lid and turn the pan over quickly, dropping the frittata on to the plate. Then slide the frittata back into the pan and brown the other side for a few minutes.

Turn the frittata out on to a serving plate and, just before serving, cut it into wedges. It may be eaten hot, cool or, best of all, at room temperature.

For an antipasto, turn to SALADS AND COLD VEGETABLES and see recipes for Flageolet Salad, Rice Salad Vinaigrette, Florentine Bread Salad, White Bean Salad, Salad Torcoloti, Aubergine Caviar, Chick-pea Salad, Peperonata, Gnocchi Salad, Insalatone and Fresh Mozzarella Salad. For two versions of Pasta i Fagioli, turn to SOUPS. In DESSERTS, see Spumoni Cake and Zuppa Inglese.

SPANISH
SPECIALITIES

I𝐓'𝐒 𝐇𝐀𝐑𝐃 𝐓𝐎 𝐂𝐇𝐎𝐎𝐒𝐄 𝐅𝐀𝐕𝐎𝐔𝐑𝐈𝐓𝐄𝐒, but if you twisted my arm, I'd have to admit that the bars in Spain are the best in the Western world. Vienna, as everyone knows, has the best pastries, Italy brews the best cup of coffee, the German trains run most reliably and Spain has the greatest bars.

Many European countries enjoy bars of great social, and even culinary, importance, so the competition is keen. In Britain, of course, pubs, especially in the country, are the social centres of their neighbourhoods. Most of them are very pleasant places to pass an evening and many serve a perfectly edible lunch.

Italian bars, dominated by big, gleaming espresso machines and full of life from the earliest hours of the morning, are the place to have breakfast – foaming cappuccino and a fresh pastry. Then, they are a place for innumerable coffee breaks through the day, a place to enjoy an occasional game of pinball, to have a snack and even to have a drink sometimes. Families run Italian bars and families patronize them. Often enough, the bar downstairs is the place to make and receive phone calls as well as to keep up on the local news.

But Spanish bars, which do not lack in any of the recommendations mentioned above, add one more distinction, which puts them at the top: Spanish bars serve *tapas*. Now, while it is true that *tapas* are snacks or small portions of various foods meant to be nibbled with a glass of wine, they cannot be so easily explained. *Tapas* are not so much a food as they are a phenomenon, and snacking, in Spain, is not so much a way of eating as a way of life. To understand *tapas*, it is first necessary to become acquainted with the rhythm of Spanish life and particularly with the custom of the *paseo*. The Spanish day starts early, usually with *café con leche* and crusty rolls (in a bar). By lunch-time, which is about two in the afternoon, appetites are honed, and instead of dashing out in shifts for a sandwich and a cup of coffee, the Spanish close down their shops, offices, banks and various businesses and settle down at home or in a restaurant for a leisurely and plentiful meal. About two hours later, refreshed and relaxed Spaniards return to their worldly concerns and attend to them until early evening.

The dinner hour, particularly on long, warm summer days, does not begin until about ten o'clock. During that very pleasant part of the day when late afternoon is slipping into early evening – about seven or eight o'clock in the summer – the greater portion of the population of every Spanish town and village streams out into the streets for a walk. But this is no solitary ramble or constitutional: it is the *paseo*, a charming social custom that knocks on ritual. Schoolgirls, linked arm-in-arm, merchants and office clerks, mothers pushing prams and whole families come out to take the air.

On all the main streets and avenues they stroll in two strong, lively currents, down one side of the road and back up the other, nodding and greeting each other and stopping to chat. And it is then, during the *paseo*, that the *tapa* bars are at their wonderful best. Oh, you can stop for a *tapa* almost any time of day. You can have *tapas* for lunch, *tapas* in the afternoon or late into the night, but *tapas* and the *paseo* truly go hand in hand. The same bar where you had a quiet cup of coffee in the morning, be it small or large, simple or elegant, is, at this time of day, invariably bright, cheerful, noisy and tempting.

There are certain districts in Madrid where the *tapa* bars are magnificent in size and justly famous. By four or five in the afternoon, the long, polished surface of the bar in such places is lined with twenty, thirty – sometimes as many as forty – platters and bowls holding a marvellous array of toothsome edibles. There are marinades and salads reminiscent of an Italian antipasto, and stuffed eggs. There are large *tortillas*, those round, golden Spanish omelettes that are cut in wedges, still warm and redolent of onions. There are olives in all their variety, *bocadillo* rolls and cheeses, roasted peppers and even hot dishes – little plates of garlicky cooked mushrooms or brown-crusted croquettes, prepared in moments on request. In the summer there is always sangría and icy gazpacho by the cup, and there might be caramel custard, in great pans or in little ceramic cups, and trays of fresh fruit, and more.

It looks like some kind of madly generous buffet, and the bartenders presiding over it dart quickly back and forth, pouring *chatos* of wine and serving up the delicacies to go with it. There are no stools or chairs in most of these establishments; you just find an opening somewhere in the line-up of eager customers and there you stand, one elbow firmly planted on the counter, as you look over the selection. Then name what you want, or point – a slice of this or a portion of that – and in a twinkling the little plates appear before you, next to your glass. When you've finished one *tapa*, you try another and another, as the mood strikes you, and when you're ready to go on and favour a different bar for a while, the amazing bartender, who has kept track of your nibbling by some secret, invisible method of his own, tots up a scrap of a bill (it's never very much), and you're off. You join the *paseo* once more and stroll along until some other display of *tapas* lures you in to pause again, enjoy another glass of wine and have another bite.

In this gratifying manner you revive your spirits and your strength at that rather peckish time when dinner is still a few hours off and lunch already forgotten. Of course, if the *tapas* are abundant in your part of town, you can all too easily make a meal of several such visits and lose interest in dinner altogether, but what of it? Nor do *tapas* vanish at ten, when restaurants are filling up. It's hard to resist stopping for just a taste of something before going to your table and ordering a serious meal. And finally, after an evening out at the cinema, theatre or wherever, how nice if you can contrive to pass a *tapa* bar on the way home and indulge in a last little bite or two with a night-cap.

Real *tapas* don't exist outside of *tapa* bars. There's no such thing, in Spain, as eating *tapas* at home. But I can't think of Spanish food without recalling those delicious evenings in the bars, and because I can't, unfortunately, transport myself to Madrid or Barcelona or Segovia whenever I get the urge, I worked out some recipes for a few of the dishes that are so particular to the *tapa* bars and included them here with my other Spanish favourites. Sometimes on summer days, when nobody especially wants a heavy, hot meal and when I'm smacking my lips in recollection of sangría, I like to prepare three or four of those *tapas*, put them out buffet-style, together with some pickled peppers, cheeses, breads and fruits, and call all hungry people.

Spanish cooking does not begin and end with *tapas*, however. It is, in fact, one of the most diverse and delicious European cuisines.

Two main influences helped shape the character of Spanish cooking, European from the north and Moorish from the south, making an interesting and happy marriage of flavours. Another quality of the cuisine is the great variety that has been preserved by virtue of intense regionalism. It is impossible to find a Spaniard in Spain! Everyone is either a Castilian, a Basque, a Catalonian – in short, a native of his or her own province. The result of this strong regional feeling is a collection of connected but individual cooking styles.

When I was in Spain, I lived most of that time in Madrid and Segovia, so the ideas and recipes I brought back were largely Castilian. One of my immediate and lasting favourites is the Tortilla Española, which needs a bit of introduction. First of all, it has nothing to do with Mexican *tortillas*, which are a bread; this is an omelette. Second, as omelettes go, it has very little to do with the French sort, except that both are made mainly of eggs. The Spanish *tortilla* is round, thick, golden brown on both sides and full of potatoes and onions sautéd in olive oil. It is further recommended by the fact that its delicious flavour is equally compelling when it is hot and when it is quite cool.

Also not to be missed is the experience of drinking a cup of Spanish hot chocolate. This concoction starts appearing in the Segovian bars in late autumn and warms the inhabitants through the bitter cold of a Castilian winter. Not one of those puny, watery liquids that are called cocoa in other parts of the world, this one is almost like a pudding, so rich and thick that it is eaten with a spoon.

Finally, a word about Spanish wine. Everyone drinks wine in Spain, from early childhood onward (though I have yet to be treated to the sight of a Spanish drunkard), so it follows that the wine must be plentiful, cheap and perfectly drinkable, which it is. This happy generality is punctuated by spectacular moments, though, in the form of certain red wines from the Rioja region. The best, and best known, of the Rioja wines are Marques de Murrieta and Marques de Riscal. If your wine merchant can supply you with one of them – buy it; drink it. These excellent wines, made by old, traditional methods, have a robust but sophisticated character. Don't drink them with reverence – that's a little uncomfortable – rather, with respect and a happy spirit.

As to sangría and the making of it, I can only say that properly made and served at the appropriate time, it is very, very easy to drink. On a hot summer day it practically drinks itself. But beware: drink it at lunch-time only if you're planning a siesta.

To make a good sangría, you must start with a decent wine; not a rare or expensive wine, please, but a good, dry, drinkable red wine, and fresh, ripe fruit. It must be prepared shortly before it is to be consumed because it doesn't improve with keeping and it certainly cannot be bottled. And, like any Spanish potable, it must be drunk with friends so that all can lift their glasses and toast each other with *'Salud, pesetas y joventud, y tiempo para gastarlos!'* – 'Health, money and youth, and the time to enjoy them!'

ENSALADILLA RUSSA

SERVES 8–10

3 large, white-skinned potatoes	*1½ tsp salt*
1 cup cooked peas	*pepper to taste*
1 cup cooked diced carrots	*mayonnaise to taste*
½ cup cooked chopped red	GARNISH
peppers	*parsley sprigs*
½ cup minced onion	*carrot slices*
2 fl oz/55 ml olive oil	*slivers of pepper*
2 fl oz/55 ml wine vinegar	*chopped hard-boiled egg, etc.*

Boil the potatoes in their skins until tender. When they are cool, peel them and cut them into very small dice, about ¼ in/6 mm.

Put the diced potatoes in a large bowl. Add a generous cupful of cooked fresh peas, a generous cupful of cooked diced carrots, the red peppers and the onions.

Toss all the ingredients together thoroughly with the oil, vinegar, salt and pepper. Taste, and correct seasoning.

Add a few spoons of mayonnaise, according to taste, and toss again until everything is very well combined.

Mound the salad carefully on an oval serving dish and shape it with the side of a knife until it is smooth and even. Spread mayonnaise over the salad until it has a smooth, even coating over the entire surface. Then decorate it with various garnishes, making pretty patterns, and chill before serving.

BARCELONA WHITE BEAN SALAD

(A *tapa*)

SERVES 6–8

1 cup dried white beans, washed	*3 tbsp olive oil*
1 large onion	*5 tbsp wine vinegar*
1 large green pepper	*salt to taste*
2 ripe tomatoes	*pepper to taste*
2 hard-boiled eggs	*minced garlic (optional)*
10 cured black olives	

Cook the beans in boiling salted water to cover until they are just tender, about 1–1½ hours. Drain and cool.

Peel the onion and cut it into 1-in/25-mm pieces. Blanch them in boiling water for a few minutes.

Grill the pepper, turning it frequently, until the skin is blistered and a little charred. Allow the pepper to cool until you can handle it easily and then peel it and seed it. Cut the pepper into 1-in/25-mm squares.

Cut the tomatoes into thin wedges, and halve and slice the eggs. Cut the olives away from their pits in several pieces.

Combine all the ingredients in a bowl and toss with the oil and vinegar and seasonings. Taste, and correct the seasoning.

Serve this salad cold as a *tapa* in a buffet or as a course on its own.

STEWED CHICK-PEAS

(A *tapa*)

SERVES 6–8

3 tbsp olive oil

3 cloves garlic, chopped or thinly sliced

1 tbsp paprika

2 medium-sized, ripe tomatoes, puréed in blender

1½ cups cooked chick-peas (see p. 152)

1 tbsp red wine vinegar

salt

pepper

In a large, deep frying pan heat the olive oil and add the garlic and paprika. Stir constantly for a few minutes, until the garlic begins to turn golden, then add the fresh tomato purée and the chick-peas, along with about 8 fl oz/225 ml of their cooking liquid.

Stir in the red wine vinegar and add salt and pepper to taste. Continue cooking on a low heat until the sauce is quite thick. Serve hot or warm.

ROASTED AUBERGINE AND PEPPERS IN OIL

(A *tapa*)

SERVES 4–6 (MORE AS A *tapa*)

1 lb/450 g aubergine (5 or 6 small)

2 large green peppers

2 large red peppers

2 tbsp olive oil

2 tbsp lemon juice

1 clove garlic, minced or pressed

salt to taste

fresh-ground black pepper to taste

Grill the aubergines and peppers under a very hot grill, turning them often, until their skins are blistered and turning brown all over. Remove and allow to cool.

When you can easily handle the vegetables, strip off the skins. Seed the peppers and cut away the white ribs.

Cut both peppers and aubergines into strips about ½ × 1 in/ 12 × 25 mm.

Toss the vegetables with the oil, lemon juice, garlic, salt and pepper. Allow to marinate for a few hours before serving. Serve cool or at room temperature.

CHAMPIÑÓNES ALLA PLANCHA

This is one of the most popular hot *tapas* served in the bars in Spain. It is served steaming hot in little individual casseroles, with slices of crusty bread. I've adapted the recipe for six people. Make it in one large casserole and serve it either as part of a '*tapa* dinner' or as a wonderful first course. It would also make a delightful light lunch, preceded by a gazpacho or salad and served with cheese, bread and wine.

SERVES 6

2 lb/900 g fresh mushrooms
2 oz/55 g butter
6–7 cloves garlic, chopped
¾ cup chopped parsley

8 fl oz/225 ml dry white wine
salt and fresh-ground black
    pepper to taste

Wash the mushrooms and trim the dry ends off the stems. If the mushrooms are large, halve or quarter them. Melt the butter in a frying pan or fireproof casserole and sauté the chopped garlic in it quickly, just until it shows the slightest bit of colour. Add the mushrooms and parsley and sauté them over high heat, stirring frequently, until the mushrooms begin to release water – just a few minutes. Add the white wine, some salt and fresh-ground black pepper, and cover the pan or casserole.

Simmer the mushrooms in the wine until they are quite tender, correct the seasoning and serve hot in preheated bowls or individual casseroles.

TORTILLA ESPAÑOLA

SERVES 4

1 large potato	*salt to taste*
1 large onion	*pepper to taste*
2½ tbsp olive oil	*5 eggs*

Peel the potato and cut it into small dice, about ½ in/12 mm. Peel and chop the onion. Heat the olive oil in a large frying pan and sauté the potatoes and onions, stirring very often, until the potatoes are just tender. Season the mixture with salt and pepper, stir, and then spread more or less evenly in the frying pan.

Beat the eggs lightly, salt them and pour them over the potato mixture. The eggs should barely cover the vegetables.

Cover and cook over very low heat until the top of the tortilla is firm, about 15 minutes. Turn a large plate upside down and place it over the pan like a lid. Holding the plate in place, turn the pan over, dropping the tortilla on the plate. Slide the tortilla carefully back into the pan and brown the other side for a few minutes.

Employing the same technique, turn the tortilla out on to a large, round plate to serve. The tortilla may be eaten hot, warm, cool, cold, or at room temperature, and is always delicious.

AUBERGINE TORTILLA

SERVES 3–4

3 tbsp olive oil	*1 tsp lemon juice*
1 large clove garlic, minced	*salt to taste*
½ large onion, chopped	*pepper to taste*
2½ cups small aubergine, cut in ¼-in/6-mm dice	*5 eggs*

Heat the olive oil in a large frying pan and add the garlic, onions and aubergine. Sauté the vegetables, stirring often, until the onions are transparent and the aubergine tender. Season with the lemon juice, salt and pepper.

Beat the eggs lightly, seasoning them with salt and pepper. Pour the beaten eggs over the aubergine mixture in the pan and spread it round evenly. The eggs should barely cover all the aubergine.

Cover the pan and turn down the heat. Cook over very low heat until the tortilla is firm on top. Gently slide a spatula round the edges and underneath it to be sure it is not sticking.

Take a large plate and turn it upside down, placing it over the pan like a lid. Holding the plate in place, turn the pan over.

Slide the tortilla from the plate back into the pan and allow it to brown on the other side for a few minutes.

Employing the same technique, flip the tortilla back on to a large plate for serving.

The tortilla may be eaten hot, cold or at room temperature. One of the more convenient aspects of Spanish tortillas is that they really are delicious at any temperature.

TORTILLA ALLA PAESANA

SERVES 3–4

1 small potato	*½ cup diced (grilled and peeled)*
½ medium-sized onion	*red pepper*
2½ tbsp olive oil	*1 clove garlic, crushed*
1 medium-sized carrot	*salt and pepper*
½ cup shelled peas	*5 eggs*

Scrub the potato, peel it if you wish and cut it into small dice. Coarsely chop the onion. Heat the olive oil in a 9–10-in/225–250-mm pan and start sautéing the potatoes and onions, stirring often.

Scrape the carrot, cut it into small dice and boil or steam it until it is barely tender. In another saucepan, boil the peas for a few minutes until they are barely tender. Drain the carrots and peas and add them to the potatoes and onions, together with the diced red pepper and the crushed garlic. Continue to sauté all the vegetables for a few minutes more – until the potatoes are nearly soft. Season the mixture to taste with salt and pepper.

Beat the eggs lightly with a little salt and pepper and pour them over the vegetable mixture in the pan. Shake the pan gently to distribute the mixture evenly, reduce the heat to very low, cover the pan and cook the tortilla for about 10 minutes, until the eggs are set.

Loosen the edges of the tortilla with a knife or spatula and give the pan another shake.

Turn a large plate upside down and place it over the pan like a lid. Holding the plate in place, turn the pan over quickly, dropping the tortilla on to the plate. Slide the tortilla carefully back into the pan and brown the other side for a few minutes.

Employing the same technique, turn the tortilla out on to a serving plate. The tortilla may be served at any temperature, from hot to very cool, but I like it best at room temperature. Cut it into wedges to serve.

ASPARAGUS TORTILLA

This one is just a little richer than most tortillas; it's a bit heavier on egg yolks and uses butter as well as the olive oil.

SERVES 3–4

6–8 oz/170–225 g trimmed fresh asparagus	pepper to taste
	1 tbsp olive oil
5 whole eggs	1 oz/25 g butter
1 egg yolk	1 medium-sized onion, finely
½ tsp salt	chopped

Thinly peel the thick bottom parts of the asparagus stalks and cut them in ½-in/12-mm pieces. Cut the tender tops of the asparagus in 1-in/25-mm pieces and keep them aside. Drop the toughest pieces into boiling salted water and boil them for 3–4 minutes, then add the tops and boil another 4–5 minutes. Drain the asparagus.

Beat the eggs and extra yolk with the salt and a little pepper.

Heat the olive oil and butter in a 10-in/250-mm frying pan and sauté the chopped onions in it until they begin to colour. Add the asparagus and stir gently for about 2 minutes. Pour the beaten egg evenly over the vegetables in the pan, lower the heat, cover and cook 8–10 minutes, or just until the eggs are set.

Turn the tortilla out on to a plate, then slide it back into the pan to brown the other side for a few minutes. Turn it out on to a serving plate, let it cool to lukewarm if desired and cut it in wedges to serve.

MENESTRA DE VERDURAS: I

This is a dish that I ate innumerable times in Spain. Whatever the restaurant, some version of this *menestra* was almost sure to be on the menu. Although the ingredients and proportions would vary with the cook, artichokes, French beans and peas appear to be essential and always, always olive oil. Here is a version hearty enough to serve as a main course, preceded by a Spanish tortilla or garlic soup and followed by fresh fruit and cheese.

SERVES 6–8

3–4 cloves garlic
½ lb/225 g onions (about 2 medium sized)
1 lb/450 g small white-skinned potatoes
¾ lb/340 g carrots
¾ lb/340 g French beans
6 tbsp olive oil
½ lb/225 g mushrooms
1 tsp salt
2 tbsp sweet paprika
fresh-ground black pepper to taste

8 fl oz/225 ml Vegetable Broth (pp. 60–61)
3 cups peeled, chopped tomatoes (with their liquid)
2 bay leaves
pinch of hot paprika
½ lb/225 g fresh asparagus
½ lb/225 g cooked artichoke bottoms
2 cups shelled green peas
GARNISH
ripe green olives and quartered hard-boiled eggs

Peel and thinly slice the garlic. Peel, halve and thickly slice the onions and the potatoes. Scrape the carrots and cut them in ½-in/ 12-mm lengths. Trim the French beans and cut them in 1-in/25-mm long pieces.

Heat the olive oil in a large, heavy-bottomed saucepan and sauté the garlic and onions in it until the onions are transparent. Add the potatoes, carrots and French beans and sauté them for 10 minutes, stirring almost constantly.

Wash and trim the mushrooms and add them to the pan along with the salt, sweet paprika and some fresh-ground black pepper. Continue sautéing the vegetables for 5 minutes more, stirring constantly, then add the vegetable broth, tomatoes, bay leaves and a pinch of hot paprika. Simmer the mixture, uncovered, over low heat for 45–50 minutes. Stir it occasionally.

Peel the bottom ends of the asparagus stalks and cut the stalks in 1–2-in/25–50-mm pieces. Thickly slice the artichoke bottoms. Add the peas, asparagus and artichoke bottoms to the *menestra* and simmer it, covered, stirring often, for 10–15 minutes more, or just until all the vegetables are tender. The liquid should be greatly reduced by this time.

Serve the *menestra* hot and garnish each plate with a quartered hard-boiled egg and a few ripe green olives.

MENESTRA DE VERDURAS: II

(A Simpler One)

SERVES 4–6 GENEROUSLY

4–5 cloves garlic
1 large red onion
2½ fl oz/70 ml olive oil
1 lb/450 g French beans
1 lb/450 g tomatoes
4 fl oz/115 ml dry sherry
1 large green pepper
1 large red pepper
½ lb/225 g mushrooms

1½ cups shelled peas
6 fl oz/170 ml Vegetable Broth
  (pp. 60–61)
3 tbsp tomato paste
2 tsp salt
1 tsp fresh-ground black pepper
½ cup sliced stuffed Spanish
  olives

Slice the garlic cloves very thinly. Quarter the onion and cut it in thick slices. Simmer the garlic and onions in the olive oil in a large, covered frying pan until the onions are wilted.

Trim the French beans and cut them in 1-in/25-mm pieces. Cut the tomatoes in thin wedges or large chunks. Add the beans and tomatoes to the onions, along with the sherry and simmer the vegetables, covered, for 15–20 minutes.

Cut the peppers in quarters or eighths, seed and derib them, and cut the pieces crossways in ¼-in/6-mm strips. Wash, destem and halve the mushrooms. Add the peppers, mushrooms, peas, vegetable broth, tomato paste, salt and pepper to the vegetables in the pan. Cover the mixture and cook for about 10 minutes, then uncover and simmer for about another 15 minutes, stirring often, or until the liquid is somewhat reduced and thickened.

Add the sliced olives, stir once more and serve hot.

COCIDO

Cocido is a peasant dish, variations of which have developed in all the different Spanish provinces. This is my simple version of the Cocido Madrileño that the ever-smiling Delfina used to prepare for us on cold, wet winter days in Segovia. The broths from the chick-peas and other vegetables combine with *fideos* (vermicelli) to make a light soup for the first course. Then serve the vegetables and those strange paprika-and-saffron-flavoured dumplings. Finish the meal with a very simple, crisp tossed salad. To go with it all, try a red Spanish wine.

SERVES 8

1 lb/450 g dried chick-peas, rinsed
pinch baking soda
3 onions
3–4 tbsp olive oil
salt
1½ lb/680 g potatoes (white-skinned if possible)
1½ lb/680 g cabbage
1 lb/450 g trimmed leeks (about 2¼ lb/1 kg untrimmed)
¾ lb/340 g carrots

fresh-ground black pepper
3 oz/85 g broken vermicelli
DUMPLINGS
1 egg
3–4 tbsp water
1 tbsp vegetable oil
½ tsp salt
½ tsp paprika
¼ tsp crushed saffron threads
¾ cup whole-wheat flour
¾ tsp baking powder

Soak the chick-peas overnight in 6½ pt/3.6 l of water with a pinch of baking soda. Then add 2 peeled onions, 1 tablespoon of the olive oil and 1 teaspoon salt, and bring the water to a boil. Lower the heat and simmer the beans until they are perfectly tender, probably about 1½ hours.

Meanwhile, prepare the vegetables. Peel the remaining onion and cut it in 1-in/25-mm chunks. Peel the potatoes and cut them in large cubes. Trim and core the cabbage and cut it in wedges or large pieces. Cut off the green tops of the leeks, trim the bottoms and slice them in half lengthways, almost to the bottom but leaving the two parts connected at the base. Scrape the carrots and cut them in 2-in/50-mm lengths.

Put all the vegetables in a large saucepan with 3–4 pt/2–2.25 l of water – just enough to cover them comfortably – and about 2 teaspoons salt. Bring the water to a boil and cook the vegetables 30–40 minutes or until they are all tender.

To make the batter for the dumplings beat together the egg, water, vegetable oil, salt, paprika and saffron. Sift the flour and baking powder together and stir them into the egg mixture.

About 30 minutes before you want to serve dinner, drain the chick-peas, discarding the 2 onions and reserving the liquid. You should have at least 1⅗ pt/900 ml. Leave the chick-peas in just enough broth to keep them moist, cover them tightly and place in a warm oven. Drain the other vegetables, again reserving the broth, and keep warm, moist and tightly covered, as the chick-peas.

Add 1⅗–2 pt/900 ml–1.1 l of the vegetable broth to the chick-pea broth, heat them together and season to taste with salt and pepper. Toss in the broken vermicelli and simmer until the noodles are tender – just 6–7 minutes. At the same time bring a saucepan of salted water to a boil and drop the dumpling batter into it by scant teaspoonfuls. Cover the saucepan and leave the dumplings to cook for 20 minutes. They'll be ready when you've finished eating the soup course.

Pile the hot chick-peas in the centre of a very large serving dish or shallow casserole and the other vegetables in a ring round them. Drizzle the beans and other vegetables with a few tablespoons of the remaining olive oil and sprinkle them with salt and pepper. Lift out the dumplings with a slotted spoon, arrange them at either end of the serving dish and serve.

Sangría

MAKES ABOUT 7 PT/4 L

6⅔ pt/3.6 l dry red wine	2 fl oz/55 ml curaçao
⅓ cup sugar	ice cubes
2½ fl oz/70 ml brandy	8–12 fl oz/225–340 ml soda
3 large oranges	water, to taste
2 large lemons	

Pour the wine into a punch bowl and stir in the sugar and the brandy. Cut 2 of the oranges into eighths and 1 of the lemons into quarters. Squeeze the juice from each piece of cut fruit into the punch bowl. Stir again and chill for 1–2 hours with the fruit.

At this point the cut, squashed fruit can be removed if you want a more elegant sangría or it can be left in if you don't care about looks. Halve and thinly slice the remaining orange and lemon. Add the sliced fruit to the sangría, floating it on top. Stir in the curaçao and just enough ice to keep the sangría cold. Just before serving pour in some soda water. Give it one final stir, pour and drink.

This is a basic sangría recipe. You may want to elaborate by adding some sliced apples, sliced bananas or other fruit, or by slightly varying some of the proportions. All variations are perfectly acceptable as long as they taste good.

Turn to SOUPS for two kinds of Gazpacho and a garlic soup. In DESSERTS see Caramel Custard and Castilian Hot Chocolate.

MEXICAN DISHES

I N THE *Popol Vuh*, the book of Mayan tribal legends that has been roughly equated with the Christian Bible, the story of the creation of humanity takes some very appealing turns. The Mayan gods seem to have been rather human themselves and did not always succeed at first try when they set out to do something. So, when they decided that it was time to people the world, they did not immediately seize on the perfect raw material for their task. Early prototypes were made from mud and then wood and rushes, but these people didn't quite work, and the gods returned to their drawing board.

In a stroke of divine inspiration they made people from maize, and these beings took to life with a success far beyond the gods' fondest expectations. In fact, they were rather too good. The maize people saw too far and understood too much. They were dangerously close to being gods themselves; their creators were impelled to 'blow a mist' into their eyes and fog their vision so they could see only what was near to them and not know more than they needed to.

This is telling evidence that the native inhabitants of Mesoamerica had a pretty high opinion of maize, and it's easy to understand why when you realize that it was, even more than wheat was to other peoples, the very stuff of life. Maize, in its numerous varieties, was the fundamental and indispensable food of all the Central American Indians, the food on which their cuisines, some of which reached high levels of sophistication, were firmly based.

To a very large degree this is still true today, certainly in Mexico. Maize is an important ingredient of countless Mexican dishes, and corn-meal and water are the sole ingredients of the Mexican tortilla, the staple food of the country. The tortilla is an ancient bread that has remained virtually unchanged through the centuries, though it is now cranked out on conveyor belts in tortilla bakeries.

I dare not guess how many millions of these thin, deliciously golden, pancake-like breads are consumed each day in Mexico, but I'm sure the figure is astounding. They are eaten plain and with butter, fried for crisps and used in some of the most popular Mexican dishes. Enchiladas are soft tortillas rolled round a filling and served hot with a sauce. Tacos are tortillas folded over a filling, sometimes left soft and sometimes fried crisp, and eaten like a sandwich. A large tortilla, folded round a filling envelope-style, with the ends tucked in, is called a *burrito*. But most important, no meal is served without a basket of fresh tortillas, still hot, to accompany it and I've seen good eaters put away a dozen or so at one sitting with some especially searing, chilli-laced dish.

This is not an exaggeration, nor is it even an example of unusual over-indulgence. Tucking into a basketful of hot tortillas, newly made from fresh *masa* and spread with some melted butter, is a real epicurean experience; it revealed in me, at any rate, a tortilla-eating capacity that I had hitherto little suspected. I was no novice at tortilla eating when my real moment of revelation came, in the big rustic kitchen of a country house in the lush Mexican interior. We were staying with the Gonzalez-Madrid family, friends of my husband, in the tiny village of San José de Gracia. On our first morning there, we were hospitably gathered in the kitchen round a big table and treated to one of the heartiest, hottest breakfasts I've ever eaten. There were sweet rolls and *chilaquiles* with rich, refried beans, fresh fruit and delicious Mexican hot chocolate, but oh, those tortillas.

The quiet Indian Nacha, who was the family's cook, presided over the stove, patting out perfect little circles of *masa* with deft flicks of her hand, snatching them off the griddle the instant they were done and passing them immediately to the table. They were tiny – a mere 4–5 in/100–125 mm across – with an irresistibly sweet flavour, and so soft and tender that they really almost melted in our mouths. It was then that I began to suspect that maybe people were made of maize, or if they weren't, perhaps they should have been (and might be all the sweeter for it).

The cuisine of Mexico today is still basically an amalgam of several Indian cuisines. The influence of Aztecs, Toltecs, Zapotecs and Mayans is felt much more strongly than that of their conquerors. Certainly the Spanish conquest made great additions to the indigenous kitchen, but in spite of that, there is little resemblance between the cooking of these two countries today.

Spanish cooking is mild – almost bland – by comparison with the fiery drama of Mexican cooking. In Mexico the food that is second only to maize in its importance is the chilli, which is cultivated and enjoyed in hundreds of varieties, ranging enormously in colour, size and intensity. Even in the *Popol Vuh* chillis were named as one of the first foods enjoyed by those maize people, and their popularity in Mexico has never waned. The market-place of every town or village has a generous space devoted to hills of fresh and dried chilli peppers, from the tiniest red ones that are like little flames to the largest, mildest green varieties. They have melodic names like serrano, poblano, jalapeño, pasilla, cascabella and xcatique – and their power is awesome.

As many sauces as France may have, Mexico has more, and every one of them contains some kind of chilli in one form or another. The chillis are often combined with onion and tomatoes as well as with some other particularly Mexican ingredients – *tomatillos* and fresh coriander leaves. *Tomatillos* look like green tomatoes with parchment-like outer skins covering them and have a fresh, tart flavour. Coriander leaves have a distinct, pungent taste and fragrance, unmistakable in any dish.

Some kind of freshly made chilli sauce is ever-present on the tables of restaurants and homes alike; it is as essential to Mexican cooking as salt. The flavour of those chillis explodes inside the mouth in a wonderfully exciting way and the heat that goes with it can be counteracted, not by drinking water or any cold liquid, but by eating tortillas, of course! Mexicans, who have eaten chillis all their lives, can swallow great amounts of them with ease, but foreigners must beware and develop their tolerance gradually. In the recipes I've written down for this book, I've gone very easy with the chillis, but feel free to increase them to your taste.

When cooking with chillis, always exercise great care. Remember that the seeds are the hottest part of a chilli; leave them in for a more intense, fiery effect and remove them for a more subdued flavour. And always, always, after handling chillis, wash your hands very well with soap and water. Then, even though you've washed carefully, keep your hands away from your eyes for an hour or more, as the tiniest trace of oil from a really hot chilli can make your eyes extremely uncomfortable at the least contact.

Another food that is indigenous to Mexico and to which Europeans took like ducks to water is chocolate. Bernal Díaz del Castillo, one of Cortez's foot soldiers, wrote an account called *The Conquest of New Spain*, and in it he described how Montezuma, the great Aztec emperor, was served large cupfuls of a strange, dark, foaming hot beverage called *cacao*. It was a substance that was unheard of in Spain at that time, but one that would soon be prized. Mexican hot chocolate is still a foaming drink, beaten with egg whites and almond paste and subtly perfumed with cinnamon and vanilla.

The people of Mexico eat and drink with gusto, and they express their exuberant enjoyment of their food in the way they refer to it. In Spanish an *-ita* or *-ito* added to the end of a word forms an affectionate diminutive. *Papas* are potatoes, *tortas* are little cakes and *frijoles* are beans, but one rarely hears the words spoken in their ordinary forms. I often remember taking a walk through a park in the lovely colonial town of Guanajuato and hearing the Indian women who were vending freshly cooked snacks calling out in their singsong voices, *'Tortitas! Calientitas! Con papitas, frijolitos!'*

The foods are savoury and delightful, fully worthy of the fondness with which they are named. In Guadalajara and Mexico City I was rarely served a dish swimming in its sauce or heavy with too much oil, and I found the lavish use of the chillis, in all their delicious variety, to be quite addictive. One of my husband's friends, a Mexican-American, asked his mother once, 'Why do Mexicans eat such hot food?' She summed up the whole issue admirably when she replied, 'Because it tastes so good.'

TORTILLAS

Making your own fresh tortillas needn't be very difficult or time-consuming, and the rewards in flavour are great. Tortillas do suffer with keeping, and if you've never had them freshly made, hot off the griddle, look forward to a real treat.

However, it's only fair to give warning that if you intend to shape your tortillas by hand, you're in for a long stretch of work. Although I've seen practised tortilla makers slap out perfect circles, thin and tender, in mere seconds, the first time I tried it, I found myself surrounded by crumbs of dough, holding a shapeless, broken lump. I discovered that a first-timer could turn out decent tortillas, but only by the painstaking process of rolling each one out between two sheets of waxed paper, slowly and carefully.

Fortunately, however, there exists a simple and cheap tool that reduces tortilla-making to a snap. The tortilla press, which can be purchased in most stores that sell ingredients for Mexican food, as well as in some stores which handle ingredients for Indian food (chapatis being similar to tortillas), is the miracle worker. I heartily recommend obtaining one if you are at all fond of tortillas.

As for the ingredients, the *masa harina* from which tortillas are made is nothing more than maize treated with lime water and specially ground to a very fine meal. Do not attempt to substitute corn-meal for *masa harina* – it is much coarser and will not work.

MAKES 12 TORTILLAS

2 cups masa harina   ¾–*1 tsp salt*
8 fl oz/225 ml water

Place the *masa*, water and salt in a bowl and stir until thoroughly combined. Knead gently with your hand for 1–2 minutes, until the dough holds together. A few more drops of water may be added if the dough seems too dry and crumbles away easily. It should be moist but firm. Divide the dough into 12 pieces of equal size and roll each piece into a ball.

If you are not using a tortilla press, place a ball of dough between two sheets of waxed paper and roll it out carefully into a circle about 6–6½ in/150–160 mm across.

If you do have a press, begin by placing the thin plastic sheet that comes with the press on the bottom section. Place a ball of dough on it in the centre of the press. Fold the plastic over the dough, leaving enough room for the dough to spread equally in all directions. This is simply a lining, to keep the tortilla from sticking to the press.

Fold the top of the press down, flip the handle over from the other side and push it down. Open the press up again and there will be your tortilla, perfectly round and thin, shaped in about 5 seconds. Peel back the plastic on top, turn the tortilla over on to the flat of your hand and gently peel back the plastic from the bottom. Keep the uncooked tortillas layered between sheets of waxed paper.

To cook the tortillas, preheat an ungreased heavy pan until it is hot enough to make a drop of water jump and sizzle.

Drop a tortilla on to the hot pan and, keeping the heat quite high, cook it for about 30–40 seconds. Turn it over with a spatula and cook the other side the same amount of time. The tortilla may start to puff up. This is fine – just press very gently on it with the flat spatula to keep the bubble or bubbles even.

Turn the tortilla twice more, giving it a total of about 2 minutes in the pan. When a tortilla is done, it has a pale golden colour, with a few dark brown spots or freckles here and there.

You can keep the tortillas warm for a little while by stacking them, wrapped in a tea-towel or cloth napkin, in a close, woven basket or a bowl. Otherwise you can reheat them in a hot skillet, one at a time for a few seconds on each side.

Serve as soon as possible with any kind of Mexican food. Fresh, hot tortillas spread with a little butter are also marvellous just by themselves.

SPINACH ENCHILADAS SUIZAS

SERVES 5

1½ lb/680 g trimmed spinach	SAUCE
3 tbsp olive oil	½ oz/15 g butter
½ oz/15 g butter	1 tbsp flour
½ large onion, chopped	8 fl oz/225 ml milk, heated
2 cloves garlic, minced	8 fl oz/225 ml soured cream, at
salt to taste	room temperature
¾ lb/340 g Gruyère cheese,	½ cup diced medium-hot green
grated	chillis
10 fresh Tortillas (p. 297)	OPTIONAL GARNISH
vegetable oil	soured cream and hot sauce

Wash the spinach leaves carefully, drain them and chop them. Heat the olive oil and butter in a large frying pan and sauté the onion and garlic in it until they are golden. Add the spinach and toss it in the hot oil until all of it is wilted. Salt it to your taste and continue cooking it over medium heat, stirring often, until all the liquid is gone.

Grate the cheese coarsely. Take a tortilla, brush it very lightly with vegetable oil and heat it quickly on both sides in a frying pan until it is very soft and flexible. Spread a heaped tablespoon of grated cheese in a line down the centre of it, then spread a heaped tablespoon of the spinach over the cheese. Fold one end of the tortilla over the filling and roll it up. Continue in this manner until all the tortillas and spinach are used up.

Lightly oil a large, shallow casserole and arrange the enchiladas in it in such a way that they won't unroll.

To make the sauce, melt the butter in a saucepan and stir in the flour. Cook this roux over low heat, stirring constantly, until it is golden. Add the heated milk and stir with a whisk until it is slightly thickened. Add the soured cream, diced chillis and the remaining cheese from the filling and cook the sauce over low heat until all the cheese is melted and the sauce is quite smooth. Season it lightly with salt and pepper and pour it over the enchiladas.

Cover the casserole and bake the enchiladas in a preheated oven at 350°F/180°C/Mark 4 for about 20–25 minutes. They should be very hot all the way through. If you like, you can uncover the casserole and brown the sauce under the grill for a few minutes before serving.

Serve the enchiladas hot, garnished with extra soured cream and hot sauce if desired.

EGG ENCHILADAS

SERVES 5

6 oz/170 g lightly salted,
  shelled pumpkin seeds
5 fl oz/140 ml Vegetable Broth
  (see pp. 60–61)
3½ tbsp lemon juice
2 cloves garlic, minced
½ cup plus 2 tbsp chopped
  medium-hot green chillis
¼ tsp salt, and more to taste
½ tsp fresh-ground black pepper,
  and more to taste
8 fl oz/225 ml double cream

10 large eggs
2 tbsp water or milk
2 tbsp fresh-chopped coriander
  leaves
1¼ oz/35 g butter
1 tsp dried crushed red chilli
  peppers
10 Tortillas (p. 297)
vegetable oil
GARNISH
½ cup chopped spring onions

Put the pumpkin seeds, vegetable broth, lemon juice, garlic and green chillis in the container of a blender and whirl at high speed until the mixture is puréed. Add the salt, pepper and cream and blend again for a very short time.

Beat the eggs in a large bowl with the water or milk, some salt and pepper, and the chopped coriander leaves. Melt the butter in a large frying pan, heat the crushed red chillis in it for a moment, then add the eggs. Cook the eggs, stirring them constantly, until they are set but still moist.

Heat a tortilla by brushing a hot frying pan with vegetable oil and placing the tortilla on it for 30 seconds–1 minute on each side. The tortilla should be completely flexible.

Spread about 2–3 tablespoons of the cooked eggs down the centre of the tortilla, then pour about 1 tablespoon of the pumpkin seed sauce over the eggs and roll up the tortilla over the filling. Continue until all the eggs are used up.

Arrange the enchiladas, seam side down, in a lightly oiled, shallow baking dish and spoon the remaining sauce over them. Bake the enchiladas in a preheated oven at 350°F/180°C/Mark 4 for about 20–25 minutes, then place them under the grill for a few moments to brown the top.

Sprinkle the enchiladas with chopped spring onions and serve.

ENCHILADAS SALSA VERDE

SERVES 6–8

2 lb/900 g tomatillos*
4 medium-sized jalapeño
  peppers, peeled, seeded and
  minced †
6 tbsp chopped fresh coriander
  leaves (packed)
1 tsp salt
1 cup finely chopped onions

vegetable oil for frying
16 Tortillas (p. 297)
1 lb/450 g fresh mozzarella
  cheese, cut in thin strips
½ lb/225 g mild white cheese,
  crumbled (see p. 204)

OPTIONAL GARNISH
Hot Paprika Sauce (see p. 107)

Peel the dry skins off the *tomatillos*, wash them and boil them in lightly salted water for 7–10 minutes, or until they are just soft. Drain, purée them in a blender and put them in a saucepan with the minced jalapeño peppers, 4 tablespoons of the chopped coriander leaves, the salt and ½ cup of the chopped onions. Simmer the sauce gently for about 40 minutes.

Heat a very small amount of vegetable oil in a pan and fry a tortilla in it for about 20 seconds on each side. Put 1 oz/25 g of the cheese strips on it, spread about 1 teaspoon of the green sauce over the cheese, and sprinkle 1 rounded teaspoon of the remaining onions over the sauce. Roll the tortilla securely round the filling. Continue filling the tortillas in this manner until all the tortillas and cheese are used up. Add a little more oil to the pan whenever necessary.

Arrange the enchiladas seam side down and close together in a lightly oiled baking dish and spoon the remaining sauce over them. Bake the enchiladas in a preheated oven at 350°F/180°C/Mark 4 for 15–20 minutes, then sprinkle the crumbled cheese and the remaining coriander leaves over them and serve immediately.

Hot sauce can be passed separately for those who really want to clear their heads.

*A kind of Mexican green tomato – small, hard and covered with a dry husk. Do not confuse *tomatillos* with unripe common tomatoes. The *tomatillos* have a distinct, tart flavour and are inedible unless cooked.
† If they are not available fresh, jalapeño peppers can be bought canned. Be sure to wash your hands carefully after handling hot peppers, and don't touch your eyes for at least 1–2 hours afterwards.

BEAN AND POTATO TACOS

SERVES 4–6

2 medium-sized potatoes (about
  1 lb/450 g)
½ onion
1½ oz/40 g butter
salt and pepper
14 fresh Tortillas (p. 297)

vegetable oil for frying
1½ cups Refried Kidney Beans
  (p. 307)
Hot Paprika Sauce (p. 107)
GARNISH
chopped cabbage and tomatoes

Peel the potatoes and cut them into small cubes. Boil them in salted water until they are almost tender, then drain. Chop the onion and sauté in the butter for a few minutes and add the potatoes. Continue sautéing this mixture, stirring often, until the potatoes are tender and slightly golden, about 10 minutes. Season to taste with salt and pepper.

Warm the tortillas quickly, one at a time, in a hot pan. If you like, you may brush them very lightly with oil before warming. Be sure to take them off the heat quickly or they will become crisp. They should be soft and flexible.

Put a rounded tablespoon of the refried beans on a tortilla and spread it across in a thick line down the centre, almost to the ends. Add a heaped tablespoon of the potatoes and arrange them the same way on top of the beans. Fold one side of the tortilla over the filling and roll it up or, if you prefer, simply fold the tortilla in half over the filling.

Just before serving, fry the tacos in a little bit of oil until they are crisp on both sides. Sprinkle them with hot sauce and chopped cabbage and tomatoes, and serve hot.

AVOCADO TACOS

SERVES 5–6

3 medium-sized ripe avocados
juice of 1 large lemon
salt to taste
½ clove garlic, pressed or
   minced
¼ cup minced onions
12 Tortillas (p. 297)
vegetable oil for frying

8 fl oz/225 ml soured cream
1 onion, chopped
6–8 oz/170–225 g white
   cheese, crumbled
GARNISH
Fresh Tomato Hot Sauce (p.
   109)

Peel and mash the avocados, then stir in the lemon juice, a little salt, the garlic and minced onions. Taste, and add more salt if you like.

Take one of the tortillas and heat it for a moment on each side in a lightly greased pan. The instant it is warm enough to roll without cracking, spread a heaped tablespoon of the avocado filling in a slightly off-centre line across the tortilla and roll it up round the filling. Continue until all the filling is used up.

Fry the rolled up tortillas in about ⅓ in/8 mm of hot vegetable oil, on both sides, until they are just crisp. Drain them quickly on kitchen towels and arrange them on plates.

Put a dollop of soured cream on each one, sprinkle with the chopped onions and crumbled cheese, and serve warm with Fresh Tomato Hot Sauce on the side.

CHILAQUILES

The first time I ate *chilaquiles*, that thick, porridge-like mixture of fried tortillas, cheese, chillis and changeable other ingredients, was when we were staying at the house of a friend in the little village of San José de Gracia, in the Mexican countryside. In the big, comfortable kitchen we were served a breakfast of *chilaquiles*, fresh-made tortillas, hot sauce, *frijolitos* (as our host affectionately called his refried beans) and foamy hot chocolate. It was an eye-opening, sinus-clearing breakfast and these *chilaquiles* are but a cool shadow of the fiery dish we ate that morning.

Good for breakfast, lunch or dinner and quite hot enough for most British palates, is this version of *chilaquiles*.

SERVES 6–8

10 Tortillas (p. 297)
vegetable oil for frying
salt
*1 lb/450 g tomatillos (see
  p. 301)*
1½ lb/680 g ripe red tomatoes
2 medium-sized onions
1½ tbsp olive oil
¾ cup diced mild green chillis
*2–3 jalapeño peppers, seeded and
  minced (see p. 301)*

*2 tbsp chopped fresh coriander
  leaves (packed)*
½ tsp sugar
*1 lb/450 g Cheddar cheese,
  grated*
4 fl oz/115 ml milk
4 fl oz/115 ml soured cream
GARNISH
3 hard-boiled eggs, chopped
3–4 spring onions, chopped
soured cream

Cut the tortillas into eighths and fry them in hot vegetable oil until they are crisp. Drain them on kitchen towels and sprinkle them lightly with salt.

Peel the dry skins off the *tomatillos*, wash them and plunge them into boiling water. Boil them for 7–8 minutes, or until they start to split. Drain them immediately and purée them in a blender.

Boil the red tomatoes for about 3 minutes, peel them and purée them as well.

Peel and coarsely chop the onions and sauté them in the olive oil in a large frying pan, until they are golden. Add the puréed *tomatillos* and tomatoes, the diced green chillis, the minced jalapeños, 1¼ teaspoon salt, coriander leaves and sugar. Simmer this mixture for about 10 minutes. Taste, and correct the seasoning if necessary with more salt or a tiny bit more sugar.

Spoon a little of this sauce into the bottom of a large casserole. Spread ⅓ of the crisp tortilla pieces over the sauce, and arrange ⅓ of the cheese evenly over the crisps. Spoon ⅓ of the remaining sauce over the cheese. Make 2 more layers the same way.

Stir together the milk and the soured cream and pour the mixture over the top of the casserole. Slip a knife through the top layer of sauce in a few places to allow some of the milk mixture to seep down.

Cover the casserole tightly and bake in a preheated oven at 375°F/190°C/Mark 5 for 20–25 minutes, then remove the lid and bake for 10 minutes more.

Serve hot, and pass little bowls of chopped eggs, chopped spring onions and soured cream.

CHILAQUILES WITH MUSHROOMS

SERVES 6

8 Tortillas (p. 297)
vegetable oil for frying
salt to taste
1 lb/450 g mushrooms
2 tbsp olive oil
4 cloves garlic, minced or pressed
pinch of thyme
pinch of oregano
pepper to taste
1 cup sliced spring onions

1 lb/450 g tomatoes, peeled and puréed
6 tbsp chopped medium-hot green chillis
3 tbsp chopped fresh coriander leaves
½ lb/225 g Cheddar cheese, grated
3 eggs
8 fl oz/225 ml milk

Cut the tortillas into strips about 1 × 2 in/25 × 50 mm and fry them in vegetable oil until they are crisp and golden. Drain the crisps on kitchen towels and salt them lightly.

Wash the mushrooms and slice them. Heat the olive oil in a large frying pan and sauté the garlic in it until it begins to colour. Add the sliced mushrooms and toss them over medium-high heat until they have released their water and most of it has evaporated. Add the thyme, oregano, some salt and pepper and toss again until the seasonings are evenly distributed. Put the mushrooms aside.

Heat about 1½ tablespoons of vegetable oil in a frying pan and sauté the spring onions in it for a few minutes. Add the tomatoes, chillis, coriander leaves and some salt and pepper, and cook over medium heat for about 5 minutes. Add the mushrooms to the tomato sauce.

Lightly oil a large casserole and cover the bottom with ⅓ of the fried tortilla strips. Sprinkle ⅓ of the grated cheese over them and spoon ⅓ of the tomato-mushroom mixture over the cheese. Make 2 more similar layers.

Beat together the eggs and the milk and pour this custard over the casserole, slipping a knife through the top layer in a few places to allow the liquid to drain through evenly.

Cover the casserole and bake it in a preheated oven at 350°C/180°C/Mark 4 for about 30 minutes. Serve quickly with a salad and fresh, hot tortillas.

RAJAS CON QUESO

These peppers with cheese make an excellent sauce or filling for omelettes.

SERVES 6 AS A FIRST COURSE OR 4 AS A MAIN COURSE

2¼ lb/1 kg green peppers
 (about 5 large)
1½ lb/680 g tomatoes or 4–5
 canned tomatoes and 8 fl oz/
 225 ml juice
1 large yellow onion

1 large red onion
3 tbsp olive oil
1½ tsp salt
1 small hot green chilli, minced
8 oz/225 g cream cheese

Grill the peppers, turning them often, until their skins are evenly charred and blistered over the whole surface. Remove them from the grill and put them in a paper bag for a few minutes to sweat. Then take them out and slip off the skins.

Remove the seeds and ribs from the peppers and cut them up in ¼-in/6-mm strips.

If you are using fresh tomatoes, plunge them into boiling water for a few moments, then take them out, peel them and cut them into thin wedges. Reserve all the juice that drains away as you handle the tomatoes.

Peel the onions, cut them in half lengthways and slice the halves $1/4$ in/6 mm thick. Heat the olive oil in a large frying pan and sauté the onion slices in it until they are golden.

Add the tomatoes, the reserved tomato juice, the salt, the minced green chillis and the pepper strips. Simmer this mixture until the tomatoes are soft (6–7 minutes), then slice the cream cheese and add it. Continue simmering the mixture, stirring often, until the cream cheese is melted and the sauce slightly thickened. Serve hot in bowls with warm tortillas.

REFRIED KIDNEY BEANS

SERVES 4–6

6 tbsp vegetable oil
1 oz/25 g butter
1½ onions
1 clove garlic, minced (optional)
4½ cups cooked kidney beans
16 fl oz/450 ml cooking liquid
  from beans

salt to taste
GARNISH
grated mild cheese, such as mild
  Cheddar

Heat the oil and the butter together in a large, heavy frying pan. Chop the onions and sauté them in the oil and butter until they are golden. If you want to add garlic, sauté it with the onions at this point.

Add the beans and their cooking liquid and lower the heat slightly. Cook the beans, stirring often, until most of the liquid has been absorbed. Mash some of the beans with a wooden spoon – some people prefer to mash all the beans; I like mine about half-mashed, but this is just a matter of taste. Continue cooking and stirring for perhaps 30 minutes until the beans have the consistency of a fairly thick paste.

Serve hot as a side dish or use as a filling for tacos, either alone or with cooked potatoes. If served as a side dish, some grated cheese should be sprinkled on top or stirred in.

SPICY REFRIED BEANS

SERVES 6

1½ cups dried red kidney beans
2½ pt/1.4 l water
2 tbsp corn oil
1½ onions
3 tsp salt
2 fl oz/55 ml olive oil
3 cloves garlic, minced
1 cup peeled, chopped tomatoes

2 small jalapeño peppers, seeded
    and minced (see p. 301)
2 tbsp lemon juice
¼ tsp cinnamon
⅛ tsp cloves
½ oz/15 g butter
1 cup grated Cheddar cheese
    (optional)

Rinse the beans and put them in a large saucepan with the water, corn oil, ½ an onion, chopped, and 2 teaspoons of the salt. Bring the water to a boil, then turn down the heat, cover the pan and simmer the beans gently for about 1½ hours. Remove the cover and cook the beans a little while longer, until completely tender and the remaining liquid is thick.

In a very large frying pan heat the olive oil and sauté the remaining onion, chopped, and the garlic until golden. Add the tomatoes, jalapeño peppers, lemon juice and spices. Pour the beans, together with their liquid, into the seasonings and stir.

Over a low heat, and stirring often, cook the beans together with the seasonings until the mixture is quite thick, but still moist. Time will vary, but it could take as long as 45 minutes. If the beans become too dry, just add a little water. Stir in the butter and, if desired, the grated cheese. Continue stirring the beans over a low heat until both butter and cheese are melted.

TORTITAS CON QUESO

We were having margaritas before dinner one evening in a wonderful restaurant in Mexico City and thought we should have something to nibble with them. The young waiter read our minds – he knew just what we wanted even though we had never heard of it and brought us a plate of fresh, hot *tortitas*. The rest of the dinner has long faded from memory, but ah! those *tortitas*.

They were little pastries, made of *masa*, just like tortillas, but fatter and with edges. I never did find out the name of the cheese but have recaptured its slightly goaty flavour by combining simple dry white cheese with some feta.

MAKES 14–15 TORTITAS

2 cups dry masa harina
8 fl oz/225 ml water
salt
vegetable oil (about 2 tbsp)

2–2½ fl oz/55–70 ml medium-
   hot green chilli sauce
4 oz/115 g mild white cheese,
   crumbled (see p. 204)
2 oz/55 g feta cheese, crumbled

Combine the *masa harina* and the water in a bowl, add a little salt and work it into a dough. Divide the dough into 14–15 even bits the size of large walnuts. Shape each one into an even, flat round, about 3–4 in/75–100 mm across, and turn up the edges to make a ¼-in/6-mm rim. Brush the insides of these shells lightly with vegetable oil.

Bake the *tortita* shells for 20–25 minutes in a preheated oven at 450°F/230°C/Mark 8. They should be slightly darker and almost crisp round the edges.

When they are cool enough to handle, spread each one evenly with a scant teaspoon of the green chilli sauce. Combine the two cheeses in a bowl and crumble them together until they are thoroughly integrated. Divide the cheese evenly among the *tortitas*, sprinkling it over the chilli sauce.

Serve the *tortitas* with any tequila drink or with beers as an hors-d'oeuvre.

MEXICAN RICE

SERVES 8

2 large onions
3–4 cloves garlic, minced
2 fl oz/55 ml olive oil
½ tsp ground ginger
½ tsp ground coriander seeds
¼ tsp ground cloves

¼ tsp fresh-ground black pepper
2 cups long-grain white rice
1⅓ pt/680 ml puréed tomatoes
2 tsp salt
12 fl oz/340 ml boiling water

Peel and coarsely chop the onions, mince the garlic and sauté them both in the olive oil until the onions are golden. Add the ginger, coriander, cloves and pepper, stir, then add the rice. Continue sautéing the mixture, stirring often, until the rice is slightly coloured.

Add the puréed tomatoes, the salt and the boiling water. Stir the mixture once, then cover and simmer the rice over low heat for another 25 minutes. All the liquid should be absorbed.

Serve the rice hot with enchiladas, Rajas con Queso (p. 306) or anything at all!

GUACAMOLE

SERVES 6–8

2 lb/900 g ripe avocados
2 fl oz/55 ml lemon juice
¼ cup minced onion
¼ cup chopped fresh coriander
   leaves

½ lb/225 g tomatoes (about 2
   medium sized)
5 tbsp finely chopped green
   chillis
1¾ tsp salt

Cut the avocados in half lengthways, remove the pits and scoop out the meat. In a medium-sized bowl, mash the avocado with a silver fork or wooden spoon.

Add the lemon juice, onions and coriander leaves. Coarsely chop the tomatoes and add them to the avocado, along with the chillis and the salt. Stir everything together thoroughly and serve chilled with fried tortilla crisps.

STRAWBERRY WATER

SERVES 6

2 lb/900 g fresh, ripe
  strawberries
16 fl oz/450 ml water

2½ fl oz/70 ml honey
2 tbsp lemon juice
10–12 ice cubes

Hull and wash the strawberries and purée them in a blender with the water in 2–3 batches. Strain the purée through a fine sieve and discard the seeds.

Stir in the honey and lemon juice thoroughly, and when the honey is completely dissolved, chill the mixture well. Just before serving, add the ice cubes and stir again.

CANTALOUP WATER

SERVES 6–8

5½ lb/2.5 kg ripe cantaloup (about
  3 medium sized)
8–12 fl oz/225–340 ml cold water

2 fl oz/55 ml honey
10–12 large ice cubes

Peel and seed the cantaloups and cut the fruit into chunks. Purée the fruit in a blender, doing about 2–3 cups at a time and adding a little cold water as necessary.

When all the fruit is puréed, stir in the honey and continue stirring until the honey is completely dissolved into the fruit juice. Add the ice cubes, stir and chill for about 30 minutes before serving. If the liquid is too thick for your taste, add a little more cold water.

Delicious with spicy Mexican food.

See SOUPS for Tortilla Soup Tlaxcalteca, Crema de Verduras, Creamed Avocado Soup and Cold Avocado Soup.

INDIAN FOODS

I'VE NEVER BEEN TO INDIA, but I have been to what must be the next best place for sampling and enjoying Indian food – London. The culinary pleasures of that city are vastly enriched by a wealth of Indian restaurants which reflect all the variety of that ancient, sophisticated cuisine, and I've spent many a glad hour pursuing my interest in it at the tables of those fragrant establishments.

A gratifying range of the simpler and more adaptable dishes can be concocted with relative ease: it takes only a modicum of effort to procure a few unusual but definitely obtainable spices, and you're on your way. The recipes that follow are but a tiny sampling, a few favourites of my own that can be successfully reproduced here without extraordinary measures. The cooking of India is so wonderful and involves such a highly developed meatless cuisine, that it would be a sin to bypass it. You probably needn't go far to find the spices and herbs you'll need. A well-stocked supermarket will provide most of your needs, and the few harder-to-find items can often be found in Indian and Chinese grocery stores. Occasionally, substitutions can be made, but certain ingredients cannot be changed for others without a substantial loss in the texture or flavour that makes a dish what it is. I recommend making the effort to search out what you need.

Fresh coriander leaves, for example, have a delightfully pungent taste and aroma that no amount of parsley can ever duplicate, although this substitution is suggested in some cookbooks. Fresh ginger is a very different thing from the ground dried ginger you'll find in the spice rack – each has its own uses. And there is no substitute for saffron. Turmeric provides a pleasant yellow colour at a fraction of the cost, but only saffron tastes like saffron. It is the costliest spice in the world because it is made from the stamens of crocus blossoms, and thousands of them are needed to make a very small amount of saffron. But the good news is that a little goes a long way.

I've always found the actual cooking of Indian food a pleasurable experience. The kitchen is filled with the heady aromas of spices from the very start, aromas that conjure up mysterious, distant lands. The colours are beautiful, and the sizzling and popping mustard seeds or ginger when they are heated in oil keeps one wide awake. Another part of the fun is finding out that curries need not all taste alike, as they do when commercially bottled curry powders are used. As soon as you start using recipes that call for individual mixtures of spices, you'll happily notice that each curry has a distinctive flavour and character of its own. But the nicest surprise is how fast it all goes. A recipe with a list of ingredients as long as your arm shouldn't put you off: it will all find its way into the saucepan with gratifying speed. Before long you'll be tasting, and then the real enjoyment starts.

Finally, such dishes always look so exotic and brilliant when they are served. Nothing is easier than serving an Indian meal, for all the dishes are put on the table at once – even the sweet can be brought out with the rest, though we usually succumb to our Western habits in that case and serve it later. The effect is opulent and colourful. In addition to the five or six dishes that make up a well-designed meal, the table is also peppered with an intriguing array of little bowls full of chutneys, pickles, fruits, nuts, raisins and other condiments – all in all a dazzling spread.

Everyone proceeds according to his or her own inclination, sampling and combining to taste from the rich assortment. Spicy and hot foods are pleasingly contrasted with cooling yoghurt *raitas* or fresh fruit, and dry dishes with moist, rich ones. The quick, hot Indian breads, perfect for scooping up all these things, should be provided in quantity. Puris and chapatis (see BREADS section) are easy to make and delicious. Both are unleavened and made of whole-wheat flour. Puris are fried in oil and puffed like little balloons; chapatis are flat and a little thicker.

The perfect drink to sip with Indian food is a good pale ale, icy cold, or a gin and tonic with a slice of lime. A hot, sweetly spiced tea can also be very pleasant. I don't recommend wine, as I have not yet discovered the wine that can bring out the best in Indian foods and that is, in turn, enhanced by that well-spiced cuisine.

If you take a fancy to Indian cooking, as I have, you'll see that the strange and bewildering will soon become very manageable and familiar, but with such foods, never ordinary. It is one of the great cuisines of the world, and even the rather elementary level at which it is sampled here does not fall short of gastronomic excitement.

Ghee

Ghee is nothing more complicated than clarified butter, and it is one of the staple ingredients used in all types of Indian cooking. Sometimes regular unclarified butter can be used in a recipe that calls for ghee, but often clarified butter is absolutely necessary. Unclarified butter will quickly burn at high temperatures, whereas ghee will not, and that is a quality that will earn your gratitude when you start to cook Indian food. Clarifying butter is quite a simple procedure and well worth the small trouble for the superior results it will yield.

Once clarified, butter will keep for weeks and weeks in the refrigerator, and for quite a while even without refrigeration, so you need to do this job only once in a long while.

To make ghee, melt 1 lb/450 g or more of butter over low heat in a heavy-bottomed saucepan, being careful not to let it brown. When it is entirely melted, skim off all the foam from the top and discard it. Raise the heat until the butter foams up again, then skim off the foam once more. Repeat this procedure another couple of times or until all the foam is gone and a clear, golden liquid is left.

Remove from the heat and carefully pour the melted butter off into a bowl or other container until only the fine sediment at the bottom of the pan is left. Discard the sediment.

CURRIED VEGETABLES WITH COCONUT

SERVES 6–8

2 fl oz/55 ml vegetable oil
3 cloves garlic, minced
1 tbsp peeled and grated fresh
  ginger
½ cup chopped onions
1 tsp mustard seeds
2 tbsp ground coriander
1 tsp ground turmeric
¼ tsp cayenne pepper
1 cup thin-sliced carrots
½ lb/225 g French beans, cut
  in 1-in/25-mm lengths

1 cup sliced spring onions
2 green peppers, stemmed,
  seeded and cut in strips
1 small, hot green chilli, minced
1 cup flaked unsweetened
  coconut
16 fl oz/450 ml water
1½ tsp salt
2 tsp sugar
½ cup peeled, sliced red pepper
5 fl oz/140 ml yoghurt

Heat the oil in a large, heavy-bottomed saucepan and sauté the garlic, ginger and onions in it until the onions begin to show colour. Add the mustard seeds, coriander, turmeric and cayenne, and stir over medium heat for about 2 minutes.

Add the carrots, French beans, spring onions, pepper and hot chilli and toss with the spices for a few minutes, then add the coconut, water, salt and sugar. Stir well, cover and simmer for about 20 minutes. Remove the lid and continue simmering, stirring often, until the liquid is reduced by over half.

Stir in the red pepper strips and yoghurt, cook a few minutes more over high heat and taste. Correct the seasoning if necessary and serve hot with rice and raita.

CURRIED CABBAGE AND PEAS

SERVES 6–8

1 medium-sized head green
  cabbage
3 tbsp vegetable oil
1 tsp crushed dried red chillis
½ tsp ground ginger

½ tsp whole mustard seeds
½ tsp ground cumin
2 bay leaves
1 tsp ground coriander
½ tsp ground turmeric

2 tsp salt

8 fl oz/225 ml water

2½ cups fresh peas

½ oz/15 g butter

1½ tsp garam masala (p. 335)

1 tbsp lemon juice

½ tsp sugar

1–2 tbsp yoghurt (optional)

Shred the cabbage coarsely. Heat the vegetable oil in a large frying pan and stir in the crushed red chillis, ginger, mustard seeds, cumin, bay leaves, coriander, turmeric and salt. Heat the spices gently for about 2 minutes, stirring often.

Add the shredded cabbage and sauté it, stirring often, until it is all evenly coated with the spices and beginning to wilt, 10–15 minutes. Add the water and the peas, cover and cook over medium heat for 20 minutes.

Remove the cover, stir in the butter, garam masala, lemon juice and sugar, and simmer, uncovered, for another 10–15 minutes. There should be very little or no excess liquid at this point.

Stir in a little yoghurt if desired and serve hot with rice and raita.

EGG AND POTATO CURRY

SERVES 8

SPICE PASTE

1 large onion, grated

2 cloves garlic, minced or crushed

1 tsp crushed dried red chillis

1 tbsp peeled and grated fresh
   ginger

2 tsp minced green chillis

½ tsp ground turmeric

½ tsp ground cumin

2 tsp ground coriander

2 tbsp water

½ tsp salt, and more to taste

CURRY

2 lb/900 g potatoes

3 tbsp vegetable oil

5 fl oz/140 ml water

3 large tomatoes, cut in thin
   wedges or chopped

2 bay leaves

7 hard-boiled eggs

Combine all the ingredients for the paste and pound them together in a large mortar or blend them for several minutes in a blender or food processor.

Scrub the potatoes and cut them in 1-in/25-mm cubes, then sauté them in the vegetable oil, stirring constantly until they start to show some colour, about 10 minutes. Add the spice paste and continue stirring over medium heat for another 5 minutes.

Add the water, the tomatoes and the bay leaves, stir, cover and simmer over low heat for 20 minutes. Uncover the curry and simmer another 10 minutes, stirring occasionally.

Coarsely chop the hard-boiled eggs, add them to the vegetables and stir over low heat for several more minutes, just until the eggs are heated through. Add a little more salt if needed and serve.

CAULIFLOWER CURRY

SERVES 4

1 large head cauliflower
1 medium potato (6–8 oz)
4 tbsp vegetable oil
1 tsp black mustard seeds
1 tsp ground turmeric
½ tsp ground cumin
½ tsp ground coriander
½ tsp cayenne pepper

1 clove garlic, minced or
   crushed
½ onion, slivered
1 tsp salt
½ pt/285 ml water
1 medium-sized tomato, chopped
2 tbsp lemon juice

Trim and wash the cauliflower and break it up into very small florets. Scrub the potato and boil it in salted water until it is nearly tender, but not quite done.

Heat the oil in a fairly large frying pan over medium–low heat and add the mustard seeds, heating until the seeds pop, just a few minutes. When the mustard seeds have finished popping, add the turmeric, cumin, coriander, cayenne, garlic and onions. Sauté this mixture over medium heat, stirring constantly, for 3–4 minutes.

Add the cauliflower and sauté, stirring often, for 4–5 minutes, then add the salt and water and cover the pan tightly. Allow the curry to simmer, covered, for 5 minutes, while you cut up the parboiled potato into 1-in/25-mm cubes.

Add the potato, stir, cover again and leave to simmer for 10 minutes. Then add the tomato and the lemon juice and stir, uncovered, over medium heat, for another few minutes.

Serve hot with rice, raita, chutneys and other condiments.

CURRIED CHICK-PEAS

SERVES 4–6

½ oz/15 g butter or 1 tbsp oil
1 tsp ground coriander
1 tsp ground cumin
1 tsp ground turmeric
¼ tsp cayenne pepper, or to taste
⅜ tsp ground cloves
⅜ tsp ground cinnamon
3 cloves garlic, minced
⅓ tsp ground ginger

salt to taste
3 cups cooked chick-peas, with
    reserved liquid (see p. 152)
2 tbsp lemon juice, and more to
taste
1 tbsp chopped fresh coriander
    leaves, and more to taste
1 firm tomato, cut in ½-in/
    12-mm dice

Melt the butter in a saucepan and over low heat stir in the spices. Allow them to heat, stirring often, for a few minutes.

Stir in the chick-peas and enough of the reserved liquid to just barely cover them. Stir well, and mash a few of the beans with a fork or potato masher.

Cook the chick-peas over a medium heat for about 20 minutes, or until the sauce is quite thick, stirring often. Remove from heat.

Stir in the lemon juice, the chopped coriander leaves and the diced tomato. Taste, and correct the seasoning.

SPICED AUBERGINE

SERVES 6–8

2 lb/900 g aubergine
1⅕–1⅗ pt/680–900 ml Akni
    (p. 333)
2 tbsp ground coriander
1½ tsp salt
½ tsp ground black pepper
¼ tsp cayenne pepper

2 tsp peeled and minced fresh
    ginger
3 tbsp fresh lemon juice
1½ oz/40 g butter or ghee (p. 317)
GARNISH
chopped chives or fresh coriander
    leaves

Peel the aubergines and cut them in strips lengthways, 1 in/25 mm wide and about ½ in/12 mm thick. Cut the long strips in 2-in/50-mm lengths.

Heat the Akni in a medium-sized enamelled saucepan and simmer the aubergine strips in it for about 15 minutes or until they are just tender. Drain them well.

Combine the coriander, salt, black pepper, cayenne, minced ginger and lemon juice in a small bowl and mix into a smooth paste.

Melt the butter or ghee in a fairly large frying pan and sauté the aubergine strips for 5 minutes only, stirring and tossing them constantly. Add the spice paste and stir often over medium heat for about 10–15 minutes, or until all the aubergine strips are evenly coated with spices and nearly dry, with no excess moisture.

Serve the aubergine hot, sprinkled with chopped chives or coriander leaves.

GREEN CURRY

So called because of its colour, but red-hot from the seasoning point of view. Don't be frightened off because it's truly delicious, but on the other hand, this isn't the curry to start with if you've never made one before and are unaccustomed to spicy foods. (Serve it with plain rice pilau and some yoghurt or raita.)

SERVES 6–8

1 lb/450 g potatoes
1 lb/450 g French beans
¾ lb/340 g courgettes
1 lb/450 g spinach
2½ oz/70 g butter
1½ lb/680 g onions
10 medium-sized cloves garlic
2 tsp ground turmeric
1 tbsp ground coriander
1 tbsp ground cumin
½ tsp hot paprika
½ tsp cayenne pepper
½ tsp black pepper
¼ tsp ground cinnamon
1½ tsp salt
1½ tbsp peeled and grated fresh ginger
4 tbsp chopped green chillis
2 tbsp lemon juice
6 fl oz/170 ml water

Scrub or peel the potatoes, quarter them lengthways, and slice thickly. Boil in salted water for 5 minutes only, drain and set aside.

Trim the French beans and cut them in 1-in/25-mm pieces. Boil them in salted water for 5 minutes, drain and set aside.

Slice the courgettes rather thickly, boil them in salted water for 3–4 minutes only, drain and set aside.

Wash and coarsely chop the spinach and set it aside.

Melt the butter in a large saucepan. Halve and thickly slice the onions and crush or mince the garlic, and sauté them in the butter until the onions begin to colour. Then add the turmeric, coriander, cumin, hot paprika, cayenne, black pepper, cinnamon and salt.

Stir this mixture over a medium heat for a few minutes, then add the prepared vegetables, the ginger, green chillis, lemon juice and water. Stir all the vegetables and spices together thoroughly and simmer, stirring again frequently, until most of the water is gone and the vegetables are just tender.

SMOTHERED POTATOES

SERVES 6

2 lb/900 g potatoes	2½ fl oz/70 ml yoghurt
2 tsp ground turmeric	1½ oz/40 g butter
1 tbsp garam masala (p. 335)	2 bay leaves
2 tsp salt	1 tsp crushed dried red pepper
½ tsp ground cumin	1 tsp sugar
½ tsp black pepper	

Peel the potatoes and cut them in 1-in/25-mm chunks. Boil them in salted water until they are about half done, 8–10 minutes. Drain them and prick them a little with a fork.

Make a paste of turmeric, garam masala, salt, cumin, black pepper and yoghurt. Roll the hot potatoes in this paste until they are all thoroughly coated.

Melt the butter in a medium-sized, shallow, fireproof casserole and add the bay leaves and red pepper, stir them over low heat for a few minutes, then add the sugar. In a few minutes, when the sugar just begins to caramelize (to turn light brown), add the potatoes, stir and toss them gently for a few minutes, then cover the casserole tightly and bake in a preheated oven at 350°F/180°C/ Mark 4 for about 30 minutes.

PURÉE OF SCORCHED TOMATOES

SERVES 6–8

2 lb/900 g ripe, red tomatoes
1 oz/25 g butter
1 tsp dried basil, crushed
1 tsp black pepper

½ tsp crushed saffron threads
¼ tsp thyme
salt to taste
2 fl oz/55 ml double cream

Put the tomatoes under a grill and turn them often until they are lightly charred all over. Let the tomatoes cool slightly or hold them under cold running water, and slip off the skins. Cut the tomatoes into chunks and purée them in a blender.

Melt the butter in a large frying pan and add the basil, pepper, saffron and thyme. Sauté the herbs and spices, stirring, for 2 minutes, then pour in the tomato purée and stir in 2 teaspoons of salt, or more to your taste.

Simmer the purée very gently, stirring occasionally, until it is very thick, about 1½ hours. Stir in the cream and stir over high heat, just long enough to regain the right consistency: that of a thin paste.

The purée can be served hot or cool, but I prefer it hot. Serve it as a rich, mild accompaniment to spicy Indian dishes.

DAL

Any purée or soup-like dish of spiced lentils, thin or thick, hotly or mildly spiced, is called dal. The variations on this theme are endless.

SERVES 4–6

1 cup lentils
1⅗ pt/900 ml water
1 tsp salt
2 tbsp peeled and grated fresh
  ginger
¼ tsp ground turmeric
crushed seeds from 4 cardamom pods

¼ tsp cayenne pepper
1¼ oz/35 g butter
½ tsp crushed dried red pepper
½ tsp ground cumin
2 tbsp chopped fresh coriander
  leaves
lemon juice

Rinse the lentils and combine them in a medium-sized saucepan with the water and salt. Bring the water to a boil, then lower the heat and simmer for 1 hour, skimming off the top as needed. Add the grated ginger, turmeric, crushed cardamom seeds and cayenne and continue simmering until the lentils are perfectly tender. Add more water if the mixture gets too thick – it should have the consistency of a thick soup.

Melt the butter in a small frying pan and sauté the crushed red pepper and cumin in it for a few minutes. Stir the butter and spices into the lentils, along with the fresh coriander leaves and a little lemon juice.

Serve the dal hot with curries and rice.

PLAIN PILAU

This is a fragrant, delicate, slightly sweet rice dish, perfect with a searingly hot curry. It is called plain because some others are very much more complicated, but it is actually not plain at all; rather, quite wonderful.

SERVES 6–8

2 oz/55 g butter	¾ cup blanched, slivered almonds*
2 cups long-grain white rice	½ cup raisins
¼ tsp cinnamon	1 cup shelled fresh peas
crushed seeds from 8 cardamom pods	1⅗ pt/900 ml hot water
	1½ tsp salt

Melt the butter in a large, fireproof casserole and fry the rice in it over low heat until it just starts to colour. Add the cinnamon and the crushed cardamom seeds. Stir and continue frying for 1–2 minutes.

Add the remaining ingredients and stir briefly. Bring the water to a boil, then lower the heat, cover the casserole tightly and let the rice steam for about 20 minutes. All the water should be absorbed and the rice just tender but not mushy.

*To blanch almonds, drop them for a minute in boiling water, then slip off the brown skins as soon as they are loose enough.

VEGETABLE PILAU

This pilau is a rather elaborate and satisfying dish and makes a nice meal when served with yoghurt or raita, an assortment of chutneys, some chapatis and fresh fruit. With the addition of dal and a vegetable curry, the meal becomes a feast.

SERVES 6–8

2½ oz/70 g butter or ghee
    (p. 317)
2 large onions, chopped
2 bay leaves, crushed
½ tsp ground cloves
½ tsp ground cinnamon
1 tsp peeled and grated or
    minced fresh ginger
½ cup potato, cut in small dice
½ cup cauliflower, coarsely
    chopped
½ cup shelled fresh peas
½ cup carrots, cut in small dice

½ cup French beans, cut in
    ½-in/12-mm pieces
½ cup summer squash, cut in
    small dice
½ cup green pepper, cut in
    small dice
2½ cups long-grain white rice
½–¾ tsp crushed saffron
    threads
2 pt/1.1 l water
2 tsp salt
⅓–½ cup coarsely chopped
    cashews
⅓–½ cup raisins

Heat the butter or ghee in a large saucepan and sauté the onions and bay leaves in it until the onions begin to colour. Add the cloves, cinnamon and ginger and stir over medium heat for 1 minute, then add all the prepared vegetables, the rice and the saffron. Toss over medium heat for about 5 minutes, then add the water and salt. Bring the water to a boil, turn the heat down to low, cover the pot tightly and cook for 25–30 minutes. All the water should be absorbed.

Add the cashews and raisins and mix everything together by gently lifting and tossing with wooden spoons. Spoon the mixture into a large, well-buttered casserole, cover and bake in a preheated oven at 350°F/180°C/Mark 4 for about 20 minutes. Serve the pilau steaming hot from the casserole.

SAFFRON RICE

SERVES 6–8

½ tsp crushed saffron threads
3 tbsp warm milk
1 oz/25 g butter
⅓ cup currants
⅓ cup shelled, chopped pistachio
nuts

1½ cups long-grain white rice
1⅕ pt/680 ml water
1 tsp salt
1 tbsp sugar
large pinch of ground cinnamon

Dissolve the saffron in the warm milk.

Melt the butter in a medium-large saucepan and add the currants, pistachio nuts and rice to it. Stir over low heat for several minutes, then add the water, salt, sugar, cinnamon and dissolved saffron.

Stir once, raise the heat and bring the water to a boil, then lower the heat, cover and barely simmer for 25 minutes. Serve immediately.

TOMATO RAITA

SERVES 6–8

1 lb/450 g ripe tomatoes
1 cup shredded coconut
2 tbsp minced green chillis
½ tsp salt

16 fl oz/450 ml yoghurt
1 tbsp vegetable oil
1½ tsp whole mustard seeds
½ tsp crushed dried red pepper

Chop the tomatoes coarsely. If you have fresh-grated or pre-grated but unsweetened coconut, combine it with the tomatoes in a bowl. If, as sometimes happens, you are able to find only the sweetened kind, soak it first in several rinses of water, then drain thoroughly and add to the tomatoes. Add the chillis, salt and yoghurt and mix it all up.

Heat the oil in a small frying pan and fry the mustard seeds and crushed pepper in it until the mustard seeds start to jump and snap. Pour this all into the yoghurt mixture and stir it in quickly.

Chill the raita for several hours before serving.

CUCUMBER RAITA

SERVES 4–6

1 large cucumber
2–3 tbsp finely chopped onions
16 fl oz/450 ml yoghurt
¼ tsp ground cumin

⅛ tsp cayenne pepper
salt
chopped fresh coriander leaves

Peel the cucumber, seed it and coarsely grate it. Stir together the cucumber, onions and yoghurt.

Heat the ground cumin for a moment in a small enamelled pan, then remove it from the heat and quickly stir in a little of the yoghurt mixture. Return the yoghurt–cumin mixture to the rest and stir thoroughly.

Stir in the cayenne, salt to taste and as much chopped coriander leaves as you like. Serve chilled with curries or other Indian dishes.

AUBERGINE RAITA

SERVES 6–8

1 large aubergine (about
    1½ lb/680 g)
2 tbsp vegetable oil
⅓ cup chopped onions
1 tsp peeled and grated fresh
    ginger
1 tsp garam masala (p. 335)

¼ tsp cayenne pepper
1 small tomato, coarsely
    chopped
1 tsp salt, or more to taste
16 fl oz/450 ml yoghurt
1 tbsp coarsely chopped fresh
    coriander leaves

Prick the aubergine with a fork in several places and bake it in a preheated oven at 400°F/200°C/Mark 6 until it is completely soft and collapsed – about 1 hour. Allow it to cool slightly, then split it in half and scoop out all the pulp. Drain off the excess liquid and coarsely chop the pulp.

Heat the vegetable oil in a medium-sized saucepan and sauté the onions in it until they are transparent. Add the grated ginger, garam masala and cayenne. Stir over low heat for about 2 minutes, then add the chopped tomato. As soon as the tomato is starting to get soft, remove the pan from the heat and stir in the aubergine pulp, salt, yoghurt and coriander leaves. Taste, and adjust the seasoning with more salt if necessary.

Chill the raita for 1–2 hours before serving.

BANANA AND COCONUT RAITA

SERVES 6–8

1 oz/25 g butter or ghee (p. 317)
1 tsp mustard seeds
¼ tsp cayenne pepper
½ cup flaked unsweetened coconut

2 ripe bananas, mashed
½ tsp salt
1 tsp sugar
16 fl oz/450 ml yoghurt

Heat the butter or ghee in a medium-sized, heavy-bottomed saucepan and add the mustard seeds. Stir the seeds over medium heat for 1–2 minutes, then stir in the cayenne. After another minute, add the coconut and bananas, remove from heat and stir quickly. Add the remaining ingredients, beat together lightly with a fork and chill for several hours before serving.

CACHUMBER
(An Indian Salad)

SERVES 4–6

2 large tomatoes
1 large cucumber
½ cup chopped spring onions
½ cup thinly sliced radishes
2 tbsp coarsely chopped fresh
   coriander leaves

2 tbsp lemon juice
¾ tsp salt
1 tsp finely minced green chillis
black pepper to taste

Cut the tomatoes in ½-in/12-mm chunks. Peel and seed the cucumber and cut it in ½-in/12-mm dice. Combine the tomatoes, cucumber, spring onions, radishes and coriander leaves in a bowl.

Mix together the lemon juice, salt and minced green chillis, and pour over the vegetables. Toss everything together so that it is thoroughly combined and add a little black pepper to taste. Chill for about 30 minutes, toss again and serve.

UPPAMA

(Semolina with Vegetables and Spices)

SERVES 8–10

2 fl oz/55 ml vegetable oil
1 medium-sized onion, chopped
1½ tsp whole mustard seeds
1 green chilli, minced
1 tsp crushed dried red chillis
1 cup semolina
2 pt/1.1 l hot water

½ cup sliced spring onions
⅓ cup finely diced carrots
1 large, ripe tomato, diced
2 tsp salt
OPTIONAL GARNISH
lemon juice and coriander leaves

Heat the vegetable oil in a large saucepan and sauté the onions in it until they are translucent. Add the mustard seeds and both chillis and stir over medium heat for 1–2 minutes. Add the semolina and stir for another few minutes.

Still stirring, gradually add the hot water. Beat lightly with a whisk to get rid of any lumps. Add the spring onions, diced carrots and tomato, and the salt. Simmer the mixture, stirring often, until it is quite thick and the vegetables are tender. This may take as long as 45 minutes–1 hour over low heat.

KHAGINA

(Indian Spiced Omelette)

SERVES 4–5

5 large eggs
5 tbsp chick-pea flour
dash of black pepper

¼ tsp ground coriander
crushed seeds from 4–5
  cardamom pods

½ tsp salt
½ cup minced or finely
  chopped onions

2 tbsp chopped fresh parsley
3–4 tbsp yoghurt
1½ oz/40 g butter

Beat the eggs, gradually sprinkling in the chick-pea flour, then add all the remaining ingredients except the butter and beat together thoroughly.

Melt the butter in a 9-in/225-mm frying pan and pour the egg mixture into it. Cook over low heat, covered, until the eggs are set on top. Flip the omelette out on to a plate and slide it back into the pan on the other side. Cook it for a few minutes more, just enough to brown the other side lightly. Turn it out on to a serving dish.

Serve the omelette in wedges as an accompaniment to a vegetable curry or with a chutney. It can be served warm or at room temperature.

RAISIN AND TAMARIND CHUTNEY

MAKES ABOUT 12 FL OZ/340 ML

1 cup raisins
1 tbsp tamarind concentrate*
6–8 tbsp water

½ tsp ground ginger
¼ tsp cayenne pepper
¼ tsp salt

Combine all the ingredients in a blender or food processor and purée, scraping down as necessary, until there are no lumps left. Add a bit more water if needed to make a mixture that is thick and not stiff.

This chutney is ready to use immediately, and will keep for 1–2 weeks if properly covered and refrigerated.

*Tamarind concentrate is a very thick, dark paste which can be purchased in speciality stores stocking Indian foods. The thick tamarind juice that is reconstituted from the concentrate has a pungent, tart flavour and combines wonderfully with the sweetness of raisins.

PAKORAS
(Hot Vegetable Fritters)

Pakoras are spicy fritters, ideal to serve hot as an hors-d'oeuvres or snack, with a tall, cool drink. Try them with a gin and tonic, or a Pimm's and soda with a slice of cucumber in it.

SERVES 4–6

⅔ cup chick-pea flour
¼ tsp baking soda
5 tbsp cold water
¼ tsp ground cumin
¼ tsp cayenne pepper
1 scant tsp salt
¼ tsp ground turmeric
pinch of crushed saffron threads

½ cup finely diced potato
½ cup slivered onions (paper-
thin slices, 1–1½ in/25–37
mm long)
2 tbsp finely chopped fresh
coriander leaves
16 fl oz/450 ml vegetable oil

Mix together the chick-pea flour, baking soda and cold water, stirring or rubbing the dough between your fingers until it is absolutely smooth and free from lumps. Add the cumin, cayenne, salt, turmeric and saffron and stir again until well combined. Stir in the potato, the onions and the coriander leaves.

Heat the vegetable oil in a 10–12-in/250–300-mm wok until it is about 350°F/180°C. Stir up the batter, scoop up a teaspoonful of it and, with a second spoon, slide it off into the hot oil. Fry 6–7 pakoras at once, for about 8 minutes, or until they are a light golden brown all over. Scoop them out with a slotted spoon, drain on kitchen towels and serve hot.

AKURI
(Spiced Scrambled Eggs)

SERVES 3–6

6 eggs
2 fl oz/55 ml milk
½ tsp salt
black pepper to taste

3 tbsp chopped fresh coriander
leaves
1½ oz/40 g butter or Ghee
(p. 317)

½ onion, finely chopped
1 small green chilli (jalapeño),
  minced
1 tbsp minced fresh ginger

½ tsp crushed dried red pepper
½ tsp ground turmeric
½ tsp ground cumin

Beat the eggs lightly with the milk, salt, pepper and chopped coriander leaves.

Heat the butter or ghee in a large frying pan and sauté the chopped onions in it until they begin to colour. Add the chillis, ginger, red pepper, turmeric and cumin. Stir over medium heat for about 2 minutes.

Raise the heat slightly and pour in the beaten eggs. Stir constantly until the eggs are just set but still creamy. Serve immediately with chapatis or puris and some spiced vegetables.

AKNI

Akni is a delicate, aromatic broth made with a combination of spices. It is used to poach or flavour certain Indian foods, and can be kept for several days in the refrigerator.

¾ oz/20 g butter or ghee
  (p. 317)
1 onion, coarsely chopped
4 cloves garlic, sliced
2 tbsp coriander seeds, crushed

1 tsp fennel seeds
1 tbsp peeled and chopped fresh
  ginger
1⅗ pt/900 ml water

Heat the butter or ghee in a medium-sized saucepan and sauté the onions and garlic in it until they are soft. Add the coriander seeds, fennel seeds and ginger and stir over medium heat for 2 minutes. Add the water and simmer the broth for 30 minutes, then strain.

POTATO CHAT PURIS

SERVES 6–8 AS AN HORS-D'OEUVRE OR SNACK

18 small Puris (p. 53)
⅓ cup slivered onions
2 cups cubed, cooked white-
skinned potatoes (waxy)
1½ cups cooked chick-peas (see
p. 152)
1 tbsp minced hot green chillis
3 tbsp coarsely chopped fresh
coriander leaves

2 tbsp lemon juice
½ tsp salt
½ cup Raisin and Tamarind
Chutney (p. 331)
½ cup mango chutney
1 cup crisp saveth noodles*

Punch in the tops of the little puris so that they have the shape of rough-edged little bowls.

Combine the slivered onions, cubed potatoes, chick-peas, minced chillis, chopped coriander leaves, lemon juice and salt, tossing everything together until it is thoroughly combined. The ingredients should be at room temperature.

Thin the Raisin and Tamarind Chutney with a little water, using just enough to give it a pourable consistency. Purée any sweet mango chutney and thin it likewise.

Fill the puris with the potato–chick-pea mixture, mounding a couple of heaped tablespoons in each puri. Pour a teaspoonful or so of each of the thinned chutneys over the vegetable mixture in each puri. Sprinkle the filled puris with the crisp *saveth* noodles and serve.

---

* Saveth noodles are tiny, thin, crisp noodles made from chick-pea flour and are available in shops that stock Indian foods. They are similar in texture to dry chow mein noodles, which could be substituted if absolutely necessary.

GARAM MASALA

A masala is a mixture of spices, either dry or in the form of a paste, and there are many masalas for many uses. This one is a fragrant blend of spices – not especially hot – that is sometimes added to food during cooking and sometimes sprinkled over a dish just before serving. It is not curry powder. It can be used alone, but more often it is blended with other seasonings.

¼ cup cardamom pods
2 tbsp peppercorns
2 tbsp cumin seeds
2 sticks cinnamon, each 2 in/
  50 mm long

2 tsp whole cloves
1 tsp ground mace
2 tbsp ground coriander
1 bay leaf

Spread the spices out on a large metal baking sheet and roast them in the oven at 225°F/110°C/Mark ¼ for about 20 minutes, stirring them often and making sure they don't scorch.

Remove them from the oven and shell the cardamom seeds, discarding the pods. Crush the cinnamon sticks by wrapping them in a towel and pounding them with a wooden mallet or other blunt instrument.

Combine all the spices and grind them, in batches if necessary, in an electric blender or food processor until they are a powder. If you don't have a blender, you can grind the spices in a stone or ceramic mortar and good luck to you.

Keep the masala in an airtight container at room temperature.

See PRESERVES for several chutneys. Turn to BREADS for Puris and Chapatis, and to DESSERTS for Carrot Halva.

DESSERTS

FROM MY EARLIEST RECOLLECTIONS, the importance of an occasion in our family could be gauged by the opulence of sweets in which we indulged. Each birthday or anniversary was marked by my mother's gloriously rich walnut torte, spread with generous layers of coffee buttercream. More a confection than a cake, this elegant pastry had to be cut in small pieces and nibbled slowly to savour all of its sweetness and sophisticated flavour. For Easter, a very special time, there were tall, light babas and delicate almond cakes, as well as sturdier ones that were dense with raisins and nuts.

As preparations for Christmas began, a nearly tangible excitement filled the air and aromas of honey and spice enveloped us when we came into the kitchen after school, cold and wet with snow. It is a feeling that still haunts me each year, and spicy *pierniki*, like Proust's madeleines, bring it back with greatest clarity. At Christmas there were fruit-cakes and marzipan and *pierniki*, of course, flavoured with honey and spices and aged in tins for weeks or even months to ripen, and there was a beautiful thing called *chrust* (hröōst), which means 'frost': these were light, lacy, brittle pastries, fried in hot oil and dusted heavily with icing sugar. With all this, there was still a great quantity of pale, crumbly butter biscuits, dried fruits, several kinds of nuts, candied orange rind, the finest chocolates that could be found and, of course, the traditional poppy-seed-filled *struçla* (strudel). On Christmas Eve, after the gala supper, these things were arrayed in all their splendour and abundance on a prettily decorated sideboard by the Christmas tree. Those who still had room could pick and choose from that phantasmagoria for the length of the happy evening (of course, everyone had room because, as we all know, dessert goes to a different stomach).

Rich desserts, along with such things as great wines and rare spices, are certainly among the luxury items in the world of food, so one must dismiss all ideas of practicality in even thinking of them. It is fine to be practical when planting a lawn or cooking soup for the family on a cold day, but that is altogether the wrong attitude for choosing tickets for the opera, buying perfume or diamonds, or making a special dessert. I just attend to quality rather than quantity and all is well. Pure marzipan and chocolate, pounds of butter, cupfuls of sugar and honey, drenchings of brandy and rum, and high, soft mounds of whipped cream are the wonderful stuff that great desserts are made of. Of course, we cannot lap up such things every day (for we are vain enough to think of slim figures), but now and then, in a party mood, how agreeable it is to forget time, forget expense, forget calories and treat ourselves and everyone around us to a memorable sweet.

SPONGE CAKE

MAKES 1 LARGE CAKE

6 eggs, separated
1 cup sugar
2 fl oz/55 ml boiling water
1 tbsp lemon juice
½ tsp vanilla extract

1½ cups flour
1½ tsp baking powder
pinch of salt
2 oz/55 g butter, melted and
   cooled

Beat the egg yolks until they are creamy and light, then gradually add the sugar a bit at a time while you continue beating. Beat the yolks and sugar together until the mixture is pale coloured and fluffy – another 10 minutes or so. Gradually add the boiling water, lemon juice and vanilla and beat another few minutes.

Sift together the flour and baking powder and fold it into the egg yolk mixture. Beat the egg whites with a pinch of salt until they hold firm peaks and fold them gently into the batter, using as few strokes as necessary. Pour the melted, cooled butter over the batter, leaving out the milky sediment at the bottom of the pan. Again using as few strokes as necessary in order not to deflate the egg whites, scoop in the butter.

Spoon the batter into a buttered and floured 9–10-in/225–250-mm spring-form cake tin. Smooth the batter lightly in the tin.

Bake in a preheated oven at 325°F/170°C/Mark 3 for 40–45 minutes if you're making 1 large cake, slightly less time if you're making 2 layers. The cake is done when it is golden on top and shrinking away from the sides and when a toothpick inserted in the cake comes out clean. Let the cake cool in the tin for a few minutes, then transfer to a rack until it is completely cool.

Sponge cake, as its name indicates, is ideally suited for all those splendid tortes and desserts in which a quantity of rum or brandy is meant to be soaked up by the cake layers.

GENOESE

One of the very best basic cakes, from which any number of tortes can be made, Genoese is especially good for soaking up rum or brandy, as in a Zuppa Inglese.

MAKES 1 VERY LARGE CAKE OR 2 LARGE LAYERS

8 eggs
1½ cups sugar
grated rind of 1 lemon

1¾ cups sifted flour
4 oz/115 g butter, melted and cooled

Break the eggs into a large bowl. Place that bowl inside an even larger one, which is about half full of hot water. Add the sugar and grated lemon rind to the eggs and beat them with an electric mixer for 8–10 minutes. They should be puffed up to 3 times their former volume, creamy white in colour and they should fall in a thick ribbon when scooped up with a spoon.

Take the bowl of beaten eggs out of the hot water and put it in a bowl of cold water. Beat the eggs for several more minutes, until they are cool. Sprinkle the sifted flour over them and fold it in with a small spatula or flat wooden spoon, using the minimum number of strokes needed to blend the flour into the eggs.

Pour the melted and cooled butter over the cake batter, leaving out only the milky sediment in the bottom of the saucepan. Again, fold in the butter with light, smooth strokes, stopping as soon as it is incorporated.

Pour the batter into a 10-in/250-mm buttered and floured spring-form tin, or into 2 9-in/225-mm buttered and floured layer tins. Smooth the batter very gently in the tins, and bake in a preheated oven at 350°F/180°C/Mark 4 for about 45–50 minutes, or until the cake is golden brown on top and pulling away from the sides of the pan.

Remove the cake or cakes from the tins and cool on cake racks.

SWEET PASTRY CRUST

MAKES ENOUGH FOR 1 (11-IN/275-MM) TART

1⅓ cups flour
1 tbsp sugar
¼ tsp salt

4 oz/115 g butter
2½ fl oz/70 ml ice water

Sift together the flour, sugar and salt in a mixing bowl. Slice the cold butter rapidly and drop the slices into the flour mixture. With a pastry blender or two sharp knives, cut in the butter until the mixture resembles breadcrumbs.

Sprinkle the ice water over the flour-butter mixture and stir it in quickly with a fork, until the dough gathers together. Form the dough into a ball, wrap it in waxed paper or foil, and chill it for about 2 hours.

LEMON TORTE

SERVES 10

½ pt/285 ml egg whites
2 cups icing sugar
2 tbsp cornflour
¼ tsp almond extract
1⅔ cups ground almonds
  (unblanched)

Lemon filling (see below)
GARNISH
blanched almond halves

Beat the egg whites with 1 cup of the icing sugar until they hold soft peaks. Sift together the remaining sugar and the cornflour, add it to the egg whites along with the almond extract and continue beating until the egg whites are stiff.

Fold in the ground almonds.

Butter and flour two 10-in/250-mm cake tins and divide the beaten egg white mixture between them, spreading it as flat and smooth as possible. Bake the layers in a preheated oven at 275°F/140°C/Mark 1 for 1½ hours. They should be pale gold in colour and shrinking away from the sides of the tins.

Allow the layers to cool slightly in the tins, then carefully remove them and let them finish cooling on racks.

Spread a little more than half the lemon filling on one layer and place the second layer on top of it. Spread the remaining filling over the top and sides of the top layer, leaving the sides of the bottom layer exposed. Decorate the torte very simply with a few blanched almond halves or just swirl the lemon topping evenly with a butter knife and leave it plain. Chill the torte for at least 1 hour.

Lemon Filling

MAKES ABOUT 16 FL OZ/450 ML

4 tbsp cornflour
6 fl oz/170 ml cold water
2½ fl oz/70 ml fresh lemon
  juice

1 cup sugar
1 tbsp finely grated lemon zest
3 egg yolks
¾ oz/20 g butter

Combine the cornflour, water, lemon juice, sugar and grated lemon zest in a medium-sized, heavy-bottomed saucepan. Stir over very low heat for 15–20 minutes, or until the mixture begins to thicken. Stir with a whisk, if necessary, to keep the mixture smooth.

When it is quite thick, remove it from the heat and beat in the egg yolks, one at a time. Return the mixture to low heat and heat it for 3 minutes only. Remove it from the heat and stir in the butter. Allow the filling to cool, stirring it occasionally.

CHOCOLATE CHEESECAKE

You only live once, so do it.

SERVES 12–14

1½ cups fine digestive biscuit
  crumbs
4 oz/115 g butter
2 cups plus 3 tbsp sugar
1½ lb/680 g soft cream
  cheese
3 eggs
½ lb/225 g semi-sweet
  chocolate

3 tbsp double cream
16 fl oz/450 ml soured cream
2 fl oz/55 ml dark rum
¾ tsp cinnamon
¾ tsp almond extract
1 cup icing sugar
approximately 1 cup fresh
  strawberries

Mix the digestive biscuit crumbs with the butter and 3 tablespoons of the sugar, working it together with your fingers until it is all well blended. Press the mixture evenly on to the bottom of a 10-in/250-mm spring-form cake tin, using a potato masher to make a flat crust.

Beat the cream cheese with an electric mixer until it is fluffy, then gradually beat in the remaining 2 cups sugar and the eggs. Continue beating or spin the ingredients in a food processor until the mixture is perfectly smooth.

Melt the chocolate together with the double cream in a small saucepan and beat the mixture into the cheese, along with 8 fl oz/225 ml of the soured cream. Add the rum, cinnamon and almond extract and beat for a few minutes more.

Pour the cheese mixture into the prepared spring-form tin and bake in a preheated oven at 350°F/180°C/Mark 4 for 55–60 minutes. The sides will probably be puffed up higher than the centre – don't worry, this is easily dealt with. Allow the cake to cool and carefully remove the sides of the tin. With a long sharp knife, slice the uneven edges off the top. Because this cheesecake has such a moist, creamy consistency, you can smooth the sides and the trimmed top with a butter knife until it is as lovely and evenly shaped as you wish.

Beat together the remaining soured cream and the icing sugar and spread it over the top of the cake, but not down the sides. Wash the strawberries, hull them and slice each one in half lengthways. Arrange the strawberries, cut side down and tips pointing in to the centre in a solid ring round the edge of the cake. Chill the cake until serving, at least 1½ hours.

KATE'S CAKE
(Chocolate Cream Torte)

So named because it was designed and first made for Katherine Bradley, a very wonderful lady, on the occasion of her eighty-fifth birthday.

SERVES 8–10

5 oz/140 g butter
1¼ cups sugar
⅔ cup ground walnuts
5 oz/140 g semi-sweet
   chocolate, melted and cooled
½ tsp almond extract
7 eggs, separated

1¼ cups flour
3–6 tbsp brandy
16 fl oz/450 ml double cream
1 cup icing sugar
chocolate curls or shaved bitter-
   sweet chocolate

Cream the butter with ½ cup of the sugar, then beat in the ground walnuts, the melted chocolate, the almond extract and the egg yolks. Beat the egg whites with the remaining sugar until they hold soft peaks and fold them into the chocolate mixture. Finally, sift in the flour and mix it in gently until it is completely incorporated.

Pour the batter into a buttered 8–9-in/200–225-mm spring-form cake tin and bake it in a preheated oven at 325°F/170°C/

Mark 3 for about 1¼ hours (it may be a little longer) or until a toothpick inserted near the centre comes out clean and dry.

Allow the cake to cool slightly in its tin, then remove it and let it finish cooling on a rack.

Cut the cake in 3 thin, even layers and drizzle 1–2 tablespoons of brandy over each layer.

Whip the cream with the remaining icing sugar until it is stiff. Spread ⅓ of the whipped cream on top of the first layer and place the second layer carefully over it. Spread another ⅓ of the cream on the second layer, put on the top layer and spread it as beautifully as you can with the remaining cream, bringing it out just to the edge but not letting any get on the sides of the cake. The three dark layers and the cream filling should make a dramatic striped effect round the sides.

Arrange chocolate curls or sprinkle bits of shaved chocolate inside the edge of the whipped cream on top in a 1-in/25-mm-wide ring. Chill the cake.

SPUMONI CAKE

In the restaurant Torcoloti in Verona we ate one of the most sublime cakes in the world. After the first long moment of silent ecstasy had passed, we asked our extremely friendly waiter if he could tell us a little something about it. We found out that it was made every day by the aged and talented mother of the owner, that it was called Spumoni Cake, and a little something more – but the recipe was not revealed.

On returning to my own kitchen I experimented with several variations of the obvious basic ingredients and finally came up with a cake that, though it is not exactly the same, is a great deal like the Verona one – and *awfully good*!

SERVES 8–10

¾ cup icing sugar
⅓ cup flour
2 eggs
2 egg yolks
16 fl oz/450 ml milk
½ oz/15 g butter
½ tsp vanilla extract

4½ fl oz/125 ml brandy
4 fl oz/115 ml strong, cold
    espresso
1 1-day-old Genoese layer,
    9 in/225 mm across and about
    2 in/50 mm thick (p. 341)
2–3 tbsp sweet powdered cocoa

Mix together the icing sugar and the flour. Beat together the eggs and the yolks, and mix them into the dry ingredients, stirring until you have a thick, smooth paste.

Scald the milk and stir it quickly into the egg paste. Heat the mixture over a low heat, stirring constantly with a whisk, until it begins to simmer. Continue beating it with the whisk, over the lowest heat, for 3 more minutes. Remove the custard from the heat, stir in the butter, vanilla and 1 tablespoon of the brandy and beat it again until it is perfectly smooth.

Allow the custard to cool, stirring it occasionally to prevent a skin from forming.

Combine the cold espresso and the remaining brandy in a measuring cup. Using a long, very sharp knife, cut the Genoese into 2 even layers. Place the bottom layer on the 9-in/225-mm false bottom of a cake tin. Spoon ⅓ of the espresso–brandy mixture over it, moistening it evenly but lightly.

Spread the cold custard over the moistened cake layer in an even layer. Place the top of the cake on the custard layer and spoon the remaining espresso-brandy mixture over it. Go slow with this part of the operation: you don't want the liquid to run off the top layer and be soaked up by the bottom one. It is important that the bottom layer be less moist than the top one or you will have difficulty serving the cake when you cut it.

When all the espresso and brandy have been used up, put several tablespoons of sweet cocoa in a fine sieve and sift it evenly over the top of the cake. The layer of cocoa should be fairly thick, or it will have dark spots where the moisture from the cake seeps through.

Place the cake, false bottom and all, on a serving platter and chill it for several hours before serving. Cut the cake with a thin, sharp knife, and wipe the knife clean with a napkin between slices. Serve fresh hot espresso with the cold cake.

WENIA'S MAZUREK
(Věnyä's Mäzōōrĕk)

This wonderful cake was first made for me by my Aunt Wenia in Poland and I immediately demanded the recipe. It is the perfect cake for a very special occasion, a baroque, luscious creation that really looks like a celebration.

SERVES 10–12

1 sponge cake, baked in a
   10 × 14-in/250 × 350-mm
   tin (p. 340)
4–5 fl oz/115–140 ml rum
1 cup plum jam
1 cup raisins
1 cup chopped walnuts

½ cup chopped candied orange
   rind
1 recipe Chocolate Buttercream,
   chilled till firm but not stiff
   (p. 349)
1 tsp unsweetened powdered
   cocoa

With a long, sharp, serrated knife, slice the sponge cake into 2 even layers. Sprinkle the rum evenly over both layers. Spread the plum jam over the entire surface of the bottom layer, right out to the edges. Toss together the raisins, chopped walnuts and chopped candied orange rind. Sprinkle about ½ of this mixture evenly over the plum jam.

Spoon ⅔ of the buttercream over the fruit and nut layer, and spread it lightly and smoothly out to the edges of the cake. Place the top cake layer gently on the buttercream layer.

Spread the remaining buttercream over the top of the cake, bringing it out to the edges but not down the sides. Through a very fine sieve, dust the cocoa over a 3 × 6-in/75 × 150-mm rectangle in the centre of the cake. Don't worry if the edges of your rectangle aren't perfect – the next step will fix that.

Take the remainder of the fruit and nut mixture, a little at a time, and sprinkle it over the top of the cake, covering the buttercream *around* the rectangle that has been dusted with cocoa. To make a straight edge around the rectangle, hold a long, wide knife along the line on one side of the rectangle and sprinkle the fruits and nuts along the blade on the buttercream side. Repeat on all sides of the rectangle, then fill in the remaining areas out to the edges of the cake. Press the fruit and nut mixture very gently into the buttercream, just enough to make it stay.

If there are creases in the buttercream from holding the knife on it to make the straight edge, press the fruits and nuts immediately next to the cocoa rectangle very lightly towards the middle, just enough to hide the crease.

The finished cake should look like this: on the sides all layers will be visible – cake, then jam, then buttercream, cake again and more buttercream. On top the surface will be covered with fruit mixture, except for a rectangular chocolate 'window' in the centre.

Chill the cake until just before serving it (at least 1 hour) and slice it with a very sharp, serrated knife, using a tiny, sawing motion.

Chocolate Buttercream

MAKES ABOUT 1 PT/570 ML

4 egg yolks
1¼ cups sugar
3 tbsp unsweetened powdered
  cocoa

5 fl oz/140 ml milk
4 oz/115 g soft butter

Beat the egg yolks until they are creamy, then beat in ¾ cup of the sugar and continue until pale and fluffy. Beat in the cocoa.

Bring the milk to a boil and add it to the egg yolk mixture, a little at a time, while continually beating. When all the milk has been added, transfer the custard to a heavy-bottomed saucepan and stir it with a wooden spoon over very low heat until it thickens enough to coat the spoon heavily. Don't even let it simmer.

When the custard has thickened, return it to the mixing bowl and set this inside a larger one ½ full of cold water. Beat the custard until cool.

In another bowl, beat the soft butter with the remaining ½ cup sugar until it is fluffy. Add the chocolate custard and beat the two together until they are one perfectly smooth, creamy mixture. Chill the buttercream for about 30 minutes before using it.

RUM AND CHOCOLATE FRUIT-CAKES

Make these before the end of November if you want to eat them at Christmas – they need ageing to develop proper flavour.

MAKES 8 MEDIUM-SIZED CAKES

1 lb/450 g dried apricots, cut in small pieces

12 oz/340 g pitted prunes, cut in small pieces

8 oz/225 g pitted dates, cut in small pieces

1 lb/450 g currants

12 oz/340 g golden raisins

12 oz/340 g candied citron

4 oz/115 g candied lemon peel

4 oz/115 g candied orange peel

8 oz/225 g shelled pecans or hazelnuts, or a mixture, chopped

1½ cups whole-wheat flour

1½ cups white flour

2 tsp bicarbonate of soda

1 pt/570 ml honey

½ lb/225 g butter, melted

4 fl oz/115 ml dark rum

2 tsp ginger

2½ tsp cinnamon

½ tsp ground cloves

1 tsp ground cardamom

¾ cup ground sweet chocolate or powdered cocoa

6 eggs

⅔ cup redcurrant jelly

brandy or rum*

In a large bowl mix all the chopped fruit, currants, raisins, candied peel and nuts. Sift together the two flours and the bicarbonate of soda and sprinkle this over the fruit. Toss the mixture until all the bits of fruit are separate and coated with flour.

In another bowl, combine the honey, melted butter, rum, spices and chocolate. Beat together the eggs and the redcurrant jelly until the mixture is thick and foamy, and then beat it into the honey

---

* The amount will vary – from 1 to 1½ pints or more – depending on your taste and the number of soakings you want to give the cakes as they age.

mixture. Pour this over the floured fruit and stir with a large wooden spoon until the batter is smooth and homogeneous.

Butter 8 medium-small ($3\frac{1}{2} \times 7\frac{1}{2}$ in/85 × 185 mm) loaf tins or a smaller number of large tins, line them with greaseproof paper and butter the paper. Divide the batter among the tins and smooth it down with a wet spoon. Bake the cakes in a preheated oven at 300°F/150°C/Mark 2 for 2–2½ hours, depending on their size. The cakes are done when a toothpick inserted near the centre comes out clean and dry.

Allow the cakes to cool, remove them from the tins and peel off the paper. Wrap each cake in several layers of cheesecloth and soak the cloth with brandy or rum, then wrap them securely in cling film or foil to keep the moisture in. Put the cakes away in a cool, dry place to age for about 1 month.

ZUPPA INGLESE

It is called 'English Soup' because its base is English custard, but it's really a marvellous, moist Italian confection – cake soaked with rum, layered with marmalade and custard, and covered with a meringue. The curious name presumably derives from a resemblance to trifle.

SERVES 10–14

½ cup sugar
½ cup flour
pinch of salt
16 fl oz/450 ml hot milk
4 egg yolks, lightly beaten
2 tbsp Marsala or brandy
¼ tsp vanilla extract
1 large sponge cake, preferably
   stale

8 fl oz/225 ml dark rum
¾ cup apricot or peach
   marmalade
4 egg whites
pinch of salt
pinch of cream of tartar
¼ cup sugar

Mix together the sugar, flour and salt in a medium-sized, heavy-bottomed saucepan. Pour the hot milk over the dry mixture and beat it with a whisk until it is smooth. Heat it gently, stirring all the while with a whisk, until it begins to thicken, about 4–6 minutes. Whisk in the egg yolks and continue stirring over low heat a few minutes more, until the custard is very thick and glossy. Remove it from the heat and stir in the Marsala or brandy and the vanilla. Allow the custard to cool completely, stirring it occasionally to prevent a skin from forming.

Cut a stale sponge cake in ¾-in/18-mm strips. Arrange a layer of the sponge cake strips in the bottom of a large, ovenproof serving dish. Sprinkle the cake with ½ the rum, then spread the marmalade over it evenly and, over the marmalade, carefully spread about ⅔ of the custard.

Arrange the remaining cake strips in an even layer on top of the custard and sprinkle the rest of the rum over it. Spread the remaining custard over the second layer of cake. Chill the *zuppa*.

Beat the egg whites with a pinch of salt and a pinch of cream of tartar until they hold stiff, glossy peaks. Gradually beat in the sugar.

Cover the *zuppa* with the meringue and swirl it round with a spoon or small spatula so that it forms peaks in an attractive pattern. Bake the *zuppa* in a preheated oven at 325°F/170°C/Mark 3 for 10–12 minutes, or until the meringue is golden brown on its peaks. Chill for 1–2 hours before serving.

APPLE STRUDEL GRANDMA CLAR
(as passed down to Flora Clar Mock)

Where it came from before Flora's grandmother started calling it her own, nobody knows, but this is not a classic version of apple strudel. It is as unusual as it is tasty.

When Flora makes this strudel, she makes double or more the amount given here, but not everyone has such an immense table on which to stretch the dough, so I've reduced the quantities a bit. You'll still need a table about 5 ft/1.5 m long and 2–3 ft/0.5–1 m wide, covered with a clean sheet or smooth tablecloth, for preparing the pastry, and though you can do it alone, the whole process is more fun if you have a friend or two around to help. Stretching the dough is not as difficult as it sounds, and spreading the sugar, cinnamon, nuts, coconut, jam and apples over such a large surface is a complete delight. Flora says, 'When it starts to look like a Jackson Pollock painting, you know you're getting there.'

MAKES 2–3 LARGE STRUDELS

4 cups flour
½ pt/285 ml water
4 fl oz/115 ml corn oil
½ cup sugar
approximately 2 tsp ground
 cinnamon
1 cup shredded sweetened coconut
1 cup strawberry or raspberry jam

¾ cup raisins
½ cup finely chopped walnuts
1¼ lb Granny Smith apples,
 peeled, cored, quartered and
 thinly sliced
additional sugar and cinnamon
 to sprinkle on top

Put 3 cups of the flour in an ample bowl and gradually stir in the water until you have a sticky, pasty mass, a little more moist than a normal bread dough. Work it a little with your hands – just enough to get out the lumps but no more. Gather the dough into a ball and dust a little more flour over it, patting it smooth as you do, until it has a nice, even shape, dry and flour-coated on the outside but very soft inside.

Spread a clean sheet or smooth tablecloth over a large, preferably oblong table and dust it evenly with the remaining flour. If the table is oblong, shape the dough gently into a loaf with proportions similar to those of the table-top. For a round table, leave it in a ball.

Put the dough down in the centre of the table and flatten it slightly with a rolling-pin. Turn the dough over and roll it out a little more, rolling always from the centre to the edges. Continue turning the dough over and rolling it out, always making sure the area under it is well floured and keeping the shape as even as possible, until it is about ¼ in/6 mm thick. Now slide your hands under the dough, palms up, and begin pulling it out very gently and carefully, letting it slide off your hands as you draw them back out to the edge. This process is really nothing but a very light 'stroking' of the sheet of pastry from underneath. Begin at the centre and work your way round, pulling it out only a little at a time. Continue stretching the pastry this way until it is paper-thin and quite transparent. Try to avoid putting holes in it, but don't panic if a little one appears here or there: they'll disappear in the rolling up.

When the dough is as thin and fine as a piece of silk (it should nearly cover the surface of the table), press out the inevitably bumpy edges with your fingers and then drizzle not quite 4 fl oz/ 115 ml of corn oil over it. Spread the oil over the pastry with your hands until coated all over.

This is where the real fun begins. Sprinkle the pastry sheet evenly with sugar, then sprinkle on about 2 teaspoons of cinnamon, or more if you like. Next sprinkle on the coconut, always covering the surface of the pastry as evenly as you can, and then drizzle or dab on the jam. After the jam, sprinkle on the raisins and the walnuts (it's starting to look like a Jackson Pollock) and finally the apple slices. You're ready to roll.

Oil 2–3 large baking sheets very generously and have them ready, along with a very sharp knife. Starting at one of the narrow ends, lift up the sheet or cloth and shake it lightly to loosen the pastry so that it starts to roll up. Continue gathering up the cloth and lifting it evenly, rolling the strudel up until it looks about as thick as you want it: about 2 in/50 mm is good. Slice off the rolled up part with a sharp knife, cut into manageable lengths and transfer them with spatulas to the baking sheets.

Now gather up the cloth, lift and begin rolling again, proceeding the same way until all the pastry is rolled up, cut and on the baking sheets. Sprinkle the strudels with a little sugar and cinnamon and bake them in a preheated oven at 375°F/190°C/Mark 5 for 15–20 minutes. They are done when the pastry is golden brown on top. Flora recommends cutting off a little slice and tasting the strudel to determine when it is ready, but I find it hard to maintain any objectivity about such matters when the first bite of strudel is actually in my mouth.

If it is allowed to cool and then wrapped well in greaseproof paper, the strudel will supposedly keep for several days to a week – but I've never been able to keep any that long!

DARK BRANDIED FRUIT-CAKES

These should be aged at least a month so that they can develop their full flavour.

MAKES 6 MEDIUM-SIZED CAKES

2 cups coarsely chopped dried figs
2 cups chopped dried apricots
½ cup chopped candied lemon peel
1½ cups sultanas
1½ cups chopped dates
2 cups chopped pecans
⅔ cup green candied cherries, halved
⅔ cup red candied cherries, halved
1½ cups whole-wheat flour
1½ cups white flour

1 tsp baking powder
¾ tsp ground nutmeg
½ tsp ground cinnamon
½ tsp ground cloves
½ tsp ground cardamom
½ lb/225 g butter, well chilled
6 eggs
1½ cups sugar
8 fl oz/225 ml Sauterne wine
½ tsp bicarbonate of soda
2 tbs water
approximately 1¼ pt/710 ml brandy

In a large bowl, combine the figs, apricots, lemon peel, sultanas, dates, pecans and cherries.

In another bowl sift together the flours, baking powder and spices, and cut in the chilled butter using two knives or a pastry blender until the mixture has the texture of breadcrumbs. Add the flour mixture to the fruit and toss them together until all the bits of fruit are separate and coated.

Beat the eggs with the sugar until they are light and pale lemon coloured. Stir in the Sauterne. Dissolve the bicarbonate of soda in the water and stir it in, too.

Combine the egg mixture with the flour and fruit mixture and stir them together thoroughly.

Butter 6 medium-small (3½ × 7½-in/85 × 190-mm) loaf tins or a smaller number of larger ones, line them with greaseproof paper and butter the paper. Divide the batter among the tins, smooth down neatly with a moist spoon and, if you like, arrange some pecan halves or cherry halves in a design on the cakes.

Bake the cakes in a preheated oven at 275°F/140°C/Mark 1 for 2 hours or slightly longer, until they are browned and a toothpick inserted near the centre comes out clean.

Allow the cakes to cool, remove them from the tins and peel off the paper. Wrap each cake in several layers of cheesecloth and soak the cloth with as much brandy as it will absorb. Wrap the cake again, securely, in foil or cling film to keep the moisture in.

Put the cakes away in a cool place for 2 weeks, then check them. If the cheesecloth is quite dry, drizzle a little more brandy on it. Replace the foil or cling film and put the cakes away for another 2 weeks or for as long as you like.

APPLE PUDDING

SERVES 6–8

3 large Granny Smith apples
2 oz/55 g butter
3 tbsp sugar
½ tsp ground cinnamon
¼ tsp ground cloves
1 tsp grated lemon rind
BATTER
3 eggs
½ cup flour

12 fl oz/340 ml milk
3 tbsp sugar
2 tbsp brandy
½ tsp vanilla extract
dash of nutmeg
GARNISH
¼–½ cup icing sugar

Quarter, peel and core the apples and cut the quarters in thin slices. In a shallow, fireproof casserole, sauté the apple slices in butter for several minutes. Add the sugar, cinnamon, cloves and lemon rind and continue to cook the apples, stirring often, for another 5 minutes, or until the apples are just tender.

Beat together the eggs, flour, milk, sugar, brandy, vanilla and nutmeg, or blend them in a blender. Pour the batter over the apples and bake the pudding for 25–30 minutes in a preheated oven at 400°F/200°C/Mark 6, or until it is puffed and golden brown on top.

Sift icing sugar over the top of the pudding and serve it warm with coffee or milk.

APPLE TART

SERVES 8–10

CRUST

1⅓ cups flour
¼ tsp salt
1 tbsp sugar
4 oz/115 g butter, well chilled
2½ fl oz/70 ml ice water

FILLING

2 lb/900 g Granny Smith apples
juice of 1 large lemon
½ cup sugar
2½–4 fl oz/70–115 ml apricot
    glaze (optional, see p. 358)

To make the crust, mix together the flour, salt and sugar, then cut in the butter with a pastry blender or two sharp knives until the mixture resembles coarse breadcrumbs. Sprinkle the ice water over it and toss together quickly until the flour is evenly moistened and the dough is starting to hold together. Form the dough into a ball and chill it for 1 hour, then roll it out in a 12-in/300-mm circle and fit it into a 10½-in/265-mm false-bottom quiche tin or flan ring.* Trim off the excess, leaving a ¼-in/6-mm rim above the pan, and flute the rim with the blunt edge of a butter knife. Chill the shell for 30 minutes.

Line the shell with foil and fill it with dried beans or rice.† Bake in a preheated oven at 425°F/220°C/Mark 7 for 8 minutes, then remove the beans and foil, prick the shell in several places with a fork and put it back in the oven for 4–5 minutes, just until the bottom of the crust begins to colour.

Meanwhile, peel and core the apples and cut them in even, lengthways slices, no thicker than ¼ in/6 mm at the outside. Put the apple slices in a bowl with the lemon juice and ½ cup of the sugar, toss lightly, and leave them there for 45 minutes. Drain the apples and reserve the liquid.

The partially baked crust can be painted with apricot glaze before the apples are arranged on it. This is one more way to fight the

---

* If you don't have a quiche tin or flan ring, you can use a shallow 10-in/250-mm pie tin, but I recommend getting a false-bottom quiche tin – they're inexpensive and very useful.
† The dried beans or rice are used as a weight, to keep the crust from slipping down the sides and puffing up in the middle. Keep the beans or rice in a jar – they can be reused for this purpose indefinitely.

soggy crust problem. Heat up the glaze and brush it on lightly with a pastry brush.

Arrange the apple slices neatly in the crust by very closely overlapping them in concentric circles, starting at the outside edge. Use all the apples. Sprinkle the remaining sugar (about 3 tablespoons) evenly over the apples. Bake the tart for 30–35 minutes in a preheated oven at 375°F/190°C/Mark 5. The apples should just be starting to brown at the edges.

While the tart is baking, boil the reserved liquid from the apples until it is reduced to a medium-thick, glaze-like consistency. When the tart is done, brush the apples lightly with this glaze or drizzle it over them.

Serve the tart warm or cool, with or without the apricot glaze.

Optional Apricot Glaze

½ cup apricot preserve or jam   *1 tbsp sugar*

To make an apricot glaze, rub the apricot preserve or jam through a fine sieve, add the sugar and boil for a few minutes. The mixture will be thick and sticky. Keep it warm over hot water until you need it, and while using it. If it gets too thick to handle, it can be thinned out with a few drops of water.

PUMPKIN PIE: I

This is my favourite. I love ginger, and this one is particularly spicy.

MAKES TWO 9-IN/225-MM PIES

*pastry for two 9-in/225-mm 1-
  crust pies (p. 342 or 357)*
¾ cup brown sugar
¼ cup white sugar
1 tbsp molasses
¼ tsp salt
½ tsp ground cinnamon
¾ tsp ground ginger

¼ tsp ground nutmeg
¼ tsp ground cloves
*12 fl oz/340 ml thick purée of
  cooked pumpkin*
3 eggs
*13 fl oz/370 ml undiluted
  evaporated milk*
3 tbsp sweet dark rum

2–3 tbsp chopped crystallized
  ginger (optional)

GARNISH
sweetened whipped cream

Prepare two 9-in/225-mm pastry shells with high fluted rims. Chill the shells for about 15 minutes while you preheat the oven to 400°F/200°C/Mark 6. When the shells are cold and firm, line them with greaseproof paper or foil and fill them with raw rice or dried beans.

Bake the shells for 10 minutes, then remove the paper or foil and rice or beans, prick the shells in several places with a fork and bake them for another 10 minutes.

In a bowl combine the two sugars, molasses, salt, spices and puréed pumpkin. In another bowl beat the eggs with the milk and rum. Combine the two mixtures and mix them thoroughly.

Sprinkle the chopped crystallized ginger evenly across the bottoms of the pastry shells. Ladle the filling carefully over the ginger, dividing it evenly between the two shells.

Bake the pies for 35–40 minutes, or until a knife inserted near the centre comes out clean.

Cool the pies on a rack and serve with sweetened whipped cream.

PUMPKIN PIE: II

This one is slightly milder in flavour – but delicious!

MAKES TWO 9-IN/225-MM PIES

pastry for two 9-in/225-mm 1-
  crust pies (p. 342 or 357)
¾ cup sugar
½ tsp salt
½ tsp ground ginger
¼ tsp ground nutmeg
1 tsp ground cinnamon
½ tsp ground cloves

12 fl oz/340 ml thick purée of
  cooked pumpkin
3 eggs
12 fl oz/340 ml single cream
2 tbsp sweet dark rum
GARNISH
sweetened whipped cream

Prepare two 9-in/225-mm pastry shells with fluted rims. Preheat the oven to 400°F/200°C/Mark 6 while chilling the shells for about 15 minutes. Line the shells with greaseproof paper or foil and fill them with raw rice or beans. Bake the shells for 10 minutes, then remove the paper or foil and rice or beans, prick the shells in several places with a fork and bake for another 10 minutes.

Combine the sugar, salt, spices and puréed pumpkin and mix them thoroughly. Beat together the eggs, cream and rum and then beat together the two mixtures.

Divide the filling evenly between the two pastry shells and bake the pies for 10 minutes at 400°F/200°C/Mark 6, then lower the temperature to 350°F/180°C/Mark 4 and bake them for another 25–30 minutes, or until a knife inserted near the centre comes out clean.

Cool the pies on racks and serve them with sweetened whipped cream.

CHERRY AND AMARETTO SOUFFLÉ

SERVES 4–6

1½ oz/40 g butter
4 tbsp flour
5½ fl oz/155 ml milk
2½ fl oz/70 ml single cream
⅔ cup sugar
4 egg yolks
2 tbsp Amaretto liqueur

1 cup halved, pitted dark
   cherries (preferably fresh)
5 egg whites
pinch of cream of tartar
GARNISH
Raspberry Sauce (p. 361)

Melt the butter in a medium-sized, heavy-bottomed saucepan and stir in the flour. Stir the roux frequently as it cooks for several minutes over very low heat. Meanwhile, combine the milk and cream, and heat them to just below simmering.

Pour the milk and cream into the roux and stir vigorously until the mixture is smooth and thick. Stir in the sugar, and as soon as it is completely dissolved and incorporated into the sauce, remove the saucepan from the heat.

Beat in the egg yolks, one at a time, then return the sauce to very low heat. Stir constantly for a few minutes, just until the egg yolks begin to thicken. Remove from the heat and stir in the Amaretto and the halved cherries.

Preheat the oven to 400°F/200°C/Mark 6 and prepare a soufflé dish with a buttered collar (see p. 119).

Beat the egg whites with the cream of tartar until they hold stiff peaks but are still glossy. Stir ⅓ of the egg whites into the thick sauce, then gently fold in the remaining egg whites.

Pile the soufflé mixture into the prepared dish and place it gently on the middle rack of the preheated oven. Turn the heat down to 375°F/190°C/Mark 5. Bake the soufflé for 35–40 minutes and serve it immediately, alone or with Raspberry Sauce.

Raspberry Sauce

MAKES ABOUT 16 FL OZ/450 ML, BUT THE AMOUNT
WILL VARY AS INGREDIENTS ARE FLEXIBLE

3–4 cups fresh raspberries*   *2–3 tbsp kirsch*
sugar

Press the washed raspberries through a fine sieve. Sweeten the purée to your own taste with sugar and beat it with a whisk or whip it in an electric blender until all the sugar is dissolved. Beat in the kirsch.

Serve the sauce with ice cream, puddings or a sweet soufflé.

* At a pinch, frozen berries can be used.

CLAFOUTI OF CHERRIES

Clafouti is a very simple pudding, best eaten warm. A mixture similar to pancake batter is poured over fruit and baked – that's all there is to it.

SERVES 6–8

4 eggs
1 cup flour
16 fl oz/450 ml warm milk
¾ cup sugar
1 oz/25 g butter, melted
2 tbsp kirsch

pinch of salt
1 lb/450 g sweet, dark cherries,
    washed, stemmed and pitted

GARNISH
sieved icing sugar
double cream, well chilled
    (optional)

Beat the eggs lightly and gradually stir in the flour. When the mixture is smooth, beat in the milk, sugar, melted butter and kirsch, along with a tiny pinch of salt.

Preheat the oven to 425°F/220°C/Mark 7. Very generously butter a large, shallow baking dish and pour a very thin layer of the batter across the bottom of it. Put it in the hot oven for 2–3 minutes, or just long enough for the batter to begin to set.

Arrange the pitted cherries evenly over the layer of batter and pour the remaining batter carefully over them.

Reduce the heat to 400°F/200°C/Mark 6 and bake the *clafouti* for about 30–35 minutes. It should be golden brown and slightly puffed.

It's a good idea to check it once or twice during the baking and if it is starting to puff unevenly in large bubbles, pierce it with a skewer or fork.

Sprinkle the hot *clafouti* with sieved icing sugar and serve it hot or warm. I've found that it's especially wonderful with some cold double cream poured over it.

COFFEE MOUSSE

SERVES 6–8

1½ cups icing sugar
8 fl oz/225 ml milk
6 tbsp triple-strength espresso
¼ tsp ground cinnamon
2 tbsp gelatin

4 fl oz/115 ml cold water
2 egg whites
16 fl oz/450 ml double cream
1 oz/25 g shaved bitter-sweet
  chocolate

Combine the sugar and the milk in a medium-sized saucepan and heat it over a medium heat, stirring constantly, until all the sugar is dissolved. Stir in the espresso and the cinnamon.

Dissolve the gelatin in the cold water and then stir it into the milk. Heat the mixture until the gelatin is completely dissolved, then remove it from the heat and allow it to cool, stirring occasionally.

Beat the egg whites until they hold stiff peaks, and in a separate bowl whip the cream until stiff.

As soon as the cooled gelatin mixture begins to thicken, stir in the whipped cream and fold in the beaten egg whites. Pile the mousse into 6–8 individual dessert dishes, decorate it with the shaved chocolate and chill it for about 2 hours before serving.

CARAMEL CUSTARD

SERVES 6–8

3 whole eggs
3 egg yolks
1¾ cups sugar

16 fl oz/450 ml milk
8 fl oz/225 ml double cream
½ tsp vanilla extract

Beat the eggs and yolks with ¾ cup of the sugar until thick and creamy. In a small saucepan, combine the milk and cream and heat to just below the simmering point. Pour the hot milk and cream gradually into the egg mixture, beating as you do. Stir in the vanilla.

Slowly heat the remaining sugar in a heavy-bottomed saucepan until it starts to melt. Continue heating gently, stirring constantly, until the sugar has been turned into a light-brown syrup, or caramelized. This will probably take about 5–8 minutes. Divide the hot caramel between 6–8 custard cups, and quickly tilt them round so that it coats the bottoms and part of the sides. The caramel will set almost immediately.

When the caramel has set, pour the custard mixture into the cups. Place the cups in a baking tin half full of hot water, cover the tops of the custards with a sheet of aluminium foil to prevent them from browning too much and bake in a preheated oven at 350°F/180°C/Mark 4 for 45–50 minutes.

The custard is done when a sharp knife inserted in the centre comes out clean. Cool the custards, then unmould them by running a thin knife round the edges and turning them over into rimmed plates or shallow bowls.

Serve the custard cool or chilled, as you prefer.

BRANDY CREAM

One of the simplest of all desserts to make, and sensationally rich and flavourful.

SERVES 6

8 fl oz/225 ml double cream,
   well chilled
⅓ cup icing sugar
2½ fl oz/70 ml honey

2½ fl oz/70 ml brandy
OPTIONAL GARNISH
chocolate curls or sliced glacé
   cherries

Whip the chilled cream with the icing sugar in a large, deep mixing bowl until it just begins to hold firm peaks. Stir the honey and brandy together until they are well blended. Pour the liquid into the whipped cream and continue beating it until it is perfectly smooth and thick. It won't get stiff enough to hold peaks, but it will thicken considerably.

Spoon the cream into 6 dessert or shallow wine glasses. If you like, you can decorate each serving with a few chocolate curls or with some sliced glacé cherries. Chill the dessert for 2 hours before serving.

PASKHA

This rich, sweet, white cheese dessert is a great delicacy and a Russian Easter tradition. It takes two days to make and is worth every moment of it.

SERVES 15–18

5 egg yolks
3 cups sugar
8 fl oz/225 ml milk
½ tsp vanilla extract
6 oz/170 g butter
3 lb/1.25 kg fresh mild white
   cheese (see p. 204)

4 fl oz/115 ml double cream
2 tsp grated lemon rind
½ cup finely chopped blanched
   almonds (optional)

Beat the egg yolks with 1 cup of the sugar until they are pale and fluffy. Add the milk and vanilla, and heat the mixture very gently, stirring constantly, until it thickens – this may take about 20 minutes. Add the butter and continue stirring until it melts. Cool the mixture, whisking it occasionally to keep it smooth.

Press the cheese through a sieve to remove any lumps and whip the cream until it is stiff. When the sauce is completely cool, beat in the remaining sugar, the sieved cheese, the lemon rind and the whipped cream. If you want to add almonds, stir them in at this point.

Paskha is traditionally shaped in a special carved wooden mould, but we must proceed on the assumption that the average kitchen does not have one. So . . . line a colander with 2 pieces of muslin or 6–8 layers of cheesecloth. Pour the paskha mixture into the lined colander, gather up the cloth around it, pull it together as tightly as you can and tie it firmly with string. Put a plate on top of the paskha and place a weight on the plate (a cast-iron saucepan should be heavy enough). Stand the colander over a bowl or deep dish to catch the drips and put it away in a cool place for 24–36 hours. Quite a bit of liquid will drain off. The paskha is ready when it is firm enough to keep its shape and be cut in slices.

Unwrap the paskha and turn it over carefully on to a plate. Slice it or cut it in little wedges and serve it alone or with a yeast cake. The paskha will keep for several days in the refrigerator if it is well covered.

CARROT HALVA
(Gajar Halva)

This Indian dessert is a rich and sweet confection with a hint of exotic flavour. After a dinner of curries, raitas, chutneys and other wonderful things, take a break for an hour or so; then serve halva in small wedges, with cold, unsweetened cream poured over it, and drink a fragrant tea.

SERVES 8–10

1½ lb/680 g carrots
2⅖ pt/1.4 l milk
1 cup sugar
⅓ cup raisins
¼ tsp crushed saffron threads
pinch of ground cardamom

¼ tsp rose extract
½ oz/15 g butter
⅓ cup ground blanched almonds
⅓ cup slivered blanched
  almonds
unsweetened cream, well chilled

Trim and scrape the carrots and shred them as finely as possible. Combine the carrots with the milk in a large, heavy saucepan and bring the milk to a boil. Lower the heat and simmer the mixture very gently, stirring often, for about 2 hours, or until it is reduced by more than ½ and is thick enough to lightly coat a spoon.

Stir in the sugar, raisins, saffron, cardamom and the rose extract and continue simmering until the mixture is thick enough to hold a soft shape. This could take another long while, so relax. Add the butter and ground almonds and stir over low heat for about 10 minutes more, taking care not to let the mixture scorch. It should now be thick enough to form a solid mass.

Remove it from the heat and allow it to cool slightly. Turn the halva out on to a plate and shape it into an even mound. Decorate it with the slivered almonds and serve it either warm or cool, with cream.

CRÈME À LA IRENA

SERVES 6–8

½ cup raisins
4 fl oz/115 ml cognac
2 oz/55 g semi-sweet
  chocolate
1 cup chopped fresh pineapple

16 fl oz/450 ml double cream
½ cup sugar
1 tsp vanilla extract
GARNISH
pirouette biscuits*

Soak the raisins in the cognac for several hours. Coarsely chop the chocolate.

Divide the fresh pineapple among 6–8 shallow dessert glasses.

Beat the cream with the sugar and vanilla just until it holds fairly stiff peaks. Drain the raisins, reserving the cognac, and add them to the cream along with the chopped chocolate. Stir the mixture thoroughly.

Put a large dollop of the whipped cream on top of the pineapple in each dessert glass. Pour a spoonful of the cognac over the whipped cream and garnish it with a pirouette biscuit. Serve immediately.

FROZEN STRAWBERRY MOUSSE

SERVES 8–10

about 1½ lb/680 g fresh
  strawberries
1½ cups sugar
1 tbsp gelatin
4 fl oz/115 ml cold water
8 fl oz/225 ml double cream

4 fl oz/115 ml egg whites
pinch of salt
2½ fl oz/70 ml curaçao
GARNISH
additional fresh strawberries

Hull and wash the strawberries and purée them in a blender. Pass the purée through a medium-fine sieve and discard the seeds. Combine the purée with 1 cup of the sugar.

Soften the gelatin in the cold water, then heat it gently until it is

*A delicate biscuit, rolled into the shape of a little cylinder; any biscuit of this general type will do.

completely dissolved. Add the remaining sugar and stir over low heat until the liquid is clear. Stir in the strawberry purée and let the mixture cool in the refrigerator until it just begins to thicken – don't forget to check frequently or you'll be sorry! I check it at least every 10 minutes, at first, then every 3–4 minutes when the mixture is already cool to the touch.

Beat the cream until it begins to hold fairly stiff peaks. Beat the egg whites with a pinch of salt until they are stiff.

When the purée begins to thicken, first stir in the curaçao, then fold in the whipped cream and finally the beaten egg whites.

Spoon the mixture into an oiled charlotte mould or into individual serving dishes and freeze without stirring for 4–6 hours. Unmould on to a serving dish if you have used a charlotte mould.

If you must leave the mousse in the freezer for a longer time and it gets too hard, just let it sit at room temperature for 15–20 minutes before serving.

Garnish the mousse with fresh strawberries.

CASTILIAN HOT CHOCOLATE

This is the thickest hot chocolate you'll ever drink – any thicker, and it would be a pudding. In Segovia it is one of the most popular winter drinks: a cup of this will take the chill off any icy day.

SERVES 6

½ cup unsweetened powdered cocoa

1 cup sugar

2 tbsp plus 1 tsp cornflour

4 fl oz / 115 ml water

1⅗ pt / 900 ml milk

Rub the cocoa and sugar together. Dissolve the cornflour in the water and combine it in a medium-sized saucepan with the cocoa and sugar. Stir this mixture until it is a smooth paste.

Begin heating the mixture, stirring it with a whisk, and gradually pour in the milk. Continue stirring with the whisk as you bring the liquid to a simmer.

Simmer the chocolate, stirring often, for about 10 minutes, until it is thick, glossy and completely smooth. Serve steaming hot.

APPLE-SAUCE CRÊPES

SERVES 6

16 fl oz/450 ml apple sauce   *butter for the pan*
12 Basic Crêpes (p. 239)   *¼ cup sugar*

Spread 1½ tablespoons of the apple sauce over half a crêpe and fold the other side over it. Spread another tablespoon of apple sauce over half the surface of the folded crêpe, and fold it in half once more. The crêpe will be folded in a triangle, with a layer of apple sauce between each layer of crêpe.

Fill all the crêpes in this manner. Shortly before serving, sauté the crêpes in butter for a few minutes on each side, until they are golden brown and hot through. Put two of the folded crêpes on each dessert plate and sprinkle each serving with about 2 teaspoons sugar. Serve hot.

FRESH LEMON DESSERT CRÊPES

SERVES 5–6

¾ cup white flour   *½ tsp fresh-grated lemon rind*
½ tsp salt   *½ tsp ground nutmeg*
3 eggs   *2 tsp sugar*
16 fl oz/450 ml milk, scalded   *butter for the pan*
    and cooled   *3–4 whole fresh lemons*
1 oz/25 g butter, melted   *1–2 cups sifted icing sugar*
2 tbsp cognac

Mix together the flour and the salt. Beat in the eggs until you have a smooth paste, then beat in the milk, melted butter, cognac, lemon rind, nutmeg and sugar. Let the batter rest for 1–2 hours.

Heat a crêpe pan and brush it with butter. Pour 3–4 tablespoons of the batter into the pan and tilt it round to distribute the batter evenly. Cook over medium heat for about 1 minute, then turn the crêpe over and cook for another minute on the other side.

To keep the crêpes hot, stack them on a warm plate, cover with a slightly damp tea-towel and keep them in a very low oven.

To serve, fold the crêpes in quarters or roll them loosely. Arrange 2–3 on each warm plate. Cut the lemons in wedges and pass the lemons and a bowl of icing sugar when you serve the crêpes. Each person should squeeze a generous amount of lemon juice over the crêpes then sprinkle them with the sugar and eat!

HUNGARIAN WALNUT CRÊPES

SERVES 8

16 medium-sized, pale crêpes
  (p. 239)
butter for the pan
FILLING
4 fl oz/115 ml milk
¾ cup sugar
½ oz/15 g butter
2 cups coarsely ground walnuts
½ tsp ground cinnamon
¼ tsp almond extract
2 tsp rum

¾ cup fine dry breadcrumbs
grated rind of 1 lemon
SAUCE
4 fl oz/115 ml strong coffee
6 oz/170 g semi-sweet
  chocolate
½ cup sugar
1½ oz/40 g butter
2 tbsp brandy
GARNISH
walnut pieces (about ¾–1 cup)

Heat the milk to scalding and stir in the sugar and the butter. As soon as the butter is melted, add the liquid to the ground walnuts along with the remaining ingredients for the filling. Stir well until the mixture is thoroughly combined and quite thick.

To make the sauce, heat the coffee and chocolate in a small, heavy-bottomed saucepan until the chocolate is melted. Add the sugar and butter and stir gently over medium-low heat until the sugar is dissolved and the butter is melted. The sauce should be glossy and smooth.

Remove the sauce from the heat and let it cool for a few minutes. Stir in the brandy. The sauce can be kept warm for a short while over very low heat or it can be reheated just before serving.

Place about 2 level tablespoons of walnut filling on a crêpe and spread it out in a small oblong shape, about 1 × 3 in/25 × 75 mm. Fold the sides of the crêpe over the filling, then fold over the ends to make an envelope, snugly fitted round the filling. When all the crêpes are filled in this manner, sauté them in a little butter for several minutes on each side until they are golden brown and hot through.

Place 2 of the hot crêpes on each dessert plate and spoon a few tablespoons of the hot chocolate sauce over them. Garnish each serving with a few walnut pieces and serve immediately.

BAKED APPLES

SERVES 6–8

6–8 large baking apples
⅔ cup flour
⅔ cup brown sugar
4 oz/115 g butter
grated rind of 1 lemon
½ tsp ground cinnamon

¼ tsp ground nutmeg
½ cup chopped raisins
2 fl oz/55 ml brandy
2 fl oz/55 ml curaçao
2 fl oz/55 ml water
double cream, well chilled

Core the apples, cutting out a generous round cavity in each one but not breaking through the bottom.

Mix together the flour and brown sugar and cut in the butter with a pastry blender or work it in with your fingers. Add the lemon rind, cinnamon, nutmeg and raisins and mix thoroughly. Stuff the apples with this mixture.

Arrange the apples in a medium-sized, shallow casserole. Combine the brandy, curaçao and water, and pour the liquid over the apples.

Bake the apples in a preheated oven at 400°F/200°C/Mark 6 for 40–45 minutes, basting them with the liquid every 6–7 minutes.

The filling will puff up and form hard little caps on top where the sugar caramelizes. When you take the apples out of the oven, let them cool for about 15 minutes, then cut the stiff, dark-brown sugar crusts off the filling, leaving just the soft, tender part. Spoon any remaining liquid over the warm apples. Serve them either warm or cool, with double cream.

PEACHES IN RED WINE

SERVES 6–8

2–2½ lb/900 g–1.1 kg small
  perfect peaches
1⅘ pt/1 l red wine

¾ cup sugar
1 stick cinnamon, 2 in/50 mm
  long

Wash the peaches, handling them gently to avoid bruising. In a fairly large enamelled saucepan simmer the wine with the sugar and cinnamon until all the sugar is dissolved. Add the peaches and simmer very gently for 8 minutes. Remove the saucepan from the heat and leave the peaches in the hot wine for about 30 minutes.

Spoon out the peaches and allow them to cool slightly, then carefully slip off their skins. Arrange them in an attractive serving dish, pour the wine over them and chill for at least 1 hour.

ORANGES IN WINE

SERVES 6–8

6 large navel oranges
¾ cup sugar
8–10 whole cloves
1 stick cinnamon, 1 in/25 mm
  long

½ pt/285 ml dry white wine
  (a good one, please)
2 tbsp brandy
seeds from 1 pomegranate

Peel the oranges with a sharp knife, cutting away all the white pith and outer membrane. Slice the oranges very thinly, cutting 6–7 slices from each one. In an attractive medium-sized serving bowl arrange the orange slices in layers, sprinkling each layer with some sugar and adding a few cloves and a bit of the cinnamon stick here and there.

When all the oranges and sugar are used up. slowly pour the wine over the slices, being careful not to wash all the sugar down to the bottom. The wine should just barely cover the orange slices. Drizzle on the brandy, cover the bowl tightly and let the oranges marinate in the refrigerator for several hours.

Just before serving sprinkle the fresh pomegranate seeds over the orange slices.

MELONS IN VERMOUTH

Fresh, ripe melons and an excellent vermouth are the requirements for this dessert, but proportions of one melon to another can be altered to your taste, and sliced or cubed melons will do very well if you don't have a melon scoop.

SERVES 8–10

2 cups honeydew melon balls
3 cups cantaloup melon balls
3 cups watermelon balls

8 fl oz/225 ml sweet Italian
vermouth

Seed and cut the melons and combine them in a deep bowl. Pour the vermouth over them and, using wooden spoons, lift the melon pieces from the bottom several times. Cover and chill for at least 2 hours, carefully stirring the mixture 2–3 times in the course of the chilling.

Serve in an attractive glass or crystal bowl.

PEACHES AND CREAM

Brandy-drenched and not overly sweet, this is marvellous tasting and very refreshing.

SERVES 6

4 medium-sized peaches
3 medium-sized bananas
juice of ½ large lemon
4 fl oz/115 ml brandy
⅛ tsp ground cinnamon
8 fl oz/225 ml double cream

⅓ cup icing sugar
⅓ cup slivered blanched
almonds
1–2 tsp powdered sweet
chocolate

Peel the peaches as thinly as possible and slice them in thin wedges. Peel and slice the bananas. Toss the fruit gently in a bowl with the lemon juice, then add the brandy and the cinnamon. Toss again until evenly coated, then refrigerate for 30–45 minutes.

Whip the cream with the icing sugar until it holds fairly stiff peaks.

Put the fruit and brandy mixture in an attractive, shallow serving bowl and sprinkle it with the slivered almonds. Spoon the whipped cream over the fruit in swirls and peaks. Through a fine sieve, sprinkle on the powdered chocolate. Serve immediately.

RUM BABA

SERVES 10–12

1 tbsp dried yeast
5 fl oz/140 ml warm milk
½ cup + 1 tbsp sugar
2¼ cups flour
4 eggs
pinch of salt
½ tsp vanilla extract
¼ tsp almond extract
4 oz/115 g soft butter
grated rind of 1 lemon
½ cup seedless raisins

fine dry breadcrumbs
RUM SAUCE
6 fl oz/170 ml water
⅔ cup sugar
2 tbsp lemon juice
4–5 fl oz/115–140 ml dark
  rum
GARNISH
light sweetened whipped cream
several glacé cherry halves
  (optional)

Dissolve the yeast in the warm milk, stir in 1 tablespoon of sugar and 1 cup of flour. Put this sponge in a medium-sized bowl, cover it with a light towel and leave it in a warm place to rise for about 30 minutes or until it has puffed up to nearly twice its original size.

Beat the eggs lightly with the remaining sugar. Add the salt, vanilla and almond extracts, and the remaining flour, and beat vigorously until the batter is perfectly smooth. Add the sponge and beat vigorously again, either by hand with a wooden spoon or with a strong electric mixer, until the batter is smooth and elastic and beginning to blister.

Cover the bowl with a light towel and leave the batter in a warm place to rise until it has doubled in bulk, about 45–60 minutes. Stir the batter down, add the softened butter and beat vigorously once more until the butter is completely incorporated and the batter is glossy and elastic. It will be quite soft and should fall away easily from the spoon and the sides of the bowl.

Stir in the grated lemon rind and the raisins. Butter a medium-sized ring mould and dust it with very fine dry breadcrumbs. Pour the batter into the mould: the batter should fill about half the mould at this point. Cover it with a light towel and let it rise in a warm place for 30 minutes.

Put the mould gently into a preheated oven at 400°F/200°C/ Mark 6. After 5 minutes, lower the heat to 350°F/180°C/Mark 4 and bake 30–40 minutes more, or until the cake tests done; a toothpick inserted near the centre should come out clean and dry.

Make the rum sauce: combine the water, sugar and lemon juice in a medium saucepan and boil for 10 minutes. Let the syrup cool to lukewarm, then add the rum.

When the cake is done, tip it delicately out of the mould on to a cake rack and let it cool to lukewarm, then put it back into its mould. Pierce the top of the baba carefully in about a dozen places, either with a thin skewer or the point of a very sharp knife. Spoon the rum sauce over the cake gradually, letting some of it seep in where the top was pierced and some of it run down the sides and centre. Cover tightly with aluminium foil and leave to ripen for several hours.

Turn the baba out on a serving dish and let it rest in that position for about 30 minutes before serving. Decorate it with *glacé* cherry halves if desired. Garnish each serving with a large dollop of lightly sweetened whipped cream.

Preserves and
Relishes

H AVING A ROW OF PRETTY, JEWEL-LIKE JARS of marmalade, chutney, jam and other such preserved delicacies secreted away somewhere in the cool, dim recesses of your kitchen cupboards is a wonderful feeling and, at the same time, both sensible and opulent. In the summer and autumn, when fruits and vegetables are abundant, we delight in eating everything fresh and ripe and hardly open that cupboard, unless it's for a chutney. But in the winter, there are days of little enough light and less warmth, and what a pleasure it is then to open one of those jars and spoon out a rich, sweet-flavoured concentration of summery goodness. Homemade jams, fruit butters and chutneys are always more satisfying that way than anything you can buy in a shop. It isn't just a matter of the sunny memories that are sealed up with the jam and that drift out with its fruity perfume when you prise off the lid – I think the flavours really are superior.

Preserving things in jars is not as mysterious a process as it is sometimes given out to be. After all, not so long ago it was a perfectly ordinary and frequent activity in nearly every household. What your grandmother could do, you can do as well: you need only to put in a small stock of easy sealing Kilner jars and have on hand some very large saucepans or a preserving pan and a few other basic pieces of equipment that you probably already have and use for other things. Then, when ripe fruit is abundant, you can cheerfully take advantage, and in the less bountiful months that follow you can spread your toast with ambrosial fruit butter or garnish a dinner with a piquant relish.

It will take several hours to put up a batch of any one of these things, but how little time that seems when you realize how long and how variously you'll be enjoying the product of your labours. Month after month I turn quite ordinary fare into something exciting or exotic by dipping into my stores. A bit of spicy Tomato-Apple Chutney added to a mild cheese in an omelette turns that 10-minute meal into something special. A sumptuous breakfast or tea can be arranged by putting out a selection of sweet conserves, jams or butters to spread on the toast. Pickled onions or spiced pickled peaches, served in small quantities to garnish a mild, creamy dish, also multiply the interest and effect of a meal. And a perfectly elegant dessert can be produced at a moment's notice by opening a jar of brandied apricots.

I've collected here a small sampling of my personal favourites. There is a definite emphasis on fruit butters and spicy concoctions of various kinds, which reflects my taste. In general, I prefer butters to jams for the great latitude possible in the proportion of sugar to fruit and the possibility of creating subtle blends of flavours. I like chutneys and spicy relishes for the incomparable way that they enhance and enliven a multitude of other foods. But most of all, I like preserves that are unusual – unavailable in the supermarket at any price and therefore doubly exciting.

Start now with a little batch of something or other – there's always *something* in season, no matter what time of year it is – and if it's your first try, well, all the more reason to make it something very special. Before long you'll amass a tidy little collection of gleaming jars, full of gold, red, green and russet brown riches, and amazing amounts of flavour for such tiny spaces.

Making Preserves

Before you start making any preserves be sure you have the following things: accurate kitchen scales, a couple of very large saucepans or a preserving pan, sharp knives, long-handled wooden spoons, sieves and plenty of suitable jars. A funnel for filling jars and tongs for lifting them out of boiling water or while they are hot are both a great help. It's also a good idea to have a supply of labels – small office labels will do the job – and to label jars with contents and date as soon as they are cool. You may think, after a few hours over your cooker, that what went into each jar is burned into your memory for ever, but when a few months go by and you've made more than one kind of preserve, it can get very confusing.

I recommend using either the screw-band or rubber band and clip type of preserving jars, which are essential for bottling fruit, for jams and chutneys as well. The jars are an investment, but you will reuse them many times, buying only new metal tops and rubber bands each time. All the recipes that follow give filling and sealing instructions for such jars, although for jams and chutneys you can, of course, use the traditional method of sealing by placing a waxed paper circle (waxed side down) on the surface of the jam, stretching a dampened cellophane cover (damp side *upwards*) smoothly over the top of the jar and holding it in place with an elastic band.

There are basic steps to be followed in any kind of preserving and they vary according to the kind of food being used and the type of preserve. Certain rules must be followed or the preserved food could be susceptible to spoilage and unsafe to eat. The recipes here, however, are all relatively high acid foods, which are much less susceptible to bacteria. So at least we needn't bother with pressure canners and only sometimes with a boiling-water bath.

STERILIZING JARS

If the preserve is not going to be processed in a boiling-water bath, the jars you are using must be sterilized. If a boiling-water bath is used, then the jars will be sterilized along with the contents. To sterilize jars, cover them completely with water and boil them for 20 minutes. I use a tall spaghetti saucepan for this job, with a small rack in the bottom to keep the jars from bouncing round. Leave the jars in the hot water until just before you want to use them, then remove them with tongs, drain them and fill them while they are still hot. Self-sealing lids with rubber strips should not be boiled. Just put them in a bowl, pour boiling water over them and leave them there until you need them.

SEALING JARS

Jars with two-part metal lids are essentially self-sealing. Fill them with the hot preserve, leaving the specified amount of headroom. Wipe the rim dry. Depending on the type of jar you are using, put the clean, dry rubber band or lid on the jar and clip or screw down the ring securely. Allow the jars to cool gradually. As they cool, the hot air in the top (that's why you need headroom) will begin to contract, creating a vacuum and sealing the jar.

Note: If you are making a jam or preserve with large chunks of whole fruit in it, allow it to cool for about 10 minutes, stirring often, before filling the jars. This will prevent the pieces of fruit from floating to the top.

THE BOILING-WATER BATH

Some preserves, such as the brandied apricots, are processed in a boiling-water bath. This simply means that the filled and sealed jars are placed on a rack in a large saucepan with enough boiling water to cover them by 2 in/50 mm, and boiled for a specified amount of time. Both the jar and contents are sterilized, while the air trapped in the contents of the jars and in the headroom left in the top is forced out. A vacuum seal is formed almost immediately after the jars are removed from the boiling water.

Some screw-band lids must be screwed on tightly, then unscrewed about half a turn to allow for expansion; follow the maker's directions. The clip type jar should be closed firmly, as the clip allows for expansion.

COOLING, LABELLING AND STORING

The hot jars should be allowed to cool gradually. When they are quite cool, the screw-on rings can be removed. The jars should be wiped perfectly clean, the seals checked and every jar labelled with contents and date. Store preserves in a cool, dry place.

MAKING JAMS

Slightly underripe fruit, freshly picked if possible, is best for jam-making. Overripe fruit tends to lose some of its natural pectin, the substance in the fruit which makes it set. Without sufficient pectin, what you intend to be jam will, in fact, remain syrup.

The fruit should be sorted carefully and any soft or blemished pieces discarded. It should then be quickly and gently washed, and, when necessary, peeled, cored or pitted. Hard fruits should be cut into small pieces. Soft fruits, such as berries, should be slightly crushed so that some juice is released and the fruit can be heated without adding water.

The prepared fruit and the sugar should both be carefully weighed. It's not a good idea to double quantities when making jams – a very large quantity will take longer and could easily boil over the top of your pan, causing you no end of grief.

The prepared fruit is cooked until it is tender, with frequent stirring to prevent scorching. Then the premeasured sugar is stirred in. The sugar can be warmed slightly beforehand to keep it from lowering the temperature of the fruit very much and help it dissolve more quickly, but this is not a do-or-die step. When the sugar is dissolved, the mixture must be brought to a rolling boil, and that means it's boiling so hard that it spits. No compromise allowed here. Jam cooked at too low a temperature won't set. The jam will foam up considerably at this point; thus the need for a very large saucepan or preserving pan. The hard boil must be maintained until the jam sets. This could take 5–25 minutes, depending on the type of fruit, its ripeness, and so on.

The easiest way to test for set is to drop a small amount of jam on to a cold plate and let it cool. If it thickens enough to form a skin and wrinkle when touched, it's time to put it in jars.

Spoon the jam into sterile, hot jars, wipe the rims dry, and seal tightly. Label when the jars are cool and store in a cool, dry place.

MAKING FRUIT BUTTERS, CHUTNEYS, RELISHES AND KETCHUP
These are the most foolproof of all preserves, as no 'setting' is involved. The ingredients are prepared according to a recipe and cooked together until the proper consistency is reached through reduction. When the substance is as thick as you want it, it's done and that's that. Just fill your hot, sterile jars and seal immediately. Since pectin is not necessary to butters and chutneys, completely ripe fruit can be used, but don't try to save fruit that is really past its prime by turning it into any kind of preserve: the flavour will suffer.

One point to remember about making fruit butters is that it could be dangerous to adjust the seasoning and spicing too early in the cooking. Remember that as the butter thickens, all those flavours will be concentrated, so wait until the consistency is nearly right before adding those final touches.

Do not overcook chutneys, unless you are prepared to have them turn into pulp. I prefer chutneys with whole chunks of fruit or vegetable in them. As soon as a chutney is thick, it is ready to be put into jars.

And remember that, in any recipe involving vinegar or brine, glass, stainless steel or enamelled utensils should be used. Avoid brass, copper, iron and tin.

One final note: chutneys, pickles and relishes of all kinds invariably improve with some ageing. Put them away and forget about them for a few months, then taste them and see how marvellously the flavours have ripened.

RASPBERRY JAM

MAKES ABOUT 2 PT/1 L

2 lb/900 g fresh, clean raspberries	*4 tsp fresh lemon juice*
	2 lb/900 g sugar

Wash and sterilize five 8-oz/225-ml jars.

Put the clean berries in a large enamelled saucepan along with the lemon juice. Squash some of the berries with a wooden spoon to start releasing the juice. Heat the berries slowly, stirring constantly and gently until they are boiling, then lower the heat and simmer them for 5 minutes, stirring often.

Meanwhile, spread the sugar in a metal roasting pan and heat it in a low oven for about 5 minutes.

Add the warmed sugar to the simmering berries and stir over low heat until the sugar has completely dissolved. Turn the heat up as high as possible, bring the jam to a boil and boil it hard for 5–6 minutes. Stir often with a long-handled wooden spoon.

Test the jam for set by dropping a bit of it on a saucer that has been chilled in the freezer. Put the saucer back in the freezer for about 2 minutes. If the jam has thickened by the time it is cool and forms a surface that wrinkles when touched, it has set and is ready to be bottled.

Ladle the jam into sterile, hot jars, leaving about ¼ in/6 mm of headroom. Wipe the rims until they are perfectly clean and dry, and seal the jars. Label them and store in a cool, dry place.

STRAWBERRY JAM

MAKES 2²/₅ PT/1.4 L

2½ lb/1.1 kg fresh, firm
strawberries

2½ lb/1.1 kg sugar (about 6
cups)
2 fl oz/55 ml fresh lemon juice

Wash and hull the berries. Cut them in half if they are very large; leave smaller berries whole.

Combine the prepared berries, the sugar and the lemon juice in a large enamelled saucepan.

Stir often and carefully with a wooden spoon over very low heat until the sugar is completely dissolved and the syrup clear.

Turn the heat up very high and, stirring constantly, bring the jam to a full, spitting boil. Boil hard, and continue stirring gently until the jam sets – this could take up to 15–20 minutes, depending on the pectin content of the fruit.

As soon as the boiling jam starts to make a heavy plopping sound, test for set (see p. 383). When it is starting to set, remove the jam from the heat. Let it cool for a few minutes, stirring occasionally. Ladle it into hot, sterile jars, leaving at least ¼ in/6 mm of headroom. Wipe the rims until they are perfectly clean and dry, and seal immediately.

Label the jars, and store in a cool, dry place. ·

APPLE BUTTER

MAKES ABOUT 2²/₅ PT/1.4 L

3½ lb/1.6 kg tart green apples
16 fl oz/450 ml apple juice
1 cup white sugar
1 cup brown sugar
½ tsp ground allspice

½ tsp ground cinnamon
¼ tsp ground cloves
⅛ tsp salt
2 tbsp molasses

Quarter, peel and core the apples. Cook the peels and cores in the apple juice, covered, for about 30 minutes. Strain the juice and discard the solids.

Add the apples and all remaining ingredients to the juice and simmer the mixture, stirring often, until the apples are very soft. Press the mixture through a fine sieve or purée it in a blender.

Continue cooking the apple butter over a low heat, stirring often, until it is very thick and smooth. Spoon it into hot, sterile jars, leaving about 1/3 in/8 mm of headroom, and seal.

CRANBERRY-FIG CONSERVE

MAKES ABOUT 2¾ PT/1.5 L

1 lb/450 g cranberries
1 lb/450 g fresh figs
2 firm, tart green apples
2 lemons

4 fl oz/115 ml water
2 lb/900 g sugar
2 tbsp kirsch

Wash the cranberries and pick them over, discarding any that are soft or brown. Trim the stems off the figs, quarter the figs lengthways and slice them thinly. Peel and core the apples and coarsely chop them. Slice 1 of the lemons and remove all the seeds, then chop it finely, peel and all, or put it through the coarse blade of a food mill. Squeeze and reserve the juice of the second lemon and discard the rind.

Combine the cranberries, figs, apples, chopped lemon, lemon juice and water in a large, heavy-bottomed enamelled saucepan and heat gently, stirring, until the berries begin popping and releasing their juice. Bring the mixture to a simmer and cook it, stirring often, until all the fruit is tender.

Add the sugar and stir over low heat until it is completely dissolved. Bring this mixture to a hard, spitting boil, and keep it boiling, stirring often with a long-handled wooden spoon, until it sets (see p. 383) – about another 8–10 minutes. Add the kirsch, stir it in and cook another minute or so, then ladle into hot, sterile jars, leaving about 1/4 in/6 mm of headroom, and seal. Allow the jars to cool, then wipe them off, label and store in a cool, dry place.

APRICOT OR PEACH BUTTER WITH BRANDY

Because a fruit butter does not depend on pectin to set, the proportions of fruit to sugar can be varied. I like mine slightly less sweet than jam (which still leaves plenty of room to be sweet). The spices also can be increased or decreased to taste.

MAKES 2½–3 PT/1.4–1.7 L,
DEPENDING ON HOW CONCENTRATED YOU LIKE IT

8 cups peeled, pitted and
    coarsely chopped apricots or
    peaches (about 6 lb/2.75 kg
    whole)
2 tbsp lemon juice

3 cups sugar
½ tsp ground cinnamon
¼–½ tsp ground ginger
¼–½ tsp ground allspice
2 fl oz/55 ml brandy

Combine the prepared fruit and the lemon juice in a large enamelled saucepan and heat very gently until the fruit starts to release its juice. Simmer, stirring often, until it is tender.

Purée the fruit in a blender, in batches of several cups, and return the purée to the saucepan. Add the sugar and spices and simmer again, stirring often, until the mixture is as thick as you want it. This may well take 1–2 hours, so be patient.

Add the brandy and cook for a few minutes more, just until the proper thickness is regained.

Spoon the hot fruit butter into hot, sterile jars, leaving about ⅓ in/8 mm of headroom, and seal immediately.

PICKLED SPICED PEACHES

MAKES ABOUT 2¾ PT/1.5 L

4 lb/1.8 kg firm, unblemished
    peaches
26 fl oz/740 ml cider vinegar
2 cups sugar
1 stick cinnamon

1 tbsp ground allspice
1 tbsp whole cloves
½ tsp ground ginger
zest of 1 lemon, peeled off in
    thin strips

Put the peaches carefully into a large saucepan of boiling water and let them simmer for 3 minutes, then remove them with a slotted spoon. Run a little cool water over the peaches and slip off their skins. Halve the peaches, remove the pits and put the fruit in a bowl of cool, salted water.

In a large enamelled saucepan heat the vinegar with the sugar and spices.

When the sugar is completely dissolved, add the peach halves and simmer them, turning them occasionally with wooden spoons so that they cook evenly, until they are just tender, about 20–25 minutes.

Arrange the peach halves carefully in sterile glass jars. Strain the vinegar and return it to the saucepan. Boil it for 5–10 minutes, or until it has the consistency of thin syrup. Pour the spiced vinegar over the peaches, covering them completely and leaving about 1/2 in/ 12 mm of headroom. Wipe the rims and seal the jars immediately. Let the peaches ripen for about 3 months.

WHOLE APRICOTS IN BRANDY

MAKES APPROXIMATELY 4⁴/₅ PT/2.7 L

4 lb/1.8 kg firm, ripe apricots	*1³/₅ pt/900 ml water*
4 cups sugar	*8 fl oz/225 ml brandy*

Use only firm, blemish-free apricots for this recipe and follow it carefully.

Wash the apricots. Heat the water and sugar together in a large saucepan. When the sugar is completely dissolved and the syrup is boiling, add the apricots and simmer them for 4 minutes *only*. Remove them gently with a slotted spoon, being careful not to bruise them or break the skins.

Fit the apricots in clean, hot jars. Don't crush them, but do fit them as closely as you can. Pour in 4 tablespoons of brandy to each 1-pt/570-ml jar. Fill the jars with the hot sugar syrup, leaving only 1/2 in/12 mm of headroom, wipe the rims and screw down the lids. Process in a boiling-water bath for 15–20 minutes (see p. 382). Remove the jars and allow them to cool gradually.

TOMATO KETCHUP

MAKES ABOUT 2½–3 PT/1.4–1.7 L,
DEPENDING ON CONSISTENCY OF KETCHUP

9 lb/4 kg ripe, red tomatoes
4 medium-sized onions, chopped
1 red pepper, seeded and
   chopped
8 fl oz/225 ml cider vinegar
   plus 2 to 3 tbsp (optional)
1 tsp whole allspice
1 tsp whole cloves

5 sticks cinnamon, broken
1 tsp celery seeds
½ tsp dry mustard
⅛–¼ tsp cayenne pepper
4 tbsp brown sugar
5 tbsp honey
1 tsp salt, or more to taste

Cut the tomatoes in quarters and purée them in a blender, in batches, together with the chopped onions and red pepper. Strain the purée through a coarse sieve to eliminate the tomato skins and pour it into a large, enamelled saucepan.

Cook the mixture over a low heat, stirring often, until it has thickened considerably, possibly as long as 1 hour.

Wrap the allspice, cloves, cinnamon and celery seeds in a piece of cheesecloth and put them in a small saucepan with the vinegar. Heat the vinegar and bag of spices together for about 30 minutes, then remove the bag of spices.

Add about ½ the spiced vinegar to the tomato mixture, stir it in and taste. For a spicier flavour, add a little more of the spiced vinegar. If it is already sufficiently spicy for you, just add 2–3 tablespoons of plain cider vinegar. This seasoning must be done to your taste. Then add the mustard, cayenne, sugar, honey and salt.

Cook the mixture again, stirring often, until it has reached the consistency that you prefer for ketchup. Time will vary, depending on what consistency you want, but it could take another hour. Taste it, and correct the seasoning if necessary. Pour into hot, sterile jars and seal, leaving at least ½ in/12 mm of headroom.

PEACH CHUTNEY

MAKES ABOUT 4 PT/2.25 L

4 lb/1.8 kg peaches
1 lb/450 g brown sugar
10 oz/285 g raisins
2 lb/900 g onions, minced or
  ground
16 fl oz/450 ml cider vinegar
2 oz/55 g peeled and finely
  chopped fresh ginger (about ⅓
  cup)

1 tbsp chilli powder
2 tbsp whole mustard seeds
1 tbsp salt
grated rind and juice of 1 lemon
grated rind and juice of 1
  orange
¼ tsp ground cayenne pepper
½ tsp ground cinnamon

Peel and remove the pits from the peaches and cut them into smallish bits, but don't chop them. Combine all the ingredients in a large enamelled saucepan and simmer gently, stirring often, until quite thick. This could take over 1 hour.

Spoon the boiling hot chutney into hot, sterilized jars, leaving ¼ in/6 mm of headroom, and seal.

TOMATO CHUTNEY

MAKES 2–2½ PT/1.1–1.4 L

4 lb/1.8 kg red tomatoes
¾ lb/340 g onions
6 oz/170 g raisins
4 oz/115 g pitted prunes, sliced
½ pt/285 ml cider vinegar
½ cup brown sugar

1 tsp ground ginger
1 tsp cayenne pepper
2½ tbsp salt
½ tsp ground cloves
1½ tsp ground coriander
1 tsp whole mustard seeds

Blanch the tomatoes in boiling water and peel them, then halve them (or, if very large, quarter them) and cut them in fairly thick slices. Peel and chop the onions. Combine all the ingredients in a large enamelled saucepan and simmer until the mixture is quite thick – it may take over 1 hour.

Spoon the chutney immediately into hot, sterile jars, leaving at least ¼ in/6 mm of headroom, and seal. The flavour will mellow with time.

TOMATO-APPLE CHUTNEY

MAKES ABOUT 2½ PT/1.4 L

4 lb/1.8 kg ripe tomatoes
2 lb/900 g tart green apples (8–9)
1 pt/570 ml cider vinegar
2½ cups brown sugar
3 large onions, peeled and chopped

1 tbsp mustard seeds, crushed
¼–½ tsp cayenne pepper
2 tbsp salt
4 tsp ground ginger
1½ cups raisins

Cut the tomatoes into quarters and purée them in the blender in batches. Strain the purée through a coarse sieve to eliminate the skins.

Peel and core the apples and cut them into ½-in/12-mm chunks.

Combine all the ingredients in a large enamelled saucepan and simmer gently, stirring often, until the mixture is very thick. Cooking time will probably be about 1½ hours. Spoon the hot chutney into hot, sterile jars, leaving at least ¼ in/6 mm of headroom, and seal.

DILL PICKLES

MAKES APPROXIMATELY 3⅕ PT/1.8 L

2¼ lb/1 kg pickling cucumbers
16 fl oz/450 ml cider vinegar
12 fl oz/340 ml water
3 tbsp sugar
2 tbsp salt
1 bay leaf

5–6 whole cloves
¼ tsp celery seeds
½ tsp whole peppercorns
½ tsp mustard seeds
1 tsp dill seeds or 2 heads fresh dill weed

Wash the cucumbers and quarter them lengthways.

Combine the vinegar, water, sugar, salt and bay leaf in an enamelled saucepan. Put the cloves, celery seeds, peppercorns, mustard seeds and ½ teaspoon of the dill seeds in a muslin bag and add it to the vinegar mixture. (If using fresh dill, omit the dill seeds here.) Bring this liquid to a boil, lower the heat and let it simmer for 15 minutes.

Remove the bay leaf and spice bag from the vinegar. Put $^{1}/_{4}$ teaspoon dill seeds, or 1 head fresh dill weed, into each of two clean 2-pt/1-l jars. Fit the cucumber spears as compactly as possible into the jars and pour the hot vinegar mixture over them. The cucumbers should be completely covered with the liquid, and there should be at least $^{1}/_{2}$ in/12 mm of headroom at the top.

Screw down the lids and process the jars in a boiling-water bath (see p. 382) for 20 minutes. Allow the pickles to cool, check the seals and label the jars.

The pickles will improve in flavour if left to ripen for a few months.

WILLIAM BRYAN'S PICKLED ONIONS

MAKES 3–4 PT/1.7–2.25 L

3 lb/1.25 kg small white onions
3$^{1}/_{5}$ pt/1.8 l water
$^{1}/_{2}$ lb/225 g salt
16 fl oz/450 ml distilled white
  vinegar
16 fl oz/450 ml cider vinegar
2 sticks cinnamon
$^{1}/_{2}$ tsp whole cloves
1 tsp mace
1 tsp ground allspice
$^{2}/_{3}$ cup sugar
2–2$^{1}/_{2}$ tsp crushed dried red
  chillis

Peel the onions. Heat the water and dissolve the salt in it. Let the brine cool to room temperature and pour it over the onions in a large glass or ceramic bowl or crock. All the onions should be covered. Leave the onions in the brine for 24 hours.

Put the 2 vinegars in an enamelled saucepan with the cinnamon, cloves, mace and allspice. Bring it to a boil, then turn off the heat, cover it and let it steep for at least 2 hours. Strain the vinegar through a cheesecloth-lined sieve and discard the spices. Add the sugar to the vinegar and stir till it is completely dissolved.

Arrange the onions in sterile 1-pt/570-ml jars, leaving at least $^{1}/_{2}$ in/12 mm of headroom. Put $^{1}/_{2}$ teaspoon of crushed red chillis into each jar and cover the onions with the spiced vinegar. Seal the jars and put them aside for 1 month.

OPEN-JAR DILL PICKLES

A great-tasting pickle to make in small quantities all summer long, these are ready in a few days, at their prime in a week and no trouble to make. But only make as many as you'll want to eat in a week's time, as they don't keep well.

MAKES ABOUT 2½ LB/1.1 KG

2½ lb/1.1 kg pickling
   cucumbers
3⅕ pt/1.8 l water
⅓ cup sugar
¼ cup salt

1½–2 oz/40–55 g fresh dill
   (stalk, seeds and all)
3–4 cloves garlic
8 large grapevine leaves

Scrub the cucumbers clean. Combine the water, sugar and salt, stirring until all the sugar and salt are dissolved. Break or bend the stalks of dill into pieces about 3 in/75 mm long, and peel and thickly slice the garlic.

Put 2–3 grapevine leaves in a 6½-pt/3.6-l jar, then a few pieces of dill and a few pieces of garlic, and on top of this arrange a layer of cucumbers. Put down a couple more grapevine leaves, some more dill and garlic, and another layer of cucumbers. Continue in this fashion until the ingredients are used up. Pour the brine over the layered cucumbers.

Place a small plate or saucer on top of the cucumbers and put a weight on it (a jar full of water will do) to keep all the cucumbers completely submerged in brine. Place the jar on a deep plate or in a shallow bowl, as the brine will start to foam over a bit as it ferments.

Leave the jar at room temperature for 6–7 days, skimming off the top of the brine whenever necessary. The pickles are ready to eat, right out of the jar, as soon as they taste sour and salty enough to suit you.

CRANBERRY RELISH

MAKES ABOUT 2 PT/1 L

12 fl oz/340 ml water
2 cups sugar
3 cups clean, picked-over
  cranberries
1 medium-sized navel orange

1 tsp ground ginger
dash of cinnamon
dash of ground cloves
crushed seeds from 4 cardamom
  pods

Combine 8 fl oz/225 ml of the water and the sugar in a medium-sized saucepan and heat until the sugar is dissolved. Add the cranberries and simmer them, covered, for 10 minutes, then uncovered for another 10, stirring occasionally.

Cut the unpeeled orange into chunks and put it through a food grinder or chop it finely. Add the remaining water to the cranberries along with the ground-up orange, the ginger, cinnamon, cloves and crushed cardamom seeds. Simmer the mixture for about 20 minutes, stirring often. Chill the relish before serving.

QUICK PICKLED PEPPERS

Serve the peppers as a relish with rich, mild-flavoured dishes.

MAKES ABOUT 1³⁄₅ PT/900 ML

4 large green peppers
1³⁄₅ pt/900 ml water
8 fl oz/225 ml cider vinegar
½ cup sugar

2 tsp pickling spice
1½ tbsp salt
1 clove garlic, peeled

Cut the peppers into thick strips or 1-in/25-mm squares. Do not discard the tops and seeds.

Heat the water in an enamelled or stainless steel saucepan with the vinegar, sugar, pickling spice, salt and garlic. Add the peppers, including the tops and seeds, and let them simmer gently for about 15 minutes, or until they are just tender. Turn off the heat and let them stand for another 15 minutes, then transfer the peppers to a jar, strain the liquid and pour in as much as is needed to cover the peppers completely. Cover the jar with waxed paper and let it stand for 24 hours.

TINY OPEN-FACED
SANDWICHES

LITTLE OPEN-FACED SANDWICHES are popular all through eastern Europe as an hors-d'oeuvre or an accompaniment to tea. In Vienna an astonishing variety of these tiny sandwiches is displayed in windows or glass cases in certain restaurants at lunch-time. Set out in rows on big trays, they are pretty enough to rival the displays of pastries and make a quick but elegant lunch for the busier Viennese.

These are really canapés, much smaller than the famous open-faced sandwiches of Scandinavia. They're perfect as hors-d'oeuvres or for a cocktail party, but I also like to have them for dinner sometimes – 7 or 8 different little sandwiches with a glass of champagne make a pleasant meal in hot weather.

One of the best things about them is that you can create a marvellous-looking tray in a very short time out of whatever titbits you have on hand. The ingredients are all very flexible and meant to be used as a guideline, so no specific amounts are given. In any case, most people don't like to make more than a few of one kind unless it's for a large affair because an assortment is always more fun. So, I've just written down descriptions of how I put together my favourites and you take it from there.

COTTAGE CHEESE AND
SPRING ONION SANDWICHES

slender sourdough or French bread,	*small-curd cottage cheese*
or pressed pumpernickel bread	*chopped spring onions*
butter	*salt and pepper to taste*

Cut thin slices from a sourdough baguette, or cut slices of square, pressed pumpernickel into quarters. Butter the bread and put a heaped tablespoon of small-curd cottage cheese on each slice.

Shape the cottage cheese evenly over the entire slice, then sprinkle about 1 tablespoon of chopped spring onions over it and press the onions in very slightly so that they do not fall off quite so easily. Salt the sandwiches lightly and grind a little black pepper on them if you wish.

CREAM CHEESE AND RADISH SANDWICHES

cream cheese
slender sourdough bread

radishes
salt to taste

Spread a thick layer of cream cheese on thin slices cut from a sourdough baguette. Wash and trim some radishes, and slice them about 1/8 in/3 mm thick. Arrange the radish slices over the cream cheese in rows, overlapping them so that at least 10–12 slices fit on each sandwich. Salt the radishes lightly.

SMOKED CHEESE AND TOMATO SANDWICHES

pressed pumpernickel bread
butter
tomato slices

sprigs of fresh parsley
smoked cheese slices
salt to taste

Cut square slices of pressed pumpernickel into quarters and butter them generously. Cut some medium-sized tomato slices in half. Put 1/2 a tomato slice on each sandwich so that the cut edge goes diagonally from corner to corner. Tuck a few small sprigs of fresh parsley in under the cut edge of the tomato slice so that they peek out in a pretty ruffle.

Cut a few thin slices of a good smoked cheese and, using little aspic cutters,* make cut-outs in nice shapes no bigger than 1 in/25 mm across. Salt the sandwiches lightly before placing one of the cheese cut-outs on top of each tomato slice.

*If you don't have aspic cutters, use very tiny biscuit cutters; failing that, simple shapes of the appropriate size could be cut out free-form with a sharp-pointed knife.

EGG AND CUCUMBER SANDWICHES

pressed pumpernickel bread　　　*hard-boiled eggs*
butter　　　　　　　　　　　　*stuffed cocktail olives*
cucumber

Cut square slices of pressed pumpernickel into quarters and butter them generously. Score a large, firm cucumber with a fork and slice it about ¼ in/6 mm thick. Put a cucumber slice in the centre of each piece of bread. Peel some hard-boiled eggs and carefully slice them about ¼ in/6 mm thick as well. Using only the slices that have some of the yolk, centre 1 slice of egg on each cucumber slice.

Cut several medium-sized pimiento-stuffed cocktail olives into 4–5 slices each and put 1 olive slice in the centre of each egg slice.

EGG AND ONION
SANDWICHES WITH PARSLEY

slender sourdough bread　　　*salt*
butter　　　　　　　　　　　　*sprigs of fresh parsley*
hard-boiled eggs　　　　　　　*pickled cocktail onions*

Cut thin slices from a sourdough baguette and butter them generously. Peel several hard-boiled eggs and slice them about ¼ in/6 mm thick. Use only the larger slices that have part of the yolk in them.

Put 1 slice of egg in the centre of each sandwich and salt to taste. Put medium-sized sprigs of fresh parsley at intervals round the edge of each sandwich, tucking the stems under the egg. Put a tiny pickled cocktail onion in the centre of the egg slice and attach it to the sandwich with a cocktail stick.

CREAM CHEESE AND
CUCUMBER SANDWICHES

*slender sourdough bread or
    pressed pumpernickel bread
cream cheese*

*cucumber
salt to taste
paprika to taste*

Cut thin slices from a sourdough baguette, or cut slices of square pressed pumpernickel into quarters. Spread each slice rather thickly with cream cheese. Score a large, firm cucumber with a fork to give it a pretty pattern and slice it about ⅛–¼ in/3–6 mm thick. Put a slice of cucumber in the centre of each sandwich and salt it very lightly, then delicately sprinkle some paprika down the centre of the sandwich so as to make a bright red line straight across it.

SMOKED CHEESE AND
PICKLE SANDWICHES

*pressed pumpernickel bread
butter*

*smoked cheese
large dill pickle(s)*

Cut square slices of pressed pumpernickel into quarters and butter them generously. Slice some good smoked cheese thinly and trim the slices to fit the small pumpernickel squares.

Using aspic cutters (see p. 399), make dainty little cut-outs from the bits of cheese you have trimmed off or from additional slices. Slice a large dill pickle, slanting the slices to make them a little larger.

Put a square slice of cheese on each piece of bread, then a large slice of dill pickle and on top of that 1 of the small cheese cut-outs.

CHEDDAR CHEESE
AND CHILLI SANDWICHES

slender sourdough French bread   *strips of green chillis*
butter   *Cheddar cheese*

Cut medium-thin slices from a long, slender loaf of sourdough French bread and butter them.

Cut some long, peeled and seeded green chillis into ¼-in/6-mm strips. Thickly slice some Cheddar cheese and cut the slices into bits about ½ × 1½ in/12 × 37 mm.

Wrap 2–3 of the green chilli strips round each piece of cheese in a coil pattern and put 1 such piece on each slice of bread. If the chilli strips are too short or uneven, cut them into shorter pieces and just lay the chillis over the cheese in slanting stripes.

EGG AND PICKLED
MUSHROOM SANDWICHES

slender sourdough French bread   *Marinated Mushrooms (see*
butter   *p. 154)*
hard-boiled eggs   *salt and pepper (optional) to*
long strips of red pepper   *taste*

Cut thin slices from a long, slender loaf of sourdough French bread and butter them generously. Peel some hard-boiled eggs and carefully slice them about ¼ in/6 mm thick. Cut a large, peeled and seeded red pepper into long ¼-in/6-mm strips.

Using only the larger slices that include part of the yolk, put 1 slice of egg in the centre of each piece of bread. Wrap a strip of red pepper round the outside of the egg slice. Place a small marinated or pickled mushroom cap on top of the egg slice and secure it with a cocktail stick if necessary.

Salt the sandwiches lightly and dust them with a little black pepper if desired.

CREAM CHEESE AND
WATERCRESS SANDWICHES

slender sourdough French bread   *cherry tomatoes*
cream cheese   *salt to taste*
watercress

Cut thin slices from a long, slender loaf of sourdough French bread and spread them generously with cream cheese.

Wash and trim a bunch of watercress, shake or pat it dry and break it up into sprigs. Arrange 4–5 sprigs of watercress on each sandwich and put ¹/₂ a cherry tomato, cut side down, in the centre. Salt the sandwiches lightly.

INDEX